Ethics & International Affairs

Ethics & International Affairs

A Reader
Second Edition

Edited by Joel H. Rosenthal

Carnegie Council on Ethics and International Affairs

Georgetown University Press / Washington, D.C.

Georgetown University Press, Washington, D.C. 20007-1079
 Printed in the United States of America.
10 9 8 7 6 5 4 3 2 1 1999
THIS VOLUME IS PRINTED ON ACID-FREE OFFSET BOOKPAPER.

Library of Congress Cataloging-in-Publication Data

Ethics and international affairs : a reader / edited by Joel H.
Rosenthal. — 2nd ed.
p. cm.
"Carnegie Council on Ethics and International Affairs."
Includes index.
ISBN 0-87840-725-1 (paper)
1. International relations—Moral and ethical aspects.
I. Rosenthal, Joel H., 1960– . II. Carnegie Council on Ethics & International Affairs. III. Title: Ethics and international affairs.
JZ1306.E87 1999
172′.4—dc21 98-45147

FOR

ROBERT J. MYERS

President, Carnegie Council on
Ethics and International Affairs
New York, N.Y.
1980–94

CONTENTS

PREFACE
to the Second Edition

Four years have passed since the first publication of this reader. In that time, we have learned to live with the derivative and already stale label "post–Cold War era." If this is indeed destined to become the signature phrase of our time, it does at least suggest the interim nature of our current system. As Michael J. Smith put it recently, when it comes to describing the international system, "we know from what but not to what" we are moving.

Despite this uncertainty, there is one fixed point from which we can reckon our position: the ethical approach to international affairs. While acknowledging the political reality expressed by the wisdom of the realist sages, this approach also recognizes the very real weight of conscience, principle, and restraint. Understanding the ways in which moral imperatives can affect the struggle for power and peace among nations is the animating force and unifying theme of all the articles presented in this volume.

As Reinhold Niebuhr reminded us, to be good students of politics we must never forget the timebound nature of our current circumstances and the timeless nature of the human condition. The effort to understand and strengthen the connection between moral commitments and political reality will continue in perpetuity. It is only the "crisis" of the moment that changes. It is our belief that those who are equipped with the requisite philosophical, historical, and social science tools will be best equipped to deal with current challenges. And it is for them that we continue to generate this new literature in the field of ethics and international affairs.

—Joel H. Rosenthal,
President
Carnegie Council on
Ethics and International Affairs 1998

ACKNOWLEDGMENTS

This book—and much recent scholarship in ethics and international affairs—owes its existence to Robert J. Myers, president of the Carnegie Council on Ethics and International Affairs (New York) from 1980 to 1994.

As president of the Carnegie Council, Bob Myers launched numerous initiatives to reinvigorate and legitimize the field. All of those who participated in his conferences, symposia, workshops, and publication efforts know of his unique and unparalleled contribution. It is with gratitude for his wisdom and generosity of spirit that this book is dedicated to him.

Two staff members of the Carnegie Council deserve special recognition for their roles in producing this work. Matthew E. Mattern served as managing editor of *Ethics & International Affairs* from 1994 to 1997. Deborah F. Washburn is the current managing editor. It is their hard work that has made this book possible.

Special thanks are due also to the members of the Editorial Advisory Board of *Ethics & International Affairs:* Lisa Anderson, Charles R. Beitz, Alberto R. Coll, Stephan Haggard, Russell Hardin, David C. Hendrickson, Dorothy V. Jones, Anthony Lake, Terry Nardin, Augustus Richard Norton, Robert L. Phillips, Michael J. Smith, Kenneth W. Thompson, and Gregory F. Treverton. Their guidance has been indispensable.

Joel H. Rosenthal

Introduction: Ethics through the Cold War and After

In the inaugural issue of *Ethics & International Affairs* (1987), Editor in Chief Robert J. Myers explained that the first objective of the new annual was to counter the cry "What does ethics have to do with international affairs?" With the end of the Cold War not yet in plain sight, the biggest challenge facing the new publication was its allegedly oxymoronic title. For a number of reasons, this problem is now behind us.

The field of ethics and international affairs has reached a point of maturity. A close look at the literature reveals that even the most ardent skeptics have always been willing to discuss international issues and foreign policy on ground that extends beyond the vicissitudes of self-interest and the quest for power represented by crude Machiavellianism and narrow conceptions of national interest.[1] Yet the end of the Cold War has helped to bring this ethical dimension to the fore. Anticommunist *raison d'état* in the West has gone the way of Marxist-Leninist *raison d'état* in the East. Both are now finished, and their reflexive appeals to the "necessity" rationale for all policy decisions must now yield to more nuanced views and substantive analyses.

Another reason for this maturity is the achievement of a new critical mass in the field. Within the past fifteen years, a new literature has been introduced, producing cumulative results. In the late 1970s and early 1980s, the field was influenced by debate over the Vietnam War, the loss of trust in government symbolized by the Watergate scandal and the Church committee hearings on

CIA activities, and concern over the nuclear stalemate. Landmark books and articles were written by Michael Walzer, Stanley Hoffmann, Charles Beitz, Henry Shue, Terry Nardin, the Roman Catholic Bishops, and others.[2] Along with the pioneering work of Hans J. Morgenthau, Reinhold Niebuhr, George Kennan, and Kenneth W. Thompson, these efforts laid the foundation for vigorous debate focusing on ideas such as deterrence, intervention, human rights, and international distributive justice.[3]

The fact that these categories are by no means new should not be surprising: it has been said that in the field of political philosophy, novelty is not a virtue. If there is any trend to be detected in the development of this literature, it is not the manufacturing of something new but, rather, a return to basics. Plato, Aristotle, Augustine, Aquinas, Locke, J. S. Mill, and Kant are not far from the surface. The philosophical issues at the heart of ethics and international affairs have remained constant through the ages, including through the Cold War and after. These permanent issues include: (1) how to balance justice and order; (2) how to balance moral commitments with political realities; and (3) how to relate the insights of philosophy and history to contemporary problems.[4]

It is telling that for all of the rapid changes we have witnessed since the end of the Cold War, we find ourselves today with the same objective as Joseph S. Nye, Jr., who wrote in the first article to appear in *Ethics & International Affairs* that we must confront our choices in their full complexity, rather than "escape with one dimensional rationalizations." Of course Nye, writing in 1987 under the title of "Superpower Ethics: An Introduction," was arguing against what is now an artifact of Cold War history: the fallacy of moral equivalence. Today it is no longer necessary to argue over whether the United States and the Soviet Union are "two terrorist states [who] speak exactly the same language," as E. P. Thompson suggested in 1984.[5] Such arguments may be over, but the essential task of ethics and international affairs remains the same: to show how policy decisions can be firmly rooted in ethics while avoiding the perils of moralism and absolutism on the one hand and empty relativism on the other.

The field of ethics and international affairs as represented in this volume has developed along two branches, each feeding off the other. The first is the study of the sources of morality, or the traditions that provide the vocabulary and the guidelines for ethical judgment. The second is the study of specific issue areas such as sovereignty, just war, and human rights, as well as larger analytical issues such as cultural relativism, public and private morality, and the role of prudence in political leadership.

There are a number of ways to categorize the sources of morality that serve as guides to ethical reasoning. Robert J. Myers identifies four fundamental sources: religion, deontology, utilitarianism, and virtue.[6] Terry Nardin and David R. Mapel in their encyclopedic *Traditions of International Ethics* (1992) cast a wider net (including sources such as Marxism and liberalism, among others) and conclude by classifying the traditions with a taxonomy that distinguishes between rule-oriented and consequence-oriented approaches. As Nardin points out, "When we argue about international affairs we draw directly or indirectly on established traditions of ethical discourse."[7]

For Nardin, Mapel, and others who write about traditions of international ethics, "ethics" is the process by which sources of morality (or traditions) are digested and applied to problems of the social world. In theory these sources of morality exist discretely and are discernible as separate entities; yet in practice they are often blended together. Much of the literature in this area is premised on the notion that it is important for decision makers (citizens and statesmen alike) to understand the sources of morality to which they appeal when they make ethical judgments. It is instructive to see how and why elements from disparate sources often overlap, and how and why they are sometimes mixed and matched.

The second aspect of the literature in ethics and international affairs looks at the question "How do the sources of morality apply to actual problems?" In short, what is their relevance to policy?

This sets up inquiries into areas of normative agreement and disagreement, as well as the theme of moral choice. Ethnic violence, regional conflict, demographic shifts, economic rivalries, and environmental protection have moved to the center of the international agenda. New motivations and restraints have emerged in dealing with these issues, primarily the reality of limited resources and the difficulties of sustaining cooperation among allies. And along with these new elements, old considerations of national interests remain powerful and often decisive. Given this mix of changing and enduring interests, many new choices have to be justified in new or at least different terms.[8]

The possibilities and limitations of normative agreement on ideas such as the sovereign equality of states, human rights, the presumption of nonintervention, the principle of self-determination, and just war are themselves a main theme within the field of ethics and international affairs.[9] There is a robust literature on the history and purpose of codified norms such as those found in the United Nations Charter, the Universal Declaration of Human Rights, and the Geneva conventions and their additional protocols. Yet this is just a baseline, for the literature goes on to explore normative ideas that are not codified in documents and in law. It becomes apparent in virtually every discussion of ethics and international affairs that the role and resonance of international moral norms cannot be reduced solely to a discussion of international law. The difference between ethics and law—between what is codified as a moral minimum and what is required in terms of right and good conduct—often varies according to circumstance and interpretation.[10]

All of the work in this reader explores the connection between moral traditions and the decision-making process; the overarching theme is "moral choice." Each author relates the timeless insights of philosophy and our collective historical experience to the hard choices of our own age. The root of ethics is human agency—real people making real decisions, acting in history. Despite their focus on the international system, the conditions of anarchy, and the primacy of power and interests, political theorists such as Hans J. Morgenthau and Kenneth W. Thompson conclude: "Ethical rules have their seat in the conscience of individual men. Government by clearly identifiable men who can be held personably responsible for their actions is therefore the precondition for the existence of an effective system of international ethics."[11] Principles must be discussed in light of specific cases; moral choice must be discussed as the product of individuals dealing with historical tradition, political circumstance, and the enduring demands of human nature, including the considerable claims of self-interest and the struggle for power.

Each chapter in this volume takes traditions and values seriously, and each seeks to show where and how these traditions and values have mattered in terms of policy. The intellectual roots of current thinking are examined with an eye toward avoiding the excesses of both moralism and nihilism. Complications posed by cultural differences and age-old debates over universality versus particularity are fully considered. Yet these endless philosophical tensions and paradoxes are rendered in a constructive rather than a paralyzing manner.

The most difficult thing about ethics and international affairs is defining it. What frameworks do we have? What pathways offer the most promising routes to increased understanding? What organizing principles do we have for thinking about morality and foreign policy? This collection is not meant to be the final word on these questions, but it is offered with the hope that its readers will find it a promising place to start.

NOTES

1. Michael Joseph Smith, *Realism from Weber to Kissinger* (Baton Rouge: Louisiana State University Press, 1986); Charles W. Kegley, Jr., *Controversies in International Relations Theory: Realism and the Neoliberal Challenge* (New York: St. Martin's Press, 1995). See also Fareed Zakaria, "Is Realism Finished?" *National Interest* 30 (Winter 1992/93), 21–32, who observes: "Far from being philosophic skeptics, realists like Max Weber, Reinhold Niebuhr, and Hans Morgenthau have devoted years of their lives and hundreds of pages of text in order to establish moral imperatives in the international arena. It is no accident that today's most prominent realist statesman, Henry Kissinger, and its most prominent realist scholar, Kenneth Waltz, have both written serious works on Immanuel Kant."

2. Michael Walzer, *Just and Unjust Wars* (New York: Basic Books, 1977); Charles R. Beitz, *Political Theory and International Relations* (Princeton: Princeton University Press, 1979); Stanley Hoffmann, *Duties beyond Borders* (Syracuse: Syracuse University Press, 1981); Henry Shue, *Basic Rights: Subsistence, Affluence, and U.S. Foreign Policy* (Princeton: Princeton University Press, 1980); Terry Nardin, *Law, Morality, and the Relations of States* (Princeton: Princeton University Press, 1983); and National Conference of Catholic Bishops, *The Challenge of Peace* (Washington: United States Catholic Conference, 1983). For a summary of this literature, see Charles R. Beitz, "Recent International Thought," *International Journal* 43 (Spring 1988), 183–204; and Charles R. Beitz et al., *International Ethics: A Philosophy and Public Affairs Reader* (Princeton: Princeton University Press, 1985).

3. The canon includes Hans J. Morgenthau, *Politics among Nations,* 6th ed. (New York: Alfred Knopf, 1985); George F. Kennan, *American Diplomacy 1900–1950,* expanded ed. (Chicago: University of Chicago Press, 1984); and Kenneth W. Thompson, *Ethics and National Purpose* (New York: Church Peace Union, 1957).

4. The best summary of the enduring characteristics of political philosophy and its relevance to international affairs is Kenneth W. Thompson, *Fathers of International Thought* (Baton Rouge: Louisiana State University Press, 1994). Thompson writes: "Despite the absence of a world state, political theory and international theory share a common universe of discourse. If they suffered from mutual neglect in the 1950s, they show signs of reinforcing each other in the 1990s. It seems clear that political philosophy illuminates historic concepts like authority, justice, community, and power. Political theory throws light on recurrent issues such as the relation between peace and order, morality and politics, equality and freedom, and change and continuity."

5. Joseph S. Nye, Jr., "Superpower Ethics: An Introduction," *Ethics & International Affairs* 1 (1987), 1–7.

6. Robert J. Myers, "After the Cold War," *Society* 28 (March/April 1991).

7. Terry Nardin and David R. Mapel, eds., *Traditions of International Ethics* (New York: Cambridge University Press, 1992). Also representative of this approach are Cho-yun Hsu, "Applying Confucian Ethics to International Relations," *Ethics & International Affairs* 5 (1991), 15–31; and James Turner Johnson, *The Quest for Peace: Three Moral Traditions in Western Cultural History* (Princeton: Princeton University Press, 1987).

8. For an overview see Charles W. Kegley, Jr., ed., *Controversies in International Relations Theory: Realism and the Neoliberal Challenge* (New York: St. Martin's Press, 1995); Gaddis Smith, "What Role for America?" *Current History* 92 (April 1993), 150–54.

9. This is best represented in Dorothy V. Jones, *Code of Peace: Ethics and Security in the World of the Warlord States* (Chicago: University of Chicago Press, 1991).

10. See Terry Nardin, "International Ethics and International Law," *Review of International Studies* 18 (1992), 19–30. Nardin observes that "international law is a source as well as an object of ethical judgments. . . . The authority of international law is determined by criteria internal to the institution of international law, not by exogenous tests of moral validity. . . . [A]s a consequence of this, international legal obligation is independent of moral obligation."

11. Kenneth W. Thompson, *Political Realism and the Crisis of World Politics* (1960; reprint, Washington: University Press of America, 1982), 157.

Part I: THEORY

ROBERT J. MYERS
Speaking Truth to Power: The Quest for Equality in Freedom

STANLEY HOFFMANN
The Political Ethics of International Relations

JACQUES BARZUN
Is Democratic Theory for Export?

ALBERTO R. COLL
Normative Prudence As a Tradition of Statecraft

Robert J. Myers*

Speaking Truth to Power: The Quest for Equality in Freedom

Professor Hans J. Morgenthau's career was marked by his primary concern with moral philosophy and an attendant imperative to speak truth to power. He was convinced of the validity of the enterprise, despite occasional reverses. "In the long run . . . the voice of truth, so vulnerable to power, has proved more resilient than power. It has built empires of the mind and the spirit that have outlasted, and put their mark upon, the empires of power. On January 22, 1967, about thirty people demonstrated in Pushkin Square in Moscow against the arrest of four persons who had transcribed the court records in the trial against Andrei Sinyavsky and Yuli Daniel. One of the organizers of the protest, Khaustov, who was sentenced to three years at hard labor, admitted at his trial that he had read Kant and Hegel and that his reading of Kant made 'him see a lot of things in a new light.' The experience of the 1960s has dispelled the illusion that truth can show power the way in direct confrontation. But historical experience reassures us that truth can indeed make people see a lot of things in a new light. And when people see things in a new light, they might act in a new way."[1]

There are many themes that one can constructively pursue if one wishes to discuss the legacy and political wisdom bequeathed

*The author presented this paper at the Eleventh Morgenthau Memorial Lecture on Ethics & Foreign Policy, sponsored by the Carnegie Council on Ethics and International Affairs, in New York City on October 10, 1991.

to us by Professor Hans J. Morgenthau. From what I hear and observe, there are a number of biographies of Professor Morgenthau in process on particular aspects of his life. My only concern in regard to these ongoing projects—and the cottage industry at the University of Virginia where the Morgenthau papers are currently located—is that some day he may suffer the fate of Plato: there are so many books about Plato that it is allegedly impossible for anyone in a single lifetime to consult the extant bibliography, let alone write anything about the whole personality. Yet something of that fate for Professor Morgenthau seems inevitable. The title that I have chosen, "Speaking Truth to Power," adumbrated by the opening quotation, may give some insight into both Professor Morgenthau and our current political condition.

I will discuss three interrelated subjects that preoccupied Professor Morgenthau—the creation of his realism doctrine and its influence on American foreign policy, some enduring dilemmas of American democracy, and finally the threat of nuclear death, of the mass destruction of humanity. While it was the development of "realism" as a distinct theory of international relations that is likely to remain his claim to historical significance, these other two topics are well worth exploring, not only to demonstrate the range of his intellectual interests but also as lasting contributions to his vision of the purpose of America.

After all, what is the truth that Professor Morgenthau presented to power? One is struck by a persistent message in his works—equality in freedom. This is articulated best in *The Purpose of American Politics,* but it reverberates powerfully in all his writings. The purpose of foreign policy is to assure our security, so that each citizen can have the opportunity for life, liberty, and the pursuit of happiness. As Hamilton put it, "No government could give us tranquility and happiness at home, which did not possess sufficient stability and strength to make us respectable abroad."[2] Thus secure, our democratic system provides the possibility for each citizen to fulfill his potential. The just society requires equality in freedom.

Morgenthau's distress at the deficiencies of American foreign policy at the end of World War II was forged in his personal experience in Germany in the interwar years. Born in 1904 in Coburg, he had a largely fragmentary memory of World War I; but his life under the Weimar Republic and the coming of Naziism was vivid indeed. He suffered personal indignities because he was a Jew, such as his humiliation as the baccalaureate speaker upon graduation from high school (he was shouted at and spit upon) and his difficulty in finding suitable employment for his talent in Germany, then Switzerland and Spain. Finally, he reached the United States in 1937, friendless and poor; his exceptional ability and determination resulted in two books that set him apart on the American intellectual scene, *Scientific Man vs. Power Politics* in 1946 and *Politics among Nations* in 1948. Intellectually, he concluded that in the light of interwar history, America simply had not learned how to use power with responsibility. The very word "power" seemed to cloud any American foreign-policy enterprise; the natural tendency of American foreign-policy makers was to prefer idealistic solutions that eschewed power. Power politics, a true tautology, was considered a phrase of opprobrium. How should he go about educating the American leadership, as well as the academy and the people in general, about how the world really worked so that the egregious blunders of the past would not be repeated? This was a self-appointed task of great magnitude for an assistant professor of political science at the University of Kansas City.

As it developed, he had a two-part strategy, which somehow evolved in his thinking about the world and America. His first level of criticism of American international politics was its facile assumption of the solubility of all problems, including political problems, through a naive faith in the sciences. The success of Newton in the physical sciences would be repeated in the social world. Reason would find solutions to all of our political, economic, and social ills. The Enlightenment and European philosophers, such as Condorcet, Bentham, Marx, and Spencer, were convinced that the advances in the physical sciences and the biological sciences could be applied to the newly discovered "social sciences" of government, history, sociology, economics, and so on. This was, in effect, the public-administration approach to problems of politics, the assumption that identifying the problem (let's say the division of income, a border dispute, the class structure, the balance of trade) paved the way to its actual solution, totally disregarding the role of power and interest in why things were as they were. It was this simplistic faith that convinced Morgenthau that people trained in this type of philosophy, this utopian, wide-eyed view of the world, would once again commit the same blunders that had all but destroyed Western civilization in World Wars I and II.

A corollary of scientific man was his lack of understanding of the weakness of human nature, despite the cautions from religion, in its capacity for evil, as well as the limitations of human competence to understand complex situations fully, let alone act on them intelligently for both self-interest and national interest. Americans particularly did not understand the tragic nature of political choice and political action, that their efforts to do good often met the biblical admonishment in Romans 7 that trying to do good often creates evil results. They had not yet learned that the experience of making fateful moral choices was the only way they could learn both moral courage and moral wisdom. Instead, they learned nothing, relying on feeble institutions, such as the League of Nations or the United Nations, to do what they could not do in the international world: confront power with superior power.

These views, expressed in *Scientific Man,* formed two of the six principles of Morgenthau's theory of political realism, which he published two years later in 1948 in his seminal work, *Politics among Nations.* The first point, to repeat, was the imperfection of man's nature, the tendency to do evil while trying to do good. He called our attention to the fact that human nature, "in which the laws of politics have their roots, had not changed since the classical philosophies of China, India, and Greece endeavored to discover these laws. Hence, novelty is not necessarily a virtue in political theory, nor is old age a defect."[3] The second principle is: "Political realism is aware of the moral significance of political action. It is also aware of the ineluctable tension between the moral command and the requirements of political action." These two carryover principles from *Scientific Man* were joined by three others to make up the difference between realism and any other school of political thought. The additions were, first, the necessary focus on "interest defined as power"; second, the assertion that interest is not "defined once and for all," that the content and manner of the use of power is conditioned by the political and cultural environment; and third, the denial by realism that moral aspirations of particular states are the same as universal moral laws—no state can claim a monopoly on virtue. These five principles result in the sixth, that politics constitutes an autonomous sphere, that the politician thinks of interest defined as power, "just as the economist thinks of interest as defined as wealth." To this philosophical base were added four fundamental diplomatic rules: (1) diplomacy must be divested of the crusading spirit; (2) the objectives of foreign policy must be defined in terms of the national interest and must be supported with adequate power; (3) diplomacy must look at the political scene from the point of view of other nations; and (4) nations must be willing to compromise on all issues that are not vital to them.[4]

What was the significance of this new formulation of the philosophy of international relations? First of all, it was welcomed as an intellectual and practical alternative to the failures of the past, particularly the failures begun in the Woodrow Wilson era. Wilson's efforts to head off World War I and the whole sorry sequence of circumstances leading through the interwar period, from the rise of the future Axis powers—Germany, Italy, and Japan—to the appeasement policy of the European allies, once again led to war. The failure of the League of Nations was apparent to all, but the lesson seemed to be that the answer was to create a better League, the United Nations, which still contained many of the weaknesses of the old. The principal defect was no effective check on the sovereignty of states. Such policies and blinded vision were "utopian," or idealistic. Morgenthau's realism, to be brief, was a call for clear-eyed concentration on the national interest—at that time, a word that did not seem to require a detailed explanation—due regard for the international balance of power, and adequate armaments and allies to counter the new threat after the Axis: the Soviet Union and its apparent mission to communize the world. This was an altogether new peril, and America was uncertain how to deal with this unprecedented menace.

"Political realism" then was the answer to the misfortunes of the past and the sure guideline to durable and successful foreign policy in the future.[5] His message came at the right moment, just as Churchill called our attention to the iron curtain. The American nuclear monopoly was soon compromised, and the new balance of power was inherently dangerous and unstable. Foreign policy held the key to peace and the preservation of civilization. This is the way Morgenthau expressed his dedication to this field, despite personal preferences. "After World War II, I made a conscious choice in concentrating my efforts on foreign policy because I realized that the existence of the United States and even of mankind depended on a sound foreign policy. What good was it to speculate on philosophical topics if in a couple of years or decades the world would be reduced to radioactive rubble? So ever since, for more than twenty years, I have been caught in this self-imposed public service which by no means coincides with my real intellectual interests."[6] Yet his foray into world politics, with no diplomatic or political experience of any kind, was an incredible success. He spoke truth to power, and power listened in the intellectual vacuum that existed. Realism was the answer on how to deal with the Cold War. The textbook *Politics among Nations* was an enormous success, and the "powers that be" sought his advice. By preserving the strength of the republic, he was helping to assure what he saw as the purpose of America in freedom.

In the domestic area, Morgenthau found the going more difficult as he applied his principles to the workings of American democracy. The connection between international relations and domestic politics in America came to Morgenthau easily if imperfectly. "When I first arrived in the United States," he writes, "my conception of the American scene was primarily formed by two influences: class B Hollywood movies and the novels of Upton Sinclair. I realized that those impressions were not completely at variance with the American reality, but also that the American reality was much more variegated and complex than the original sources of my knowledge would indicate."[7] And in another passage: "Intellectually, I was quite unprepared for the United States. I had read William James in German translation but I had found him rather flat, commonsensical, and not particularly interesting. I had been brought up in a tradition entirely different from American pragmatism. That tradition had been influenced by such people as Max Weber and Hans Kelsen. So I was quite taken aback by the optimism and pragmatism characteristic of the American intellectual tradition."[8] He was also not acutely aware of the "can-do tradition" that remains an American characteristic, and has produced great triumphs and great disasters. One of these was the Vietnam War; in criticizing that war early on, Morgenthau found himself in the unaccustomed position of being an outside critic—like most critics, he preferred the insider position. And so he was surprised at the controversy that rose like a black cloud over his 1965 article in the *New York Times Magazine* in opposition to the Vietnam War.

The *New York Times Magazine* piece questioning American involvement in the Vietnam War was based on one of Morgenthau's basic foreign-policy aphorisms—"Never put yourself in a position from which you cannot retreat without losing face and from which you cannot advance without grave risks." In *Politics among Nations,* his examples were Napoleon III on the eve of the Franco-Prussian War of 1870 and Austria and Germany just before World War I. He probably learned from the Vietnam article that examples from the distant past are safer than those of the contemporary political scene. "Unfavorable reaction to this article on the part of the administration was not long in coming. President Johnson expressed himself privately in quite unflattering terms about my position. I was no longer invited to the White House. I was fired as a consultant to the Defense Department. The White House established a desk called 'Project Morgenthau' for the purpose of getting something on me."[9] The efforts of the Johnson administration to discredit Morgenthau were not successful, and those who participated in that enterprise were left with nothing to be proud of. The experience, however, left Morgenthau in a pensive mood, as revealed in a volume of his essays published in 1970.

> I find my faith, suggested by some of these essays, in the power of truth to move men—and more importantly statesmen—to action the more curious since about twenty five years ago I launched, in *Scientific Man vs. Power Politics,* a frontal (and, as it turned out, premature) attack against these and other liberal illusions. The disavowal of that faith by political experience was absorbed by me and many, if not the great mass, of my contemporaries not as an isolated incident but as the definitive refutation of one of the main tenets of liberal philosophy. We came to realize now, through political experience, what some of us had concluded before by way of philosophical reflection, that power positions do not yield to arguments, however rationally and morally valid, but only to superior power. We also came to realize that the distribution of power in America favors the continuation of policies that we regard to be indefensible on rational and moral grounds.[10]

After this disappointing experience, he took time to reflect on the democratic principle of dissent, a subject on which he had become an unwilling expert. In a piece published in August 1968, he outlined his view on the access in American society to the truth and on the crucial role of minority rights, in the largest sense, if democracy is to be preserved. This was a central issue for equality in freedom. Like Arthur Schlesinger, Jr., he believed that relativism is the operative philosophy of the American democracy—that everyone has access to the truth, with no one having a monopoly, and that inherent in the American democratic system is the possibility that today's minority may be tomorrow's majority. Rising above this relativism and making it workable, however, is the transcendent notion of a "higher purpose" that guides American democracy and acts as a brake on simple majoritarianism. That kind of problem was anticipated by James Madison in *Federalist* 10. The will of the majority is not, then, by definition the absolute truth and can in most cases be modified by incremental changes in what seems to be right or true. This process allows for mediation at the margins of political conflict and, since it is an open-ended process, oils the democratic preference. There is not a permanent majority and a permanent minority on political issues. Changing consensus on the Vietnam War is a good example of such a shift in public and official viewpoint and appreciation of what the right policy should be, after a seemingly unending process of trial and error. Professor Morgenthau had a wry and ironic conclusion to this particular Vietnam ordeal, often the fate of anyone who is prematurely correct about public policy: "For those who have made it their business in life to speak truth to power, there is nothing left but to continue to speak, less frequently perhaps than they used to and certainly with less confidence that it will in the short run make much of a difference in the affairs of man."[11]

In some other observations on the American domestic scene, his instincts for analyzing the key problems were as astute as in the international field, relying, as he generally did, on how the strength of the powers that be stood in relationship to reform. "What is disquieting in our present condition [he wrote in 1967] is the contrast between the gravity of the two great domestic problems that require solutions—race relations and unemployment—and the complacency permeating the thoughts and actions of government and public alike."[12] These problems are still very much with us and have not only been a blot on the American conscience but stand as a disfigurement of how American democracy wants to be perceived and what it sees in the mirror. One of his concerns was that these twin evils could result in greater violence in society and a lessening of the prospects for equality in freedom.

The content of democracy in America and elsewhere, that is, its quality, has to be a source of constant scrutiny. Its shortcomings and intransigent problems lead to the conclusion of E. J. Dionne, for example, in *Why Americans Hate Politics,* that the process of politics for resolving such problems has become so flawed and the results so unsuccessful that there is a sense of helplessness in the land. He longs for a participatory democracy that revitalizes the body politic. "In our efforts to find our way toward a new world role, we would do well to revive what made us a special nation long before we became the world's leading military and economic power—our republican tradition that nurtured free citizens who eagerly embraced the responsibilities and pleasures of self-government. With democracy on the march outside our borders, our first responsibility is to ensure that the United States becomes a model for what self-government should be and not an example of what happens to free nations when they lose interest in public life. A nation that hates politics," he concludes, "will not survive as a democracy."[13]

Michael Oakeshott, the British philosopher, thinks that part of this problem comes about because of the increasing difficulty of the individual in society to cope; the autonomous individual in today's world is often unable to make all the determinations and decisions required of him or her as they are thrust upon one in terms of political beliefs, job preferences, religious alliances, and so on. People in this situation, Oakeshott says, become "individual manques," who opt out of the "civic association" and therefore don't participate in solving such pressing problems as race relations and distributive justice, if one can still talk about distributive problems in our "free market" society. The philosopher David Norton sees this as a towering problem for the kind of democracy he prefers, a democracy populated by virtue-loving individuals who seek the "good life" and are motivated to pursue, through active participation, the politics of their community.[14]

Morgenthau's ongoing concern about the treatment of African-Americans in America was the denial of what he saw to be the purpose of America, equality in freedom. He expressed it this way: "The contrast between the legal and moral commitment to equal opportunity for all and the actual denial of that opportunity to a collectively defined group of citizens constitutes a tragic denial of the American purpose. Its tragic quality stems from its inescapability, its imperviousness to the good intentions of either the reformer or the paternalist."[15]

This inequality, to quote Jefferson, is a "moral reproach." Slavery, Morgenthau says, could be handled by a single legal stroke, the Emancipation Proclamation. Segregation can be attacked by law, but that does not resolve the matter. "All states of the Union are segregationists in different degrees, with regard to different activities and by virtue, or in spite, of different legal arrangements. Even where the law requires integration in all fields of social interaction, segregation is still a social fact." The prospect, as he saw it, was for a three-cornered escalation of domestic violence: "the black man against government, the lower white middle class against the black man, and the government against both."

The issue of black inequality was intimately connected to the unemployment question. The American economy, Morgenthau thought, was now in a position to move from scarcity to abundance. "Morally," he wrote, "we have accepted the obligation to provide all citizens with a modicum of economic well-being and security as a precondition for having an equal opportunity to realize this human potential in freedom. It is only outmoded economic theory and practice that stands in the way of our using our productive power for this moral end."[16] He does not explain what the "new economic theory" might be—he was often criticized for the relatively small attention he paid to economic matters—but his message was clear. These injustices must be ameliorated or, once again, the level of violence will rise in the unequal struggle of the individual, lacking equality and opportunity, in a confrontation with the state.

Surely the purpose of America was more noble; issues like racial equality and unemployment needed to be raised to the level of public debate, giving different versions of America's destiny. He cited as historical precedents Pinckney-Hamilton, Lodge-Wilson, Borah-FDR. Instead, writing in 1959, he lamented "the lack of relevant controversy, for where nothing is clearly stated, there is nothing to oppose."[17]

The truth he was pointing out to the powers that be was that problems of this gravity, these weeds of injustice, could not be removed by the status quo. In international politics, the status quo is ordinarily highly valued for its reliability and general convenience; but in American domestic politics, if we are to be democratic, allowing for the waxing and waning of majority views, an intransigent status quo is often dangerous to the improvement of the prospects for equality in freedom. Change was urgently and immediately required. Power once again did not agree with Morgenthau, but like Immanuel Kant, he had done his duty.

Finally, in analyzing Morgenthau's international and domestic politics, we come to a related core concern, how the individual faces the world and its institutions. He wonders how the individual can save himself from the mindlessness of mass destruction, caused by science and technology gone amuck. He wonders whether technology and science will obliterate him. His thoughts on these matters are interspersed in many of his works, but principally in his essays on *Science: Servant or Master?* Man is threatened by technology as applied science, which can destroy man and his social and material environment by war, social dislocation, and pollution. "Technology has created a potential economy of abundance, while tens of millions of people in the United States and hundreds of millions throughout the world live in poverty." If this situation were not bad enough, science has compromised man's "inner freedom," through which a limited autonomy was possible. Now even the simplest activities require reliance on technology—water, transportation, light. All these technological advances carry with them the possibility of totalitarian control and the loss of individual autonomy.[18]

Morgenthau sees a change away from the view of the ancients that science for science's sake was its own reward. "We are no longer capable of that self-assurance . . . that salutes each new knowledge as a new victory carrying its justification within itself." The difference between the ancient and modern view of scientific advance is like that between the soldier and the statesman. "For the soldier, victory is justified by itself; the statesman must search for its political meaning. For the soldier, victory is an end in itself; for the statesman, it must be a means to an end."[19] The critique of science is not against science per se, however, but what man has tried to do with science, by not subjecting the scientific enterprise to a transcendent standard. "Action is neutral as concerns human life: it is as willing to keep millions alive with the means science has put at its disposal as it is to kill them. The same technologies produce medicines and poison gas, machines and weapons, nuclear energy and nuclear bombs. Action, like theoretical knowledge, is divorced from transcendent meaning. As in the sphere of science it is at best still possible to distinguish between true and false, so in the field of action one can still distinguish between useful and useless, but no longer between good and bad, valuable and worthless."[20] Science, however, is not an independent actor, simply setting about to do what it wishes, as the title of the essays suggest, but, rather, its performance is subject to human volition. The failure comes from humankind's inability to "set science tasks that affirm life and enlarge it" (even though he acknowledged that goal-oriented science might destroy the very system of scientific inquiry).

The development of nuclear weapons spurred enormously the disparity between "people power" and the government. The knowledge of the overwhelming force of government power—despite the unlikelihood of a government using nuclear weapons on its own people—strengthened the status quo. The impossibility of popular revolution in a modern state run by a determined leadership was a powerful boost for the status quo, the powers that be. On the international scene, the existence of these nuclear weapons was creating irrational policies based on the idea that nuclear weapons were just another weapon, a logical extension of block-busting, air-sucking conventional weapons. Morgenthau was convinced of the unusability of nuclear weapons, beyond their deterrence value for those who saw deterrence as a feasible and moral proposition. He was scathing in his criticism of such nuclear warriors as Herman Kahn, who tried to make nuclear war thinkable and winnable. Morgenthau summarizes the Kahn position: "We can survive, and recuperate from, a nuclear war, provided we make the necessary preparations and our calculations are correct; yet the first proviso is improbable and the second, dubious. Thus a massive undertaking, which sets out as a demonstration of the acceptability of nuclear war and generally has been debated as such, ends up as a hypothetical intellectual exercise, a piece of political science fiction, divorced from reality by improbable and dubious empirical assumptions."[21]

The nuclear war thesis had two potentially disastrous consequences: there is no rational relationship between means and ends (even the Napoleons and Hitlers, he wrote, paid attention to this principle), and it raises the specter of nuclear death. This was the final assault and indignity against one's individual existence as a single human being, someone who matters. Equality is in fact the essence of democratic government; each person should be treated as though each is as worthy as the other, in accord with equality in freedom;[22] "nuclear destruction destroys the meaning of death by depriving it of its individuality."[23]

The meaning of life and death, Morgenthau wrote, is in part dependent on being remembered after death; with the possibility of millions dying simultaneously, the quantity of deaths might be remembered, but no individual quality. As long as nuclear weapons exist and science and technology expand the possibilities of mankind's destruction beyond the control of humanity itself, the threat of nuclear death remains: "It would indeed be the height of thoughtless optimism to assume that something so absurd as a nuclear war cannot happen because it is so absurd."[24]

Can anything substantial be done about this situation? Not likely, if one remembers the apparent irreducibility of human nature. Seeing things in a new light may not be enough. The eight thousand years of recorded history show little change in mankind's moral behavior. Eight thousand years is not long, to be sure, in the course of evolution. But how long must we wait, if that is the only solution? One possibility is to concentrate on improving each individual's interest and capacity for freedom and intellectual and moral growth. Looked upon this way, the three areas I have discussed today—the realist theory of international relations, democracy, and nuclear war—all point to the sacredness of each person. This is not an atomistic approach, in which each person is or should be fully autonomous. Within this autonomy, there must be a sense of community and common purpose at the international, national, and local levels. As Bellah's book, *Habits of the Heart,* demonstrates, there is a balance between the individual and community, full of new possibilities. This is reinforced by a study of Hans Morgenthau's life and his works. In speaking truth to power, I conclude with this observation: "Man's future," Morgenthau wrote, "depends ultimately upon himself. Although he cannot live without social ties to other men, he alone, in the solitude of his autonomous reflection, decides his future as man."[25] For those interested in Morgenthau's search for equality in freedom, speaking truth to power, there is hope that this decision will be for the reaffirmation of man's spirit and onward destiny, a happy reliance on Machiavelli's recommendation of the pillar of virtue, which is in our own hands, and the pillar of fortune, which is beyond our reach.[26]

NOTES

1. Hans J. Morgenthau, *Truth and Power: Essays of a Decade, 1960–70* (New York: Praeger, 1970), 8–9.

2. Ibid., 12.

3. Hans J. Morgenthau, *Politics among Nations,* 3rd ed. (New York: Alfred A. Knopf, 1962), 4.

4. Ibid., 563–64.

5. For a full treatment of the realist philosophy, see Joel H. Rosenthal, *Righteous Realists* (Baton Rouge: Louisiana State University Press, 1991). Also see Greg Russell, *Hans J. Morgenthau and the Ethics of American Statecraft* (Baton Rouge: Louisiana State University Press, 1990); and Michael J. Smith, *Realism from Weber to Kissinger* (Baton Rouge: Louisiana State University Press, 1986).

6. Kenneth W. Thompson and Robert J. Myers, eds., *Truth and Tragedy* (New Brunswick: Transaction Press, 1984), 381.

7. Ibid., 378.

8. Ibid., 378–79.

9. Ibid. 382–83.

10. Morgenthau, *Truth and Power,* 5.

11. Ibid., 8.

12. Ibid., 209.

13. E. J. Dionne, Jr., *Why Americans Hate Politics* (New York: Simon and Schuster, 1991), 351.

14. David Norton, *Democracy and Moral Development* (Berkeley: University of California Press, 1991), 110.

15. Hans J. Morgenthau, *The Purpose of American Politics* (New York: Alfred Knopf, 1962), 39.

16. Morgenthau, *Truth and Power,* 211–13.

17. Morgenthau, *The Purpose of American Politics,* 4.

18. Hans J. Morgenthau, *Science: Servant or Master?* (New York: New American Library, 1972), 3–5.

19. Ibid., 9.

20. Ibid., 28.

21. Ibid., 136.

22. Will Kymlicka, *Contemporary Political Philosophy* (Oxford: Clarendon Press, 1990), 5.

23. Morgenthau, *Science: Servant or Master?* 149.

24. Ibid., 152.

25. Ibid., 71.

26. Morgenthau, *The Purpose of American Politics,* 323.

Stanley Hoffmann*

The Political Ethics of International Relations

The two major developments in the literature on international relations during the past ten years have been widely different and yet, as we shall see, they are not unrelated. One is the growth of a "scientific" theory of conflictual cooperation. It applies game theory to the study of the conditions and possibilities of cooperation under anarchy. The most characteristic contribution to this literature was the October 1985 issue of *World Politics,* which tries to show how game theory could be used to bridge the gap that has developed between the study of diplomatic-strategic behavior and that of the international political economy.

The other major development is the appearance, especially in the United States and in Britain, of a new literature about the ethical aspects of international relations and particularly of foreign policy. These works are both analytical and prescriptive. They are analytical insofar as they concern themselves not only, like so many writings on international affairs, with the facts of power and the description of interests but also with the moral choices faced by decision makers or by citizens when they have to engage in transactions among different societies or deal with those domestic issues that affect foreigners. These works also concern them-

*The author presented this paper at the Seventh Morgenthau Memorial Lecture on Ethics & Foreign Policy, sponsored by the Carnegie Council on Ethics and International Affairs, in New York City in the fall of 1988.

selves with the moral consequences that decisions entail even when the decision maker is unaware of the moral nature of his choices. Principally, however, this new literature is prescriptive; this is probably its most daring aspect. It asks the following question: given the nature of international politics, given the constraints that operate on any foreign policy, what are, on the one hand, the moral *restraints* that actors (states, international or regional organizations, transnational actors such as multinational corporations, and so on) should observe and, on the other hand, what are the moral *objectives* that they ought to give themselves?

This new body of work rests on three assumptions. The first assumption is that all politics is a goal-oriented activity (indeed, one of the weaknesses of many of the attempts at turning the study of international relations into a science is that they concentrate on means instead of starting with goals, or else they consider the actors' goals as given or fixed, which is a serious mistake). One major difference between, say, international politics and sports is that the goals of foreign policy are multiple; they are selected by the state and they consist of both material objectives and "milieu" targets that embody a conception of the good, a notion of right and wrong. The second assumption is that international relations is a domain of moral choice. It is not the realm of pure necessity, nor is it a field in which the moral code is different from the code that exists in personal life, in the life of groups, or in domestic politics. The limits within which this moral code operates may be much more stringent, and the possibilities of moral action may be more limited, but the code itself is not radically different. Although the substance of morality does not vary with the sphere of action, it remains true that the world is characterized by a great diversity of moral codes actually observable in different cultures or societies, and it is also true that there are many competing moral systems or theories, that is, there are serious disagreements about what constitutes a moral imperative, about how we define the criteria of morality and rank our values. The third assumption is that this diversity does not vitiate or preclude efforts at moral reasoning in any field of applied ethics.

The new literature on ethics and international affairs has many authors; some are philosophers (see for instance the 1985 issue of the journal *Ethics* on nuclear issues). Indeed, philosophers seem to have had a field day trying to cope with the formidable problems raised by nuclear weapons, often at an extremely high level of abstraction. But much of the new literature comes from political theorists, such as Michael Walzer or Charles Beitz, and political scientists, such as Joseph Nye and Robert W. Tucker. I will now turn to some remarks about the antecedents of this literature; I will then ask myself why it has developed now; I will briefly review the major contributions so far and finally make a few more personal remarks.

The Antecedents of the New Literature

The new literature has august antecedents. The philosophies of international relations that have dominated the intellectual history of the field always had an ethical dimension. In succession, the field has been marked by the Christian philosophy of just war, the liberal conception that emerged when the modern state system appeared, and the Marxist approach to world affairs. The Christian doctrine of just war was based on the model or assumption of a worldwide Christian community under natural law, with the Church playing the role of authority and official interpreter of that law. The doctrine entailed an attempt not at banning the use of force but at imposing limits on it. In other words, it recognized, or implied, the inevitability of evil but tried both to contain it and to harness evil impulses to the common good. Hence the complex system of restraints on the ends and means of force, a remarkable mix of absolute prescriptions (such as those concerning the ends toward which force could legitimately be used, or the principle of the immunity of noncombatants) and of calculations of consequences.

The liberal conception had deep Christian roots. One of its major branches, that which affirmed the existence of natural rights and whose greatest founding fathers were Locke and Grotius, had its own origins in the traditional Christian conception of natural law. Both the natural-rights branch and the utilitarian one were (and still are, insofar as liberalism is alive today) oriented toward the future. Liberalism advocated and predicted a society of self-determined, self-governing nations that would settle their conflicts without war, nations in which the powers of the state would be sharply curtailed by the free transnational activities of individuals (such as travel and trade). It thus offers a vision of both an interstate society and a transnational society. The Kantian variant of liberalism contains a strong emphasis on the state: it stresses the need for certain proper, that is, constitutional, institutions, and the league for peace that Kant envisaged rested on agreements among states. Anglo-Saxon liberalism put less of an emphasis on the state and much more on the role of individuals, who would reduce the state to a collection of public services controlled by domestic and world public opinion. Clearly, there was a definite conception of the political good in these visions.

Finally, the Marxist philosophy of history predicted the final abolition of class conflicts and of states; the end of alienation would be at the same time the end of social struggles and the end of state quarrels. Although the stages of human history that precede this nirvana offer nothing but false moralities, that is, ideologies in which the conceptions of the good merely disguise the interests of the powerful, the final vision is, once again, clearly a moral one.

All these conceptions express dissatisfaction with the moral implications of what has sometimes been called, since Rousseau, the "state of war," that is, the state of permanent tension and recurrent violent conflict among the temporal units into which the world is divided. Now, this state of war is itself both a latent, and often manifest, reality in the so-called Westphalian system of international relations and an intellectual tradition of its own. I am referring to what is probably the most distinguished school of thought in the history of international relations, realism (the best recent study of it is that of Michael Smith, *Realist Thought from Weber to Kissinger* (Louisiana University Press, 1987).

Realists, who assert and describe the permanence and inevitability of violent conflict in an anarchical milieu deprived of common central power and almost devoid of common values, have always been bothered by the ethical issue. Some realists have simply denied that ethics has much to do with international affairs. For Machiavelli, indeed, all politics, domestic as well as international, is a state of war, and the Christian morality that is often observed in private life is irrelevant to and destructive of the political universe. For Max Weber all politics, again, entails violence, but the structure of international affairs, which rules out a monopoly on the legitimate use of force, condemns the world to inexpiable clashes of values and power. The statesman, whose primary responsibility is to his own nation, cannot morally transcend its borders. Other realists have, in effect, smuggled a certain brand of ethics into their stark and bloody universe. It is the ethics of moderation or of the least evil, and one can analyze the superficially cool but deeply passionate work of Thucydides, the writings of Hans Morgenthau, and those of George Kennan, the most articulate critic of the legalistic and moralistic approaches in international relations, as pleas for an enlightened or moderate conception of the national interest that would certainly not eliminate but would at least mitigate conflict and allow for a modicum of comity among states.

As the density of relations and of processes among states and across states increased in the last two centuries, ethical considerations became important in the actions of states, particularly in two kinds of cases that brought about profound changes of behavior, regimes, and maps. On the one hand, we find the sudden, recurrent appearance of revolutionary actors who try to reshape international relations according to certain principles: France during the French Revolution, Russia after the October Revolution, and Nazi Germany. All these actors went way beyond the traditional kinds of possession goals, onto attempts at recasting the milieu in their own image. On the other hand, after the major wars that marked the breakdown of an international system, ambitious peace settlements have tried to create conditions for stability that very clearly derived from a combination of political and moral principles. I am referring to the Congress of Vienna and its reassertion of monarchic legitimacy and, of course, also to the Wilsonian settlements of 1919, as well as to the failed attempt at building a new world order in 1945.

And yet we encounter a paradox. Despite these intellectual traditions and this massive intrusion of political-ethical considerations at important moments in modern international affairs, the ethical dimension seemed to disappear in the scholarly literature of international relations. Why? A first cause appears to be the general tendency toward "value-free" research and theory. In the social sciences, research and theory were conceived as a reflection on or an explanation of what *is,* in reaction against the mixing of the *is* and the *ought* that had prevailed before. In other words, social science has wanted to conquer its independence from all aspects of philosophy. This ambition did not appear until late in the nineteenth century; it is interesting in this respect to compare Tocqueville and Weber. The latter is the real father of the value-free conception, whereas Tocqueville, in his analyses of democracy in America, France, and England, in his writings on revolutions, and in his analytic history of the development of the French state, never tried to dissociate the *is* from the *ought,* his analytical concepts from his value preferences. To be sure, the Weberian conception never conquered everything and everyone: as one of Weber's most brilliant disciples, Raymond Aron, pointed out, scientific analysis in sociology and political science is almost inevitably followed by, or almost inevitably leads to, an ethical-political evaluation. The grip of the scientific ideal, however, appears to be most tenacious in the study of international relations. Harsh criticisms, including those of Raymond Aron, have not dispelled the dream of a science of international relations built on the models of the natural sciences and of modern economics—a science consisting of formal models in which the preferences of the actors are treated as givens and in which attempts are made at quantifying the multiple imponderables of international affairs.

A second cause for the disappearance of the ethical dimension in the literature is the deep mark of the realist intellectual tradition. It was a double impact. On the one hand, realists seemed to be arguing that there was no room for ethical considerations in a Hobbesian universe; such considerations make sense only within a well-ordered state. This conception has been most recently restated by Felix Oppenheim, who argues, in his article "National Interest, Rationality, and Morality," that foreign policy is nothing but the quest for the most effective means to reach unavoidable or necessary goals; it is a domain not of moral principles but of rational choice.[1] On the other hand, realist works also try to show that international affairs could be seriously damaged and made more violent or irrational by the introduction of ethical considerations. This is what George Kennan pointed out; E. H. Carr had previously stated that ethical notions in foreign policy were likely to be either a hypocritical disguise or a sign of ethical confusion.

As a result, ethical considerations have for a long time been relegated almost exclusively to the literature of international law. Here they appear inevitable, since international law is about how states *ought* to behave, and the key issues in the theory of international law—the foundations of obligation, the nature of sovereignty—all raise questions about the nature and direction of international relations. The answers reproduce the traditional philosophies: positivism (the international-law translation of realism), natural law, liberalism, and Marxism. But international relations theory has reacted against international law, which it has tried to describe, deconstruct, or demythologize as a mere tool of states and their interests.

Confronting a New International System

Why has a new literature on ethics and international relations developed in the last ten years? As usual, we have to look for an answer in the evolution of international relations themselves. The density of those relations has increased even more than it had in the nineteenth and early twentieth centuries. We now live in the first truly global international system and it is characterized by two highly important phenomena. The first is the nuclear revolution. The invention of nuclear weapons has created formidable new dimensions of insecurity and, as one statesman after another has proclaimed, highlighted the bankruptcy of the traditional approach to security as a zero-sum game. The second phenomenon is economic interdependence in an increasingly integrated world economy. This has meant both that domestic politics, and particularly domestic public policies in economic and social matters, are at the mercy of outside forces and that domestic needs and demands can often be met only by international cooperation. The nuclear revolution and economic interdependence amount to a huge change in the significance of sovereignty. Sovereignty now does not mean authority abroad (including the authority to accept voluntary limitations); it means only the authority to cope with a host of external penetrations, obstacles, and constraints.

These new phenomena put an enormous emphasis on the problem of change. Letting things happen, behaving as states have traditionally behaved, following the customary logic of conflict and competition among a hugely increased and diversified crowd of actors could easily be catastrophic, and yet the political logic is almost inevitably driven by the quest for short-term gains. One key innovation, the result of the multiple crises of the twentieth century, has been the attempt by states to achieve, at home and abroad, deliberate, planned change—the welfare state at home, agreements among superpowers on rules of the game, the establishment of international regimes, efforts at regional integration, the turn to international organizations, and so on. Now, planned change necessarily involves values, because planned change reintroduces the dimension of "ought-ness" in international affairs.

There are also purely intellectual reasons for the development of the new literature. One notices a certain dissatisfaction with the "value-free" conception of social science. One could almost argue that the more international relationists, to use Hedley Bull's expression, try to square the circle by turning the study of international affairs into science, the more other scholars realize the philosophical limitation of the attempt. After all, in dealing with human affairs the scholar's role is not exhausted by the familiar dialectic of explanation and interpretation. Explanation means trying to identify the causal connections that led to an event; interpretation is an attempt at exploring the meaning of the event or phenomenon. When one is through with explanation and interpretation, there remain an extra dimension and task: evaluation, or judgment, which goes beyond the quest for the historical significance or meaning of the event or phenomenon and implies a moral position. Let us take the example of the Cuban missile crisis. It is easy to see how, after one has tried to explain the surprising Soviet move and the American reaction, and after one has interpreted the place of this crisis in Soviet and American foreign policy and its significance for the international system, one is still left with the need to take a moral stand on the risks and choices that characterized the diplomacy and strategy of the two antagonists, and on the solution they reached.

There has also been considerable dissatisfaction with realism. Quite a number of years ago Arnold Wolfers showed how unconvincing arguments about necessity were in the realm of national security: there are, in fact, always choices, and the idea that survival and national security are beyond moral judgment, or can be envisaged apart from moral judgment, is both shortsighted and dangerous. Insofar as morality, driven out of the main door, is smuggled in through the rear window in the works of some realists, one is left in a very uncomfortable position. Max Weber's conception of international relations as a clash of national assertions and cultures and his conception of the duties of the statesman resulted in a view according to which a German statesman could have no other political and moral horizon than the unmitigated pursuit of the German national interest. This position was arbitrary (since in the Weberian universe there seems to be no reason why one national set of goals ought to be judged morally superior to another), and yet it was presented as an absolute. As for Hans Morgenthau's conception of the national interest, it did not make sufficiently clear the fact that the definition of this interest is derived not only from geopolitical considerations but also from values, most of which originate in domestic beliefs and intellectual traditions (this is as true for the way in which survival is defined as for the selection of goals other than survival and security). As I explained thirty years ago in *Contemporary Theory in International Relations* (Englewood Cliffs, N.J.: Prentice-Hall, 1960), Morgenthau's assumption that a correctly defined national interest would be ipso facto moral and lead to an international politics of moderation strikes me as very time-bound; it assumes a universe of statesmen who do not have to take the passions of nationalism too much into account.

Finally, there was a reason intrinsic to political philosophy for the emergence of political ethics in international relations. Political philosophy has traditionally been about the good state. Indeed, the current critique of liberalism, which accuses it of "bracketing" the search for the good and concerning itself only with the definition of rights, forgets that behind this emphasis on rights there is a conception of a good state, which happens to be the state that grants such rights and allows for a free competition among divergent views of the good. Traditional political philosophy did not go much beyond the state, not only because the state was correctly seen as the highest focus of human allegiance but also because it was conceptualized as a largely self-sufficient, sovereign unit. But as the international system became more and more obviously a major constraint on states—indeed, one particularly influential theory of international relations, that of Kenneth Waltz, presents the international system as the determinant of state behavior in a universe of anarchy—as this system began to develop a host of institutions of its own, traditional ethical-political concerns could not but be transported from the level of the state to the level of the international system itself.

Thus we find an interesting convergence of two very different strands. On the one hand, there is the explicitly ethical reasoning of works such as those of Beitz, Nye, or myself, which examine the possibilities and limits of ethical behavior in foreign policy. On the other hand, there is the question that underlies the apparently purely "scientific" research of such writers as Robert Keohane and the other students of international regimes, or the research of Robert Axelrod and the other enthusiasts of game theory. This question is whether, in a world in which self-help can easily be counterproductive or disastrous, cooperation that is mutually and genuinely beneficial to states can emerge in the midst of anarchy and on the basis of calculations of interests. Even if some of its champions deny it, the literature on the emergence of cooperation is not value-neutral; both this literature and the works on game theory seek a way out of conflict within the constraints of the Westphalian system. Indeed, even the vocabulary is not neutral, insofar as game theory relies on a somewhat simpleminded dialectic of cooperation versus defection! The explicit ethical strand asks, in a variety of ways, for moral progress in international affairs; the scientific literature tries to prove that such progress is possible under certain conditions.

Philosophical Debate and Political Achievements

It is impossible in a brief account to do justice to the many contributions that the new literature has already made. I would like to comment first on what could be called the philosophical debate within the literature, and then on the political achievements with which it can be credited.

Philosophically, this literature has rediscovered some of the most fundamental and intractable questions of moral philosophy. Three appear as particularly vexing. First, practically every moral theory or system rests on assumptions of universality, on the belief that moral reasoning can persuade individuals of different societies and beliefs, or that the moral intuitions of human beings are not fundamentally irreconcilable or intransitive. And yet, as I indicated before, there is an undeniable diversity of moral conceptions and standards. To what extent is the advocacy of a single moral code a form of hubris or of hypocrisy, the attempt to impose one particular philosophy on others? Conversely, does the recognition of diversity entail a resignation to moral cacophony and conflict? Thus the issue of relativism versus universality is one which has to be faced, even if it cannot easily be resolved.

Second, there is the tension, so familiar to moral philosophers, between two approaches to morality: the deontological approach, which relies on imperatives and commands and which is best exemplified by Kant, versus the various moral approaches that emphasize the need to take consequences and context into account (utilitarianism is only one of these approaches). It is hard to imagine a statesman who does not seek to evaluate consequences and whose decisions are made without reference to the context, but there is of course a constant danger of diluting or ditching principles and slipping into mere opportunism when consequences (which are in any case hard to foresee) and context become the dominant considerations.

Third, there is the question, raised, for instance, by Charles Beitz in his influential book *Political Theory and International Relations*

(Princeton: Princeton University Press, 1979), whether morality and self-interest are basically incompatible. Is a moral act one that is purely disinterested? In this case the argument for an ethics of foreign policy becomes pretty hard to sustain. To be sure, there is a danger of assuming all too easily that self-interest and morality necessarily coincide, or that morality is simply another name for an enlightened self-interest; clearly, there are cases in which morality and even a broad conception of self-interest will be in conflict, but how far can one go in demanding altruism or self-abnegation of states and their representatives?

I turn now to the intellectual contributions of the ethical literature to our understanding of international politics. They appear in three realms. First, the new literature has intellectually sharpened some of the underlying dilemmas of contemporary international relations. In the realm of force, it has made us look more closely at the effects of different strategies and it has raised important questions of trade-offs. For instance, insofar as deterrence is concerned, we have asked ourselves about the ethical significance of a peace preserved by a threat of indiscriminate destruction. On the other hand, if pulling away from such a threat (either by moving toward more accurate and discriminating nuclear weapons, as Albert Wohlstetter or Fred Iklé would want us to, or by moving toward nuclear disarmament) would actually weaken deterrence or make the world safe for conventional war, does this represent moral progress? Philosophers and political theorists have raised ethical questions about the reliance of statesmen and citizens on the expectation that deterrence would remain solid forever and that crises could always be managed. At this stage the ethical literature is torn between two currents. There is a literature of total condemnation of the nuclear universe, deterrence and all, a condemnation that is often (although not always) based on absolute principles but that may well be not only unrealistic but potentially dangerous. Another strand tries, often in rather tortured ways, to vindicate deterrence, not merely as a fact of life but as a morally acceptable position, and even to find "centimeters" of possible moral use of nuclear arms, which is of course not without enormous risks of its own.

To the conundrum of deterrence must be added the conundrum of nonproliferation. The ethical goal of limiting the spread of nuclear weapons, especially in areas where the conditions that have kept deterrence reasonably stable between the superpowers may not be reproduced, raises a conflict between the value of international security and the value of national sovereignty. Then there are all the moral problems of intervention, a domain that remains insufficiently explored in the new literature. In a world where nonintervention is practically impossible, in which intervention takes many forms other than military assistance and violent intrusion, are there possible guidelines? I am referring to guidelines concerning the nature and seriousness of the threat necessary to justify military intervention; or guidelines concerning the capacity to affect positively the political, economic, and social life of another society, for instance through economic or humanitarian intervention, without violating this society's autonomy; or guidelines concerning covert operations—a subject that Gregory Treverton's recent book has very sharply put into focus (*Covert Action: The Limits of Intervention in the Postwar World.* New York: Basic Books, 1987). Even if such guidelines are possible, what would be their meaning and effects in a universe of self-help?

In the realm of human rights and distributive justice there are, again, many conflicts and trade-offs highlighted by the ethical literature. There is the conflict between self-determination, or sovereignty, and justice. National sovereignty can be a formidable obstacle to attempts at achieving justice across borders or at instituting effective international or regional human-rights regimes; sovereignty is also a colossal obstacle to attempts at what might be called international centralization or centralized decision making for the solution of problems that are way beyond the means of any one state. Furthermore, there are conflicts between the different dimensions of human rights and of justice (justice for the state versus justice for individuals in a state, equality of opportunity versus equality of outcomes, trade-offs between equity and efficiency, and so on). There are also conflicts between widely different philosophical conceptions of our responsibility to others who happen to live outside our borders.

Secondly, the new works have important implications for the theory of international relations. By underlining the poverty of traditional realism and of what is sometimes called neorealism, they offer major corrections to such theories. The new ethical writings also confirm that there are many different ways of "reading" the nature of international relations. The "scientific" literature is dominated by the old realist reading or by the structural reading of Kenneth Waltz's neorealism. In other words, it is dominated by the "anarchy" formulation. There are several alternatives that the new literature has brought forward. One is the conception of the international milieu as an international society—partly conflictual, partly collaborative because of common interests, institutions, and norms. This could be called a neoliberal reading of international affairs and is to some extent derived from the remarkable treatment by Hedley Bull in his book *The Anarchical Society: A Study of Order in World Politics* (New York: Columbia University Press, 1977), which was itself grounded in a Grotian interpretation of international affairs. It offers a "statist" conception of international morality, insofar as it looks at the international order as above all a society of states, but it is a statist conception that, instead of stressing anarchy and conflict, stresses the social and cultural underpinnings of interstate relations. There exists also a far more radical alternative to the realist approach, the idea of an emergent world (and not just international or interstate) society or world community. This appears in two very different versions: that of Charles Beitz, who takes as his point of departure the writings on interdependence and the erosion of sovereignty, and that of the whole literature on dependency, which of course entails a much gloomier reading of interdependence but, again, differs drastically from the "horizontal" approach of anarchy.

Another correction is provided by the importance that much of the ethical literature grants to what Kenneth Waltz, in his famous earlier book *Man, the State, and War,* had called the second image, that is, the domestic political and economic regime, a factor quite often neglected by realists—and by Waltz himself in his *Theory of International Politics* (Reading, Mass.: Addison-Wesley, 1979). With respect both to war and to human rights, the new literature emphasizes that moral progress seems to be linked to the development of democracy. Finally, the new literature corrects international relations theory insofar as these works stress both urgency and discontinuity; they tend to show that merely trusting historical forces will not provide sufficient moral opportunities to prevent disasters. In other words, they state, and sometimes scream, that the international system is not self-regulating; that in the realm of force, deterrence, left to itself, may well self-destruct; that even if it lasts between the superpowers, it still leaves room for the chaos and violence of limited wars and intervention; that it has no answer to the problems of nuclear proliferation; that in the realm of economic interdependence, the long-term mutuality of interests in a world of rabidly uneven economic and social conditions still leaves room for highly disruptive state temptations to engage in short-term zero-sum games; and that the spread of disorder may come not only from the deliberate manipulation of interdependence but from the unforeseen effects of domestic political decisions. The ethical literature tells us that the processes of change on which the world has relied are today often far too dangerous, insofar as they entail the use of force, and are probably irrelevant, given the transformations of power and of the international system.

The great merit of this literature is to show the need for new approaches, for what Mr. Gorbachev now calls "new thinking"; indeed, the fundamental question that it asks is whether the traditional realist model is compatible any longer with the realization of essential human values. Obviously this model embodies some such values, such as self-determination, but at what cost? While the ethical writers are aware of the limits of moral opportunity and action in international affairs, they tend to reject the view that self-interest is the only possible morality of states, especially as self-interest is itself a dependent variable defined in the light of external circumstances, internal structures, and values and ideologies.

The third major political achievement of the new literature lies in its approach to the future. Much contemporary literature in international relations asks what is politically likely and desirable. But its answers are unconvincing. First, this literature is unsatisfactory because of the very indeterminacy of international affairs. Some broad trends are certainly predictable, but what are not predictable are crises, actual policy choices, and how these interact with trends. Hence the endless multiplication of often equally plausible scenarios among which it is quite impossible to choose. Second, as a result, much of this literature smuggles in preferences and is thus doubly deficient, analytically and ethically, because these preferences are rarely made explicit. The new ethical writings move from indeterminacy to freedom. They point out that the future is indeed open. These works' contribution to futurology is important, both because they shed the pretense of scientific forecasting, and because they inject into reflections on the future the indispensable element of intentionality; this allows for the fruitful cooperation of political scientists and philosophers trying to answer the question: under what political conditions could certain values become effective policies?

All this being said, the new literature has, of course, weaknesses of its own. The philosophical foundations of the writers' preferences and arguments are not always made sufficiently clear, as Hedley Bull pointed out years ago in his review of Michael Walzer's *Just and Unjust Wars*. Moreover, there may well be an overconcentration of talent and ingenuity in the realm of the superpowers' nuclear conflict. The thorny issues of nuclear ethics are certainly the most terrifying, but they are not the only ones in this world, and I personally wish that less energy would be spent on what I would call the two theologies of nuclear strategy, the theology of strategic studies and the more ethical theology. More attention ought to be paid to the formidably complex problems of human rights and, above all, justice in a world of considerable misery, population explosion, unregulated migrations, environmental disorders, and so forth. In a sense, it is the very abstractness of the nuclear issue that seems to excite the authors; writing intelligently about the other issues requires a much broader range of empirical knowledge and experience.

Extending the Debate

I would like to end these remarks with some more personal suggestions. I hope to develop them at far greater length in a book that Michael Smith and I plan to write. I believe that those of us who are interested in the ethical dimensions of foreign policy must begin by recognizing that in today's world the states are simply not ready to commit hara-kiri; that statehood still represents a good; and that statehood is the object of the aspirations and hopes of individuals in most of the world (observe the Palestinians). In other words, sovereignty, however much it may be leaking, is not merely a reality but a value. Therefore, ethics cannot hope to establish the nirvana of a world government in the short run; it can aim only at moralizing state behavior, on the one hand, and, on the other, at enlarging in a variety of ways what could be called the cosmopolitan sphere of international affairs, both through interstate institutions and regimes and through the establishment of a transnational society.

While the opportunities for moral action are clearly limited, a margin for action exists. Here, as in many other realms of human endeavor, necessity is the mother of morality. The fear of violent death and the fear of economic collapse are the international-relations equivalent of that famous threat of hanging which so powerfully concentrates the mind. Both these fears give rise to imperatives that can also be seen as a result of learning—learning the two very different lessons of 1914 (that is, the danger of an unstoppable war mechanism) and of 1939 (the dangers of appeasement), and learning the lessons of the Great Depression. These imperatives are reenforced by the transformations of power, the sharp limits on the usefulness of force, and the restraints that operate on economic power in an interdependent realm—transformations I have tried to analyze at some length in previous books.

There are, of course, preconditions to moral action. The first is moral awareness: awareness of the fact that morality is an integral part of public policy, an element that is present even when it is not consciously included in the calculations of statesmen. We are aware of this in our private life and in our domestic political life, at least in democracies. We are much less aware of it in foreign-policy making, partly because of the absence of a world community, partly because of the grip of the realist tradition. Yet our decisions always have moral effects on others, and even decisions that we think are based on considerations of prudence and expediency turn out to be grounded in an underlying conception of the good. It is this implicit theory of the good that determines our explicit definition of the prudent.

Thus there is a need for a moral vision in the statesman and the citizen. Morality is not reducible to cost-benefit analyses (in most issues, evaluating what is a cost and what is a benefit is highly subjective and indeed dependent on one's values); nor does it mean accommodating all claims (one has to listen to them, of course, but a final judgment is still necessary on which claims are right and which are wrong; political strategy may require prudence in dealing with the claims that are wrong, but a moral strategy requires such judgment). In other words, the statesman and the citizen need to begin with a moral conception, that is, with certain principles to be applied while taking into account their consequences, since political ethics needs to be an ethics both of ends and of consequences.

Not only is moral awareness needed; political awareness is indispensable as well. Next to cynicism, the greatest threat to morality is disembodied idealism. Indeed, the difficulty of ethical action in international relations results from the fact that moral concern has to be both prior to an event or given situation (that is, one must already know what one wants) and entirely immersed in it, since there can be no purely mechanical application of principles. Thus, the ethical practitioner desperately needs a correct analysis of situations. Both law and morality provide rules for certain categories of situations; but we need to be able to say, when we take up a case, in what category it belongs. When, as so often happens, the answer is ambiguous, we need to go deeper and analyze the dynamics of the conflict—which is exactly what the American bishops did in their famous letter on nuclear weapons. In other words, the first duty of an ethicist is to be an expert, just as the first duty of an international relationist is to be morally aware.

The strategy I have recommended before and continue to believe in is a transformist strategy—one that aims at building a satisfactory world order while defending the interests of one's state. No statesman can neglect such a defense, but these interests are less and less likely to be safeguarded by self-help alone or by reliance on preordained harmony. In moral terms, the problem we face is that of the rights of others beyond our borders: not merely the moral rights of other states, which have been enshrined in international law for a long time, but the rights of other human beings, either as members of other communities or simply as human beings. Since it is difficult for a statesman to be a pure cosmopolitan, he has, if he is morally aware, a choice among three moral strategies. One is moral warfare (we are good, other states have moral rights only insofar as they share our values, international relations is a clash between good and evil). This is an unacceptable position, because it makes an agreement on values a precondition for the recognition of rights; it violates the moral duty of impartiality. Moreover, the political consequences are unacceptable: endless political-military warfare and a selective treatment of misery or human rights. A second approach is incrementalism. This is unsatisfactory, because it does not go to the roots of the moral blemishes that proliferate in international affairs and because it still relies essentially on the dynamics of self-help, whose occasional good results are too easily reversible. The third strategy is what I call transformism. Essentially, it aims at reforming the present world order so as to introduce as much interstate and transnational society into the framework of anarchy as is possible. Such a strategy requires certain kinds of leaders and certain kinds of citizens. The leaders should not be narrow tribalists, or heroes, or ideological crusaders; they need to be compassionate, open, and capable of making informed decisions. The citizens must be able and willing to pressure, to prod, to censure their government, and also to act independently across borders.

This whole approach aims both at avoiding the worst and at pushing as far as possible in a more cosmopolitan direction. It recognizes the fact that moral fulfillment is still linked to the national community and that peace and justice are often, although certainly not always, best achieved within it. But there is nothing morally sacred about a national community: it is good only if it is based on certain moral-political principles of legitimacy, and even when the national community is morally admirable, it stops being so if it becomes exclusive and inflates its own worth. It is admirable when it is the concrete embodiment of universal moral rules, but certainly not in other cases.

How all these abstract notions are turned into concrete suggestions is, of course, another story. The philosophical foundation of this approach is another story as well, although it is easy to see that Kant, however diluted and modified, is not very far behind.

Be this as it may, it is necessary to salute the new literature with all its battles, its own sound and fury, and its flaws as a major contribution both to moral philosophy and to our understanding of politics. The fact that this literature, until now, is largely Anglo-Saxon is, of course, a source of worry, both because of the silence of other countries and because of the dangers of innocent, or not so innocent, parochialism. What is now being achieved, however, is a leap of philosophical concern from the horizon of the state to the still hazy one of the world as a whole. It is also a new way of amending, completing, and enriching realism, one that aims at reconciling those two forces whose battle enlivened the field of international politics some forty years ago, realism and idealism. Reflecting upon Hans Morgenthau's remarkable work, I wrote recently that we are all realists now. But it is a realism that encompasses not only—in its analytical dimensions—all the reasons for, and forms of, cooperation in a world that is still anarchic but also a prescriptive dimension that tries to transcend gradually the most perilous and morally unacceptable flaws of an anarchic milieu.

NOTE

1. Felix Oppenheim, "National Interest, Rationality, and Morality," *Political Theory* 15 (August 1987).

Jacques Barzun*

Is Democratic Theory for Export?

I sent two of our men. They traveled for three days and found people and houses without number, but they were small and without government; therefore they returned.

—CHRISTOPHER COLUMBUS,
First letter from the New World, March 14, 1493

A permanent feature of American opinion and action in foreign policy is the wish, the hope, that other nations might turn from the error of their ways and become democracies: "They are a great people,[1] why can't they manage their affairs like us?" A corollary has been "Let us help those governments that are democratic, make them our allies, and let us oppose the others—indeed, if necessary, take action to coerce them." A current example is the agitation about South Africa, which rages from the campus to Capitol Hill and from the boardroom to the living room. In these rooms, anyone not in favor of "doing something" against South Africa is deemed a traitor to the very spirit of this country, these democratic United States.

But there remains a question on this subject that has long bothered the thoughtful. What is it exactly that we want others to copy? What is the theory of democracy that we mean to export?

*The author presented this paper at the Sixth Morgenthau Memorial Lecture on Ethics & Foreign Policy, sponsored by the Carnegie Council on Ethics and International Affairs, in New York City on September 17, 1986.

Not all democracies are alike. Whose constitution is the best? On what theory is it based? The demand for a theory has been especially urgent during the last forty years because of the striking success of the opposite theory, Marxist-Leninist communism. In one region after another it has conquered what often looked like rising democracies. The rival theory was apparently more attractive, more convincing. We attribute these results to eloquent agents who had an easy time because "we" weren't there with a theory of our own. Who such missionaries for our side might be, given the democratic idea of the self-determination of peoples, is something of a puzzle, but it is secondary to yet another, greater one: What are these missionaries to preach? Where do we find the parallel to the writings of Marx and Lenin, and what do those writings tell?

Different persons would give different answers, which is a weakness to begin with. Some would point to the Declaration of Independence and the federal Constitution; others, to Rousseau, Edmund Burke, Thomas Paine. Then there is Tocqueville's *Democracy in America* in two volumes and a wonderful little book by Walter Bagehot on the English Constitution, not to mention the *Federalist* papers and many eloquent pages from John Adams, Thomas Jefferson, and Abraham Lincoln. Taken loosely together, these writings would be regarded by many as making up the theory of democracy.

Of course, they don't all agree; they don't form a system. The *Federalist* writers are afraid of democracy;[2] John Adams disputes Tom Paine and goes only part way with Jefferson.[3] Burke and Rousseau sound like direct contraries. Tocqueville calls for so many of the special conditions he found here that his conclusions are not transferable. And Bagehot does the same thing for Great Britain: you have to be Englishmen to make the English Constitution work.

All these *ifs* and *ands* make a poor prospect for unified theory, but there is worse. When we actually read these documents, we find that each theorized about a few subjects among many that very properly go by different names. We have: democracy, republic, free government, representative government, constitutional monarchy. There are besides natural rights, civil rights, equality before the law, equal opportunity. Then there are also universal suffrage, majority rule, separation of powers, and the two-party system. Nor should we forget another half-dozen other topics that are found associated in modern times with the so-called democratic process—primary elections, the referendum, proportional representation, and so on.

That array of ideas and devices cannot but be daunting to the propagandist for democracy. Which are essential? How should they combine? The very need to explain what the terms mean bars the way to easy acceptance and enthusiasm. In addition, the key words do not mean the same thing to all the theorists. To cap these troubles, nowhere in the West has there been a central authority to define an orthodoxy, even a shifting one, such as there has been on the communist side.

On that side, there is the advantage not only of unity but of broad abstraction: the class struggle, history as dialectical materialism, surplus value, society shaped by the forms of economic production, the contradictions in capitalism preparing its decline and fall, the aim and training of the revolutionist, and the dictatorship of the proletariat leading to the withering away of the state. These eight "big ideas," energized by resentment and utopian hope, make up a scheme that has the ring of high intellectuality. The scheme is readily teachable as a series of catchwords that, as experience shows, can appeal to every level of intelligence. It offers not only a promise of material advantage but also a drama—a struggle toward a glorious end, unfolding according to necessity.

Compared with a scripture and prophecy, which amount not to theory but to ideology, the concrete plans and the varied means of the writers on democracy present a spectacle of pettifogging and confusion. Common opinion reinforces this lack of order and unity. The democratic peoples suppose that free governments did not exist before the population at large got the vote, which is not true, or that democracy is incompatible with a king and an aristocracy, though England is there to show that a monarchy with a House of Lords can be democratic. Was the United States a democracy when senators were not elected directly by the people? Were we a free government when we held millions in slavery or segregation? Finally, it takes no research to find out that the democracies of France, Italy, and Sweden, those of Brazil, Mexico, and the Philippines, and of Thailand, India, and the United States are far from giving people the same freedoms by the same means.

Take two recent illustrations. In France, the last elections brought to power in the National Assembly, and hence in the office of the prime minister, a party opposed to that of the president, whose term was to continue for another two years. This vote caused immediate and prolonged consternation. Would there be a violent clash, or would government stop dead in a stalemate between the president and his prime minister, backed by the Assembly? A few daring souls said that "cohabitation" (which in French has no sexual overtones) might be possible. But debate raged on. It so happened that a young musicologist from Smith College was in Paris when the dismay was at its height. Being fluent in French, he wrote a letter to *Le Monde,* which published it as remarkable. It said, in effect: "Good people, don't be upset. What bothers you has happened in the United States quite often. Democracy won't come to an end because two branches of government are in the hands of different parties."[4]

He was right. Cohabitation has begun, but it is working in ways that surprise American friends of democracy—for instance, by the use of ministerial decrees that become law or of the closure, called guillotine, by which debate is cut off in the Assembly. The point of the example is clear: one Western democracy is nearly stymied by a lawful result of its own system and gets over the trouble by means that would be unthinkable—antidemocratic—in another democracy, where that same trouble of divided authority seems no trouble at all. What unified theory could cover both versions of the democratic process?

The second example comes from the Philippines, where a national election was held in circumstances of violence and coercion and yielded an outcome that could therefore be questioned. A delegation from the United States Congress had to go and inquire into the events surrounding the vote before this country could assume that the democratic process had in fact been carried out; for as we saw, common opinion holds that the vote of the people is the diagnostic test of democracy.[5] But what if the voting itself is not free, as in parts of the Philippines and in many other countries where the doubt and confusion are never settled by inquiry? Are those democracies? Or must they be considered halfway cases in order to fit under the grand theory?

The truth is, the real subject for discussion is not "Is democratic theory for export?" but "Is there a theory of democracy?" We expect to find one not solely because a large part of the world boasts a rival theory but also because, in our admiration for science, we like to have a theory for every human activity. My conviction is that democracy has no *theory*. It has only a *theorem,* that is, a proposition that is generally accepted and can be stated in a single sentence. Here is the theorem of democracy: for a free mankind, it is best that the people should be sovereign, and this popular sovereignty implies political and social equality.

When I say the theorem of democracy has been accepted, I am not overlooking the antidemocratic opposition. For in one sense there is none. Look over the world of the twentieth century, and you find at every turn the claim that the government of this nation and that nation is a popular government—the People's Republic of China, the German Democratic Republic, the Democratic Republic of Yemen, and that of Kampuchea all say so in their titles. Other nations profess the same creed and point to their constitutions. The Soviet Union has one that provides for elections and delegates at various levels. Parties and voting and assemblies are found all up and down the five continents. The split comes over who "the people" are, what is meant by "party," and how the agents of government act for (or against) the people. Historically, "the people" has always been recognized in some fashion. Athens was a democracy—with slaves; the Roman emperor spoke in the name of "the Senate and the Roman people"; the Germanic tribes and the American Indians had chiefs and also general councils; kings were the "fathers" of their people—and their servants too. And the old adage *Vox populi, vox Dei*—the voice of the people is the voice of God—has always meant that rulers cannot and should not withstand the people's will.

The theorem, then, is not disputed even when tyranny flourishes under it, for it has two parts and the tyrant can boast that the blessings of the second part, equality, are due to him. We are thus brought to the great question of the machinery of government, because it is how the wheels turn, and not a theory, that makes a government free or not free. The dictatorship of the proletariat may be the theory of communism, but in fact neither the proletariat nor its single party rules. Voting and debating is make-believe set over a tight oligarchy led by one man. There is no machinery to carry out the promise that in time the proletariat will disappear and the state will wither away, and most often, there is not even a device for ensuring the public succession from one top leader to the next.

The conclusion established so far would seem to be this: democracy has no theory to cover the working of its many brands of machinery, whereas its antagonists use a single, well-publicized theory to "cover" in another sense, namely, to conceal, the workings of one rather uniform machine, the police state.

A further conclusion is that the demand for a theory of democracy shows the regrettable tendency to think entirely in abstractions, never bringing general statements side by side with the facts of experience or even noticing important differences between abstractions if they happen to be linked together by custom or usage. Democracy, for example, is thought of as synonymous with free government; "the sovereign people" is thought of as meaning all, or most, or some of the residents within the boundaries of a state. What kinds of freedom a government guarantees, how they are secured, and which groups and individuals actually obtain them and which do not are complicated questions that theorists and journalists alike prefer to ignore. They know that such details are of no use in stirring up either protests at home or virtuous indignation about others abroad. The public at large takes government itself abstractly, as a kind of single-minded entity, an engine that works only in one direction and always expresses the same attitude toward human desires. The democratic, modern style of government is the good kind, and the rest, past and present, are the bad.

For this childlike view, there is only one remedy, and that is a little history. I include under this term contemporary history, for after having excluded the possibility of a theory of democracy I am concerned to offer instead a survey, or rather a sketchy panorama, of its manifestations. I do this with a practical purpose in view: I think it is important to know how the so-called free world came into being, what ideas and conditions would be required for its extension, and, most immediate and important, what changes are occurring in our own democracy that threaten its peculiar advantages and make its export impossible.

Let us return to our theorem. It calls for three difficult things: expressing the popular will, ensuring equality, and, by means of both, distributing a variety of freedoms. These purposes imply machinery. How, for example, is the popular will ascertained? The devices we are familiar with in the Anglo-American tradition have come from two sources. One is the long, slow, haphazard growth of the English Constitution from the Parliament of Simon de Montfort in 1265 through innumerable struggles for rights won (and listed) a few at a time—Magna Carta, the Bill of Rights, and so on.[6] From this history, Montesquieu, Locke, and others variously derived the precepts and precedents that influenced the making of the United States Constitution.

The other source is antiquity—Greece and Rome—whose practices and writings on government inspired thinkers to design plans or issue warnings appropriate to their own time. The most famous scheme is that of Rousseau. His is also the most instructive, for although he is crystal clear, his interpreters divide on the tendency of his great book, *The Social Contract*. Some say it promotes freedom, others say it leads to totalitarianism. This shows how double-edged propositions can be. But let us see what Rousseau himself says. He takes democracy literally: all the people, equal in rank, come together and decide policy and choose leaders. This is the old Athenian democracy, except that there are no slaves. Rousseau goes on to point out that only a small city-state can manage that sort of government. Knowing his ancient history, he adds that such pure democracy is too good for men as they are. He agrees with the great minds of ancient Greece. Aristotle, Plato, Xenophon, Thucydides—all were against democracy; they saw dozens of democratic cities perish from inefficiency, stupidity, and corruption.[7]

Rousseau therefore falls back on representative government, which he calls, correctly, "elective aristocracy": the people elect those they think the best (*aristoi*) to run their affairs for them. He also requires a lawgiver to describe the structure of the government. For "lawgiver" substitute "constitution," a set of rules for day-to-day operations.

Why should anybody think that such a system must end in tyranny? One answer can be given through a quick reminder: Hitler did not seize power, he was voted in as head of a plurality party by a people living under a democratic government and with a constitution that combined the best features of all constitutions on record. If you add to the strength of Hitler's party that of the German Communists, you have a large democratic majority voting for totalitarian rule. To generalize from this example, if the people is sovereign, it can do anything it wants, including turn its constitution upside down. It can lose its freedom by choosing leaders who promise more equality, more prosperity, more national power through dictatorship. The theorem of popular sovereignty is honored in the breach. The dictator says, "I represent the will of the people. I know what it wants."

On the other hand, a new nation can ask, "Popular sovereignty, the vote for everybody, then what?" That question was precisely the one put to Rousseau by envoys from two nations, Poland and Corsica. He wrote for each of them a small book that shows how he would go about being a lawgiver, a constitution maker. These notable supplements to the abstract outline of *The Social Contract* are conveniently forgotten by Rousseau's critics. For, in prescribing for Poland and for Corsica, Rousseau makes the all-important point that the history, character, habits, religion, economic base, and education of each people must be taken into account before setting up any machinery. No rules or means apply universally. What works in England will fail in Poland; what the French prefer, the Corsicans will reject.

Political equality can be decreed, but freedom cannot—it is a most elusive good. Rousseau warns the Poles that they should go slowly in freeing their serfs, for fear that in their economic ignorance the serfs will fall into worse misery than before. This was Burke's great point about the solidity of English freedom, which is freedom under a monarchy and what we would surely call a nonrepresentative Parliament: based as it was on gradual change through history, freedom had taken root inside every Englishman. Burke criticized the French revolutionists because they did not revive the old assemblies and thereby give the French some training in the use of freedom. Instead, they wrote principles on a piece of paper and expected them to produce the right behavior overnight. On this central issue, Burke and Rousseau are at one, as a fine scholar long ago demonstrated to a nonlistening world in her book *Rousseau and Burke.*[8]

This element of time, of the slow training of individuals by history, carries with it a predicament and a paradox. The predicament is: how can the peoples that want to spread freedom to the world propose their institutions as models if those institutions depend on habits long ingrained? It is easy enough to copy a piece of actual machinery, such as a computer or even a nuclear weapon. It takes only a few bright, well-trained people with the model in front of them. But to copy a government is not something that a whole population can achieve by merely deciding to do it.

One may note in passing the double error of the former colonial powers: they did not teach the ways of freedom soon enough to their colonial subjects, and they let go of their colonies too quickly when the urge to independence swept the globe. The bloodshed was immediate and extensive, and it is not over. Some of the nations that emerged tried what they thought was democracy, only to succumb to military or one-party rule—always in the name of popular sovereignty, indeed of liberation. The word is not always a mere pretense, for it is liberation to be rid of a government that cannot govern. The ancient maxim is true: *Mundus vult gubernari*—the world insists on being governed.

As for the paradox, it is this: How can a people learn the ways of free government until it is free? And how can it stay free if it cannot run the type of machinery associated with self-government? On this score, the spectacle of Latin America is baffling. The several states gained their independence from Spain not long after the thirteen North American colonies gained theirs from England, during the period 1783–1823. Yet repeated efforts by able, selfless leaders have left South and Central America prey to repeated dictatorships, with the usual accompaniment of wars, massacres, oppression, assassinations, and that great diagnostic fact, uncertainty about the succession of legitimate governors.

To contrast the history of the North American colonies with the history of those of the South is not to disparage Latin America but to remind ourselves of the bases of free government. We make a great mistake in calling the American War of Independence "the American Revolution" and in bragging about the fact that it did not wind up in dictatorship like the English Revolution under

Cromwell or the French under Robespierre. In 1776 the Americans rebelled against very recent rules and impositions. What they wanted was not a new type of government but the old type they had always enjoyed. They were used to many freedoms, which they claimed as the immemorial rights of Englishmen. Once they had defeated the English armies and expelled the Loyalists, they went back to their former ways, which they modestly enlarged and codified in the Bill of Rights. Needless to say, when the people of South America threw off Spanish and Portuguese rule, they had no such tradition or experience to help them.

The evidence is overwhelming that it is not enough to be left alone by a royal or imperial power in order to establish some degree of freedom and to keep it safe, to say nothing of achieving egalitarian democracy. One should remember the travails of Spain itself throughout the nineteenth century and down to a few years ago. One should think of France, eager for freedom in 1789 but hardly settled in it during its five republics, two empires, one partial dictatorship, and twelve constitutions. For two hundred years in Central Europe, various peoples, unhappily intermingled by centuries of war and oppression, have been longing to form nations, and nations to form free states. Even under the iron heel of local communism and Russian hegemony, a working system seems beyond reach. A recent headline read, "Ethnic Mini-States Paralyze Yugoslavia."[9] The lesson here is that *the people* must first define itself through a common language and common traditions before it can hope to be *the sovereign people.*

Nor are grassroots aspirations alone enough to ensure either nationhood or liberal rule. We should recall the forgotten example of Russia. At the turn of the nineteenth century there had developed in Russia a widespread, homegrown movement toward constitutional government. In 1905 several well-organized parties, ranging from conservative and liberal to socialist and revolutionary, had obtained from the tsar a representative two-chamber assembly based on nearly universal suffrage. Important civil rights and religious toleration were granted, and able leaders arose from the middle class and professional groups; but the parties and leaders were unable to keep themselves united behind their gains, and the whole house of cards soon collapsed. Politics were, so to speak, immature and the popular will confused. A symbol of that confusion was the crowd's cheering for the Archduke Constantine to replace the tsar: "Constantine and Constitution" was the shout, and it turned out that many thought that Constitution was Constantine's wife.

That first experience was not forgotten. Ten years later, in March 1917, a second democratic revolution occurred, backed at first by everybody—not just do-or-die liberals and revolutionaries but business and professional men, trade unionists and conservative landholders, urban workers and army officers. The force behind the call for reform was the desire to win the war, and the institutions set up to carry out the one and carry on the other were perfectly adequate. Again, those in charge were unable to make the new institutions work, and in eight months they perished under the onslaught of a new autocracy led by Lenin and Trotsky. In less than ten years, then, two intelligent attempts to modernize government in Russia had failed—and Russia was a country where Western ideas had long since penetrated, a country whose educated class was at home in all the democratic capitals of Europe.

Our second large conclusion must therefore be that a democracy cannot be fashioned out of whatever people happen to be around in a given region; it cannot be promoted from outside by strangers, and it may still be impossible when attempted from inside by determined natives. Just as life on the earth depended on a particular coming together of unrelated factors, so a cluster of disparate elements and conditions is needed for a democracy to be born viable. Among these conditions one can name tradition, literacy, and a certain kind of training in give-and-take, as well as the sobering effect of national disaster—France in 1870 and Germany in 1945. The most adaptable of peoples, the Japanese, took a century to approximate Western democracy, aided no doubt by the harsh tutelage that followed a grievous defeat. And another people might have taken these same experiences the other way, as spurs to resist change.

The absence of theory and the rare occurrence, at one time and place, of the right pieces to assemble might seem enough to rule out the export of democracy from nation to nation, but there is today a third and last obstacle: the present character of free governments in the West. This difficulty may be made clear by comparing our times with the heyday of enthusiasm for democratic freedom, 1918–20. The First World War had been fought against monarchies and empires, and this country joined in to "make the world safe for democracy." There is nothing foolish in that motto of Woodrow Wilson's. Victory seemed to give the Allied powers a chance to replace two conglomerate empires with a galaxy of new, true, and free nations.[10] Russia itself seemed to have jumped the gun in March 1917.

What was not foreseen was the backlash of the war. Emotionally, it was a revulsion against four years of carnage. In practical effect, it was nothing less than a social revolution. The war itself was revolutionary, having moved the masses out of their routines—the men into the trenches, the women into the factories. What happened under Lenin in Russia, and for a time among her neighbors, advertised this social upheaval. The masses were now sovereign in their outlook and behavior. Henceforth, whatever was done must be done for their good and in their name. Their needs and wants, their habits and tastes marked the high tide of democracy as Tocqueville had foreseen it in this country. The message was clear to all, because it had been preached with growing intensity for one hundred years. Universal suffrage; the end of poverty; identical rights for everybody; social, economic, even sexual emancipation; popular culture, not elite esthetics—these demands went with a distrust and hatred of all the old orders, old leaders, and old modes of life that had brought on the four years of homicidal horror and destruction. The new modes were to be anticapitalist (obviously), anti-Victorian in morals, and antiparliamentarian as well, for many thought representative government a corrupt and contemptible fraud. Democracy needed better machinery. In that mood, it is no wonder that fascism and the corporate state triumphed so rapidly.[11] If England and France hung on to their constitutional freedoms amid this turmoil, it was due largely to historical momentum, the same force that threw Russia back into its old groove.

After all this, it would be a mistake to think that what is now called the free world is just the continuation of the liberal regimes that existed before 1914. The social revolution has changed them all into welfare states, and this transformation, which is one expression of the socialist ideal, has so altered the machinery of free government that it no longer resembles the model one could previously define by a few plain devices, such as voting, the party system, and majority rule.

Although the changes of the last sixty years in democratic nations have been similar, they have been uneven. In different countries the notions of freedom and equality have taken varying and sometimes contradictory meanings. Does a national health service increase freedom or reduce it? Does workers' compensation give equal treatment to workers and employers when it disregards contributory negligence in causing accidents? Are the rules for zoning and landmark preservation a protection of property rights or an infringement of them? More generally, can the enormous increase in the bureaucracy needed to enforce endless regulations and the high taxes levied for all the new services be called an extension of freedom or a limitation? Where it is clearly a limitation, the argument advanced is that it is imposed for the sake of equality, thus fulfilling the prediction of the earliest critics of democracy—that it begins by talking the language of liberty but ends in promoting an equality that destroys one freedom after another.

One can readily understand how the modern constraints to ensure rights came into being. The old inequalities were so flagrant, so irrational, and so undeserved, the exclusions and prejudices were so heartless and often so contrary to the laws even then on the books, that only concerted action by the government could bring the conditions of life for the masses into conformity with the democratic theorem—the popular will absolute implies equality also absolute.

But the steady drive toward social and economic parity for all has brought about a great shift in the source of day-to-day authority over individuals. The guarantor of rights and freedoms is no longer political; the government we live under is administrative and judiciary. Hence the diminished interest in political life and political rights: the poor turnout at most elections, the increase in single-issue partisanship, the rare occurrence of clear majorities, and the widespread feeling that individual action is futile. To exercise his or her freedom, the free citizen must work through channels long and intricate and rarely political.

To see this situation in perspective, open your Tocqueville and see what he saw as the essence of the American democracy. For him, the federal government is of small importance compared to the government of each state—and so it was in 1835 for every American citizen. "The government" meant the legislature at the state capital. What is more, in all the small things that affect individual life, from roads and police to schools and taxes, Tocqueville tells us that it is the township or county that is paramount. He gives New England as proof: the town meeting determines the will of the people, and the selectmen carry it out. That is democracy at work. Everybody has a voice in decisions, everybody has a chance to serve in office, everybody understands the common needs as well as the degree to which anybody's opinion or proposal is worth following.[12] The democracy is that of Athens in its best days, the one Rousseau said was too perfect for human use.

Today, the government machine is more like the circuitry of a mainframe computer, too complex for anybody but students of the science. And this elaboration of devices for equality can only be endless. The lure of further rights is ever present, because among men and women in society "equal" is a figurative term, not a mathematical one. For example, the justice of rewarding talent with higher pay has been gravely debated; the word "meritocracy" has been invented to suggest that merit violates democratic equality because merit is not earned, it is, as it were, unmerited. Other attempts are being made, under the name of comparable worth, to legislate the equality of very diverse occupations. Equality of opportunity has come to seem too indefinite and uncertain.

Please note that I am describing, not judging. The point here is not the contents or wisdom of these new rights conferred in batches on the minorities—ethnic and sexual—on the employed and the unemployed, the disabled, the pregnant, the nonsmokers, the criminal, the moribund, and the insane, to say nothing of the fanciers of old buildings, the champions of certain animals and plants, and that great silent minority, the consumers. What is in question is the effect of ever-extended rights on the conception or definition of free government. One such effect is a conflict of claims, a division in the body politic. Many complain that others have become not equal but superequal, that reverse discrimination has set in. The rights of women and those of the unborn were clearly opposite. Perhaps the smoker and the nonsmoker form the emblematic pair whose freedoms are incompatible.

The upshot is that the idea of the citizen, a person with the same few clear rights as everybody else, no longer holds. In his place is a person with a set of special characteristics matched by a set of privileges. These group privileges must be kept in balance by continual addition if overall equality is to survive.[13] This progression has a visible side effect: it tends to nullify majority rule, for in seeing to it that nobody loses through any decision, it makes majority and minority equal. Finally, progressive equality and bureaucratic delay encourage the thing known as "participatory democracy," which is in fact direct minority rule, a kind of reverse democracy for coercing authority by protests, demonstrations, sit-ins, and job actions in order to obtain the rapid satisfaction of new demands.[14] Regardless of one's like or dislike for the great complication that the original ideal of government by the people and for the people has undergone, one must admit once more that devising a theory for its actual working is impossible. To say, "Here it is, come and observe, and then copy it" would be a cruel joke. For one thing, the Western world still believes, rightly, that it is free. But though at one in the resolve to establish equality, its institutions remain wide apart in their allotment of freedoms. For example, an American citizen would find the extent of regulation in Switzerland or Sweden oppressive. He would call Switzerland's indirect elections at every level a backward, undemocratic system of representation. A Swiss (or an Australian) would retort, "You haven't advanced as far as the initiative and referendum for important national issues. You don't know what freedom is."[15]

In France, that same American would be shocked at the practices by which the police regularly gather and use information about every citizen, and would not be pacified by the reply that it is an old custom quite harmless to freedom. Elsewhere, the drag on democracy would seem to be the inability to act within a reasonable time, the result of government by coalition. In Holland, for example, because of the system of "pillarization"—the forming of groups according to religious, occupational, and ideological preference—there are over twenty parties competing at the polls, and there is no majority.[16] It is precluded by proportional representation, which many regard as essential to democracy. As for Germany and Italy, the same need for coalition works in the usual way to give extremists leverage against the wishes of the actual but disunited majority.

Which of these complexities would one recommend to a new nation eager for free government? If a detached observer turned to the American scene, he would note still other obstacles to the straightforward democratic process: gerrymandering, the filibuster, the distorting effect of opinion polls, the lobbying system, the maze of regulations governing registration for voting and nominating, the perversities of the primaries, and, worst of all, the enormous expense of getting elected, which entails a scramble for money and the desperate shifts for abating its influence, including financial disclosure, codes of ethics, and the like. Nobody wants to play according to the rules.[17] Add the use of television to make quick bids for popularity through inane, fictional dialogue, and the employment of public-relations gurus to guide the choice of ideas to propose to the electorate, and you can gauge the decay of political campaigning. A symbol of the loss is the four-yearly spectacle called a debate between presidential candidates—no debate but an amateurish quiz program.[18]

A last feature of modern democracy that should baffle would-be imitators is the contempt in which politicians are held. Here is a system that requires their existence, endows them with power, and throws a searchlight on all their acts, and yet the same people who choose them perpetually deride and denounce them. The educated, no less than the populace, resent the politician's prominence but would not trade places with him. Writers multiply more or less witty epigrams about the breed and defamatory little essays against them.[19] The title "honorable," used to address them, is obviously a bitter irony. How to explain all this to a visitor from Mars? For politicians not only represent us, they represent the scheme by which our changeable will is expressed. They are, as a group, the hardest working professionals; they must continually learn new masses of facts, make judgments, give help, and continue to please. It is this obligation, of course, that makes them look unprincipled. To please and do another's will is prostitution, but it remains the nub of the representative system.

With these many complex deeds and chaotic demands, American democracy would have little to show the world with pride if it were not for another aspect of our life that Tocqueville observed and admired, that is, our habit of setting up free, spontaneous associations for every conceivable purpose.[20] To this day, anybody with a typewriter and a copying machine can start a league, a club, a think tank, a library, a museum, a hospital, a college, or a center for this or that and can proceed to raise money, publish a newsletter, and carry on propaganda—all tax-exempt, without government permission or interference, and free of the slightest ridicule from the surrounding society. Here is where the habits of American democracy survive in full force. Robert's Rules of Order are sacred scripture, and the treasurer's report is scanned like a love letter. Committees work with high seriousness, volunteers abound, and the democratic process reaches new heights of refinement.[21]

This admirable tradition enables us to accomplish by and for ourselves many things that in other democracies require government action. But this very habit of self-help, contrasting with the huge helpless hulk of government, has lately bred the conviction that popular sovereignty, like equality, should be unlimited. More and more often it is taken for granted that every organization, from businesses and churches to magazines and universities, should become a little democracy, with everyone voting, regardless of his position or knowledge. The former governing bodies—board of directors or elected vestry—should no longer act for their constituency because their decisions "affect everybody." In some instances, indeed, the geographical neighbors of an institution have claimed a voice, on the irrefutable ground that they, too, are affected by what it does.

It is plausible to regard this tendency as a result of the feeling that government at the top is unresponsive and in some ways unrepresentative, even though it is busy enacting privileges and protections. The bureaucracy then tries to homogenize the fates of citizens; they, in turn, appeal to the courts, which establish and often widen the rule; and thus a hopefully contentious atmosphere keeps everyone's attention on his or her rights. These are the occasion for a continual free-for-all.[22] There is undoubted freedom of a kind in a free-for-all. In how many countries, for example, would it be possible for a visiting head of state to do what one such recently did in New York—to make half a dozen speeches attacking the president? Where else would avowed partisans of subversion be allowed to teach in state universities? Such things are commonplace with us, but, again, they betoken group rights. Dissenters nowadays are tolerated only when their views are already group views. On our campuses, where academic freedom is claimed by the faculty, it is not extended to unpopular lecturers from outside. Their invitations are cancelled under pressure, and their talks disrupted. The notion of a "free market for ideas," the belief that truth comes out of unrestricted debate, is vindicated only when a vocal group favors the freedom.[23]

That, unfortunately, is an old story in this country. Tocqueville observed in 1835 that "he knew of no nation in which there is so little independence of mind and real freedom of discussion."[24] He attributed this lack to the weight of majority sentiment. Now the majority is that of the group to which one belongs by profession, status, or region. But if in those early days of democracy free discussion thrived better elsewhere, it was not solely because free speech was a legal right; it was also because of property rights. Their sanctity was something all the early proponents of constitutional government insisted on. They knew that liberties must have a material base: independence of mind is wonderfully spurred by an independent income. And this underpinning has been progressively weakened, by industrial civilization as much as by public law. Even in public opinion, property has become an unsavory word.

These various developments of democratic life help to account for the generalized feeling of oppression that pervades the free world. It manifests itself in common talk, in novels and plays, in the medical concern with stress, in the rise of cults, and in the recourse to drugs.[25] Such feelings of oppression are now so pervasive that optimism and the love of life are felt to be almost indecent. Consider in this light the universal demand for liberation, or emancipation, which has come not from the former colonies but from long-united parts of great nations. The Scots, the Welsh, the Basques, the Bretons want to be free, just like the smallest islands of the Pacific or Caribbean and, indeed, of our own waters. Only a couple of years ago, Martha's Vineyard was clamoring to be free of Massachusetts. It sounded like a joke, but it expressed the widespread illusion that if only we could be "by ourselves" all our frustrations would end. It is an individual desire before it becomes a group demand, a demand generally called nationalism. But that is the wrong word. It is separatism, the very reverse of wanting to form or belong to a larger group. Hence the call for decentralization and what has been termed in this country the New Federalism, each a type of separation from the great machine built on the plan of popular sovereignty and absolute equality.[26]

Being at the end of this rapid survey, I must repeat the caution I urged before: do not take description as disparagement. We do live under a free government, and it has enormous advantages over any that is not free or only part free. We could all name these advantages and show their rational and emotional value, but that would not help our present inquiry, which is to find out what foreign nations could use to model themselves on our polity, could adopt from our complicated practices. The answer, I think, is: nothing. The parts of the machine are not detachable; the organism is in fact indescribable, and what keeps it going, the "habits of the heart," as Tocqueville called them, are unique and undefinable. In short, we cannot by any conceivable means "show them how to do it."

This must be our third and last conclusion. What is more, if Rousseau were approached today by some liberal-minded South African and asked for advice of the kind he gave to Poland and Corsica, he would be at a loss where to begin, for he would not be facing one nation trying to modify its institutions but several peoples, with diverse traditions, each trying to keep or gain its freedom by power. In the democratic theorem, the sovereignty of the people implies the practical unity of that people. How to create it when it does not exist is a different task from that of developing free institutions and is probably incompatible with it.

In answer to the question posed in the title of this discussion, I have attempted to make three points:

First, democracy has no theory to export, because it is not an ideology but a wayward historical development.

Second, the historical development of democracy has taken many forms and used many devices to reach the elusive goal called human freedom.

Third, the forms of democracy in existence are today in a state of flux. The strong current toward greater equality and the strong desire for greater freedom are more than ever in conflict. Freedom calls for a government that governs least; equality for a government that governs most. No wonder the institutions of the free world are under strain and its citizens under stress. The theorem of democracy still holds, but all of its terms have changed in nature, especially the phrase "the people," which has been changed beyond recognition by the industrial revolution of the nineteenth century and the social revolution of the twentieth.

NOTES

1. Or "a great little people."

2. Madison repeats in the *Federalist* (nos. 10, 14, 48, 58, and 63) that full or pure democracy is a menace to freedom, and he praises the Constitution being proposed to the American people for its "total exclusion of the people in their collective capacity" (no. 63).

3. See the *Adams-Jefferson Letters,* ed. Lester J. Cappon, 2 vols. (Chapel Hill: University of North Carolina Press, 1959), 199, 236, 248, 279, 351–52, 456, 519, 550, 598, and passim.

4. Peter Anthony Bloom, "La Leçon des Etats-Unis," *Le Monde* (Paris), February 28, 1986.

5. "The right to vote is surely the linchpin of peaceful change," says Lloyd N. Cutler, former counsel to President Carter, and he recommends it for South Africa ("Using Morals, Not Money, on Pretoria," *New York Times,* August 3, 1986, sec. 4, p. 23). But change to peace is far from assured. Hitler's example has been imitated again and again by well-led groups aiming at one-party rule.

6. Simon de Montfort anticipated the English Constitution by six hundred years. The Parliament of 1265 included two delegates from every shire and two burgesses from every town. The aim was that, acting as Great Council to the king, they should advise him, supervise the several divisions of government, afford redress, and approve taxes. The king's ministers should be responsible to it. In short, Montfort wanted in 1265 what slowly and painfully became general in Western Europe by the end of the nineteenth century. In 1265 the barons quarreled, resented middle-class participation in government, and resumed a war in which Montfort was conveniently stabbed in the back. But the people of England continued to worship him as a martyr, patriot, and saint.

7. Aristotle's treatise on ancient governments influenced such eighteenth-century proponents of free government as Madison in their fear of "democracy," for Aristotle says it is the corruption of free government, just as tyranny is the corruption of monarchy (*Politics,* bk. 4, chap. 2).

8. A. M. Osborne, *Rousseau and Burke* (New York: Oxford University Press, 1940).

9. *Washington Post,* June 28, 1986.

10. It is worth noting that tsarist Russia and the communist Soviet Union joined the Western powers in the last two world wars without preventing these powers from proclaiming that they were fighting to put down autocracy and advance the cause of freedom. Theories, theories!

11. The theory of the corporate state, or socialism in the guise of state capitalism, was expounded in France and Germany and promulgated in Italy. It had intellectual adherents for a time; Winston Churchill praised Mussolini, and David Lloyd George, Hitler. The defeat of the Axis powers silenced such advocates, which shows again how dependent on current events theorists are.

12. Alexis de Tocqueville, *Democracy in America,* vol. 1, part 1, chap. 5.

13. State constitutions are continually being amended. In 1984–85, the last year for which figures are available, 158 of the 338 proposed changes in state constitutions were approved. Many of these proposals dealt with rights, and of these, 77.7 percent were approved (Council of State Governments, *The Book of the States: 1986–87* [Lexington, Ky.: 1986]), 4.

14. For example, when budget cuts forced the Library of Congress to reduce its hours of service, readers staged protests by various forms of obstruction. Arrests were made, and so were concessions. Again, acting in behalf of eleven monkeys, a group of "simiophiles" camped outside the National Institutes of Health and commanded attention. Such sequences have come to be called civil disobedience, but they are not always civil and they bypass the traditional procedures guaranteed by the Bill of Rights—peaceful assembly and petition. It is felt, no doubt justly, that the old devices presuppose a different society, less hurried, better integrated, and used to articulate communication.

15. The latest "initiative" in Switzerland proposes to abolish the Swiss army. So radical a change will doubtless elicit a large turnout at the polls, but usually no more than a quarter of the electorate votes on the initiatives, of which there is usually a large backlog.

16. Pillarization was made official in 1917 to satisfy the demands of the Catholic, Protestant, and "Humanist" factions that divided the Dutch professions, trade unions, sexes, and ideological groups. Each permutation of these combining allegiances was recognized as a pillar of the state and given a place on the ballot. In the last ten years, a demand has grown for more comprehensive parties, but it has not yet made headway.

17. In addition to the deliberate evasion or twisting of the rules, their administration is inevitably slow and poor. This evil is only partly the fault of the bureaucrats, who are so readily blamed. The art of administration has not been brought up to date; no one has thought about it since Frederick the Great and Napoleon or, it often seems, since Charlemagne. Although courses and certificates are offered on every conceivable activity of the modern world, administration is ignored. There are courses in management, but they take it for granted that psychologizing and manipulating people is the sole avenue to efficiency.

18. As one listens to any current campaign or "debate," one cannot help comparing its quality and methods with those of Lincoln and Douglas in 1858 or even of later presidential aspirants, such as Woodrow Wilson, Theodore and Franklin Roosevelt, or John F. Kennedy. One difference is the attention span required. Its dwindling is suitably met by the use of "30-second spots" on the air.

19. See, for example, two sections in Rose Macaulay, *A Casual Commentary* (London: Methuen, 1925)—"Problems for the Citizen" and "General Elections." In the second, the author suggests a nationwide refusal to vote, which would result in "a ridiculous little parliament that could be ignored," to everybody's advantage.

20. Tocqueville, *Democracy in America,* vol. 2, part 2, chap. 5.

21. It is not uncommon, for example, that after a strenuous debate in committee, a vote of seven to five will prompt a chairman to say, "This business needs further thought; we shouldn't go ahead divided as we are."

22. The latest of these to arouse angry debate is "language rights," aimed at making the United States officially multilingual. It is not said how many languages other than English would be included under these rights; at the moment Spanish is the one contender. See the arguments on each side in Gerola Bikales, "Comment," *International Journal of the Sociology of Language* 60 (1986), 77–85.

23. The disruption of others' speech, coupled with the claim to free expression for oneself, seems to be triggered by something besides unpopular views, namely holding office. Members of the cabinet or of the diplomatic corps have been assailed at colleges (and at writers' conferences) even before they spoke, and university officials have apologized for issuing the invitations. Faculty members doing "government research" or aiding intelligence agencies are suspect. These symptoms of disaffection may not be grave, but they indicate something less than support for the American form of government.

24. Tocqueville, *Democracy in America,* vol. 1, part 2, chap. 7.

25. Tocqueville again has something to say on the subject: "If social conditions, circumstances, and laws did not confine the American mind so closely to the search for comfort, it might be that when the Americans came to deal with immaterial things, they would act with more maturity and prudence and would keep themselves more readily in hand. But they feel themselves to be imprisoned within bounds that they are seemingly not allowed to escape, so that once they have broken through these barriers their minds do not know where to settle down and they often rush heedlessly far beyond the limits of common sense" (vol. 2, part 2, chap. 12).

26. Students of government in the United States report that it is in the counties that flexible adaptation to modern circumstances is most visible and innovative. See Howard L. Griffin, "Stasis and American County Governments—Myth or Reality?" (address to the American Studies Association of Texas, Huntsville, Tex., November 15–17, 1984).

Alberto R. Coll

Normative Prudence As a Tradition of Statecraft

The notion of prudence, or practical wisdom, is a key element in a way of thinking, legitimately described as a tradition, about the ethical dilemmas of international relations. The hallmarks of this tradition are twofold. First, there is a recognition of the difficulty of translating ethical intentions and purposes into policies that will produce morally sound results. Theorists and practitioners of statecraft sometimes see prudence as that virtue which enables its possessor to bring moral goals into some form of approximation with the stubborn and less than hospitable realities of international politics. Thus, as a tradition, prudence often has associated itself with a sober reading of the human condition and its possibilities, resembling that of secular realists such as Thucydides and Machiavelli. The main difference is that leading prudence theorists such as Aristotle, Aquinas, and Burke have refused to acquiesce in the collapse of the "is" into the "ought." While acknowledging the dark side of human nature and politics, they have insisted on the ultimate authority of the "ought" over the "is," and on the feasibility of moral action in an admittedly recalcitrant world. Nevertheless, the philosophically conservative bent of the prudence tradition has caused it to be shunned by those traditions, religious or secular, which seek to transform radically the patterns of international politics. In the intellectual armory of radical Christian and secular millenarians, utopians, and revolutionaries there is little usefulness for prudence.

Second, the notion of prudence draws attention to the statesman's character as a key component of his ability to act morally in the political world. Writers concerned with prudence emphasize that a statesman's religious, philosophical, or ideological views are less reliable as an indicator of his capacity for prudence than a series of character traits and intellectual virtues. This focus on character makes the prudence tradition distinctive. While writers on prudence recognize the power of political philosophy and conceptions of morality, they affirm the centrality of the statesman's character and his habits of decision making and action as critical factors in the concrete fulfillment of notions of the good.

In the West, the prudence tradition has clustered around the general proposition that, although politics is distinct from morality, it is ultimately grounded in and justified by it. There are two major currents of dissent from this proposition with which the prudence tradition has had to contend. One, that of secular realists such as Thucydides, Machiavelli, and Hobbes, maintains that politics and morality are basically divorced and that for the practical man of affairs the considerations of the political realm must take precedence regularly over those of morality. Thinkers and statesmen in this camp view skeptically the Aristotelian or Thomistic claim that the morally right can be harmonized, however tentatively and tautly, with the politically good. Hence, they define prudence as the skill of discerning that course of action which best serves one's self-interest and, therefore, as unconnected to morality, which is supposedly the pure or unencumbered search for the truly good.

There are important differences between the Aristotelian and Christian understandings of prudence, on the one hand, and that of the tradition of secular political realism that encompasses Thrasymachus, the Athenian spokesmen in the Melian dialogue, Machiavelli's prince, and Hobbes on the other. In this latter tradition, prudence is equated with caution, stealth, and the successful quest for survival at all costs; its guiding norm is the survival of the self or a particular political community, with few, if any, restraints on the range of means allowed for the pursuit of this end. Like Aristotle, who distinguished true prudence from "shallow cleverness," Aquinas contrasted practical wisdom with a series of "false prudences," the most important of which is *astutia,* or cunning. The "false prudences" exalted by the secular realists have at their root the sin of covetousness, an "immoderate straining for all the possessions which man thinks are needed to assure his own importance and status . . . an anxious senility, desperate self-preservation, overriding concern for confirmation and security."[1] Unlike Machiavelli, Aquinas saw moral excellence as a requirement, albeit not a guarantee, of prudence: "It is requisite for prudence, which is right reason about things to be done, that man be well disposed with regard to ends; and this depends on the rectitude of his appetite. Therefore, for prudence there is need of moral virtue, which rectifies the appetite."[2] While rejecting the secular realists, however, Christian prudence does not embrace utopianism. "The decisions of prudence embody the duties enforced on us by things as they are; in these decisions true cognition of reality is perfected for the purpose of realizing the good."[3]

At the opposite end of the spectrum from the secular realists is an equally formidable group of religious and secular idealists that the tradition of "normative prudence" has had to face. While maintaining the supremacy of morality over politics, they view prudence suspiciously as a dangerous Trojan horse for the importation of potentially corrupting extraneous considerations into the citadels of pure moral reasoning or biblical ethics. Whereas the secular realists empty prudence of its richer meaning by reducing it to mere pragmatism, the more radical among the idealists see prudence as the first step down the slippery slope of allowing morality or biblical imperatives to be subjected to politics. Interestingly, the secular realists have been so successful in expounding their particular definition of prudence that in today's philosophical and political discourse the prudential is regularly equated with the self-interested, even by people who do not share their philosophical assumptions. The tradition of normative—as opposed to self-interested or value-free—prudence represented by Aristotle, Thomas Aquinas, Edmund Burke, and Reinhold Niebuhr has refused to disconnect prudence from morality. It has insisted that it is possible to bridge the worlds of morality and politics, to pursue and achieve moral objectives in the political world, even if the objectives themselves have to be redefined and adjusted in the process. This branch of the tradition also has maintained that whenever the intellectual skills associated with prudence are put in the service of immoral purposes, they lose their character as attributes of prudence and become merely forms of cunning or cleverness, admirable perhaps in their virtuosity but not deserving of the name of prudence. Prudence is not value-free; it remains under the guidance, however ambiguous or indirect, of moral principles.

The distinctiveness of normative prudence lies in its determined effort to maintain a connection between the spheres of politics and morality while allowing each considerable space for their inner dynamics. Under attack from moral purists who sometimes see it as little more than an incoherent form of realism, and from secular realists who believe that the effort to keep morality and politics in some form of harmonious tension with one another is hopeless, this tradition of prudence has appealed to theorists and practitioners who have sought to find a middle ground from which to search for a statecraft that is neither politically impractical nor morally bankrupt.

Insofar as this tradition of prudence posits the ultimate subjection of politics to morality and of means to ends, it is not purely instrumental. It is possible, indeed, to elaborate a vision of the common good and of the moral purposes of statecraft shared by Aristotle, Aquinas, Burke, and Niebuhr. The resultant concept of the common good, however, is broad enough to permit a great deal of diversity. With Aristotle, the ends of a well-ordered city-state serve as the standard for prudence, while in Aquinas such a standard is supplemented by glimpses of a much wider transnational human community, the common good of which must not be ignored.

Although prudence theorists have devoted considerable attention to the issue of the ends of statecraft, what makes them most distinctive is their parallel attention to instrumental concerns in general and, in particular, to the relationship of a person's character to his capacity for acting well in the political realm.

The Aristotelian Roots

Aristotle considered prudence, or practical wisdom, the highest form of virtue or excellence in political life. Without a prudent statesman at the helm, the polis was like a ship wildly tossed about by the waves of human passions and misdirected moral energies. Statesmen have practical wisdom "when they calculate well with respect to some worthwhile end, one that cannot be attained by an applied science or art."[4]

Prudence manifests itself in two dimensions of statecraft: the ends and the means. It aims at choosing a good end or virtuous action, and in so doing it requires a capacity for deciding well, for excellence or "fitness" in the process of deliberating and choosing ends. Prudence also concerns itself with the means whereby one can attain such a good end. Thus, prudence is both a defining and an instrumental virtue. A prudent statesman must choose among competing ends; he then engages in the process of considering the means by which he will attempt to achieve the chosen end. In Aristotle's view, statesmen such as Pericles were prudent because they had "the capacity of seeing what is good for themselves and for mankind, and these are, we believe, the qualities of men capable of managing households and states."[5]

It is significant that Aristotle cited the management of "households and states" as the preeminent arena for prudence. Prudence involves managing the practical dilemmas of daily life with due regard not only for that which is good but also for the inherent complexities and difficulties of social and political realities. Unlike abstract speculation or theoretical wisdom, practical wisdom is concerned "with human affairs and with matters about which deliberation is possible." The realm of prudence is that of the contingent, the relative, and the uncertain; it is fraught with fluidity, ambiguity, and "might-have-beens."

At the core of prudence is a series of character traits or secondary virtues. Not everyone is equally endowed by nature with such traits, and an individual aspiring to possess them in their ripest form needs to cultivate them over a long period of time, so that they can become habits and an integral part of a person's character. These component elements of prudence are deliberateness, self-control, and good sense.

One of the marks of prudent persons is their ability to deliberate well. According to Aristotle, "excellence in deliberation will be correctness in assessing what is conducive to the end, concerning which practical wisdom gives a true conviction."[6] Deliberation is intrinsic to moral reasoning, and it requires a degree of existential gravity and modesty; enough gravity to recognize a moral dilemma, and enough modesty to realize one's limited capacities to deal with it. The essence of deliberation is a pause and a dialogue; the pause that should precede all difficult moral decisions in statecraft, and the subsequent dialogue in which the decision maker, having paused, engages his own conscience and that of others to wrestle with the problem at hand. Aristotle observed that "no one deliberates about things that cannot be other than they are, nor about things that are not directed to some end, an end that is a good attainable by action." Deliberation is thus, like prudence, a practical virtue, concerned with practical, contingent things. Politics, which is the highest realm of prudence, is also one of the highest realms for deliberation. There can be no good statesmanship, and no healthy political life in a society, when deliberation is not acknowledged as a virtue and an indispensable prerequisite to the attainment of good political ends.

Self-control is another component of prudence. Men are easily swayed by pleasure and pain. The pleasant and painful tend to "destroy and pervert" our convictions "concerning how we should act." Aristotle explains that "in matters of action, the principles or initiating motives are the ends at which our actions are aimed. But as soon as a man becomes corrupted by pleasure or pain, the goal ceases to appear to him as a motivating principle: he no longer sees that he should choose and act in every case for the sake of and because of this end."[7] A person who has self-control, however, knows his limitations well, and also what he is capable of doing. He will withstand the swayings of pain and pleasure and persevere in his course of action, undaunted by passions or the shadows of the imagination. The prudent statesman knows that the achievement of good ends in statecraft is not a fully rational enterprise untroubled by uncertainties or calamities. He will expect considerable resistance and opposition, be it from individual passions or vested interests, or from the sheer chaos of social life. But the statesman will press on, seeking the most complete approximation he can fashion between the good ends he perceives and the recalcitrant environment that perpetually confronts him.

The third character trait or habit in Aristotle's catalogue of the elements of prudence is good sense, which he equated with sympathetic understanding. Good sense has two dimensions; one is the ability to make a "correct judgment of what is fair and equitable," the other a "sense to forgive" and to put oneself in somebody else's place. "To say that a person has good judgment in matters of practical wisdom implies . . . that he has sympathetic understanding; for equitable acts are common to all good men in their relation with someone else."[8] The two dimensions of sympathetic understanding are intimately related. A "correct judgment of what is fair and equitable" ultimately requires putting oneself in someone else's place; in some circumstances, such a judgment may call us to forgive.

The fairness and equity to which sympathetic understanding leads are far removed from strict legal demands that the last ounce of flesh be paid and that justice be done even if the heavens do fall. As Aristotle makes clear in his discussions of equity elsewhere in the *Ethics* and the *Politics,* equity and fairness are a higher and more perfect form of justice than strict legal justice as commonly understood.[9] Equity and fairness adapt the requirements of justice to the weaknesses of human nature and the vagaries and ambiguities of the human condition. This is in keeping with Aristotle's concern throughout the *Ethics* to avoid building an ethical system oblivious to the sad realities of human existence.

The role of sympathetic understanding in prudence has several politically significant implications. Prudent statesmanship calls for political sympathy and fairness. Aristotle did not pay much attention to diplomacy in his writings, but at the core of diplomatic theory and practice is the idea, so dear to practitioners of the tradition of political realism in international affairs such as Richelieu, Metternich, Bismarck, Churchill, and Kissinger, of putting oneself in the position of one's adversaries, allies, or trading partners. Only then can one assess their strengths and weaknesses, and the proper policy toward them. Diplomacy (at least in the "mercantile" version of it, as opposed to the "warrior" version, to use Harold Nicolson's classic categories) also entails the capacity for acting fairly toward others. Some of the most successful practitioners of the art are those statesmen whose word is generally reliable and whose reasonableness and fairness can provide an incentive for negotiation.[10]

Influenced by Aristotle, Edmund Burke remarked that magnanimity is the essence of political wisdom, a point Lincoln was to immortalize in his second inaugural address with his call for "malice toward none . . . charity for all." Burke was referring not so much to the Aristotelian virtue of high-mindedness, which commentators sometimes translate as magnanimity, as to Aristotle's sympathetic understanding, which is accompanied by fairness, equity, and a judicious willingness to forgive. Some of the most durable achievements of diplomacy and statecraft have exhibited this political forgiveness.

Because its purpose is action, and action involves the knowledge of particulars, practical wisdom, or prudence, is more concerned with particulars than with universals. "This explains why some men who have no scientific knowledge are more adept in practical matters, especially if they have experience, than those who do have scientific knowledge."[11] The focus of practical wisdom is not so much the knowledge of generalizations, which is useful in politics only to a limited degree, as an awareness of particulars and the complex multiplicity of variables in political life. No one ever knows all these variables, but the prudent statesman tries to acquaint himself with as many particulars as are relevant to the decision he is pondering. This is one of the reasons experience is an essential requirement of prudence.

Experience is the ripening agent without which the skills or habits of prudence fail to blend to form the character of a prudent statesman. Experience provides intimate knowledge of the possibilities open to human action. An experienced statesman has seen much of what political reality is capable of throwing on his lap; therefore, he is less likely to be caught completely unaware by the sudden twists and turnings of the human drama. He will pursue flexible and open-ended policies, eschewing rigidity of mind and action. He will recognize the amorphous texture of politics for what it is, and will try to anticipate the unexpected shapes this amorphous mass may take. Long acquaintance with particulars also will give the statesman a better sense of proportion concerning the situation he faces and the means necessary to cope with it.

In describing the subject matter of politics as "things that can be other than they are," Aristotle underscored the elements of spontaneity, unpredictability, and genuine freedom in political life. Although there is room in politics for the play of economic necessity and other conditioning circumstances, these do not cancel out the important role of chance and human freedom. The absence of uniformity thus makes politics unfit for the precision of theoretical science, requiring the more elusive faculty of practical wisdom, or prudence.

A statesman does not deserve the appellation "prudent" unless he directs his efforts to good ends. Unless virtue is its end, prudence is little more than knavery, shallow cleverness. "A man cannot have practical wisdom unless he is good."[12] "Without virtue or excellence, this eye of the soul (intelligence) does not acquire the characteristic (of practical wisdom)." According to Aristotle, "A man fulfills his proper function only by way of practical wisdom and moral excellence or virtue: virtue makes us aim at the right target, and practical wisdom makes us use the right means."[13] In sum, "it is impossible to be good in the full sense of the word without practical wisdom or to be a man of practical wisdom without moral excellence or virtue."[14]

The notion of prudence as an autonomous, amoral skill in the pursuit of self-interest was alien to Aristotle. For all its remarkable independence of means, Aristotelian prudence is ultimately subject to the "theoretical wisdom" of what we might call moral philosophy and theology. The practical wisdom, or prudence, of the political world needs the illumination of a higher wisdom. Prudence "has no authority over theoretical wisdom or the better part of our soul [the rational element that grasps necessary and permanent truths]." Prudence "issues commands" to attain theoretical wisdom and makes the provisions "to secure it," but "it does not issue [commands] to wisdom itself. To say the contrary would be like asserting that politics governs the gods because it issues commands about everything in the state."[15] In Platonic language, prudence is concerned with the contingent, and theoretical wisdom with the transcendent, the latter having ultimate authority over the former.

The Thomistic Elaboration

The Aristotelian conception of prudence was attractive to Christian theologians seeking to bridge the treacherous gap between the necessities and inner logic of a fallen political world and the transcendent vision of the gospel. Aquinas incorporated prudence into the Christian moral universe as preeminent among the four cardinal virtues and as that virtue without which justice, courage, and self-control cannot be fulfilled. Prudence is "the perfected ability to make right decisions." Its main function "is to order things well for an end or purpose. This cannot be done aright unless the end be good, and also the means be good and adapted to the end."[16] It is an intellectual virtue insofar as it directs a person to choose the right means to an end; but it also has the character of a moral virtue since its proper working requires the presence of moral virtue in the will, directing it to good ends.

There are different kinds of prudence, dealing respectively with the good of the individual, the family, and the state. The latter, also known as political prudence, is the highest and fullest form because it is concerned with the common good. Like Aristotle, Aquinas made the important point that while the virtues of a good man, a good citizen, and a good ruler have common elements, they are different kinds of virtue.

Aquinas accepted the Aristotelian categories of deliberation, good sense or sympathetic understanding, and experience as components of prudence and added several others to the list: memory, insight or intelligence, "teachableness," acumen, reasoned judgment, foresight, circumspection, and caution. Memory refers to the capacity for an "honest" or "just" memory, for recollecting our past experiences and those of others realistically, without allowing our subjective desires and illusions to warp such recollection. As he put it: "Prudence is engaged with contingent human doings. Here a person cannot be guided only by norms that are simply and of necessity true, he must also appreciate what happens in the majority of cases." In sum, "our calculations about the future should be based on what has happened in the past. Accordingly our memory of them is needed for being well advised about the future . . . recalling many facts is required for prudence."[17] This was, among other things, an implicit recognition of the value of the study of history for the development of prudent statecraft.

Drawing on Cicero and Macrobius, St. Thomas argued that intelligence and intuitive understanding (which for him were the same) were a part of prudence. He defined intuitive understanding as "a certain correct appreciation of an ultimate principle assumed as self-evident." Since "prudence is right reason in human deeds . . . its entire process derives from insight or understanding." Insight, or intuitive understanding, is a trait that requires development over the course of a long life rich with experience. It enables a person to connect in an almost intuitive fashion ultimate principles with particular, specific ends or goals in which those principles are realized in some approximation.[18]

Another important element of prudence is teachableness, or *docilitas,* a general attitude of openness to the insights of others. It includes a willingness not to close our minds to the infinite variety of surprises that reality may hurl against our designs and policies; it is a quality of spiritual, emotive, and intellectual flexibility and humility. St. Thomas recognized that this was a difficult quality to cultivate: "To be generously docile calls for much effort, that of a person who carefully, frequently, and respectfully attends to the teachings of men of weight, and neither neglects them out of laziness nor despises them out of pride." It was bound to be especially difficult for "rulers" or political leaders. "All the same," he said, "even people in authority ought themselves to be tractable sometimes, for in matters of prudence no one is wholly self-sufficient."[19]

Acumen, or *solertia,* refers to the ability to act rightly in sudden, unexpected crises and to draw upon one's inner resources when confronted by a practical dilemma that requires immediate action.

Whereas the emphasis in *docilitas* is on profiting from the experience and insight of others, *solertia* focuses on the inescapable position of immediate responsibility in which a decision maker finds himself when he has to act without the benefit of consulting or seeking the consensus of others. Just as "docility disposes us to gather sound opinions from others, so acumen disposes us to make correct assessments by ourselves." Acumen "is the flair for finding the right course in sudden encounters. . . . [It] hits upon the point, not only with demonstrations [that is, intellectually], but in practical issues as well."[20]

Prudence also requires reasoned judgment, a quality almost indistinguishable from Aristotle's "deliberateness." The "prudent man should be a good reasoner," and his judgments should be well-reasoned. While "understanding and reason are not distinct faculties, they take their names from distinct functions; understanding from a close insight into truth, reason from inquiry and discussion." Aquinas added that, although "reasoning works with more assurance in some other intellectual virtues, nevertheless the ability to reason well is most important for prudence, in order that general principles may be rightly applied to particular issues which are various and uncertain." Human beings cannot grasp truth by simple insight because their understanding is deficient, and the contingent world is less than fully intelligible to our intellect. Indeed, moral and political matters are full of uncertainty and indeterminateness. Hence, in order to attain any kind of practical certitude about such matters, we have to engage in reasoning.[21]

Foresight, or prevision, entails the ability to predict, as clearly as humanly possible, the consequences of our actions and the degree to which the particular action we are about to take will lead to the realization of our goal.[22] Foresight is essential to sound statecraft, for, as Aquinas observed, the past and the immediately present are beyond our ability to alter, leaving only "those future contingencies that a man can shape to the purpose of human life" as the subject of prudence. "Both contingency and purpose are implied in the notion of [prevision], which signifies looking ahead to something distant to which present occurrences are to be adapted."[23] Prudent statesmen are not solely concerned with having right intentions; they also weigh carefully the consequences of their actions.

The two other components of prudence that Aquinas underlined were circumspection and caution. Circumspection is a capacity for discerning the degree to which circumstances affect the applicability or appropriateness of moral principles in specific situations. Since "prudence is about individual actions . . . and these involve many factors, it may happen that a means good and suitable in the abstract becomes bad and inopportune owing to a combination of circumstances." In the same way that prevision, or foresight, looks "ahead for what is in itself suitable for a purpose," circumspection looks into whether a particular action done on behalf of a moral principle is "opportune, given the existing [present] situation."[24] A prudent statesman applies moral principles with due regard for their context.

This means that the process of moral reasoning in which a prudent statesman engages is far from subject to simple formulas. It is an intensely complex, undetermined, and personal process, at the core of which there can be a high degree of uncertainty and even existential agony. As explained by Aquinas' foremost twentieth-century commentator, Josef Pieper:

> The immediate criterion for concrete ethical action is solely the imperative of prudence in the person who has the decision to make. This standard cannot be abstractly construed or even calculated in advance. . . . The imperative of prudence is always and in essence a decision regarding an action to be performed in the "here and now." By their very nature such decisions can be made only by the person confronted with decision. . . . No one else can assume this burden. The strict specificity of ethical action is perceptible only to the living

> experience of the person required to decide. He alone has access to . . . the totality of concrete realities which surround the concrete action, to the "state" of the person himself and the condition of the here and now.[25]

Thus the tradition of normative prudence stands apart from various forms of moral casuistry that set out to enclose an ethical dilemma tightly within the bounds of distinguishing principles and formulas drawn from previous similar cases so as to resolve it definitively.

The last item in Aquinas's catalogue of the elements of prudence was caution. He defined it as an awareness of the all-encompassing presence of evil in human affairs and of the imperative to guard against its subtle manifestations. Aquinas was no believer in the perfectibility or basic goodness of man, and he had a firm theological grounding in the reality of original sin. Thus he could write that "prudence deals with contingent actions, in which bad may be mixed with good, as true with false . . . human deeds are multiform; rights are often entangled with wrongs, and wrongs wear the air of good." In the contingent world of politics not all situations are morally clear-cut cases of good pitted against evil. Even the most seemingly righteous causes are often tainted by sin. Caution is a form of skeptical discernment toward earthly absolutist claims, "a necessary ingredient in prudence if right courses are to be so followed that hazards are avoided."[26]

Like Aristotle, Aquinas believed that prudence was practical wisdom in the service of the common good. "Some men, insofar as they are good counsellors in matters of warfare or seamanship, are said to be prudent officers or pilots but not prudent absolutely; for only those are prudent absolutely who give good counsel about what concerns man's entire life." More specifically, he argued that "perversions" of rightful systems of government, such as tyranny, ignoble oligarchy, and mobocracy, "have no part with prudence," thus suggesting that while such regimes and their rulers may be capable of some prudent acts, it is improper to speak of them as prudent per se.[27]

The Burkean Mediation

The theological successors of Thomas Aquinas who developed his understanding of natural law further in the realm of political theory did not pay much attention to prudence. Such prominent theorists of international law as Franciscus de Vitoria and Francisco Suarez, while highly sensitive to the problematical relationship of morality to politics, focused their efforts on an analysis of natural law, just war, the nature of the international community, and the rights of persons, but said little about the mediating virtue of prudence or the critical importance of the prudent statesman. Among the Renaissance humanists of the fifteenth and early sixteenth centuries, a prudence tradition with classical and Christian roots flourished, especially in writers such as Pontano and Guicciardini,[28] but it was effectively eclipsed by Machiavelli, who collapsed prudence into an amoral skill to maximize power and political success.[29]

The tradition resurfaced vigorously with Edmund Burke, who indirectly derived many of his central philosophical assumptions from Aristotle and Aquinas through the seventeenth-century Anglican divine Richard Hooker. A practitioner more than a scholar, Burke did not treat prudence with a high degree of intellectual precision, but it is clearly one of the key elements in his view of the relationship of morality to statecraft. "Prudence is not only the first in rank of the virtues, political and moral," he wrote, "but she is the director, the regulator, the standard of them all." The foundation of prudence is its assumption of the unreliability of theory—by which Burke meant all forms of intellectual speculation—as a guide to practical human action. Seizing upon Aristotle's distinction between the man with scientific knowledge and the man of experience, Burke drew a similar distinction between a theorist or professor and a statesman: "A statesman differs from a professor in a university; the latter has only the general view of society; the former, the statesman, has a number of circumstances to combine with those general ideas, and to take into his consideration. Circumstances are infinite, and infinitely combined; they are variable and transient; he who does not take them into consideration is not erroneous, but stark mad . . . metaphysically mad. A statesman, never losing sight of principles, is to be guided by circumstances; and, judging contrary to the exigencies of the moment, he may ruin his country forever."[30]

Time and circumstances make a great difference in the moral appropriateness, or lack thereof, of applying a particular principle: "In every question of moral and political prudence, it is the choice of the moment which renders the measure serviceable or useless, noxious, or salutary."[31] More to the point, "circumstances (which with some gentlemen pass for nothing) give in reality to every political principle its distinguishing color and discriminating effect." Principles, therefore, are important, and a statesman is not to lose sight of them on his difficult journey. But prudence is essential as a mediator between general moral principles and the infinitely variable and complex circumstances to which those principles must be applied.

Burke's outline of the relationship between prudence and the moral principles it mediates is not free of problems. Aristotle and Aquinas formally subordinated prudence to morality or "theoretical wisdom," while insisting that in this world it was the highest political virtue. Burke seemed to move further, or at least less unequivocally, in the direction of giving prudence full autonomy when he argued that "practical wisdom [supersedes] theoretic science" whenever the two come into conflict.[32] To protect himself against Machiavellianism, Burke drew a distinction between "true prudence" ("public and enlarged prudence," which is concerned with the good of the whole and which takes within its purview a larger, long-term view of things) and "that little, selfish, pitiful, bastard thing, which sometimes goes by the name," and which is little more than cleverness or cunning.[33]

The Burkean catalogue of character traits, habits of intellect, and judgment that the prudent actor possesses was not new: the capacity to deliberate; the exercise of self-control against the passions and delusions of the mind; a profound skepticism toward any attempt to turn theoretical conclusions or "universals" directly into policy without due regard for the friction of circumstances or "particulars"; an appreciation for the value of equity and forgiveness in the making of political judgments. All these were part of the inner fabric of the prudent statesman. In addition, the prudent statesman had to learn to live with ambiguity, incompleteness, and inconclusiveness. As Burke wrote, "The decisions of prudence . . . differ from those of judicature [in that] . . . almost all the former are determined on the more or the less, the earlier or the later, and on a balance of advantage and inconvenience, of good and evil."[34]

It was on this last point and on the philosophical possibilities it opened that twentieth-century non-Machiavellian realists such as Hans Morgenthau, Reinhold Niebuhr, and Kenneth W. Thompson sought to anchor their own understanding of prudence and their adherence to the prudence tradition. Unlike E. H. Carr and the early George Kennan, who drew an impenetrable barrier between morality and policy, these realists were prepared to admit that the barrier was far more porous and that the relationship between statecraft and the absolute moral law whose reality they recognized was far more subtle and sophisticated than either Carr or the early Kennan supposed. Statecraft could not ignore the moral law, even if it could not follow it without the aid of prudence. It was mainly through Burke that they acquired the concept of prudence.

In the hands of Morgenthau, Niebuhr, and Thompson, prudence has few of its Thomistic lineaments but much that is reminiscent of Burke's emphasis on its near autonomy, his distrust of ideological abstractions and moralism, his perception of prudence as a "balancer" of competing goods and lesser evils,[35] and his sharp sense of the ambiguity and inconclusiveness at the heart of the prudential decision-making process. If the contemporary realists err, it is on the side of vagueness and imprecision about the meaning of prudence—a reflection, perhaps, of their neglect of Aquinas, whom they suspected of being excessively rationalistic and legalistic but whose understanding of prudence could have been immensely valuable to them. Yet it may be that the realists also shied away from Aquinas because of the latter's assumption that prudence could be harmonized consistently with good means and ends. In the light of the twentieth century's horrible upheavals, they were far more skeptical of such an assumption, and far more attuned to the possibility that less than good means, indeed horrible ones, might be morally justifiable in the light of ends that were either ultimately good or at least preferable to, or less evil than, the feasible alternatives. There is little of St. Thomas's quiet moral confidence and serenity in the agonized queries of Hans Morgenthau about the inevitable evil of politics or Reinhold Niebuhr's skeptical probings of the relationship of reason to man's moral and political life.

The twentieth-century realists have rendered a signal service to the prudence tradition by bringing into it an intense, almost one-sided concern with international politics. For Aristotle, Aquinas, and Burke, statecraft meant primarily the right ordering of the polity and only secondarily the polity's relationship to the vast external realm outside it. For the realists, statecraft means above all steering the ship of state through the turbulent waters of international politics at a time when, thanks to nuclear weapons and modern technology, errors in this task can have ultimate, irretrievable consequences.

Ambiguities and Criticisms

The central ambiguity in the notion of prudence is its relationship to those transcendent principles to which theoretically it remains subject even while operating with considerable freedom on the plane of day-to-day affairs. Within the Christian branch of the tradition, this ambiguity takes the form of the problematic relationship between Jesus' "radical gospel," with its seemingly uncompromising transcendent reference point, and the general tenor of prudential decision making, which tends to revolve around, and focuses on, the necessities and parameters imposed by this world. Christian thinkers have tried to lessen the ensuing tension by writing about two forms of prudence: lower prudence and higher prudence.[36] The first kind, most evident in the Old Testament and the Pauline letters, has been appropriated by Christian realists of our own day, such as Reinhold Niebuhr and Martin Wight, via St. Augustine's distinction between the City of Man and the City of God. In the realm of statecraft, lower prudence focuses on modest goals, such as limited order, tranquility, and accommodation. Its inward logic is an instrumental conception of international morality coupled with skepticism toward any radical transformational designs of world politics. Aside from its concern with limited objectives, lower prudence devotes most of its energy to the question of means, to making the inevitable struggle for power among nations less brutal and dehumanizing than it otherwise might be. Its archetypical models include Hugo Grotius's counsels to moderation in *De Iure Belli ac Pacis* and Reinhold Niebuhr's observation that the highest ethical action one can expect of a state in international relations is one that is both morally good and beneficial to that state's interests.[37]

Higher prudence, on the other hand, is more willing to take risks for the sake of exploring possibilities open to ethical action. It is, in contemporary Roman Catholic language, "a virtue infused with grace; its measure exceeds that of living merely according to reason—its measure is the mind of Christ; its purpose is not to be respectable but to be a fellow citizen of the saints and a familiar of God. . . . It springs from and lives only in charity, without which one may be shrewd but cannot be prudent."[38] The limits of this higher prudence in the political realm, however, are ambiguous, as are also the boundaries between lower prudence and secular realism. At what point does higher prudence become, in Eric Voegelin's words, a radically irresponsible and unrealizable desire to "immanentize the escathon"? And where is the line that separates lower prudence from a narrow, selfish desire to protect one's self-interest without causing undue harm to others?

A second ambiguity, present as well in Aristotle's notion of prudence, has to do with the time measurement by which one ought to evaluate a statesman's actions. In their day, Pericles, Philip II of Spain, and Otto von Bismarck were widely admired as prudent. Indeed, in the *Ethics* Aristotle cited Pericles as a paragon of the prudent statesman, in much the same way that many contemporary chroniclers treated Philip II and Bismarck. Yet the three of them set in motion policies and long-term trends that proved ruinous to their state and the international society of which they were a part. While it may be unfair to judge statesmen by consequences that would have been extremely difficult for them to foresee, is it not appropriate to judge them for the long-term costs of their deceptively brilliant short-term achievements?

The most serious charge brought against the prudence tradition is that the notion of prudence itself, even the "normative prudence" of Aristotle and Aquinas, is inadequate as a guide to ethical statecraft. According to this argument, the considerable freedom that prudence arrogates for itself—both in its choice of which ends are to receive greater priority at a particular moment and in its choice of which means are appropriate for effecting the chosen ends—signifies that in practice statesmen resort to prudence as an imprecise, dangerously broad rationalization for selfish pragmatism. In the everyday run of affairs, "lower prudence" winds up taking precedence over "higher prudence," and the prudence tradition lacks the inner intellectual and normative resources to remedy this tendency. At its best, prudence fails to give a statesman rational guidance for choosing among moral principles in specific situations; at its worst, it degenerates into an intuitionism under whose spell the grossest immoralities are condoned.

The prudence tradition has offered some tentative replies to these serious charges. Contemporary philosophers of ethics and international affairs tend to focus on the search for moral principles through which statesmen might create a more humane and ethical system of international relations. They have worked to demonstrate the validity of ethical imperatives, and of hypothetical policies derived from such imperatives, in issues such as nuclear deterrence, the global arms race, distributive economic justice, human rights, and the environment. Interestingly, the ultimate moral ends pursued by the contemporary theorists do not differ radically from those accepted by many of the theorists within the mainstream "normative prudence" tradition.

What makes the prudence tradition distinctive is its reminder that moral principles are translated into actual policies only through the mediation of a complex process in which human decision makers play a critical role. To use Aristotelian language, theoretical wisdom does not become embodied in action except through a filtering process that includes the reason, imagination, will, choices, and particular acts of particular human beings. Moral principles are ultimately realized only in specific acts that human beings choose to carry out. This is why the character of the statesman, including his foundational predispositions, attitudes, and intellectual and moral skills and habits, is an important focus of the prudence tradition. A correct set of moral principles is not sufficient to ensure that policies founded on such principles will be morally sound.

In terms of affecting the practical attitudes a statesman takes toward difficult ethical choices confronting him, prudence can be valuable in moderating some of the worst errors to which he is prone. The Aristotelian emphases on self-control, deliberation, sympathetic understanding, and the value of experience and intimate acquaintance with the particular details of the problem at hand are all valuable correctives to hubris, mean-spiritedness, self-righteousness, and the politician's tendency to give primacy to ideological abstractions over the more intractable empirical realities at the core of international relations.

Aquinas brought these Aristotelian concerns into the Christian understanding of prudence, while adding others: memory, the capacity for a memory of integrity and realism; teachableness, with its emphasis on intellectual and existential openness and flexibility; acumen, focusing on the skill of acting rightly in sudden crises; and foresight, which in spite of its theoretical difficulties has the salutary effect of forcing the statesman to ponder the wide range of future consequences that may flow from his actions.

The writers on prudence also have set themselves against the popular notion that all that is required for excellence in public service is to place a "good and decent man," or a man of good moral principles, at the helm. A decent man does not always make a prudent statesman. In order to ripen into morally sound statecraft, a person's desire to do the good requires the cultivation of those ways of thinking and acting, those intellectual and volitional habits and skills associated with the concept of prudence. Yet another misguided conventional belief, congruent with our society's technological bent, is that ethical decision making can be systematized and fully rationalized either through some sort of "moral system" such as casuistry or biblical literalism or through "scientific" techniques of decision making or systems analysis. Here, too, prudence warns against the understandable but morally pernicious yearning for simplification and certainty. Given the uniqueness of every agent and every situation, and the difficulty of balancing competing ends and means, prudence reminds us that at the core of ethical decision making is a degree of existential agony and darkness perhaps indicative of man's finiteness and of his need for a transcendent grace that, in Reinhold Niebuhr's words, may "complete what even the highest human striving must leave incomplete."[39] For Niebuhr, "faith in God's forgiveness" is what ultimately "makes possible the risk of action."[40]

More directly, one can argue that the processes of moral reasoning—weighing and balancing, and the cultivation of those inward attitudes and habits that should accompany these processes—are unavoidable for any decision maker or thinker, confronted by moral dilemmas in the political arena, who wants to bring the claims of morality in rightful balance with those of the political world. Even for those who studiously wish to avoid the use of the term, prudence may be inescapable.

In the annals of international relations, the title "prudent" has been reserved for those statesmen who have exercised the art of ruling with sufficient excellence to earn the gratitude of their contemporaries and posterity. While disagreement will continue as to whether Pericles, Philip II, or Bismarck deserve the appellation, a greater degree of consensus may be possible with regard to Washington, Lincoln, and Churchill. These rank as among the best that humanity is capable of producing. In the context of their undeniable flaws and the titanic pressures they faced, their moral wisdom is all the more remarkable. At the core of their statecraft and their moral and political reasoning was the notion, explicitly articulated or otherwise, of prudence. In their own minds prudence—or something akin to it—rather than a single moral principle or philosophy, was the mediating process and personal virtue through which they connected the moral ends they pursued with their everyday actions and policies. To argue that prudence is normatively meaningless, useless, or noxious requires refuting a formidable body of historical experience concerning one of the important instruments by which statesmen have given substance to moral principles in the political world.

NOTES

1. Josef Pieper, *The Four Cardinal Virtues* (Notre Dame: University of Notre Dame Press, 1966), 21.

2. Thomas Aquinas, *Summa Theologica,* 1a2ae, 57, 4.

3. Pieper, *The Four Cardinal Virtues,* 25.

4. Aristotle, *Nicomachean Ethics,* trans. Martin Ostwald (Indianapolis: Bobbs-Merrill, 1962), VI, 1140a, 26–32.

5. Ibid., VI, 1140b, 6–11.

6. Ibid., VI, 1142b, 32–35.

7. Ibid., VI, 1140b, 11–20.

8. Ibid., VI, 1143a, 17–33.

9. Ibid., VI, 1137b–38a.

10. François de Callieres, *De la Maniere de Negocier avec les Souverains* (Paris, 1716; reprint, Notre Dame: Notre Dame University Press, 1963); Harold Nicolson, *Diplomacy* (London: Oxford University Press, 1939); Adam Watson, *Diplomacy: The Dialogue between States* (New York: McGraw Hill, 1983).

11. Aristotle, *Ethics,* VI, 1141b, 15.

12. Ibid., 1144a, 35–37.

13. Ibid., 1144a, 6–31.

14. Ibid., 1144b, 30–33.

15. Ibid., 1145a, 6–11.

16. Aquinas, *Summa Theologica,* 2a2ae, 49, 7.

17. Ibid., 49, 1.

18. Ibid., 49, 2. As he explained: "The reasoning involved in prudence draws on a double understanding. One, the understanding of general principles, which is for that understanding classed as an intellectual virtue it is a habit of mind whereby by nature we see general principles, not only of theory but of practice as well, such as 'Do evil to nobody.' . . . The other understanding is . . . seeing the ultimate particular or factual principle. . . . This individual principle . . . is about an individual end. And so the understanding which is taken as part of prudence is a certain correct appreciation of some particular end."

19. Ibid., 49, 3.

20. Ibid., 49, 4.

21. Ibid., 49, 5.

22. See the discussion in Pieper, *The Four Cardinal Virtues,* 14–18.

23. Aquinas, *Summa Theologica,* 2a2ae, 49, 6.

24. Ibid., 7.

25. Pieper, *The Four Cardinal Virtues,* 25.

26. Aquinas, *Summa Theologica,* 2a2ae, 49, 8.

27. Ibid., 1a2ae, 57, 4; 2a2ae, 50, 1.

28. Victoria Kahn, *Rhetoric, Prudence, and Skepticism in the Renaissance* (Ithaca: Cornell University Press, 1985).

29. Leo Strauss, *Thoughts on Machiavelli* (Glencoe, Ill: Free Press, 1958); Eugene Garver, *Machiavelli and the History of Prudence* (Madison: University of Wisconsin Press, 1987).

30. Edmund Burke, speech, May 11, 1792. For the intellectual context of Burke's thought, see J. G. A. Pocock, *The Machiavellian Moment: Florentine Political Thoughts and the Atlantic Republican Tradition* (Princeton: Princeton University Press, 1975); Francis Canavan, *The Political Reason of Edmund Burke* (Durham: Duke University Press, 1960).

31. Edmund Burke, second letter to Sir Hercules Langrishe, IV, 57.

32. For an excellent discussion of the problematic nature of this effort, see Harvey Mansfield, "Edmund Burke," in Leo Strauss and Joseph Cropsey, eds., *History of Political Philosophy,* 3rd ed. (Chicago: University of Chicago Press, 1987), 692–95.

33. Harvey Mansfield, "Edmund Burke," 693.

34. Burke's first letter to Sir Hercules Langrishe, III, 304. Cited in Gerald W. Chapman, *Edmund Burke: The Practical Imagination* (Cambridge: Harvard University Press, 1967), 138. Deeply aware of the fiercely competitive relationship among the numerous moral claims on the statesman's resources and commitments, Burke counseled, "He forms the best judgment in all moral disquisitions, who has the greatest number and variety of considerations in one view before him, and can take them in with the best possible consideration of the middle results of all."

35. See, for example, Kenneth W. Thompson's discussions of prudence in *Morality and Foreign Policy* (Baton Rouge: Louisiana State University Press, 1980). In this and other works Thompson also has emphasized the centrality, to prudence and to sound statecraft, of moral reasoning, which he defines in categories not foreign to Aquinas's own definition.

36. See the discussion in Clark E. Cochran, "The Radical Gospel and Christian Prudence," in Francis Canavan, ed., *The Ethical Dimension of Political Life: Essays in Honor of John H. Hallowell* (Durham: Duke University Press, 1983), 188–99.

37. Reinhold Niebuhr, *Moral Man and Immoral Society* (New York: Charles Scribner's, 1960), 83–112.

38. *New Catholic Encyclopedia* (New York: McGraw Hill, 1967), 11:928, col. 2, cited in Cochran, "The Radical Gospel and Christian Prudence," 196.

39. See Niebuhr's closing words in *The Children of Light and the Children of Darkness* (New York: Charles Scribner's, 1944).

40. Cited in Thompson, *Morality and Foreign Policy,* 143.

Part II: CULTURE

Frances V. Harbour

Basic Moral Values: A Shared Core

Students annually torture teachers of ethics and international affairs with a long list of impossible questions. Among the hardest for me to answer has always been whether moral values have any basis other than the conventions of a particular culture or the whims of a single individual. Is morality merely a matter of either private or national taste, on a par with preferring apple pie to baklava? Or do some moral principles have a weight that extends beyond subjectivity?

When applied to international affairs, the already sticky question is made even worse by a serious empirical tangle. If morality is entirely objective, how can we explain well-known differences between cultures and between individuals on specific moral questions? But, on the other hand, if morality is merely subjective, why is there so much concurrence between societies at the most basic level of morality? These questions have pedagogical and policy implications as well. If we do not recognize and respect differences in moral values, why should we or our students practice tolerance? But if there are no objective limits, how can we avoid letting leaders like Adolf Hitler, Josef Stalin, and Idi Amin off the hook morally? This article is the result of my attempts to wrestle with these intractable questions on my own account and for my students.

Certainly the first side of the problem is better known than the second. Attempts to apply moral and ethical concepts to international affairs are widely criticized on the grounds that moral values differ too much from society to society to make valid cross-cultural judgments possible. And certainly one must acknowledge very important value differences between cultures. In some societies, for example, revenge killing may be considered a duty. In others, it is forbidden. In some societies women vote. In others they do not even drive. Sometimes the differences extend to individuals in the same culture. One American considers abortion wrong. Another does not. Differences between cultures or between individuals often make political relationships difficult inside a country, much less across borders. This insight captures an important part of the reality of the international world. But it is only one part.

The other side of the problem is less well known. As important as the variation in local codes is a surprising concurrence, on a very general or basic level, of ethical evaluations among cultures with very different traditions and circumstances. As anthropologists Alfred Louis Kroeber and Clyde Kluckhohn point out, "considering the exuberant variation of cultures in most respects, the circumstance that in some particulars almost identical values prevail throughout mankind is most arresting."[1]

How then is the scholar, practitioner—or teacher—to deal with both sides of the issue? My answer has two parts. First, a shared core of human moral values does exist, but only at the most basic level: approval of beneficence, justice, courage, and so on. My hypothesis is that secondary and tertiary moral values differ between societies because cultures build on these basic, shared building stones in different ways. Secondary values are elaborations and specifications of the general values in the form of culturally shaped definitions and principles of conduct. For example, is there a moral difference between murder and killing in war? Am I bound by my promises in business transactions? The definitions or intermediate-level principles, in turn, are used to construct specific codes of behavior at a tertiary level. What is the just punishment for murder? May I kill male noncombatants in war? Am I bound by contracts with foreigners?

If moral conventions are constructed from shared human values the observer can explain not only differences between societies but also seemingly puzzling similarities. This hypothesis does not, however, explain why there are shared core values in the first place. Many, including Kroeber and Kluckhohn, would argue that human beings simply respond in similar ways to the necessities of our nature and environment.[2] My argument is that the basic, foundation-level moral values are shared across cultures because they share the same objective property. There is a right and wrong that we perceive and to which we react by means of an emotional trace. However, since the original signal is delicate—and the secondary and tertiary levels are constructed from the basic level by fallible human beings—the further the applications get from the shared core, the less assurance we have that a given principle, character trait, or rule shares the objective property.

The main reason moral philosophers have not been very interested in the empirical issue of whether or not universal moral or ethical values exist is that they quite rightly point out that this data would not *prove* the existence of objective moral values one way or the other. All the cultures in the world might simply be incorrect. I am not claiming here that near universal acceptance proves that morality is real property in certain evaluations—that "ought" follows from "is." I am simply arguing that, if objective moral values do exist at a very general level, it would be extremely odd if there were no shared moral values at all. There are, however, a few shared moral values. This fact is consistent with and, indeed, suggestive of some underlying objective causal factor.

Defining Morality

An important problem arises when we try to explain why morality, if it is objective rather than a matter of taste or convention, is so difficult to define precisely. Here the job is not to identify the content of morality and thus to distinguish right from wrong; instead, the metaethical question is how we can tell if a judgment belongs in the domain of morality at all. That this is a controversial undertaking supports the notion that morality is "nonnatural." According to philosophers, if moral values were "naturalistic" we could simply translate them into "factual, *nonvaluational* terms" with nothing important left over.[3]

The problem, at least from the perspective of the ordinary user of moral language, is that there seems no valid answer to G. E. Moore's famous open question argument.[4] For example, if a property of good things—such as Bertrand Russell's definition of good as "that which we desire to desire"—is synonymous with goodness, we would not be able to ask sensibly, "It may be that which I desire to desire, but is it good?"[5] The reason the question makes sense is that, at least for the average user of moral language, the first clause simply does not have the same meaning as the second. Technically, it represents an open, not a closed question. The same seems to be true of any naturalistic definition of moral terms that we can offer. (For example, try asking Moore's question with the principle of utility—right consists of producing the greatest net happiness.) This means any naturalistic definition of moral terms does not fully capture the concept.

There is nothing logically wrong with stipulatively defining or proposing reform of moral language, but stipulation and proposal do not by themselves change meaning except for those who choose to accept the definition. Goodness, rightness, and other normative concepts thus do not seem to be naturalistic in and of themselves. In this sense the intuitionists seem to be correct.

The intuitionists miss something important, however, in their insistence that moral properties are not knowable by standard perceptual means, but only by the somewhat mysterious faculty of intuition.[6] What they do not take sufficient account of is that, while the moral properties do not simply consist of their naturalistic counterparts, we can recognize that such properties are present through their effects on our nervous systems. Thus, moral-sense philosophers such as David Hume and Annette Baier (and more recently political scientist James Q. Wilson) have an important insight: humans *register* morality through emotional reactions. And, as this moral-sense school points out, the emotional stimulus plays an important role in motivating us to act morally.

I would argue then that moral feelings are the naturalistic trace caused by the perception of objective but nonnatural moral properties. The problem is, individuals and societies can train themselves to ignore these feelings or even to feel similar sensations in response to inappropriate stimuli, as in genocidal behavior. Thus, there is naturalistic, value-neutral evidence that we have *correctly perceived* a basic moral value only when we both feel a sentiment of approval or disapproval and there exists a matching, persistent, intercultural pattern of positive or negative affect toward the *general category* of behavior or character represented. Values bolstered in this way may be (with only a little trepidation) regarded as authoritative.

By definition, there is no way to prove empirically the correctness of the hypothesis: the proposed property is nonnatural. There are, however, good reasons for holding the position and arguing that the objections raised to similar hypotheses do not demolish it. This is an argument like some in physics. Nonnatural, objective value at the most basic level is comparable to the hypothesized "weak" and "strong" forces at work in the nuclei of atoms. Its presence, like theirs, cannot be apprehended directly. However, there is empirical evidence for its possible, even probable, existence; its existence would explain observable phenomena that are otherwise puzzling; and objections to its existence do not appear decisive.

To say that morality cannot be fully defined in empirical terms is not to say that it cannot be recognized or that we cannot separate moral from nonmoral judgments. Here philosopher William Frankena offers some particularly useful ideas. He points out that morality as an institution is a more or less self-conscious "action-guide, some kind of standard for conduct, character formation, and life, something by which, together with the facts or what we believe or take to be the facts about ourselves, our situation, and the world, we do or may determine how we should act or shape ourselves." What distinguishes morality from other social-action guides such as law and etiquette is that the judgments are not merely tools for judging the effectiveness, prudence, or beauty of actions, and so on. Like law and etiquette, morality mostly deals with how people ought to relate to each other, but unlike law and etiquette, Frankena argues, the judgment is in some sense "ultimate or for its own sake . . . [although taken] from the point of view of the consideration of the effects of actions, motives, traits, etc. on the lives of persons or sentient beings as such."[7] Thus, a moral value is not akin to a mere preference for apple pie over baklava. Morality involves evaluations that bear on the essence of being human. Hume and Baier and other subjectivists explain these evaluations simply as conventionalized responses to the human condition, but they offer no persuasive evidence that the emotion they catalog could not be stimulated by perception of an objective property.

The Objectivity of Moral Values

Much of the metaethical debate of the twentieth century has concerned what statements such as "X is evil" mean if there is no such thing as objective moral value. Radical emotivists have suggested that a plausible translation is "X, ick!" The prescriptivist translation would be something like "No doing X, please."[8]

At least in one sense, both of these translations suffer from a serious shortcoming. They do not reflect what the "ordinary user of moral language" *means* when she makes a judgment or exhorts someone to some behavior. As J. L. Mackie points out, "the ordinary user of moral language means to say something about whatever that he categorizes morally . . . as it is in itself, or would be if it were realized, and not about, or even expressive of, his or anyone else's attitude or relation to it."[9] Mackie correctly argues that most ordinary users of moral language at least *think* they are making a statement about the actual state of some aspect of the universe. Belief is not enough to prove objectivity, of course. Nevertheless, philosophers who depend heavily on linguistic analysis of meaning but do not take this intention into account make prescriptions without having fully dealt with the nature of their empirical data.

Although the fact that this belief in objectivity is widely held does not make it true, that it is so widespread at least suggests the possibility that there is something objective that stimulates the shared experience. Moreover, it is not merely unsophisticated people who have believed that moral properties in some sense represent objective reality. Until comparatively recently the mainstream of Western philosophical thinking (including Plato, Aristotle, Aquinas, Kant, Sidgwick, and Mill) also held this view.

There is thus an empirical problem. If an objective property of morality does not exist, why is there such a persistent, *intercultural* pattern of taking morality to have objective authority? The position here is like Kant's, a view that while it is the mind that puts together the pieces of the outside world, its creation has objective force, necessity, and universality.[10] If we as human beings have similar reactions under similar conditions, it is somewhat odd to say that there is no objective condition to which we are reacting.

If a scientist were told of a belief that, like the belief that morality is objective, was shared by most human beings throughout Western recorded history but was rejected by some of the people living in one time period, the scientist would need very strong evidence for believing that what was operating was not some parochial aspect of that one group's culture or material circumstances.

Regarding moral properties as merely subjective thus leaves open an empirical problem of a persistent erroneous belief. This problem does not arise if moral principles or virtues have objective weight beyond the individual or society that affirms this authority. This suggests that subjectivism needs a very strong case in order to carry the day against the prima facie plausibility of the objectivity of at least some ethical values.

Do Variations in Ethical Codes Mean No Objective Value?

Although regarding moral properties as merely subjective is problematic, regarding all moral beliefs as equally objective leaves open a serious problem on the other side of the intercultural dilemma. Different societies assign different priorities to the general values they share. Moreover, J. L. Mackie is only one of the philosophers who spotlight "the well known variation in moral codes from one society to another." He argues that "actual variations in the code are more readily explained by the hypothesis that they reflect ways of life than by the hypothesis that they express perceptions, most of them inadequate and badly distorted, of objective values."[11]

As Mackie himself points out, the strength of this argument against objective value depends in part on how general one believes the original values reflected in resulting judgments to be.[12] If, for example, virtues such as "justice" or "beneficence," or even principles such as "do not murder," are what are intrinsically valuable, then the guidance they provide will be quite general. The values will lead to outlines and tendencies rather than to detailed codes. Thus, we should not find it surprising that some—although not all—behavior considered morally proper in one culture is not considered morally proper in another. As Stephen Toulmin points out, shared central moral values "are recognized in just about all societies and communities." It is primarily definitions of situations, the derived or secondary evaluations, the "marginal issues and considerations about which different societies, cultures, and groups display much less unanimity."[13]

If this conclusion is correct, specific definitions and rules derived from the general principles *are* in part contingent on local conditions. Only the general values and the resulting tendency to react emotionally to them are universal. For example, all societies require some individual sacrifices for the good of the community, but these sacrifices differ in degree. Some of the disagreements between China and the United States over human rights arise because Chinese culture is more communally oriented than contemporary U.S. society. But, unless we are talking about a general concept shared by both cultures, how can we compare differences between conceptions? We do not normally compare baklava to trees.

One should not assume automatically that division and discord are inherent even at the secondary and tertiary levels. For example, in September 1993, representatives of more than 125 religions signed a nine-page document called "The Declaration of a Global Ethic." Among other concepts, it condemns violence and leaders who "incite aggression, fanaticism, hate, and xenophobia." It advocates respect for nature and between the sexes. The signers were both Eastern and Western and included groups as diverse as Roman Catholics, Sikhs, Hare Krishnas, Zoroastrians, and Lutherans. What surprised Hans Küng, the author of the original draft, was that "there was no objection to any important point."[14]

Political leaders, too, have endorsed documents that indicate at least some shared values. In international law the least controversial of these include the United Nations Charter, the 1948 Universal Declaration of Human Rights, the Convention on the Prevention of the Crime of Genocide, and the Convention against Torture and Other Cruel, Inhuman, or Degrading Treatment. Certainly there are important disputes about the meaning and priority of these conventions. Nevertheless, each shares such widespread acceptance that it is considered customary international law. At minimum, genocide, slavery, and torture are globally condemned. As Norman Bowie points out, a government accused of torture does not defend the practice but, rather, denies it or accuses others of starting the practice or of being equally guilty.[15]

Judgments about the validity of a particular aspect of the local code or of an individual's version of it depend on its connection to the relevant general categories of interculturally accepted value.

Primary Values and War

The next step is to see whether conceiving morality as a nonnatural but objective general property is a workable approach. This moves the hypothesis out of the realm of metaethical musings about the nature of morality and into normative ethics. It requires the actual evaluation of the right and wrong of acts, states of affairs, and the characters and motives of people. In theory at least, an analyst armed with this approach can work at all three levels: the content of the shared primary values, the fit of given social definitions and intermediate-level constructs with the primary values, and the acceptability of specific rules and behavior, motives, and character. I intend to apply the three-level approach to the problem of war, one of the critical areas of ethics and international affairs. At the first level, I will identify and demonstrate the relevance of primary values to the conduct of war. At the second level, I will argue that both defensive war and pacifism are reasonable applications of the primary values of special beneficence and war. At the third level, I will defend the moral value of the Western just war tradition's principle of double effect.

What are some of the primary values that might be relevant to the conduct of war? How would we know them? One way to begin is to survey lists of purportedly universal values. Three fairly extensive lists of moral values that have been cross-culturally validated and aspire to universality are Christian theologian C. S. Lewis's "Illustrations of the Tao"; anthropologist Clyde Kluk-hohn's examples of values shared around the globe, including some additions by philosopher Richard B. Brandt; and psychologist M. Rokeach's list of moral and nonmoral human values, as applied transculturally by Shalom H. Schwarz and Wolfgang Bilsky.[16]

Primary Moral Values

Approval of:	
justice[ac]	
beneficence[abc]	
special beneficence to kin/compatriots[abc]	
subordinating interests of individual to group[ab]	
good faith and veracity[abc]	
courage[ac]	
self-control[abc]	
Disapproval of:	
murder[ab]	
incest or rape[abc]	

[a] Lewis, *The Abolition of Man,* 95–120.
[b] Brandt, "Relativism and Ultimate Disagreements about Ethical Principles," 38.
[c] Schwarz and Bilsky, "Toward a Theory of the Universal Content and Structure of Values," 881.

Because none of the lists is intended to be absolutely exhaustive, none can stand alone as a compendium of primary values. (By the same token, absence from all three does not prove that a value is not primary.) To minimize individual or disciplinary bias, only moral values cited by two or more of the lists are tentatively identified as primary.

Which of the primary values are relevant to fighting wars? The answer is virtually all of them. Beneficence, special beneficence, and justice are certainly central to the Western just war tradition, Islam's *jihad,* the Confucian tradition of war, and the Hindu tradition, to name only a few. Equally important, the character traits or virtues of courage, sacrifice of self for the group, good faith and veracity, and self-control are essential for a soldier to be able to fight well, in both the moral and nonmoral sense of the term. More than two thousand years ago, Taoist strategist Sun Tzu pointed out that "leadership [in war] is a matter of intelligence, trustworthiness, humaneness, courage, and sternness."[17] Plato's guardians "dedicate themselves wholly to the maintenance of freedom in the state . . . and know the essential forms of temperance, courage, liberality, magnificence, and their kindred."[18] Malham Wakin, chairman of the U.S. Air Force's Philosophy and Fine Arts Department, writes, "Loyalty and obedience, integrity and courage, subordination of the self to the good of the military unit and the nation-state—these are among the moral virtues critical to the military function and they take the form of universal obligations."[19] These emotionally charged primary values undergird any organized war that is not the hell of Hobbes's "war of all against all."

War and Murder

It is at the secondary and tertiary levels that the more complicated and controversial intellectual analysis of right and wrong in war begins, although the emotional element does not disappear. For example, the preceding table lists prohibition of murder as a primary value. The moral distinction between "murder," which is universally condemned, and killing in war, which is not, takes place at the secondary level. The distinction is not on the primary level because it is not universal—as the views of well-respected pacifists from a variety of cultures demonstrate. Second-level elaborations of "no murder" tell us that private citizens are not permitted to kill *compatriots* except under very special circumstances. The protected category of compatriots is defined in wider or narrower ways in different societies. Pacifists tell us explicitly or implicitly that any nonpacifist definition of compatriot is too narrow. Pogo's "We have met the enemy and he is us" is literally true. All people are our compatriots, not only those with whom we share nationality or other narrow affiliations.

The pacifist definition leaves us with another moral dilemma, a conflict between primary values. If killing in war is always murder, what are we to do if killing is the only way to protect those to whom we have a special duty—another universal—from an invading army, a bomber force, or other mortal threat? Many pacifists would argue that war is a very poor way to defend even our own compatriots. Nineteenth-century pacifist Adin Ballou wrote, for example, "would as many lives have been sacrificed, or as much real misery have been experienced by the human race, as have actually resulted from the general method of self-preservation, by personal conflict and resistance of injury with injury? He must be a bold man who affirms it."[20] One might argue, as do St. Thomas Aquinas and, more recently, Michael Walzer, that defense of the community justifies lethal violence against opposing military forces, whether or not they or their leaders are morally justified in going to war in the first place. From this perspective, fighting a war is not murder but a form of beneficence toward the specially protected group. The issue is the harm and the special duty to protect from harm; whether or not the perpetrator is also a compatriot is not an issue.

Thus, reasonable arguments can be offered to support both pacifism and a purely defensive war. Both of these pass the test of plausible connections to primary values. Pacifism and defensive war are disagreements at the second level of morality, the level of definitions of primary values. Each is a morally reasonable elaboration of primary principles, and thus, although diametrically opposed, both seem compatible with the primary principles of "no murder," justice, and special beneficence.

Third Level Values: Justifying the Deaths of Innocents

Other difficult moral problems with the institution of war arise because wars are almost never as simple as the defense of the homeland. On both sides, people who have done nothing to deserve punishment and who represent no real danger to the enemy suffer and die. This is an injustice. While this class is narrower than all civilians, it certainly includes children and persons with diminished capacity, such as the mentally ill. Because this is an area where considerable divergence among cultures exists and specific guides to conduct are required, dealing with the problem means moving to the third level of moral analysis.

Clearly, one answer is that of the pacifists. As Robert L. Holmes puts it, war inevitably entails killing innocents on the other side. Since we may not kill innocents, we may not fight wars.[21] The pacifist answer has not been accepted by the majority of world traditions, however. For example, eighth-century Muslim theologian Mohammad ibn al-Hasan al-Shaybani wrote that "if the Muslims stopped attacking the inhabitants of the territory of war for any of the reasons that you have stated, they would be unable to go to war at all, for there is no city in the territory of war in which there is no one at all of these you have mentioned."[22] Al-Shaybani's conclusion is thus the opposite of Holmes's: the moral urgency of war means that it is sometimes permissible to kill otherwise protected noncombatants.

Many cultures permit war but attempt to limit the amount of harm wars cause to noncombatants. For example, the traditional Western just war principle of discrimination forbids the deliberate targeting of noncombatants. Islamic law also tells believers not to kill noncombatants deliberately. The specific rules differ. Just war doctrine traditionally includes all those not engaged in the war effort.[23] Islam defines noncombatants as women and children, and perhaps the elderly.[24] An ancient Indian text is more expansive than just war tradition. It orders protection for "those who look on without taking part, those afflicted with grief . . . those who are asleep, thirsty, or fatigued or are walking along the road or have a task on hand unfinished, or who are proficient in fine art."[25] Thus the tertiary-level differences between cultures are real. In each case, however, the underlying primary value is the same: special beneficence for a protected group.

In the Western just war tradition, the principle of double effect permits some killing or harming of protected noncombatants. Conditions for doing so are relatively strict: the main act must be permissible in and of itself; the damage must be a side effect—not intended either as an end or as a direct means to an end; and the harm may not exceed the bounds of proportionality.[26] The just war tradition thus permits acts leading to *collateral* harm to noncombatants, provided the harm to be caused is less than the good expected.

Paradoxically, then, even in this rule-oriented tradition, the standard bearing on collateral deaths and other harm is related to expected consequences, although in a much more limited way than for utilitarianism. An important question is whether it makes sense to have such a rule from the perspective of primary values. The answer, I believe, is yes, or, rather, "yes but."

Using utilitarian arguments, the solution seems relatively straightforward. The central utilitarian principle is that of utility: what will maximize net happiness. This utilitarian perspective is a form of the primary principle of generalized beneficence. For a utilitarian, the principle of double effect, paired with discrimination and proportionality, maximizes utility for the following reasons. War is a more or less permanent fixture of the international system for the foreseeable future. War simply cannot be fought in such a way that no innocents are harmed or killed. The principle of double effect offers significant beneficence to children and others who are not dangerous without requiring a militarily impossible standard. When observed, it leads to fewer rather than more deaths of innocents. Because the just war tradition, long a part of Western culture, has been wrought over the centuries in the forge of real wars, it, rather than some novel higher standard, has a chance of actually being followed—or at least of affecting policy.

The second utilitarian reason for supporting a rule that offers some protection to noncombatants is that such principles benefit the international system and belligerent states as well. A strategy or tactic leading to substantial civilian casualties, particularly if they are intentional or incurred over long periods of time, may well have a corrosive effect on the morale of soldiers and the societies that support them. This is a violation of special beneficence to one's own citizens as well as of justice. So, too, a leader must consider the long-term military effects of tactics involving the deaths of civilians on the other side during the war. Avoiding enemy civilians may well encourage reciprocal limits by the other side. Moreover, other states note strategies leading to heavy civilian casualties—as in the Iran-Iraq war—and may well conduct future wars against the power that initiated them accordingly—as in the Gulf War. It is thus clear that initiating a policy that leads to indiscriminate or disproportionate noncombatant casualties almost certainly will have important negative utilitarian consequences.

The distinction is also reasonable from a deontological perspective, but the justification may be less intuitively satisfying. From a deontological perspective, acts and motives are enjoined or forbidden, not effects per se. So when we judge an effect morally we are really judging the nature of the action that produced it. In terms of primary values, we thus prohibit murderous and rapacious actions per se and admire acts motivated by a desire for justice, beneficence, and so on. Because we judge the nature of the act, motive is an important part of what makes it right, merely permissible, or out-and-out wrong. We recognize this in everyday life when we acknowledge the difference between accidently harming someone and doing so on purpose, between killing someone and not saving a distant foreigner from starvation. But is there a significant moral difference between deliberately causing harm and undertaking actions whose effects we know will be harmful?

The answer here, I think, is yes, although a full-scale examination of intention is beyond the scope of this paper. When we pursue a goal, we make it part of ourselves as people; we embrace it. The initiator of intended harm embraces the consequences of her acts because she intends them to lead causally to her goals. If those consequences are evil, then she embraces evil. Yet, as Thomas Nagel argues, "the essence of evil is that it should *repel* us."[27] To say the least, embracing evil is a violation of beneficence, justice, and so on. We do not embrace mere side effects—undesired consequences—in the same way.

The terror bomber bombing a neighborhood to "cleanse" it is morally different from the strategic bomber who hits a house while destroying a munitions factory. The terror bomber wants the good that victory will bring but has embraced the injustice of killing innocents. He would repeat the act if something should go awry and the harm not be consummated. The just war, double-effect strategic bomber, on the other hand, wants not only the good that victory will bring but also a balance of good in the war itself. He would be happy if by some chance the unintended victims escaped or took steps to reduce their danger as much as possible. The strategic bomber's motives are thus better than the terror bomber's. Because a deontologist is concerned with acts and motives, not effects per se, the balance is probably enough to make the act permissible, although not desirable.

As is appropriate for the third level of moral value, the distinction between terror bomber and strategic bomber is tenuous. Giving a little less weight to motives and widening the definition of "intended" effects produces a different evaluation. The strategic bomber, too, would persist in pursuing the desired end, even though it will also produce the deaths of innocents—as a side effect. Thus a refusal to embrace a course of action that will entail deaths of innocents is certainly plausible. Either conclusion seems a reasonable application of moral reasoning, thus supporting the permissibility of either approach.

Because the deontological judgment is so close, the other conditions of the principle of double effect take on additional importance. The deaths must be a genuine side effect, neither desired in themselves nor as a means to an end. No cynical turning aside of intention will do here. The act with the undesirable side effect must not be wrong in itself—for example, not aimed at noncombatants. And, equally important, the harmful side effects must not be disproportionate to the good expected from the act. These are formidable requirements that go far to ensure that beneficence and justice are both served. Not all actual or proposed "strategic" bombing would qualify.

The (bare) permissibility of some collateral deaths in the just war tradition in no sense justifies genocide. The intentional slaughter of innocents on a massive scale is a deliberate evil. With genocide, justice and beneficence are both impermissibly violated.

In Lieu of Conclusions

It is important to realize that at the secondary and tertiary levels very different evaluations may be morally acceptable. Both pacifist rejection of war and carefully limited just war traditions are permissible extensions of primary principles. There are some true and false statements in normative reasoning, but they are relatively few and far between. Most unambiguous evaluations are at the primary level. Murder *is* wrong. Courage *is* a good thing—and so on. In a few extreme cases, there is such a clear link between primary-level values and secondary rules and specifications that moral sense and reason alike tell us that primary values and application can be decisively linked. Prohibition of genocide comes to mind here.

More often, however, a person making moral judgments must work through contradictions: genuine perceptions of both good and evil in the same situation. The three-tiered approach does not by itself solve the problem of what to do when the object of evaluation contains elements of both right and wrong. It does not solve the tragic dilemma—a case in which, as Thomas Nagel puts it, "there is decisive support for two or more incompatible courses of action."[28] Even if an objective property underlies our perceptions and evaluations, moral reasoning requires working through the contradictions to an answer that is on balance morally plausible. The three-tiered approach provides criteria and a methodology for working toward permissible solutions.

The voice of moral value is a "still, small voice." Its signal is delicate. Like an understanding of mathematics, the ability to listen to and to read moral sense must be encouraged and developed in childhood. Even once acquired, it is highly corruptible, and the emotional response is not very precise. When, however, we find a matching, persistent, intercultural pattern of positive or negative feelings toward certain character traits or general categories of behavior, we have some reason to trust that an objective property has been perceived. The requirement for matching intercultural patterns is crucial. It serves to separate core values from derived ones. More importantly, it serves as a double check on both an individual's and a given culture's reactions. A person may be wrong. A whole society may be wrong, as with the institution of slavery.

The relationship between culture and moral value is thus a complex one. Cultures are communities in which universal moral values are combined into particular chords and more complicated melodies. Societies teach the results to succeeding generations. Cultures thus differ—and should differ—in patterns of moral evaluations and codes of behavior. However, societies also provide the arena for moral debate. In a world where cultural isolation is more and more difficult to achieve, moral debate and change are increasingly the order of the day. Thus, finding the answer to my students' question becomes increasingly urgent.

Shared basic moral values built up into different ethical edifices answer the question posed by my students in the affirmative. Some but not all moral values have a weight beyond simple taste. This hypothesis explains observable phenomena that are otherwise puzzling, and objections to the existence of nonnatural but objective moral values do not appear decisive. But more than that, the argument provides for tolerance in a diverse world without requiring us to give up our moral compass.

NOTES

1. Alfred Louis Kroeber and Clyde Kluckhohn, "Culture," in Charles L. Reid, ed., *Choice and Action: An Introduction to Ethics* (New York: Macmillan Publishing Company, 1981), 60.

2. Ibid., 59–61.

3. Tom Beauchamp, *Philosophical Ethics: An Introduction to Moral Philosophy* (New York: McGraw-Hill, 1982), 339.

4. G. E. Moore, *Principia Ethica* (Cambridge, UK: Cambridge University Press, 1903), 6–8. It does not matter for the purposes of my argument whether Moore is correct in his assessment that using a naturalistic definition of normative terms is formally a logical fallacy since I am proposing a nonnaturalistic definition.

5. Fred Feldman, *Introductory Ethics* (Englewood Cliffs, NJ.: Prentice-Hall, 1978), 199–200.

6. Beauchamp, *Philosophical Ethics,* 352–55.

7. William K. Frankena, *Thinking about Morality* (Ann Arbor: University of Michigan Press, 1980), 19.

8. Feldman, *Introductory Ethics,* 216–17.

9. J. L. Mackie, *Ethics: Inventing Right and Wrong* (New York: Penguin Books, 1977), 33.

10. Immanuel Kant, *The Metaphysical Elements of Justice: Metaphysics of Morals,* trans. John Ladd (New York: MacMillan, 1965), 14–16.

11. Mackie, *Ethics,* 36–37.

12. Ibid.

13. Stephen Toulmin, Richard Rieke, and Allan Janik, *Introduction to Reasoning,* 2nd ed. (New York: MacMillan, 1984), 397–98.

14. Lauri Goodstein, "'Declaration of a Global Ethic' Signed at Religious Parliament," *Washington Post,* September 3, 1993, 3.

15. Norman Bowie, "Moral Obligations of Multinational Corporations," in Steven Luper-Foy, ed., *Problems of International Justice* (Boulder, Col.: Westview Press, 1988), 107.

16. C. S. Lewis, *The Abolition of Man: How Education Develops Man's Sense of Morality* (New York: Macmillan Publishing Company, 1947), 95–120; Richard B. Brandt, "Relativism and Ultimate Disagreements about Ethical Principles," in Beauchamp, *Philosophical Ethics,* 38; Shalom H. Schwarz and Wolfgang Bilsky, "Toward a Theory of the Universal Content and Structure of Values: Extensions and Cross-Cultural Replications," *Journal of Personality and Social Psychology* 58 (May 1990), 881.

17. Sun Tzu, *The Art of War,* trans. Thomas Cleary (Boston: Shambhala Publications, 1991), 4.

18. Plato, *The Republic and Other Works,* trans. B. J. Jowett (Garden City: Doubleday, 1973), 83, 91.

19. Malham Wakin, "The Ethics of Leadership," in Malham Wakin, ed., *War, Morality, and the Military Profession,* 1st ed. (Boulder, Col.: Westview Press, 1979), 214.

20. Adin Ballou, "Christian Non-Resistance," in Staughton Lynd, ed., *Nonviolence in America: A Documentary History* (Indianapolis: Bobbs-Merrill, 1966), 31, quoted in Richard Wasserstrom, "On the Morality of War," in Wasserstrom, ed., *War and Morality* (Belmont: Wadsworth, 1970), 92.

21. Robert L. Holmes, *On War and Morality* (Princeton: Princeton University Press, 1989), 193.

22. Muhammad ibn al-Hasan al-Shaybani, *The Islamic Law of Nations,* ed. and trans. Majid Khadduri (Baltimore: Johns Hopkins University Press, 1966), sec. 117, as quoted in John Kelsay, *Islam and War* (Louisville: Westminster/John Knox Press, 1993), 65.

23. See, for example, John Finnis, Joseph Boyle, and Germain Grisez, *Nuclear Deterrence, Morality, and Realism* (New York: Oxford University Press, 1987), 88–90.

24. John Kelsay, "Religion and the Governance of War: The Case of Classical Islam," *Journal of Religious Ethics* 18 (Fall 1990), 129–31; see also, Sobhi Mahmassani, "International Law in Light of Islamic Doctrine," in Academie de Droit International, *Recueil des cours* 117 (1966), 307–8. Most contemporary Islamic jurists accept the legal rules embodied in the Geneva Protocols and other treaties on POWs as currently binding. See Elizabeth Ann Mayer, "War and Peace in the Islamic Tradition and International Law," in John Kelsay and James Turner Johnson, eds., *Just War and Jihad: Historical and Theoretical Perspectives on War and Peace in Western and Islamic Traditions* (New York: Greenwood Press, 1991), 198.

25. S. V. Viswanatha, *International Law in Ancient India* (Bombay: Longmans, Green & Co., 1925), 156; quoted in Michael Walzer, *Just and Unjust Wars: A Moral Argument with Historical Illustrations,* 1st ed. (New York: Basic Books, 1977), 43.

26. John C. Ford, S. J. "The Morality of Obliteration Bombing," in Wasserstrom, *War and Morality,* 26.

27. Thomas Nagel, *The View from Nowhere* (New York: Oxford University Press, 1986), 182.

28. Thomas Nagel, *Mortal Questions* (Cambridge: Cambridge University Press, 1979), 128.

Sissela Bok

Early Advocates of Lasting World Peace: Utopians or Realists?

The plans that Erasmus, the Abbé de Saint-Pierre, Kant, and others offered for moving toward a universal and perpetual peace have long been dismissed as utopian or hypocritical, at times even suppressed as dangerously heretical. These thinkers challenged the common perception of war as an immutable aspect of the human condition and the idea of lasting peace as possible, if at all, only in the hereafter—a perception that has seemed self-evident to most commentators from antiquity onward whether they espouse what has come to be called a realist, a pacifist, or a just war perspective. In the nuclear age, however, nations can no longer afford to leave that perception unchallenged. They cannot run the risk of yet another world war; even in the unlikely event that such a war could be kept non-nuclear, today's conventional weapons would bring devastation beyond anything that humanity has experienced. Likewise, prolonged regional conflicts are increasingly seen as intolerable, given the levels of impoverishment, homelessness, and suffering that they inflict, as well as the risk that they will ignite large-scale war. The social and environmental threats that nations now face collectively, moreover, call for unprecedented levels of cooperation that will be unattainable except under conditions of lasting peace.

If, therefore, self-preservation now dictates collective efforts toward a lasting world peace, no matter how difficult to achieve, it is worth reexamining the writings of those who once pioneered such an approach. To be sure, they had more than their share of quick-fix solutions; and the particulars of even the most sophisticated of their plans can hardly be adequate for today's international relations. But two aspects of the best among their writings are as relevant today as in the past: their intrepid challenges to the common assumption that war will always be with us, and their suggestions for how to create a social climate conducive to the forging of a stable peace.

In the works of Desiderius Erasmus and Immanuel Kant, these lines of reasoning are pursued with special subtlety and force. They are as relevant to practical choice by contemporary governments, organizations, and individuals as to theories of war and peace. By now, many proponents of realist, just war, and pacifist theories have come to agree on the necessity of working toward the goal of lasting peace, while continuing to differ about the means. It will help, in debating the means, to consider the coordinated, practical measures explored by these two thinkers in the light of all that we have later learned about which ones work best and why. In turn, such a study will require a rethinking, from within each of the three theoretical perspectives, of the role and the demands of morality in international relations.

The Debate through the Ages

> It will be enough for me, however, if these words of mine are judged useful by those who want to understand clearly the events which took place in the past and which (human nature being what it is) will, at some time or other and in much the same ways, be repeated in the future.
>
> —Thucydides, *The Peloponnesian Wars*

The conflict between Athens and Sparta depicted by Thucydides has been reenacted time and again over the centuries. Most thinkers since his time, whether they have gloried in war, tolerated it, or denounced it, have taken for granted that it will remain a constant in the human condition. To be sure, they have argued, it can be staved off for a time or fenced away from one or more regions of the world, but experience shows that it cannot be eradicated for good. To think otherwise is to be caught in an illusion.

They have explained the perennial nature of war by referring, as did Thucydides in the passage cited above, to human nature: to incorrigible traits such as pugnacity, vindictiveness, partisanship, and the lust for conquest and power. But they have also invoked, as did he, the external circumstances of scarcity and hardship that drive communities to fight one another in order to survive. These traits and circumstances have in turn often been seen as inflicted on human beings by fate or some supernatural power. Thus, Homer portrays the gods as prolonging the Trojan War by using participants for purposes of sport or intrigue or amusement; and the biblical God has been interpreted as imposing hardship and tribulation to punish human beings, to test them, or to separate the just from the unjust.

The debate about how to respond to such a predicament was, for centuries, largely three-cornered. Against the common background of war as a constant in the human condition, the responses accorded with one or the other of what we now call the realist, pacifist, and just war traditions—though with all the overlays, interlacings, and variations that would naturally accrue over the centuries.

Realists, often invoking Thucydides, held that it was useless and perhaps even dangerous to rail against the cruelty and immorality of anything as perennial as war; what mattered, rather, was to act according to the best available strategic estimates of what would serve a ruler's or nation's self-interest. In this way, engaging in wars for the sake of preserving or increasing a nation's independence, wealth, or power was acceptable, even commendable. Moral judgments about the rights and wrongs committed in starting any particular war or in its conduct were, according to such a view, beside the point.

Tertullian, Origen, and other early Christian pacifists argued, on the contrary, that morality and religion commanded human beings to renounce war and all killing. No matter how prevalent war might be and no matter what interests any one war might serve, the Christian's duty was to refuse all participation. Otherwise the biblical injunction to love one's enemy and to turn the other cheek would lose all meaning.

Just war theorists, from Augustine and Thomas Aquinas on, advocated, on similarly religious and moral grounds, limiting rather than renouncing the recourse to war. Among the causes these thinkers regarded as justifying going to war were, variously, wars fought in self-defense, wars in defense of an ally, and wars of conquest and crusade to punish wrongdoing and to convert unbelievers. But justice also required careful scrutiny of the conduct of warring forces, no matter how just the cause to which they laid claim.

Beginning with the sixteenth century, a fourth pattern emerged among the responses to the prevalence of war—that of Erasmus and other advocates of specific, practical steps toward what they called "perpetual peace." They challenged not only the commonly accepted thesis regarding war's perennial nature but also the specific claims of thinkers in the existing three traditions regarding when, if ever, war was legitimate. Because the proposals for a lasting peace were often summarily dismissed or even suppressed, they did not constitute a lineage of well-known fundamental texts nor give rise to the wealth of commentary generated by the other traditions. As a result, advocates of perpetual peace were rarely seen as contributing to a tradition separate from that of pacifism. By now, however, it is becoming increasingly clear that they were shaping a new tradition of thinking about war and peace fully as worthy of study as the three others. To this tradition belong, among others, Desiderius Erasmus, William Penn, the Abbé de Saint-Pierre, Immanuel Kant, and Jeremy Bentham.[1] Among its interpreters and critics are Leibniz, Rousseau, and Hegel.[2]

Thinkers in this fourth tradition had no illusions that peace was somehow a natural state for the human species. They could hardly quarrel with the historical record of recurrent aggression, injustice, and warfare. They meant, rather, to challenge what they saw as the unthinking extrapolation from that past experience to the future: the unwarranted inference from what has been to what must always be. Over time, they argued, nations could break away from the destructive patterns of the past. But they had little faith, unlike a number of utopians, in some convulsive political or religious transformation that would bring permanent harmony—the more so as they had seen at close hand the corrupting and brutalizing effects of unrestrained violence on behalf of such causes both on perpetrators and on victims, no matter how humane the original motives.

The synthesis arrived at by these thinkers was eloquently voiced by Erasmus and formulated with greater precision, clarity, and scope by Kant. It employs both the realist language of strategy and the normative language common to pacifists and just war theorists. According to this view, nations can only achieve lasting strategic benefits by respecting fundamental moral constraints, but it does little good merely to stress these constraints without setting forth concerted, practical steps to facilitate and reinforce their observance. War may indeed continue to be our lot, they admit, but we are free to choose differently. Each generation, far from being condemned to reenact the errors of the past, has the opportunity to learn from the mistakes and disasters of previous generations, and thus the capacity to move, over time, toward a state of perpetual peace.

The Complaint of Peace

What is more brittle than the life of man? How short its natural duration! How liable to disease, how exposed to momentary accidents! Yet though natural and inevitable evils are more

> than can be borne with patience, man, fool that he is, brings the greatest and worst calamities upon his own head. . . . To arms he rushes at all times and in all places; no bounds to his fury, no end to his destructive vengeance.
>
> —Erasmus, *The Complaint of Peace*, 1517

Few have spoken out more forcefully than Erasmus about the folly and cruelty of war. Already in his *Adages,* published in 1500 and reportedly more widely circulated at the time than any other book save the Bible, he had inveighed against war in an essay entitled *"Dulce Bellum Inexpertis"* ("War is Sweet to Those Who Have Not Experienced It").[3] Between 1514 and 1517, when a brief interval in the near-constant wars between European powers made a more lasting peace seem at least possible, Erasmus devoted himself wholeheartedly to helping bring it about.[4] He suggested summoning a "congress of kings"—a "summit meeting" among the kings of Europe—for the purpose of signing an indissoluble peace agreement. He revised and expanded his essay on the sweetness of war to the inexperienced for the latest edition of the *Adages*. And he wrote a manual for princes—*The Education of the Christian Prince*—to guide the young Prince Charles of Spain, who was shortly to become Charles V.[5]

This book presents a striking contrast to Machiavelli's *Prince* (written a few years earlier but still unpublished).[6] Where Machiavelli had broken away from the stress on virtues so common in previous books of advice for princes and urged the prince to resort to violence, deceit, and betrayal whenever necessary to gain or retain power, Erasmus emphasized moral virtues as prerequisites to a good reign. And whereas Machiavelli had urged the prince to study war above all else, Erasmus gave precedence to learning "the arts of peace": how to establish and preserve a rule of just laws, improve the public's health, ensure an adequate food supply, beautify cities and their surroundings, and master the diplomatic alternatives to war. A last, brief chapter, entitled "On

Beginning War," counsels the prince never to go to war at all, save as a last resort; but "if so ruinous an occurrence cannot be avoided," then the prince should wage it with a minimum of bloodshed and conclude the struggle as soon as possible.[7]

A year after publishing his *Education,* Erasmus returned to the charge with *The Complaint of Peace.*[8] This time, Erasmus sent his book to all the rulers of Europe instead of addressing it to one prince alone. Peace, speaking "in her own person, rejected from all countries," is the protagonist of this book. Her complaint addresses the irrationality and inhumanity of war. Of all the evils that beset humanity, she argues, surely war is the most puzzling, because it is self-chosen. If the insults and indignities heaped upon her went along with advantages to mortals, she could at least understand why they might persecute her. Yet, since they unleash a deluge of calamities upon themselves through engaging in war, she has to speak to them of their misfortune even more than complain of her own.

In these several works, Erasmus gives short shrift to the realist and just war schools of thinking that ruled the day at the courts of Spain and other European powers, but at the same time he distances himself from pacifist claims to nonresistance at all times. First of all, however attractive a war may seem at the outset, he argues, it appeals to dreamers, not to realists. From war "comes the shipwreck of all that is good and from it the sea of all calamities."[9] Claims to the benefits of war result, he claims, from inexperience. Those who have had to live through war are too rarely consulted; as a result, each generation foolishly undertakes to learn about war's costs from scratch. Even on the strictest strategic grounds of national self-interest, Erasmus insists, a truly realistic look at the costs of war should dissuade a prince from just about all recourse to arms.

Second, Erasmus evinces equal skepticism about claims that particular crusades and wars are just. He writes scornfully of the spectacle of clergy on both sides of so many wars declaiming the just cause of their own rulers. Who does not think his own cause just, he asks, warning that the likelihood of bias and corruption is so great in seeking reasons for going to war that "the good Christian Prince should hold under suspicion every war, no matter how just."[10] This suspicion, he held, was the more necessary since so many conquests and crusades were being fought in the name of the Christian Church, even though "the whole philosophy of Christ teaches against it."[11]

Third, Erasmus addresses pacifist concerns by holding that wars in self-defense are, indeed, legitimate, but only after all other alternatives, including arbitration, have been exhausted and only after obtaining the consent of the people, who will, after all, suffer so much more directly from any war than their rulers. If such procedures were taken seriously, it is doubtful whether any war would remain to be fought. But the decision to avoid going to war would then be made on pragmatic as well as on religious and moral grounds and would not constitute an absolutist rejection of all war, no matter what the costs.

In *The Complaint of Peace,* Erasmus advances a carefully reasoned attack on the underlying assumption widely shared in his day, as in our own: that violent conflict and organized war are somehow inherent in the human condition. He discusses each of the three most common explanations why human existence should be so burdened with the ravages and deaths that war brings: that war will always be with us because of indelible deficiencies in human nature, unrelenting outside pressures, or divine intention—perhaps because of all three.

To those who embrace the first explanation and point to greed, aggressiveness, and vindictiveness as human traits so pervasive that they eliminate all chances of a lasting peace, Erasmus responds by asking: What is it in human beings that predisposes them to war? Are they saddled with indelible personality traits that preclude all chances of a lasting peace? How do we have to envisage human nature for this to be true? If it carries with it traits that make wars inevitable, Erasmus begins, they cannot be traits shared with animals, since animals show no organized hostility to members of their own species. The conduct of human beings can be so much baser than that of animals that the word "bestiality" bestowed upon the worst forms of human conduct is unfair to animals.[12] Neither the viciousness that human beings can show one another nor the increasingly destructive machinery they were coming to employ in combat had equivalents elsewhere in nature.

What about the traits that distinguish persons from animals? Surely they are not such as to predispose us to war. Our human capacity to reason, our inability to survive alone that makes us dependent on family and society, and our "power of speech, the most conciliating instrument of social connexion and cordial love"—these traits, Erasmus argues, need hardly be conducive to war. On the contrary, they should predispose human beings to living with one another in peace, not war, he concludes. It is only our familiarity with "everlasting feuds, litigation, and murder" that produces the conduct that we mistake for a natural predisposition to war—the more readily so if leadership, education, and social reforms offer no counterbalance.

To the second standard explanation—that outside pressures of scarcity and hardship and natural calamities inevitably cause recurrent conflicts—Erasmus answers that it is surely madness to add to these undoubted outside pressures all the suffering that wars bring. The corruption into which human societies have fallen has rendered them unable to deal in the most reasonable way with conflicts engendered by such hardships. For the state of affairs in his own period, Erasmus holds rulers responsible above all others. In their greed and folly, they repeatedly and mindlessly drag their peoples into the tragedy of war. But rulers cannot wreak this havoc by themselves. Hatred and conflict have become endemic. Erasmus catalogues the groups that harbor such traits: citizens given to strife and dissension; courtiers poisoning the climate with their intrigues and grudges; scholars and theologians at daggerheads with one another; clergy and monastics tearing one another to pieces through their partisan disputes; mercenary soldiers feeding as vermin on the miseries they inflict on human communities.

The third explanation common since antiquity—that the human predisposition to war is due to divine intention—could in principle account for the first two and undercut all proposals for reform. While human nature may not by itself be destined for perennial warfare and while outside pressures might not of their own precipitate it, God may have seen to it that these conditions would nevertheless persist. In response to such theological claims, Erasmus invokes scripture: Christ's central message, quite to the contrary, is one of peace, forgiveness, and nonviolence. If anyone has intended the brutal, near-constant warfare that admittedly beset Europe in his time, he suggested, it must, rather, be Satan.

Having countered the three explanations most often brought forth to buttress ancient dogmas about the inevitability of war, Erasmus turns to the future. Though a lasting peace is possible, great changes are needed to bring it about. Peace cannot simply be ordained by religious or political authorities, nor can it be mandated merely through treaties and alliances alone. Rather, it has to be undertaken at every level of society. Kings must work together for the good of their citizens and consult them before embarking on any war. And citizens must grant kings "just so many privileges and prerogatives as are for the public good and no more."[13] Erasmus, who never ceased criticizing kings for their exploitative and brutal scheming at the expense of their peoples, here hints at the alternative of government limited by democratic consent—hard to envisage in his time and dangerous for anyone to promote. If nations submitted, further, to an international court of arbitration, they could avert many wars; if need be, peace should be purchased to prevent still others.

Bishops and priests must likewise unite against war and cease appealing to just war theory to excuse every war their king or the pope undertakes. The nobility and all magistrates must also collaborate in the work of peace. To each of these groups and to "all who call themselves Christians" Erasmus pleads, "Unite with one heart and one soul, in the abolition of war, and the establishment of perpetual and universal peace."[14] But beyond Christianity, Erasmus also wishes to suggest that the hostilities between faiths and nationalities could be tempered if only people reflected that they are, above all, members of the same human race: "If name of country is of such nature as to create bonds between those who have a common country, why do not men resolve that the universe should become the country of all?"[15]

During the remaining decades of his life, Erasmus saw the world move relentlessly in the opposite direction. Wars of conquest succeeded one another, religious and ideological persecution spread, and the religious conflicts that would later culminate in the Thirty Years' War intensified. Though frequently reprinted, Erasmus's writings on war and peace fell out of favor in many quarters. Many were burned and prohibited as heretical during the Counter-Reformation.[16] To militants of every persuasion, his insistence on arbitration and on other peaceful means of resolving conflicts seemed an endorsement of cowardice and vacillation. Over time, his work was deprecated, at times outlawed. As a result, later advocates of perpetual peace too often ignored the depth and scope of his proposals. They tended, rather, to stress purely diplomatic methods for achieving lasting peace. Thus the Abbé de Saint-Pierre proposed in 1712 a permanent league of European rulers under common laws.[17] Even today, most texts dealing with issues of war and peace mention Erasmus only in passing if at all.

Kant's Requirements for Peace

> Wars, tense and unremitting military preparations, and the resultant distress which every state must eventually feel within itself, even in the midst of peace—these are the means by which nature drives nations to make initially imperfect attempts, but

> finally, after many devastations, upheavals, and even complete inner exhaustion of their powers, to take the step which reason could have suggested to them even without so many sad experiences—that of abandoning a lawless state of nature and entering a federation of peoples in which every state, even the smallest, could expect to derive its security and rights.
>
> —Immanuel Kant,
> "Idea for a Universal History with a Cosmopolitan Purpose"

It was not until Kant published his essay on "Perpetual Peace" in 1795, building on earlier works such as his article on "Universal History," that individual and institutional change were once again brought into public debate as necessary prerequisites for arriving at a lasting peace.[18] Like Erasmus, Kant argues that such a state of peace is fully achievable, even though war, thus far, has been a constant factor in the human condition. But Kant sees greater obstacles to achieving such a peace than Erasmus ever conceded.

Kant shares, first of all, the Hobbesian view of international relations as anarchic: nations exist in a "lawless state of nature" where "the depravity of human nature is displayed without disguise," whereas within civil societies it is at least controlled by governmental constraints.[19] Unlike Erasmus, Kant had long agreed with those who held that wars had served important purposes throughout history and had most likely even been intended for such purposes by nature. Without the incentives provided by competition, lust for power, and conflict, human beings might never have developed their talents or their technology much beyond the animal stage. But wars had become increasingly destructive and risked becoming even more so, to the point where a war of extermination could bring about "perpetual peace only on the vast graveyard of the human race."[20] As a result, the time had come when nations would have to break out of the state of nature or perish.

Given Kant's concessions to the holders of the majority thesis, how did he envisage that such a change might be brought about? To begin with, he saw grounds for the hope that nature had intended such a shift for human beings. We cannot prove that this is so, nor even infer it, but it is "more than an empty chimera."[21] Each individual life is brief and flawed, but through the transmission of experience, human beings may, in the end, achieve a sufficient degree of rationality and the capacity to cooperate in achieving security for themselves and their descendants. And that it is *possible* for human beings, thus equipped, to change is clear, for although Kant acknowledges that human beings do exhibit a propensity to evil and to war, they also possess a predisposition to good. They are at all times free to choose to act according to what they recognize as right and to guide their lives differently. Though peace will not come of its own accord nor from an oversupply of human goodness, it can be instituted, chosen.

But bringing peace about will require far more than the piecemeal reforms too often advocated. Plans such as those of the Abbé de Saint-Pierre have been ridiculed as wild and fanciful, Kant suggests, in part because their proponents took for granted that the necessary changes were imminent, easy to institute, and unproblematic. Any realistic approach would have to be based on the recognition, on the contrary, that change would be slow to come, that it would require reforms at every level of national and international society, and that such reforms would be bound to fail over and over again unless measures were first taken to change the very atmosphere in which negotiations are carried out.

Accordingly, Kant began his essay on "Perpetual Peace" by proposing a set of "preliminary articles" to help prepare the social climate for the larger institutional reforms. Some of these preliminary articles set forth steps that governments could take right away to reduce the distrust standing in the way of all meaningful cooperation. If governments could negotiate peace agreements without secret reservations concerning future wars, if they could abstain from forcible interference in the affairs of other nations, and if they could, even when at war, discontinue what he called "dishonorable stratagems," such as the breach of agreements or treaties, the employment of assassins, and the instigation of treason within one another's states, then they would, at the very least, not be poisoning the atmosphere for peace negotiations.[22]

By stressing basic moral constraints not only within but also between nations—constraints on violence, deceit, breaches of faith, and excessive secrecy—Kant does not mean to say that these constraints by themselves will provide all that is needed to ensure a lasting peace.[23] He merely insists that so long as they are not taken into account, there can be no chance whatsoever of instituting such a peace. Distrust, as Hobbes had pointed out before him, undermines the incentive to cooperate. Little wonder, then, Kant argues, that a lasting peace has been out of reach: the reasons for such debilitating distrust have never been carefully addressed. But at the same time, we need not imagine that peace will continue to elude humankind once the constraints are taken seriously and once it becomes clear that they are indispensable to long-term collective survival.

Along with creating a climate that allows for institutional reform, Kant sees three "definite articles" as necessary for a perpetual peace among nations. The first calls for the achievement, over time, of a world in which more and more states have representative governments elected by free citizens equal before the law. Such a form of government will do much to cut back on the wars of any state, since citizens tend to be far less enthusiastic about wars they know they will have to pay for and fight in than autocratic leaders who impose taxes and give orders from the sidelines. But of course, citizens in such states can still be persuaded to concur in wars of conquest by skillful propaganda; as a result, additional international measures are necessary. The second article proposed by Kant calls for the joining together of states in a federation capable of keeping a just peace, and the third for respecting the human rights of visitors or outsiders to such states so as, for example, not to enslave them or conquer them.

Kant may well have been thought utopian to speak of the spread and federating of representative governments as conducive to lasting peace in 1795, when only the young American republic could lay claim to a stable form of such governance, and to invoke "a universal right of humanity" in condemning slavery and imperialistic conquest in a period when these practices were so widespread. But he insisted that such an idea was not "fantastic and overstrained. . . . Only under this condition can we flatter ourselves that we are continually advancing toward a perpetual peace."[24]

Utopians or Realists?

> In your hands rests our future. By your labors at this conference we shall know if suffering humanity is to achieve a just and lasting peace.
>
> —President Harry S Truman, speaking to delegates at the opening session of the UN Conference in San Francisco, April 23, 1945

In 1953, President Dwight D. Eisenhower spoke of the change that the cold war had brought since "that hopeful spring of 1945." At that time, "the hope of all just men . . . was for a just and lasting peace. The eight years that have passed have seen that hope waver, grow dim, and almost die. And the shadow of fear again has darkly lengthened across the world."[25]

That shadow has continued to lengthen. By now, over seventeen million people, most of them civilians, have died in wars since the end of the Second World War, and many more have been driven from their homes. The great powers have built up vast stockpiles of nuclear weapons with unprecedented destructive potential, and still more nations stand poised to follow suit. As a result, Kant's warning that a war of extermination could bring perpetual peace on the vast graveyard of humanity has taken on, over the decades of the nuclear age, a directness that even he could hardly have predicted.

The full horror of such a prospect has decisively shifted the incentives with respect to war. It has become a commonplace for world leaders to speak of the necessity of bringing about a lasting peace. In principle, if not yet when it comes to implementation, they have agreed to make every effort to avoid unleashing, even accidentally, another major war.

It is no wonder, accordingly, that we are also witnessing a realignment within the several traditions of thinking about war and peace. Their exponents are moving closer to one another and in turn—often without knowing it—to the principled yet practical stance by which thinkers in the perpetual-peace tradition combined moral and strategic considerations.

Already during the nineteenth century, many pacifists were adopting the language of the perpetual-peace tradition, its stress on step-by-step efforts to strengthen conditions for lasting peace, and its support for international organizations. Thus, British Quakers founded a Society for the Promotion of Permanent and Universal Peace in 1816.[26] They disagreed among themselves, as did other pacifists, about whether to endorse complete nonresistance in all wars or to accept resistance in clear cases of self-defense when all other methods have failed. This disagreement still persists among pacifists today. Many who, like Tolstoy, were once in favor of unilateral disarmament and noncooperation with all military activities, including strictly defensive ones, have had to weigh whether such a stance with respect to nuclear weapons might not increase, rather than decrease, the risks to humanity. "Do what is right though the earth should perish" has taken on an entirely new and more literal meaning since Hiroshima and Nagasaki.[27]

Only a minority of those active in contemporary peace movements adopt such an absolutist stance. But whether or not they do, the threat to collective survival posed by nuclear weapons has induced many to focus their attention sharply on weapons systems and government military strategy. Their research and advocacy has at times reflected back, as in a mirror, the priorities of their opponents, and the underlying moral debate has centered on issues of violence and nonviolence. But as the events beginning in the late 1980s continue to unfold, it is becoming increasingly clear that the chances for peace depend on a complex linkage of individual, domestic, and international policies; that shifts in military strategy often do not lead but, rather, follow upon a restructuring of such policies, as seen in the present thawing of the cold war; and that a more comprehensive moral framework is needed, in which nonviolence plays a central but not exclusive role. In the Philippines, in East Germany, in Czechoslovakia, and in Hungary, "people power" has shown itself victorious in the face of massively armed governments: as Václav Havel long continued to insist at great personal risk, citizens who are striving to "live within the truth" can overthrow dictatorships by nonviolent means.[28]

Realists, whether of a practical or a theoretical bent, are increasingly driven to reconsider their most fundamental presumptions in the face of the present predicament. Many among them once argued that strict national self-interest should dictate foreign policy, quite apart from what might be desirable for other nations, and that morality was beside the point in international relations. By now, the first argument has had to be sharply modified and the second abandoned. First, national self-interest now clearly mandates a concern for comprehensive international security; and international security, in turn, is affected by such factors as hunger, deforestation, and population growth the world over. Even from a strictly strategic point of view, therefore, it matters to attend to these factors. Second, doing so necessitates being alert to the role of moral claims, such as those voiced the world over regarding fundamental human rights. References to human rights abroad were once dismissed by many realists as sentimental, given political realities in most nations, and as potentially counterproductive efforts to interfere with sovereign states. But the political power of calls for human rights can no longer be denied, nor their importance to foreign relations. The same is true with respect to the action or inaction on the part of governments in matters of environmental or nuclear strategy. It is not surprising, therefore, that George Kennan, who has long argued against the assumption "that state behavior is a fit subject for moral judgment," does not hesitate to express such moral judgments when it comes to nuclear weapons. In *The Nuclear Delusion,* he cries out, in a tone that Erasmus would not have disowned, against the readiness to use nuclear weapons against other human beings, and thus placing in jeopardy all of civilization, calling it a blasphemy and "an indignity of monstrous proportions."[29]

Contemporary just war theorists, unlike those in the realist tradition, have consistently advanced moral claims in the context of war and peace. If the nuclear balance of terror has accelerated a shift, on their part, in the direction of Erasmus and Kant, it has been in reducing the range of wars seen as potentially just ones. It is hard, at present, to view many wars as likely to serve the cause of justice. Whereas Augustine and Thomas Aquinas argued in favor of certain wars to avenge wrongs, the U.S. Catholic bishops stated in 1983 that "if war of retribution was ever justifiable, the risks of modern war negate such a claim today."[30] They restate the just war position so as to exclude, in the contemporary world, nearly all wars as unjust except those of strict self-defense or defense of others under attack, and only then as a last resort. And like Erasmus and Kant, they emphasize the monumental injustice of governments in channeling such a vast proportion of the world's scarce resources into armaments, calling it "an act of aggression upon the poor."[31]

Marxists have also been narrowing the very different criteria that V. I. Lenin and Mao Zedong elaborated for when wars are just. Lenin held that wars against oppressors by wage earners and enslaved or colonized peoples were fully legitimate, progressive, and necessary: "Whosoever wants a lasting and democratic peace must stand for civil war against the government and the bourgeoisie."[32] Mao likewise argued that the only just wars are nonpredatory wars, wars of liberation: "Communists will support every just and nonpredatory war for liberation, and they will stand in the forefront of the struggle."[33] It has become increasingly difficult, however, to maintain that the fanning of regional wars has, in fact, promoted justice, and the faith that a lasting peace is bound to result from such warfare is faltering even among many committed Marxists. Similarly, Marx's castigation of moral claims—concerning justice and rights, in particular—as "ideological nonsense" is undergoing impassioned rejection throughout much of the communist world.[34]

In all these respects, Kant's essay on "Perpetual Peace" bears rereading. Nearly two centuries after its publication, and especially after the events of 1989, it no longer seems fantastic or overstrained to link the chances for peace with the respect for human rights and with the growing cooperation between nations in which those rights are protected by representative forms of government.

Just as contemporary thinkers who once rejected fundamental moral claims as irrelevant or postponed them as premature have been led to take them into consideration on strict realist grounds, so, too, have many who once based their position on strictly normative claims had to acknowledge that strategic realities affect their choices. While the goal of lasting peace may still seem out of reach, it no longer makes either strategic or moral sense for governments, policy advisers, or theorists not to try to move in the direction of that goal.

But if so many have come to take such a goal seriously as at least worth striving for, however utopian it seemed when first advocated by thinkers in the perpetual-peace tradition, then there is reason to take equally seriously the ways that they suggested for moving closer to that goal. Clearly, however, they could not have foreseen the kinds of negotiations required by today's weapons and international alignments, nor the present social and environmental threats to humanity. These developments call for responses of a complexity that no one could have predicted centuries ago. But the tradition of perpetual peace may be more helpful when it comes to exploring the crucial role of the social climate, which determines whether or not adequate levels of cooperation will be possible, and the framework of moral constraints needed at every level of society to keep that climate from deteriorating.[35]

Our century has seen the development of new strategies for bringing about change in ways that respect the social climate. The tradition of nonviolent resistance to oppression that began with Mohandas Gandhi in India and continued with the civil rights struggle led by Martin Luther King, Jr., in the United States has influenced political change in countries as different as South Korea, Chile, and East Germany. During the past year, we have witnessed a striking contrast. While peaceful revolutions produced astounding successes in one country after another in Eastern Europe, fighting dragged on with no end in sight in Lebanon, Ethiopia, El Salvador, and too many other nations and produced only further suffering. Few have doubted that nonviolent resistance is more respectful of human rights and less likely to brutalize and corrupt its participants. What is becoming increasingly clear is that with the help of modern communications media, such resistance can also bring speedier and more far-reaching results—and that both strategic and moral considerations favor such resistance. Being more protective of the social climate, it is also more conducive to the cooperation that is so desperately needed once the struggle is over.

To be sure, nothing guarantees that those who lead such movements to victory can govern well or that changes wrought with nonviolent means will not once again succumb to violence. Nor do all efforts at nonviolent resistance succeed, as Tiananmen Square and too many other examples demonstrate. Yet even when the latter efforts meet with repression, as did Solidarity for years, nonviolent movements have a better chance of ultimately succeeding than groups that resort to a violent uprising.

Only time will tell whether a cumulative process of nonviolent and principled efforts at domestic and international change can, in the long run, disprove the age-old assumption that war will always be with us. Much that Erasmus, Kant, and others suggested, such as giving citizens a voice with respect to whether or not to undertake a war, convening international parleys and federations, and submitting disputes to arbitration, must have seemed highly improbable—indeed utopian—at the time. But, the word "utopia" can have two meanings. One indicates an excellent place or society that is possible but at present merely visionary; the second refers, rather, to an unattainable society advocated by impractical idealists. In arguing that it is possible for human beings to establish a lasting world peace, Erasmus and Kant may well have been utopian in the first sense; but we have everything to lose by not trying to disprove the claim that they were also utopian in the second.

NOTES

1. For the works by Erasmus that contributed most to this tradition, see notes 3, 5, and 7 below. See also Edwin D. Mead, ed., *The Great Design of Henry IV from the Memoirs of the Duke of Sully* (1559–1641) (Boston: Ginn & Co., 1909); William Penn, "An Essay Towards the Present and Future Peace of Europe" (1693), in Fredrick B. Tolles and E. Gordon Alderfer, eds., *The Witness of William Penn* (New York: Macmillan and Co., 1957), 140–59; Abbé de Saint-Pierre, *Selections from the 2nd Edition of the Abrégé du Projet de Paix Perpétuelle* (1712) (London: Sweet & Maxwell, 1927); Immanuel Kant, "Perpetual Peace: A Philosophical Sketch" (1795), in Hans Reiss, ed., *Kant's Political Writings* (Cambridge: Cambridge University Press, 1970), 93–130; Jeremy Bentham, "Essay on Universal Peace. Essay IV. A Plan for a Universal and Perpetual Peace" (1789, first published in 1843), in Charles W. Everett, ed., *Jeremy Bentham* (London: Weidenfeld and Nicolson, 1966), 195–229.

2. Gottfried Wilhelm Leibniz, *"Observation sur le projet d'une paix perpétuelle de M l'abbé de St. Pierre,"* in *Opera Omnia*, ed. L. Dutens, vol. 5 (Geneva, 1768); Jean-Jacques Rousseau (editing and commenting upon the work of the Abbé de Saint-Pierre), *A Project of Perpetual Peace,* trans. Edith M. Nuttall (London: Richard Cobden-Sanderson, 1927);

G. W. F. Hegel, *Philosophy of Right* (1821), trans. T. M. Knox (Oxford: Clarendon Press, 1958), 208–16.

3. *The Adages* were first published in 1500. A later edition, published in 1515, contained a greatly expanded version of *"Dulce Bellum Inexpertis."* See Margaret Mann Phillips, ed., *The Adages of Erasmus: A Study with Interpretations* (Cambridge: Cambridge University Press, 1964), 308–53.

4. In 1516, France and Switzerland concluded the Treaty of Fribourg, known as *la paix perpétuelle,* which lasted until the French Revolution. The year before, Henry VIII had concluded a "permanent" but much more short-lived peace with France. For a few years, nevertheless, Erasmus, Thomas More, and other humanists had hopes for a flowering of peace that would permit the shaping of a new political and cultural order.

5. Erasmus, *The Education of a Christian Prince,* trans. Lester K. Born (New York: Octagon Books, 1973).

6. Niccolò Machiavelli, *The Prince and the Discourses* (New York: Random House, 1950).

7. Erasmus, *Education,* 249.

8. Erasmus, *The Complaint of Peace* (Boston: Charles Williams, 1813). For a more recent though not entirely complete translation, see "Peace Protests!" in Jose Chapiro, trans., Erasmus and Our Struggle for Peace (Boston: Beacon Press, 1950), 131–84. In a letter from 1523, Erasmus comments bitterly to a friend that he must "soon compose the Epitaph, rather than the Complaint, of Peace, as she seems to be dead and buried and not very likely to revive" (Cited in translator's preface to the 1813 edition of *The Complaint of Peace,* iv).

9. Erasmus, *Education,* 249.

10. Ibid., 250.

11. Ibid., 251.

12. Comparisons between animals and human beings traditionally placed humans above animals in the chain of being. Cicero, among many others, had argued that the two ways of doing wrong—by force or by fraud—were both bestial: "Fraud seems to belong to the cunning fox, force to the lion: both are wholly unworthy of man, but fraud is the more contemptible" (*On Moral Duties*, I, XIII, 41). Machiavelli had accepted the comparison only to argue that human beings ought to learn from the fox and the lion in those respects. Erasmus intended to show, on the contrary, that force and fraud on the scale practiced by humans and with the means at their disposal were of an entirely different order and that to attribute such aspects of human conduct to animals was merely to calumniate them.

13. Erasmus, *Complaint,* 51.

14. Ibid., 79.

15. Chapiro, trans., "Peace Protests!" 173.

16. See Marcel Battaillon, *Erasme et L'Espagne* (Paris: Librarie E. Droz, 1937), 2: 29.

17. Abbé de Saint-Pierre, *Selections from the 2nd Edition of the Abrégé.* See also Rousseau, *A Project of Perpetual Peace.*

18. Kant, "Perpetual Peace: A Philosophical Sketch" and "Idea for a Universal History with a Cosmopolitan Purpose," in Hans Reiss, ed., *Kant's Political Writings,* 93–130 and 41–53.

19. Ibid., 103.

20. Ibid., 96.

21. Ibid., 114.

22. Ibid., 96.

23. For a discussion of these constraints in Kant's writings and of their role in international relations, see Sissela Bok, *A Strategy for Peace* (New York: Pantheon Books, 1989).

24. Kant, "Perpetual Peace," 108.

25. Dwight D. Eisenhower, "The Chance for Peace," address delivered before the American Society of Newspaper Editors, April 16, 1953. Reprinted in Kenneth E. Alrutz et al., eds, *War and Peace,* Lynchburg College Symposium Readings, vol. 5 (Lanham, Md.: University Press of America, 1982), 621.

26. See F. H. Hinsley, *Power and the Pursuit of Peace* (Cambridge: Cambridge University Press, 1963), 93–97.

27. Kant explicitly defended this motto. But while it committed him to absolutism with respect to lying, it did not do so when it came to violence, since he regarded violence in self-defense as legitimate. See Sissela Bok, "Kant's Arguments in Support of the Maxim 'Do What Is Right Though the World Should Perish,' " *Argumentation* 2 (1988), 7–25, reprinted in David M. Rosenthal and Fadlou Shehadi, eds., *Applied Ethics and Ethical Theory* (Salt Lake City: University of Utah Press, 1988), 191–212.

28. Václav Havel, "The Power of the Powerless," in Václav Havel et al., *The Power of the Powerless: Citizens against the State in Central-Eastern Europe* (London: Hutchinson, 1985), 39.

29. George Kennan, *The Nuclear Delusion* (New York: Pantheon Books, 1982).

30. National Council of Catholic Bishops, *The Challenge of Peace: God's Promise and Our Response* (Washington: Office of Publishing Services, USCC, 1983), 39. For a secular interpretation of just-war doctrine that similarly restricts the causes for just war, see Robert W. Tucker, *The Just War: A Study in Contemporary American Doctrine* (Baltimore: Johns Hopkins University Press, 1960).

31. Catholic Bishops, *Challenge of Peace,* v.

32. Vladimir I. Lenin, "The Question of Peace," in *Collected Works* (Moscow: Progress Publishers, 1968), 21:290–94 and 297–338; see also "Socialism and War," ibid., 297–338; and "April Theses, 1917," ibid., 24:21–26.

33. M. Rejai, ed., *Mao Tse-tung: On Revolution and War* (Garden City, N.Y.: Doubleday, 1970), 67.

34. D. McLellan, ed., *Karl Marx: Selected Writings* (Oxford: Oxford University Press, 1977), 568–69.

35. See Bok, *Strategy for Peace,* chap. 4.

Cho-yun Hsu

Applying Confucian Ethics to International Relations

China is not just a country; it is a subcontinent comparable in size to Europe, surrounded by high mountains in the west and the south, a desert in the north, and the Pacific Ocean in the east. Within today's China proper, however, there is little impassable terrain separating one part from another. Ever since Neolithic days, which, generally speaking, lasted until the end of the third millennium B.C., cultural exchanges among regions had resulted in noticeable Chinese characteristics across all of China, although a number of local archaeological traditions were still distributed in major regions, such as the Yellow River Valley, the Yangtze Valley, the coastal region, and the high plateau loess of the Manchurian wooded land.[1] The Chinese geographic conditions allowed the emergence of both a universal state and a multistate system, alternating or even combining at different levels. The state of Shang in the late second millennium B.C. evolved politically from that of a chieftain leadership into a prototypical monarchy. The Shang system was a vague pattern of zoning that consisted of the royal domain, subordinate tributaries, and foreign countries.[2]

Such a "zoning system" was later institutionalized in the Chou kingdom, which followed the Shang and dominated the core region of what was then China, that is, the Central Plain in the Yellow River middle valley. The name of the Central Kingdom therefore became a synonym for China. The Chou feudal network was organized in a hierarchy of vassal states that originated from the Chou garrisons commanded by Chou princes. The political network of power delegation was deliberately made identical with a network of kinship by which the rulers of the Chou states, including the king and the rulers of the vassal states, were all Chou scions. The rulers of other satellite states who were drawn into the orbit of the Chou kingdom were made relatives of the Chou through complicated patterns of matrimony at various levels of the Chou state's hierarchy. Thus, in the Chou period China was shaped into a nation, a nation of Hua-Hsia.[3]

The Chou structure also constituted a hierarchy of zoning, just as its Shang predecessor. The Chou royal domain was the center, surrounded by the Chou vassal states and then the non-Chou states scattered along less favorable peripheries, beyond which were the "barbarians," whom the Chou addressed with derogatory titles. Beyond the barbarians were people whom the Chou regarded as insignificant and, therefore, nearly nonexistent. The *tien-hsia* or the world under heaven, was a world under the Chou order, a "civilized" world.[4] An idealized model is pictured by ancient scholars as a pattern of concentric squares. The center is the royal domain directly managed by the royal court. Surrounding the central zone are several other zones—the Yu-Kung said there were five, while in the Chou-li, it is said, there were nine. Vassal states located in each zone, it is also said, maintained distinctive relationships with the center. The closer these states were to the center, the more obligations of submission were expected. States of the inner zones served as garrisons to guard the royal domain. The ones in intermediate zones were the buffers between China and the peripheries. The farthest peripheries were zones that were only remotely related to China and were thus regarded as foreign and even barbarian. Hence, the interstate relationships in ancient China were visualized as hierarchically differentiated ones within a universal state. From the Chinese point of view, the internal and the external zones ought to have had a clear demarcation; yet, in a relative sense, the people in the external zones were considered to be a part of the internal zones if they were to become culturally assimilated or politically incorporated.[5]

The Mandate of Heaven

This system of a universal state was the embodiment of the political ethics of the "Mandate of Heaven." From the time the Chou dynasty was being founded, the Chou leaders, for the sake of establishing legitimate succession to replace the culturally superior Shang state, had claimed that the Heavenly God made a judgment upon the conduct of state rulers and shifted the Heavenly Mandate from the Shang to the Chou. The moral implication of receiving the endowment of the Heavenly Mandate based on the verdict of God is indeed an extremely crucial break from that of the old tribal deities who were worshipped by various nations in pre-Chou days. The Chou Heavenly God and his associates were the ones who transcended the old function as protectors to adopt the role of a judging god. The Chou tien-hsia was to be governed with a mandate that could also be taken away if the Chou ruling house failed to fulfill its mission as recipient of the Heavenly Mandate. The universal state of Chou, then, was the embodiment of an ethical expectation.

In poems as well as in history, the Chou princes were reminded repeatedly that the Heavenly Mandate never was given permanently to any incumbent ruling group and that the God of Heaven would manifest his will explicitly through the wishes and conduct of the ordinary people, who reflected his judgment. In other words, the Mandate of Heaven was actually reflected in the mandate of the people, who, of course, were the people of the Chou tien-hsia, excluding the barbarians and foreigners. This basic assumption of judgment, especially judgment by the people, remained throughout Chinese history fundamental to its political ethics.[6]

The Chou system, which started in the last decade of the thirteenth century B.C., collapsed in the eighth century B.C.. Although the Chou royal court nominally survived about five more centuries, China was virtually divided into a score of contending entities, most of which descended from the former Chou vassalages, while some came from non-Chou states. This period of several competing states, known in history as the Spring and Autumn period, was followed by the Warring States period, in which seven major states strove to unify China. A multistate system thus replaced the Chou universal order until one of these competitors, the state of Ch'in, defeated the other states to reunite China in 221 B.C.. Many of the concepts that developed in the modern international community, such as the balance of power, diplomatic manipulation, collective security, and interstate conferences and treaties, also developed in China during the ancient Spring and Autumn period.[7] Nevertheless, the shadow of the Chou universal state survived the advent of the Chinese multistate system, manifesting itself in the distinction that persisted between the Chinese tien-hsia and the foreigners in the peripheries of China, and in the belief that the primary concern of any ruling house should be the welfare of its subjects because of the demand of the Mandate of Heaven.

Those states of the former Chou tien-hsia, even though they were contenders among equals, generally regarded themselves as members of a big "family," since their ruling houses were originally related by blood or matrimony. Therefore, state affairs were treated in a familial manner. Interstate treaties normally included sentences regarding family business—such as the prohibition against shifting from one heir apparent to another or allowing concubines to usurp the position of the principal wife—together with concerns over boundaries, mutual aid in times of need, water rights, and tariff courtesies. The state rulers, similar to the European royal houses, addressed each other as cousins, brothers, uncles, and nephews. However, the order of seniority among relatives was even more carefully and rigidly observed, since in the Chou feudal system, which combined with the kinship structure, ranking of orders indeed carried out the function of ranking of authorities.[8]

During the Spring and Autumn period, the Chou king mainly played a nominal role in interstate affairs. An overlordship, titled a *Pa,* usually the strongest state among the equals, organized the Chou states into an alliance with the pretext of defending the Chinese from the non-Chou powers, which were called barbarians and among which the most noticeable were the southern states of Chu and Wu. Ironically, after centuries of confrontation, cultural influences and economic exchanges finally incorporated these barbarians into the world of Chou China. By the Warring States period these states, together with those of the Central Plain, formed a larger Chinese world in which each state struggled to reach supremacy and become master of an even larger unified China. Among themselves, however, they still regarded the peoples in peripheries as barbarians. The zoning structures presented previously were expandable in that the concept of the Central Kingdom actually experienced expansions during the Spring and Autumn and Warring States periods.[9]

Interstate agreement was not just based on trust by the communal spirit of fellow aristocrats but also was guaranteed by oaths sworn in the name of the Heavenly God, other deities of nature such as mountains and rivers, and the ancestors of the participants. The rituals of such a state cult had to be conducted with utmost sincerity and seriousness.[10] Mutual trust derived from common faith, therefore, was essential for holding the interstate relationships in functional order. This common faith was much like a moral expectation, although a systematic construction of an ethical system was yet to come.

Therefore, at the dawning of civilization in China, there existed the notions that a judging God of Heaven directed his mandate to the rulers, that the people were the ones who reflected the will of this God, that the Chinese states belonged to a common community of the Chou order in which the rulers of individual states were related as cousins, and that trust founded upon faith was essential in maintaining such an order. Although these notions did not yet comprise an ethical system, they formed the basic materials that Confucius would later use to lay the cornerstone for the construction of such a system.

The Foundations of Confucianism

Confucius (551–479 B.C.) lived during the Spring and Autumn period. As a descendent of a declining aristocratic household, Confucius was a marginal personality whose heritage came from both aristocrats and commoners. Though most commonly hailed as the first teacher in China, he should also be given the credit for having heuristically reinterpreted the values in the code of conduct of the old aristocracy and having conscientiously universalized these values into an ethical system.

The foundation of Confucian ethics is the concept of *jen,* which is variously translated as "love" or "benevolence" or "humanism." None of these translations, however, conveys the full connotation of *jen.* The English word "love" is too "outer-oriented" to define *jen,* which is basically a virtue, in the sense of total inner excellence.[11] The word *jen*, before the Confucian definition, had appeared as a descriptive term to mean "true manly beauties," or "perfect virtue."[12] Thus, the etymological connections may lead to a concept of *jen* as an essence of the human being that in a societal setting is manifest as care for others. Nevertheless, it is an inner-based, even inner-endowed virtue, instead of a visible behavior or an aspect of an interpersonal relationship. *Jen* is not necessarily related to a consequence; rather, it is an intrinsic characteristic in which its manifested behavior or norm of behavior is only secondary. That concept which is related to consequences is the Confucian *li,* closely related to *jen.* The distinction between *jen* and *li,* interestingly, is parallel to that between the Greek "ethics" and the Latin "moral," as Terry Nardin has correctly pointed out.[13]

As Confucius repeatedly argued in the *Analects, jen* should be the guiding force of any political or social choice or decision. Confucius commended the leader Kuan Chung for having fulfilled the principle of *jen* when he made the state of Ch'i the first overlordship in the Spring and Autumn period, effectively organizing the Chinese states into an alliance that prevented warring among its members.[14] Confucius argued that because of Kuan Chung's success in uniting the Chinese states, the Chinese world was saved from the intrusions of the barbarians and thus the Chinese way of life was preserved. Therefore, Chinese society was culturally redefined as a civilization instead of a political system. It should be noted, however, that Confucius did not intend to reserve his high principle of ethics for the Chinese world only. The same standards of behavior, such as sincerity and honesty, should be observed even in a foreign country as well.[15]

In a time of drastic social changes, Confucius preferred that certain social norms be maintained so there would be at least some order and stability. Thus he insisted that the titles of the power holders and their legitimate functions ought to match. A ruler, for example, should be both a legitimate ruler and an actual ruler. A minister, meanwhile, should obey an order issued by the ruler to discharge the mission related to his office. In one case when a usurper had murdered the ruler of the state of Ch'i, Confucius seriously advised his own ruler, the Duke of Lu, to take punitive actions against the Ch'i strongman even though the state of Lu was much weaker than Ch'i. His proposal was not adopted. Confucius nevertheless demonstrated that Lu, or any other state, had moral obligations to uphold certain ethical principles; violation of the sovereignty of another state, in this case, was regarded as a lesser consideration.[16]

Confucian ethical values on interstate affairs are well reflected in the critical historical works produced in the Confucian era.[17] Historical events were judged in accordance with criteria set forth in the Confucian ethics, which were largely an idealized reconstruction of the Chou order. Among the criteria used by the scholars were three categories relating to interstate affairs: the respect for the superior status of the Chou royal house, the observance of the legitimacy of authorities at different levels and of their mutual relationship, and the distinction between Chinese and foreigners.[18]

The first category, respect for the Chou royal house, was viewed as confirmation of a universal order under the Chou leadership. The supreme position of the Chou was not to be challenged. This, of course, was an idealized order, posed as a condemnation of any division of the Chou China by former vassal states. Any interstate meeting that was nominally presided over by a royal representative was hailed as legitimate, while those that were not attended by a royal representative were regarded as illegal. The action of the overlords *(Pa)* Duke Huan of Ch'i and Duke Wen of Chin, both of whom had rallied all the Chinese states to form an alliance in order to reestablish the Chou order, received highest praise from the Confucian scholars as defenders of the Chou system. In theory, the Chou order was not to be challenged and no exceptions were to be found within the realm of China. Therefore, even the calendar, in Confucian scholars' opinion, was to be decided and issued by the royal court on behalf of the entire world of China.[19]

The second criterion, the existence of a hierarchical differentiation within the Chou system, held that the vassal states should be subordinate to the royal house. Likewise, the roles of individuals within the feudal hierarchy should be coherent with their status. Deviation from this principle was often criticized. Usurpation of power received harsh disapproval. On the other hand, if a ruler became tyrannical, armed forces of other states who invaded to depose the unpopular ruler were given praise for having served a just cause.[20]

In the third criterion—the distinction between Chinese and foreigners—culture was posited as the defining standard, rather than race. Assimilation of foreigners by the Chinese was approved while the opposite was not. Interestingly, large and powerful states, such as Chu in the south, that were not only foreign but also challengers of the Chou world were regarded as barbarians in the Spring and Autumn period, while in every aspect thorough assimilation had gradually brought them into the Chinese world as full-fledged members of the interstate community in the Warring States period. The northern peoples, most of whom were nomads and pastoralists, remained barbarians throughout ancient Chinese history and would never be absorbed into the Chinese system. Nevertheless, Confucius did not rule out the possibility that a foreigner could be "civilized" and insisted that a number of ethical standards should prevail also in foreign lands. China should serve as a model for barbarians to civilize themselves. The Confucian scholars in their comments on history, therefore, condemned foreign intrusion into the Chinese world. Meanwhile, they considered it natural that the Chinese way of life and the sovereignty of the Chinese state need not be extended into foreign land unless the foreigners voluntarily accepted Chinese culture.[21]

These three principles remained in the Chinese history of the imperial dynasties as important guides, to be used by the Chinese to design their foreign policies.

Justice and the State

Motzu (ca. 479–390 B.C.), the first philosopher appearing in the Warring States period, gave a new interpretation to the early Confucian ethics for state and interstate affairs. In his utilitarianism, a societal and communal concern was crystallized into the term *i,* which was often translated as "righteousness." Observation of *i,* however, was required not just because it was a deontological virtue but, rather, because observation of such a societal righteousness would bestow on the collective unit—a neighborhood, a state, or the entire *tien-hsia*—a prevalence of universal love. In order to achieve this universal love, or for the sake of reaching such a goal, no state was to attack another. Motzu's principle for interstate relationships, therefore, was peace in the world.[22] His righteousness was an abstract moral goal, rather than a practical ethical criterion relevant for day-to-day decision making.

Mencius (ca. 370–296 B.C.), who also lived during the Warring States period, extended Confucianism in several aspects. One of his significant contributions was the integration of the concept of *i* with Confucian *jen* to create a new fundamental notion of the Confucian system. Probably taking a hint from Motzu's *i,* Mencius repeatedly redefined *i* as an innate virtue, with which a human being is born. Mencius argued that *jen* and *i* were both aspects of human nature. However, his *i* did stand as a rather others-oriented virtue, in contrast to a self-oriented virtue. Although he denied that he held *i* as different from *jen,* he related *jen* to a mentality of general compassion, and *i* to a consciousness of shame.[23]

Although this interpretation deviated considerably from that of Motzu's thought, Mencius still could not erase the connotation of the social context of *i.*[24] It should be noted, however, that Mencius gave *i* a content of social norm that served as a guide for human behavior because he interpreted it as analogous to a *lu* (road and path). To love one's own parents, he argued, is *jen;* to pay respect to an elder is *i.*[25] It becomes obvious that the former is spontaneous behavior while the latter results from socialization. Therefore, *i* probably should be regarded as social justice, rather than as righteousness.

To Mencius, state and interstate affairs were to be judged in terms not only of *jen* but, more often, of *i,* justice. Justice should be given even more precious weight than one's own life, if one is compelled to make a choice between them.[26] A sense of compassion *(jen)* and a sense of shame *(i),* according to Mencius, were innate in human nature and required conscientious nurturing. People often lost these natural characteristics and became vulnerable to the corrupting influence of desire and lust because they did not consciously attempt to preserve them.[27]

Jen and *i* appear to have been personal ethical concerns. Mencius, however, used these two ethical virtues as criteria to judge politics. The idealized king should be a sage and the idealized utopia was to be a state, the goal of which was realization by practice of these principal virtues. A state at least should give its subjects plenty of opportunity to make a reasonable livelihood, should achieve some extent of fairness in the distribution of resources, and should provide its subjects with education to enrich their spiritual life. At the very least, a ruler should practice *jen* by taking care of the old and lonely ones and the orphans.[28] On the other hand, a bad government that deprived people of their livelihood is just as murderous as the one that slaughters its people with weapons or lets beasts kill them.[29]

A compassionate and just government would win full support of the people, and enemies would have great difficulty conquering such a state. Mencius cited the rise of Chou from a small state to illustrate how peoples of oppressed states would welcome a true king, a king of compassion, as their savior.[30] In interstate politics, therefore, the best policy should be that of a good government at home. Extension of the popularity achieved in one's own state would attract people of all states and, therefore, was the best way to reach unification under a true king. A large state could achieve such unification by practice of *jen;* in the same manner, even a small state could achieve what the founding king of the Chou had accomplished.[31] Since there were no such kings in his time, Mencius concluded that no such achievement would be seen.[32]

Thus, an ideal king should be a sage. If a ruler corrupted the concept of *jen* and *i,* such a person would actually fail in his entrusted responsibilities as ruler. The people then had the right to remove him from the throne or even to execute him if he was blighted to such a degree. In such a case, Mencius regarded the punishment not to be an action of regicide.[33] This argument is generally regarded as recognition that the people had the right to revolt against tyranny.

To Mencius the worst policy adopted by a state would be to interrupt its people from their normal life for the sake of invading other states. Expansion of territory and accumulation of wealth were both tasks that would do just that. Officials and generals who served the government in order to accomplish such goals were, in Mencius's opinion, spoilers and blighters who should be punished rather than rewarded.[34]

Throughout Mencius's arguments, public and private ethics, and the social and personal aspects of a moral life, were not differentiated. Therefore, a virtuous personality should be the fundamental requirement expected from capable leadership. Thus, a good character and good capabilities were closely related.[35] This deontological proposition of Mencius left a long-lasting impact on Chinese political theories.

The entire Confucian system of ethics as refined and extended by Mencius is crystallized in *The Great Learning,* one of the four classics of the Confucian tradition. The authorship of *The Great Learning* is generally attributed to the grandson of Confucius, though this is not certain. Essentially, *The Great Learning* appears to have been a guidebook for Confucian students to appreciate gradually the connections between various items of virtues. The primary objects of self-cultivation consist of a triad, i.e., bringing the human virtues back to their original purity, loving the people, and maintaining a conduct that is perfectly good. The first and the third objects are ostensibly repetitions of the same issue. The first, however, may be what an individual may achieve alone, while the third goal is an elevation of personal virtue to the highest level of collective virtue by passing on to others the achievements of living a personally virtuous life.[36]

In *The Great Learning,* therefore, an individual is expected to move consciously and conscientiously step-by-step toward a perfect *tien-hsia* of tranquility and happiness. These steps are the acquisition of discernible knowledge, the development of intellectual sincerity, the rectification of emotion and sentiment, and, finally, the cultivation of a balanced personality. Once such self-cultivation is accomplished, one should serve as an example in the kinship group so that the kinsmen may be all brought to moral accomplishment. Since a state is a congregation of kinship groups, an exemplary family—especially the leading one—should move all families to reach the same level of moral accomplishment. Likewise, if all the states individually have reached a high level of moral cultivation, the whole *tien-hsia* is well ordered by tranquility and happiness.

The text of *The Great Learning* is somewhat ambiguous in defining the roles of the exemplary individual, individual family, and individual state. On the one hand, at every level, the heads of households and the state rulers appear subject to special expectations. On the other hand, all the people, families, and states are expected to participate in this process of self-cultivation. The process is a continuum of a range of private and public ethics, along which there is no differentiation of the private and the public aspects of morality.[37]

Here it should be noted that the *tien-hsia* is not simply the political order of a Chinese world. As was noted earlier, foreigners could be assimilated into China by sharing the same universal culture.[38] The sage king Hsun was originally an "eastern barbarian," and another sage king, King Wen of Chou, was originally a "western barbarian." Both, nevertheless, were exemplary rulers of the entire Chinese world.[39]

These general principles proposed by Confucius, Mencius, and *The Great Learning* were to be followed as guides of personal and collective behavior by the Chinese of later centuries. In summary, Chinese ethics is a deontological system that has a continuity spanning a range from personal to public concerns, without differentiation. A good society, a good state, and a good world all have to rest upon the foundation of good individuals. Between the world (*tien-hsia*), which is a universal, cultural order with little racial implication, and individuals, who are expected to achieve self-cultivation of virtues, are the state and the family or household, the most crucial social entities, with the individual, oneself, as the root of good order at every level.[40] These general principles formed during the time of the ancient Chinese multistate system reveal an anticipation of a universal order to arrive at some later time. The unification of China by the end of the Warring States period indeed fulfilled the expectation of the emergence of such a universal order. From then on, the Chinese often believed that the *tien-hsia,* with China as its center, was universal and that not only state boundaries within China would appear meaningless but there would also be no clear-cut boundaries throughout the entire *tien-hsia.* Instead, there would be only a gradually fading relationship between the center and the peripheries as distances from the center increased—again, a spatially and culturally arranged continuity. A hierarchy of differentiated relationships was thus the trademark of this sinocentric interstate order.

The Sinocentric Hierarchy

The very first serious test of the sinocentric concept was the relationship between China and Hsi'ung-nu during the Han dynasty (206 B.C.–A.D. 220). Just as China was being unified in the third century B.C., in northern Asia the nomadic Hsi'ung-nu empire arose on the vast stretches of the steppe lands. The Hsi'ung-nu pulled in various other tribes from along the northern border of China to form a confederation that constituted a serious challenge to Chinese supremacy in East Asia. A complex of fortifications was built by China to fend off the nomadic intruders, the famed system known as the Great Wall. Ever since the founding of the Han dynasty, China and the Hsi'ung-nu seesawed back and forth along this line, which demarcated the separation between the farming and the nomadic cultures. After the first defeat suffered by China in the reign of the Han founding emperor, the Han court established a policy of pacification by sending a Chinese girl, who some say was an imperial princess, to marry the Great Shangyu, the Hsi'ung-nu emperor. It was wished that a matrimonial bond between these two contesting powers would reduce the tensions that might lead to conflict. A Chinese courtier who advised adopting such a policy said, "A son-in-law shall not assault the father-in-law." In addition, trade along the borders was routinely conducted to benefit both sides. In Emperor Wu's reign (140–87 B.C.), however, China launched a series of successful attacks along the north, and war continued for years.

During the next imperial reign, in 81 B.C., there was a debate on the issue of the state monopoly on the production and sale of salt and iron for the sake of increasing revenues to fund the costly Hsi'ung-nu wars. The hawkish side, mainly the minister of finance and his colleagues, argued that the universal empire of Han should maintain the role of common master of all the peoples in the *tien-hsia*; that the unruly Hsi'ung-nu should be subjugated in order to achieve peace throughout China; that exchanges of valuable things between China and foreign countries should be appreciated as an influx of wealth to the central land; and that effective border defense with possible punitive expeditions against the Hsi'ung-nu should be taken as the best guarantee for peace and prosperity in and around the Chinese world. In other words, they argued that a universal state of the *tien-hsia* should leave no one out of its system. Speculation on the existence of a larger world order, as proposed by Tsou Yen, of which China made up thus far one-ninth, was cited by the minister as the reason that expansion of the contemporary world would be necessary to reach the ultimate universal world of the entire true *tien-hsia*. It should be noted that the argument presented by the minister was built upon the assumption that a universal order would be reached by pushing to the limits of the *tien-hsia* and that, therefore, the peripheries of the current world order had to be absorbed into its center.

On the other side of the debate, the Confucian scholars argued that peace was once preserved along the border by having matrimonial ties between Chinese and the Hsi'ung-nu leaders; that the Chinese world was self-sufficient and did not need the useless, luxurious items being imported; that there ought to be an order of priorities among public policies; that concerns for the livelihoods of the Chinese should surpass any other considerations; that the well-being of the people in China or near to China should outweigh that of distant peoples; and, finally, that the best policy to convince those from afar to willingly subordinate to China would be the fulfillment of the government obligation to provide the Chinese people with good livelihoods. The dovish position, therefore, represented Confucian concepts of good government and the establishment of a universal order by making internal peace and prosperity a model that would attract foreigners to join and participate.[41]

The arguments presented by both sides were more polemical than constructive. Nevertheless, they shared one common theme, namely, that there had been or ought to be a universal state with China as its center. Although the Confucian scholars opposed having limited resources wasted on warfare, their emphasis on the improvement first of the governance of central China proved that they did not rule out an expansion of the Chinese order. Confucian scholars differed most with their opponents in their view that the universalized order of the Chinese world should be a cultural order and that the only way to accommodate an expansion should be by means of an outward radiation of cultural influences. A very Confucian mentality, indeed.

Another case to illustrate the long-lasting impact of ancient Confucian ethics on international politics is the debate that occurred over the relationship between the Northern Sung China (A.D. 960–1127) and the Khitan-Liao (A.D. 916–1125). Ever since the early middle ages, namely the Sui (A.D. 581–618) and T'ang (A.D. 618–907) periods, China had been forced to face the reality of several strong neighbors. They were the newly converted Islamic nations in central Asia, such as the Tu-chueh and the Uighurs, and the powerful Tibetan empire, which received Indian cultural influence via the spread of Buddhism.[42] For relations with the latter, there existed a bilateral treaty to settle border disputes and maintain the channels of communication—the first treaty on truly equal terms between China and a neighbor.[43] China had entered an international community in which it could no longer take for granted its dominant position.

The founding emperor of the Sung dynasty reunited China after the prolonged period of civil wars and disunion known as the Five Dynasties (A.D. 907–979), when several contending states competed for the claim of the imperial court. The conditions during the Five Dynasties resembled those of the Spring and Autumn and Warring States periods. It is no surprise, therefore, that many of the interstate relationships were shaped by copying the patterns set in ancient China, essentially creating another period of a multistate system in Chinese history.[44]

As China became reunited, the internal multistate system ceased to prevail. Nevertheless, when Sung China looked beyond its borders, it saw that it was only one state among several in East Asia. In the west, right on the border of the western provinces, arose the Tangut kingdom. In the southwest, a small kingdom ruled much of the mountainous regions west of the upper stream of the Yangtze River. To the north, a powerful kingdom of nomadic pastoralists, called the Khitan, had extended its stretch of steppe homeland to occupy a good part of the northern territory of China. Beyond the Khitan, Korea rose as a power in the Far East and an important balancing factor between China and its northern neighbors.[45] Once in such a new multistate system, China had to reconsider its sinocentric mentality, formed in ancient China and reinforced in the Han period.

The Khitan was an especially significant partner with which the Sung had to deal. Originating in the Manchurian woods, the people of this formerly pastoral economy adapted well to the steppes and developed a formidable cavalry. Taking advantage of Chinese internal disturbances during the Five Dynasties, the Khitan played the Chinese states off against each other in order to win the concession of a sizable area along the present Hopei and Shansi provinces in the north. The process of cultural advancement proceeded in the Khitan from the combination of two influences:

that of the steppeland culture and that of the Chinese who had remained when the Khitan took over. Thus, in the Sung court, the advisers noted well the fact that the Khitan had in its territory Chinese human resources, a knowledge of how to organize a Chinese civil service, and, at the same time, a nomad-based military advantage. These advisers reminded the court that China should not consider the Khitan to be merely another barbarian along the northern peripheries.[46] The Sung strategists suggested three approaches to dealing with the Khitan. The first and most preferred policy was to have an effective defense along the border provinces. The key words used were: "forcefully fending the intruders away; yet no more pursuance as they withdraw." The second-best strategy was to negotiate for peace by sending generous gifts annually and marrying imperial princesses to the Khitan chieftains. The third and least desired option was to launch large-scale campaigns to penetrate the enemy's territory.[47] Obviously, because the Sung people fully realized the disparity of military strength between China and the Khitan, the last option was not used until the very end of both the Northern Sung and the Khitan dynasties in 1124.

For a long period, there was no formal diplomatic relationship between China and the Khitan, although trade was continuously carried out and only sporadic conflicts interrupted a de facto truce. In 1004, the Khitan launched a massive invasion. After a major confrontation, a stalemate was reached and a treaty signed in that same year. The treaty established a prolonged period of general peace that lasted for more than 150 years, broken only occasionally by minor confrontations. Interestingly, the wording of the treaty closely resembled that used in the treaties of the Spring and Autumn period, including sentences regarding such things as boundaries and mutual respect, and ending with an oath invoking the deities and spirits of ancestors to guarantee observance of the obligations. Meanwhile, China promised to give to the Khitan two hundred thousand pieces of silk and one hundred thousand teal of silver. What was not included in the official treaty was the establishment of a sworn brotherhood between the two emperors whereby the Sung emperor was considered an elder brother and the Khitan emperor a younger (the Khitan acknowledged the seniority of the Sung emperor due to consideration of the actual age difference between these two rulers at the time the treaty was signed). It should be noted that such a brotherhood was not merely court protocol. In later correspondence and other occasions of contact the terms of an elder-younger brother relationship and an uncle-nephew or aunt-nephew relationship were carefully and explicitly taken into consideration in order to regulate privileges and obligations as would exist between true kinsmen.[48]

In short, one would expect the Sung-Khitan relationship to have been a deviation from the sinocentric mentality. But by maintaining, on the one hand, a rather fraternal structure, Sung China still argued that the non-Chinese sector of the international order was to stay out of the universal Chinese state because of its cultural distance from central China, while on the other hand, in adopting the typical Chinese kinship terminology, it injected an all-Chinese *gemeinschaft* spirit into the international relationship—the fusion of private and public ethics as discussed previously.

In later dynasties, especially the periods of the Ming (A.D. 1368–1644) and the Ch'ing (A.D. 1644–1911), a tributary system that included trading and the exchanging of gifts brought numerous smaller satellite states of East Asia into the orbit of the Chinese empire.[49] The pretext for developing such a tributary system, nevertheless, was to fulfill the concentric sinocentric patterns of zoning as raised in this paper. It should be noted that although there were economic transactions prevalent in the tributary system, China was seldom on the gainful side because of costly expenses associated with such practices. Economic considerations were secondary to the goal of confirming Chinese supremacy.[50] The Ming and Ch'ing dynasties rarely dispatched troops into the tributary states and in even fewer cases annexed their territories.

Occasionally, China intervened militarily in disputes between tributary states, or in the domestic affairs of a certain tributary state on issues such as succession to the throne by an illegitimate son.[51] On the whole, however, China seemed content in the role of supervisor of an order of *Pax Sinica,* which was always described in terms of an ancient universal state of the Chinese empire and around which were zones of other lesser states, each of whom held a relationship with China differentiated according to its history and its cultural and spatial distance from China. Beyond the world of Chinese order were those states and those peoples who need not belong to the sinocentric order. They were to be left outside Chinese influence, as was China to be left alone by these distant nations, or barbarians.

Sinocentrism actually survived to the end of imperial China.[52] During the Opium War, the Chinese still tried to convince the British that China was self-sufficient to such a degree that trade with outsiders was totally unnecessary. When the British insisted on entering Canton City, the Chinese officials were puzzled as to why the foreigners who belonged to another world would want to stay in China. Even as the war flared up, Chinese scholars still insisted that a self-examination on the moral governance of Confucian ethics should be more important than preparation for combat strategy. All this survived until China was dragged into a new world by a British gunboat, and a new global multistate system developed in which Confucian deontological ethics on state and international affairs were set aside to allow China to shield itself from the cannonball shot from the gunboat.

NOTES

1. Cho-yun Hsu and Kathryn M. Linduff, *Western Chou Civilization* (New Haven: Yale University Press, 1988), 6–16.

2. Ibid., 24–27.

3. Ibid., 151–53.

4. Ibid., 224–26.

5. John K. Fairbank, *The Chinese World Order: Traditional China's Foreign Relations* (Cambridge: Harvard University Press, 1968), 20–22.

6. Hsu and Linduff, *Western Chou Civilization,* 101–6.

7. Richard L. Walker, *The Multi-State System of Ancient China* (Hamden, Conn.: Shoe String, 1953), 20–40.

8. Cho-yun Hsu, *Ancient China in Transition* (Stanford: Stanford University Press, 1965), 2–8.

9. Walker, *The Multi-State System,* 73–92.

10. Ibid., 83–86.

11. Benjamin I. Schwartz, *The World of Thought in Ancient China* (Cambridge: Harvard University Press, 1985), 73–85, 146–47.

12. Ibid., 75.

13. Terry Nardin and David Mapel, eds., *Traditions in International Ethics* (London: Cambridge University Press, 1992), 3.

14. *The Confucian Analects,* trans. James Legge (Hong Kong: Hong Kong University Press, 1960), XIV: 17–18.

15. Ibid., XIII: 19; XV, 5.

16. Ibid., 22.

17. Confucius himself was considered the author of a chronicle titled "The Spring and Autumn," from which the historical period receives its name. The authorship of this chronicle remains disputed. Nevertheless, two commentaries, known as the "Kung-yang" and the "Ku-liang," were composed by Confucian scholars.

18. Po-chi Liu, *Chun-Chiu Hui-meng Cheng-Chih* (International politics in the Chun-Chiu period) (Taipei: Chungua Ts'ung Shu, 1962), 399ff.

19. Ibid., 389ff.

20. Ibid., 404ff, esp. 407.

21. Ibid., 414ff, esp. 422–24.

22. Schwartz, *The World of Thought in Ancient China,* 143–51; Angus Graham, *Later Mohist Logic, Ethics, and Sciences* (Hong Kong: Chinese University Press, 1978), 451.

23. *The Works of Mencius,* trans. James Legge (Hong Kong: Hong Kong University Press, 1960), II: i–4.

24. Schwartz, *The World of Thought in Ancient China,* 147; Graham, *Later Mohist Logic, Ethics, and Sciences,* 451.

25. *The Works of Mencius,* VII: i, 15.

26. Ibid., VI: i, 10.

27. Ibid., VI: i, 8.

28. Ibid., I: ii, 5.

29. Ibid., I: i, 4.

30. Ibid., I: i, 5–6; II: i, 2.

31. Ibid., I: ii, 2.

32. Ibid., VII: ii, 2.

33. Ibid., I: ii, 6; I: ii, 8; V: ii, 9.

34. Ibid., IV: i, 14; VI: ii, 9.

35. Ibid., VI: ii, 13; VII: ii, 28.

36. *The Great Learning*, trans. James Legge (Hong Kong: Hong Kong University Press, 1960), chap. 1.

37. Ibid., chaps. 6–10.

38. *The Works of Mencius,* III: i, 4.

39. Ibid., IV: ii, 1.

40. Ibid., IV: i, 5.

41. For arguments of both sides, see *Yen-T'ieh-Lun* (The discourses on salt and iron), Chunghua gsu-pu-pei-yao edition (Taipei, 1934), passim.

42. Larry W. Moses, "T'ang Tribute Relations with the Inner Asian Barbarians," in John Curtis Perry and Bardwell L. Smith, eds., *Essays on T'ang Society* (London: E. J. Brill, 1976), 61–89.

43. Fang-Kuei Li, "The Inscription of the Sino-Tibetan Treaty of 821–822," *T'oung-pao,* 1956.

44. Morris Rossabi, ed., *China among Equals: The Middle Kingdom and Its Neighbors, 10th–14th Centuries* (Berkeley: University of California Press, 1983), 6–12.

45. Ibid., passim; Tao Jing-shen, *Two Sons of Heaven: Studies in Sung-Liao Relations* (Tucson: University of Arizona Press, 1988), 6–9.

46. Ibid., 46–48.

47. Tao, Jing-shen, *Sung-Liao Kuan-hsi-shih Yen-chiu* (A study on relations between Sung and Liao) (Taipei: lien-ching, 1984), 123; Tao, *Two Sons of Heaven,* 48.

48. Tao, *Sung-Liao Kuan-hsi-shih Yen-chiu,* 24–26.

49. Fairbank, *The Chinese World Order,* 63–89.

50. Ibid., 90–111.

51. Ibid., 165–79.

52. Ibid., 1–4.

Amartya Sen*

Human Rights and Asian Values

In 1776, just when the Declaration of Independence was being adopted in this country, Thomas Paine complained, in *Common Sense,* that Asia had "long expelled" freedom. In this lament, Paine saw Asia in company with much of the rest of the world (America, he hoped, would be different).

> Freedom hath been hunted round the globe. Asia and Africa have long expelled her. Europe regards her as a stranger and England hath given her warning to depart.

For Paine, political freedom and democracy were valuable everywhere, even though they were being violated nearly everywhere too.

The violation of freedom and democracy in different parts of the world continues today, even if not as comprehensively as in Paine's time. There is a difference, though. A new class of arguments has emerged that denies the universal importance of these freedoms. The most prominent of these contentions is the claim that Asian values do not give freedom the same importance as it is accorded in the West. Given this difference in value systems, the argument runs, Asia must be faithful to its own system of political priorities.

Cultural and value differences between Asia and the West were stressed by several official delegations at the 1993 World Conference on Human Rights in Vienna. The foreign minister of

---

*The author presented this paper at the Sixteenth Morgenthau Memorial Lecture on Ethics & Foreign Policy, sponsored by the Carnegie Council on Ethics and International Affairs, in New York City on May 1, 1997.

Singapore warned that "universal recognition of the ideal of human rights can be harmful if universalism is used to deny or mask the reality of diversity."[1] The Chinese delegation played a leading role in emphasizing regional differences and in making sure that the prescriptive framework adopted in the declarations made room for regional diversity. The spokesman for China's foreign ministry even put on record the proposition, apparently applicable in China and elsewhere, that "individuals must put the state's rights before their own."[2]

I shall examine the thesis that Asian values are less supportive of freedom and more concerned with order and discipline than are Western values, and that the claims of human rights in the areas of political and civil liberties are, therefore, less relevant in Asia than in the West. The defense of authoritarianism in Asia on grounds of the special nature of Asian values calls for historical scrutiny, to which I shall presently turn. But there is also a different line of justification that argues for authoritarian governance in the interest of economic development in Asia. Lee Kuan Yew, the former prime minister of Singapore and a great champion of "Asian values," has defended authoritarian arrangements on the ground of their alleged effectiveness in promoting economic success. I shall consider this argument before turning to historical issues.

Asian Values and Economic Development

Does authoritarianism really work so well? It is certainly true that some relatively authoritarian states (such as South Korea, Lee's own Singapore, and post-reform China) have had faster rates of economic growth than many less authoritarian ones (including India, Costa Rica, and Jamaica). But the "Lee hypothesis" is, in fact, based on very selective information, rather than on any general statistical testing of the wide-ranging data that are available. We cannot take the high economic growth of China or South Korea in Asia as proof positive that authoritarianism does better in promoting economic growth, any more than we can draw the opposite conclusion on the basis of the fact that the fastest-growing country in Africa (and one of the fastest growers in the world) is Botswana, which has been a oasis of democracy in that unhappy continent. Much depends on the precise circumstances.

There is, in fact, little general evidence that authoritarian governance and the suppression of political and civil rights are really beneficial in encouraging economic development. The statistical picture is much more complex. Systematic empirical studies give no real support to the claim that there is a conflict between political rights and economic performance.[3] The directional linkage seems to depend on many other circumstances, and while some statistical investigations note a weakly negative relation, others find a strongly positive one. On balance, the hypothesis that there is no relation between the two in either direction is hard to reject. Since political liberty and individual freedom have importance of their own, the case for them remains untarnished.

There is also a more basic issue of research methodology here. We must not only look at statistical connections, we must also examine the causal processes that are involved in economic growth and development. The economic policies and circumstances that led to the economic success of East Asian economies are by now reasonably well understood. While different empirical studies have varied in emphasis, there is by now a fairly well-accepted general list of "helpful policies," among them openness to competition, the use of international markets, a high level of literacy and school education, successful land reforms, and public provision of incentives for investment, exporting, and industrialization. There is nothing whatsoever to indicate that any of these policies is inconsistent with greater democracy and had to be sustained by the elements of authoritarianism that happened to be present in South Korea or Singapore or China.[4] The recent Indian experience also shows that what is needed for generating faster economic growth is a friendlier economic climate, rather than a harsher political system.

It is also important to look at the connection between political and civil rights, on the one hand, and the prevention of major disasters, on the other. Political and civil rights give people the opportunity to draw attention forcefully to general needs and to demand appropriate public action. The response of a government to acute suffering often depends on the pressure that is put on it, and this is where the exercise of political rights (voting, criticizing, protesting, and so on) can make a real difference. I have discussed elsewhere the remarkable fact that in the terrible history of famines in the world, no substantial famine has ever occurred in any independent and democratic country with a relatively free press.[5] Whether we look at famines in Sudan, Ethiopia, Somalia, or other countries with dictatorial regimes, or in the Soviet Union in the 1930s, or in China during the period 1958 to 1961 with the failure of the Great Leap Forward (when between 23 million and 30 million people died), or currently in North Korea, we do not find exceptions to this rule.[6]

While this connection is clearest in the case of famine prevention, the positive role of political and civil rights applies to the prevention of economic and social disasters in general. When things go fine and everything is routinely good, this role of democracy may not be badly missed. It comes into its own when things get fouled up, for one reason or another. Then the political incentives provided by democratic governance acquire great practical value. To concentrate only on economic incentives (such as the market system provides) while ignoring political incentives (such as democratic systems are equipped to provide) is to opt for a deeply unbalanced set of ground rules).

Asia As a Unit

I turn now to the nature and relevance of Asian values. This is not an easy exercise, for various reasons. The size of Asia, where about 60 percent of the total world population lives, is itself a problem. What can we take to be the values of so vast a region, with such diversity? There are no quintessential values that apply to this immensely large and heterogeneous population, that differentiate Asians as a group from people in the rest of the world.

The temptation to see Asia as one unit reveals, in fact, a distinctly Eurocentric perspective. Indeed, the term "the Orient," which was widely used for a long time to mean essentially what Asia means today, referred to the direction of the rising sun. It requires a heroic generalization to see such a large group of people in terms of the positional view from the European side of the Bosporus.

In practice, the advocates of "Asian values" have tended to look primarily at East Asia as the region of particular applicability. The generalization about the contrast between the West and Asia often concentrates on the land to the east of Thailand, even though there is an even more ambitious claim that the rest of Asia is also rather "similar." For example, Lee Kuan Yew outlines "the fundamental difference between Western concepts of society and government and East Asian concepts" by explaining, "When I say East Asians, I mean Korea, Japan, China, Vietnam, as distinct from Southeast Asia, which is a mix between the Sinic and the Indian, though Indian culture also emphasizes similar values."[7]

In fact, however, East Asia itself has much diversity, and there are many variations between Japan and China and Korea and other parts of East Asia. Various cultural influences from within and outside this region have affected human lives over the history of this rather large territory. These diverse influences still survive in a variety of ways. To illustrate, my copy of Houghton Mifflin's international *Almanac* describes the religions of the 124 million Japanese people in the following way: 112 million Shintoists and 93 million Buddhists. Buddist practices coexist with Shinto practices, often within the same person's religious makeup. Cultures and traditions overlap over wide regions such as East Asia and even within specific countries such as Japan or China or Korea, and attempts at generalization about Asian values (with forceful—often brutal—implications for masses of people in this region with diverse faiths, convictions, and commitments) cannot but be extremely crude. Even the 2.8 million people of Singapore have vast variations in their cultural and historical traditions, despite the fact that the conformism surrounding Singapore's political leadership and the official interpretation of Asian values is very powerful at this time.

Freedom, Democracy, and Tolerance

The recognition of heterogeneity in Asian traditions does not, in any way, settle the issue of the presence or absence of a commitment to individual freedom and political liberty in Asian culture. It could be argued that the traditions extant in Asia differ among themselves, but nevertheless may share some common characteristics. It has been asserted, for example, that the treatment of elderly members of the family (such as aged parents) is more supportive in Asian countries than in the West. It is possible to argue about this claim, but there would be nothing very peculiar if similarities of this or other kinds were to obtain across the diverse cultures of Asia: diversities need not apply to every field. The question that has to be asked, rather, is whether the Asian countries share the common feature of being skeptical of freedom and liberty, while emphasizing order and discipline. The advocates of Asian particularism often—explicitly or by implication—make this argument, which allows for heterogeneity within Asia, but asserts that there is a shared mistrust of the claims of liberal rights.

Authoritarian lines of reasoning often receive indirect backing from modes of thought in the West itself. There is clearly a tendency in the United States and Europe to assume, if only implicitly, the primacy of political freedom and democracy as a fundamental and ancient feature of Western culture—one not to be easily found in Asia. A contrast is drawn between the authoritarianism allegedly implicit in, say, Confucianism and the respect for individual liberty and autonomy allegedly deeply rooted in Western liberal culture. Western promoters of personal and political liberty in the non-Western world often see this as bringing Western values to Asia and Africa.

In all this, there is a substantial tendency to extrapolate backwards from the present. Values spread by the European Enlightenment and other relatively recent developments cannot be considered part of the long-term Western heritage, experienced in the West over millennia. Indeed, in answer to the question when and under what circumstances "the notion of individual liberty . . . first became explicit in the West," Isaiah Berlin has noted, "I have found no convincing evidence of any clear formulation of it in the ancient world."[8] This diagnosis has been disputed by Orlando Patterson, among others.[9] Patterson points to features in Western culture, particularly in Greece and Rome and in the tradition of Christianity, that indicate the presence of selective championing of individual liberty. The question that does not get adequately answered—indeed, it is scarcely even asked—is whether similar elements are absent in other cultures. Isaiah Berlin's thesis concerns the notion of individual freedom as we now understand it, and the absence of "any clear formulation" of this can coexist with the support and advocacy of *selected components* of the comprehensive notion that makes up the contemporary idea of individual liberty as an entitlement of everyone. Such components do exist in the Greco-Roman world and in the world of Christian thought, but we have to examine whether these components are present elsewhere as well—that is, in non-Western cultures. We have to search for parts rather than the whole—both in the West and in Asia and elsewhere.

To illustrate this point, consider the idea that personal freedom for all is important for a good society. This claim can be seen as being composed of two distinct components, to wit, (1) *the value of personal freedom:* that personal freedom is important and should be guaranteed for those who "matter" in a good society, and (2) *equality of freedom:* that everyone matters and should have similar freedom. The two together entail that personal freedom should be guaranteed, on a shared basis, for all. Aristotle wrote much in support of the former proposition, but in his exclusion of women and slaves did little to defend the latter. Indeed, the championing of equality in this form is of quite recent origin. Even in a society stratified according to class and caste—such as the Mandarins and the Brahmins—freedom could be valued for the privileged, in much the same way freedom is valued for non-slave men in corresponding Greek conceptions of a good society.

Another useful distinction is between (1) *the value of toleration:* there must be toleration of diverse beliefs, commitments, and actions of different people, and (2) *equality of tolerance:* the toleration that is offered to some must be reasonably offered to all (except when tolerance of some will lead to intolerance for others). Again, arguments for some tolerance can be seen plentifully in earlier writings, without that tolerance being supplemented by equality of tolerance. The roots of modern democratic and liberal ideas can be sought in terms of constitutive elements, rather than as a whole.

Order and Confucianism

As part of this analytical scrutiny, the question has to be asked whether these constitutive components can be seen in Asian writings in the way they can be found in Western thought. The presence of these components must not be confused with the absence of the opposite, namely ideas and doctrines that clearly *do not* emphasize freedom and tolerance. Championing of order and discipline can be found in Western classics as well as in Asian ones. Indeed, it is by no means clear to me that Confucius is more authoritarian in this respect than, say, Plato or St. Augustine. The real issue is not whether these non-freedom perspectives are *present* in Asian traditions, but whether the freedom-oriented perspectives are *absent* there.

This is where the diversity of Asian value systems becomes central, incorporating but transcending regional diversity. An obvious example is the role of Buddhism as a form of thought. In Buddhist tradition, great importance is attached to freedom, and the part of the earlier Indian theorizing to which Buddhist thoughts relate has much room for volition and free choice. Nobility of conduct has to be achieved in freedom, and even the ideas of liberation (such as *moksha*) have this feature. The presence of these elements in Buddhist thought does not obliterate the importance for Asia of ordered discipline emphasized by Confucianism, but it would be a mistake to take Confucianism to be the only tradition in Asia—indeed even in China. Since so much of the contemporary authoritarian interpretation of Asian values concentrates on Confucianism, this diversity is particularly worth emphasizing.

Indeed, the reading of Confucianism that is now standard among authoritarian champions of Asian values does less than justice to the variety within Confucius's own teachings, to which Simon Leys has recently drawn attention.[10] Confucius did not recommend blind allegiance to the state. When Zilu asks him "how to serve a prince," Confucius replies, "Tell him the truth even if it offends him."[11] Those in charge of censorship in Singapore or Beijing would take a very different view. Confucius is not averse to practical caution and tact, but does not forgo the recommendation to oppose a bad government. "When the [good] way prevails in the state, speak boldly and act boldly. When the state has lost the way, act boldly and speak softly."[12]

Indeed, Confucius provides a clear pointer to the fact that the two pillars of the imagined edifice of Asian values, namely loyalty to family and obedience to the state, can be in severe conflict with each other. The governor of She told Confucius, "Among my people, there is a man of unbending integrity: when his father stole a sheep, he denounced him." To this Confucius replied, "Among my people, men of integrity do things differently: a father covers up for his son, a son covers up for his father, and there is integrity in what they do."[13]

Elias Canetti has pointed out that in understanding the teachings of Confucius, we have to examine not only what he says, but also what he does not say.[14] The subtlety involved in what is often called "the silence of Confucius" has certainly escaped the modern austere interpreters in their tendency to assume that what is not explicitly supported must be implicitly forbidden. It is not my contention that Confucius was a democrat, or a great champion of freedom and political dissent, but there is reason enough to question the monolithic authoritarian image of him that is presented by the contemporary advocates of Asian values.

Freedom and Tolerance

If we shift our attention from China to the Indian subcontinent, we are in no particular danger of running into hard-to-interpret silence; it is difficult to outdo the Indian traditions of speaking at length and arguing endlessly in explicit and elaborate terms. India not only has the largest religious literature in the world, it also has by far the largest volume of atheistic and materialistic writings among the ancient civilizations. There is just a lot of literature of all kinds. The Indian epic *Mahabharata,* which is often compared with the *Iliad* or the *Odyssey,* is in fact seven times as long as the *Iliad* and *Odyssey* put together. In a well-known Bengali poem written in the nineteenth century by the religious and social leader Ram Mohan Ray, the real horror of death is described thus: "Just imagine how terrible it will be on the day you die,/ Others will go on speaking, but you will not be able to respond."

This fondness for arguing, and for discussing things at leisure and at length, is itself somewhat in tension with the quiet order and discipline championed in the alleged Asian values. But in addition, the content of what has been written indicates a variety of views on freedom, tolerance, and equality. In many ways, the most interesting articulation of the need for tolerance on an egalitarian basis can be found in the writings of Emperor Ashoka, who in the third century B.C. commanded a larger Indian empire than any other Indian king in history (including the Moghuls, and even the Raj, if we leave out the native states that the British let be). He turned his attention in a big way to public ethics and enlightened politics after being horrified by the carnage he saw in his own victorious battle against the king of Kalinga (now Orissa). Ashoka converted to Buddhism and helped to make it a world religion by sending emissaries abroad with the Buddhist message. He also covered the country with stone inscriptions describing forms of good life and the nature of good government.

The inscriptions give a special importance to tolerance of diversity. For example, the edict (now numbered XII) at Erragudi puts the issue thus:

> A man must not do reverence to his own sect or disparage that of another man without reason. Depreciation should be for specific reason only, because the sects of other people all deserve reverence for one reason or another.
>
> By thus acting, a man exalts his own sect, and at the same time does service to the sects of other people. By acting contrariwise, a man hurts his own sect, and does disservice to the sects of other people. For he who does reverence to his own sect while disparaging the sects of others wholly from attachment to his own, with intent to enhance the splendour of his own sect, in reality by such conduct inflicts the severest injury on his own sect.[15]

These edicts from the third century B.C. emphasize the importance of tolerance, both in public policy by the government and in the behavior of citizens to each other.

On the domain and coverage of tolerance, Ashoka was a universalist and demanded this for all, including those whom he described as "forest people," the tribal population living in preagricultural economic formations. Condemning his own conduct before his conversion, Ashoka notes that in the war in Kalinga, "men and animals numbering one hundred and fifty thousands were carried away (captive) from that kingdom." He goes on to state that the slaughter or the taking of prisoners "of even a hundredth or thousandth part of all those people who were slain or died or were carried away (captive) at that time in Kalinga is now considered very deplorable [by him]." Indeed, he proceeds to assert that now he believes that even if a person should wrong him, that offense would be forgiven "if it is possible to forgive it." He describes the object of his government as "non-injury, restraint, impartiality, and mild behaviour" applied "to all creatures."[16]

Ashoka's championing of egalitarian and universal tolerance may appear un-Asian to some commentators, but his views are firmly rooted in lines of analysis already in vogue in intellectual circles in India in the three preceding centuries. It is interesting, however, to consider another author whose treatise on governance and political economy was also profoundly influential. I refer to Kautilya, the author of *Arthashastra,* which can be translated as the "economic science," though it is at least as much concerned with practical politics as with economics. Kautilya, a contemporary of Aristotle, lived in the fourth century B.C. and worked as a senior minister of Emperor Chandragupta Maurya, Emperor Ashoka's grandfather, who had established the large Maurya empire across the subcontinent.

Kautilya's writings are often cited as a proof that freedom and tolerance were not valued in the Indian classical tradition. Two aspects of the impressively detailed account of economics and politics to be found in *Arthashastra* might tend to suggest that there is no support there for a liberal democracy.

First, Kautilya is a consequentialist of quite a narrow kind. While the objectives of promoting the happiness of subjects and order in the kingdom are strongly backed up by detailed policy advice, he depicts the king as a benevolent autocrat, whose power is to be maximized through good organization. Thus, *Arthashastra* presents penetrating ideas and suggestions on such practical subjects as famine prevention and administrative effectiveness that remain relevant even today, more than two thousand years later; yet at the same time, it advises the king how to get his way, if necessary through the violation of freedom of his opponents and adversaries.

Second, Kautilya seems to attach little importance to political or economic equality, and his vision of good society is strongly stratified according to lines of class and caste. Even though the objective of promoting happiness, which is given an exalted position in the hierarchy of values, is applied to all, the other objectives have clearly inegalitarian form and content. There is an obligation to give the less fortunate members of the society the support that they need to escape misery and enjoy life—Kautilya specifically identifies as the duty of the king to "provide the orphans, the aged, the infirm, the afflicted, and the helpless with maintenance," along with providing "subsistence to helpless women when they are carrying and also to the [newborn] children they give birth to."[17] But recognizing that obligation is very far from valuing the freedom of these people to decide how to live—tolerating heterodoxy. Indeed, there is very little tolerance in Kautilya, except for the upper sections of the community.

What do we conclude from this? Certainly, Kautilya is no democrat, no egalitarian, no general promoter of everyone's freedom. And yet, when it comes to the characterization of what the most favored people—the upper classes—should get, freedom figures quite prominently. Denial of personal liberty of the upper classes (the so-called Arya) is seen as unacceptable. Indeed, regular penalties, some of them heavy, are specified for the taking of such adults or children in indenture, even though the slavery of the existing slaves is seen as perfectly acceptable.[18] To be sure, we do not find in Kautilya anything like the clear articulation that Aristotle provides of the importance of free exercise of capability. But the importance of freedom is clear enough in Kautilya as far as the upper classes are concerned. It contrasts with the governmental duties to the lower orders, which take the paternalistic form of state assistance for the avoidance of acute deprivation and misery. Still, insofar as a view of the good life emerges from all this, it is an ideal that is entirely consistent with a freedom-valuing ethical system. The domain of that concern is narrow, to be sure, confined to the upper groups of society, but this limitation is not wildly different from the Greek concern with free men as opposed to slaves or women.

I have been discussing in some detail the political ideas and practical reason presented by two forceful, but very different, expositors in India in the third and the fourth centuries B.C. because their ideas have influenced later Indian writings. I do not want to give the impression that all Indian political commentators took lines of approach similar to Ashoka's or Kautilya's. Quite the contrary. Many positions taken before and after Kautilya and Ashoka contradict their respective claims, just as others are more in line either with Ashoka or with Kautilya.

For example, the importance of tolerance—even the need for universality in this—is eloquently expressed in different media, such as Shudraka's drama, Akbar's political pronouncements, and Kabir's poetry, to name just a few examples. The presence of these contributions does not entail the absence of opposite arguments and recommendations. Rather, the point is that in their heterogeneity, Indian traditions contain a variety of views and reasonings, but they include, in different ways, arguments in favor of tolerance, in defense of freedom, and even, in the case of Ashoka, in support of equality at a very basic level.

Akbar and the Moghuls

Among the powerful expositors and practitioners of tolerance of diversity in India must be counted the great Moghul emperor Akbar, who reigned between 1556 and 1605. Again, we are not dealing with a democrat, but with a powerful king who emphasized the acceptability of diverse forms of social and religious behavior, and who accepted human rights of various kinds, including freedom of worship and religious practice. Such rights would not have been easily tolerated in parts of Europe in Akbar's time.

For example, as the year 1000 in the Muslim Hejira calendar was reached in 1591–92, there was excitement about it in Delhi and Agra (not unlike what is happening right now as the year 2000 in the Christian calendar approaches). Akbar issued various enactments at this juncture of history, and some of these focused on religious tolerance, including the following:

> No man should be interfered with on account of religion, and anyone [is] to be allowed to go over to a religion he pleased.
>
> If a Hindu, when a child or otherwise, had been made a Muslim against his will, he is to be allowed, if he pleased, to go back to the religion of his fathers.[19]

Again, the domain of tolerance, while religion-neutral, was not universal in other respects, including gender equality or equality between younger and older people. The enactment went on to argue for the forcible repatriation of a young Hindu woman to her father's family if she had abandoned it in pursuit of a Muslim lover. In the choice between supporting the young lovers and the young woman's Hindu father, old Akbar's sympathies are entirely with the father. Tolerance and equality at one level are combined with intolerance and inequality at another level, but the extent of general tolerance on matters of belief and practice is quite remarkable. It is interesting to note, especially in light of the hard sell of "Western liberalism," that while Akbar was making these pronouncements on religious tolerance, the Inquisition was in high gear in Europe.

Theories and Practice

It is important to recognize that many of these historical leaders in Asia not only emphasized the importance of freedom and tolerance, they also had clear theories as to why this was the appropriate thing to do. This applies very strongly to both Ashoka and Akbar. Since the Islamic tradition is sometimes seen as being monolithic, this is particularly important to emphasize in the case of Akbar. Akbar was, in fact, deeply interested in Hindu philosophy and culture, but also took much note of the beliefs and practices of other religions, including Christianity, Jainism, and the Parsee faith. In fact, he attempted to establish something of a synthetic religion for India—the Din Ilahi—drawing on the different faiths in the country.

There is an interesting contrast here between Ashoka's and Akbar's forms of religious tolerance. Both stood for religious tolerance by the state, and both argued for tolerance as a virtue to be practiced by all. But while Ashoka combined this with his own Buddhist pursuits (and tried to spread "enlightenment" at home and abroad), Akbar tried to combine the distinct religions of India, incorporating the "good points" of different religions. Akbar's court was filled with Hindu as well as Muslim intellectuals, artists, and musicians, and he tried in every way to be nonsectarian and symmetric in the treatment of his subjects.

It is also important to note that Akbar was by no means unique among the Moghul emperors in being tolerant. In many ways, the later Moghul emperor, the intolerant Aurangzeb, who violated many of what would be now seen as basic human rights of Hindus, was something of an exception.[20] But even Aurangzeb should be considered in his familial setting, not in isolation. None of his immediate family seems to have shared Aurangzeb's intolerance. Dara Shikoh, his elder brother, was much involved with Hindu philosophy and had, with the help of some scholars, prepared a Persian translation of some of the *Upanishads,* the ancient texts dating from about the eighth century B.C. In fact, Dara Shikoh had much stronger claims to the Moghul throne than Aurangzeb, since he was the eldest and the favorite son of their father, Emperor Shah Jahan. Aurangzeb fought and killed Dara, and imprisoned their father for the rest of his life (leaving him, the builder of the Taj Mahal, to gaze at his creation in captivity, from a distance).

Aurangzeb's son, also called Akbar, rebelled against his father in 1681 and joined hands in this enterprise with the Hindu kingdoms in Rajasthan and later the Marathas (though Akbar's rebellion too was ultimately crushed by Aurangzeb). While fighting from Rajasthan, Akbar wrote to his father protesting his intolerance and vilification of his Hindu friends. The issue of tolerance of differences was indeed a subject of considerable discussion among the feuding parties. The father of the Maratha king, Raja Sambhaji, whom the young Akbar had joined, was no other than Shivaji, whom the present-day Hindu political activists treat as a superhero, and after whom the intolerant Hindu party Shiv Sena is named.

Shivaji himself took quite a tolerant view of religious differences. As the Moghul historian Khafi Khan, who was no admirer of Shivaji in other respects, reports:

> [Shivaji] made it a rule that wherever his followers were plundering, they should do no harm to the mosques, the book of God, or the women of any one. Whenever a copy of the sacred Quran came into his hands, he treated it with respect, and gave it to some of his Mussalman followers.[21]

In fact, a very interesting letter to Aurangzeb on the subject of tolerance is attributed to Shivaji by some historians (such as Sir Jadunath Sarkar, the author of the classic *Shivaji and His Times,* published in 1919), though there are some doubts about this attribution (another possible author is Rana Raj Singh of Mewar/Udaipur). No matter who among Aurangzeb's contemporaries wrote this letter, the ideas engaged in it are interesting enough. The letter contrasts Aurangzeb's intolerance with the tolerant policies of earlier Moghuls (Akbar, Jahangir, Shah Jahan), and then says this:

> If Your Majesty places any faith in those books by distinction called divine, you will there be instructed that God is the God

> of all mankind, not the God of Muslims alone. The Pagan and the Muslim are equally in His presence. . . . In fine, the tribute you demand from the Hindus is repugnant to justice.[22]

The subject of tolerance was indeed much discussed by many writers during this period of confrontation of religious traditions and the associated politics. One of the earliest writers on the subject of tolerance was the eleventh-century Iranian Alberuni, who came to India with the invading army of Sultan Mahmood of Ghazni and recorded his revulsion at the atrocities committed by the invaders. He proceeded to study Indian society, culture, religion, and intellectual pursuits (indeed his translations of Indian mathematical and astronomical treatises were quite influential in the Arab world, which in turn deeply influenced Western mathematics), but he also discussed the subject of intolerance of the unfamiliar.

> In all manners and usages, [the Hindus] differ from us to such a degree as to frighten their children with us, with our dress, and our ways and customs, and as to declare us to be devil's breed, and our doings as the very opposite of all that is good and proper. By the bye, we must confess, in order to be just, that a similar depreciation of foreigners not only prevails among us and the Hindus, but is common to all nations towards each other.[23]

The point of discussing all this is to indicate the presence of conscious theorizing about tolerance and freedom in substantial and important parts of Asian tradition. We could consider many more illustrations of this phenomenon in writings from early Arabic, Chinese, Indian, and other cultures. As was argued earlier, the championing of democracy and political freedom in the modern sense cannot be found in the pre-Enlightenment tradition in any part of the world—the West or the East—so we have to look at the constituent components of this compound idea. The view that the basic ideas underlying freedom and rights in a tolerant society are "Western" notions, and somehow alien to Asia, is hard to make any sense of, even though that view has been championed by both Asian authoritarians and Western chauvinists.

Intervention across National Boundaries

I want to turn now to a rather different issue, which is sometimes linked to the debate about the nature and reach of Asian values. The championing of Asian values is often associated with the need to resist Western hegemony. The linking of the two issues, which has occurred increasingly in recent years, uses the political force of anticolonialism to buttress the assault on basic political and civil rights in postcolonial Asia.

This linkage, though quite artificial, can be rhetorically very effective. For example, Lee Kuan Yew has emphasized the special nature of Asian values and has made powerful use of the general case for resisting Western hegemony to bolster the argument for Asian particularism. The rhetoric has extended to the apparently defiant declaration that Singapore is "not a client state of America."[24] That fact is certainly undeniable, and is an excellent reason for cheer, but the question that has to be asked is what the bearing of this fact is on the issue of human rights and political liberties in Singapore, or any other country in Asia.

The people whose political and other rights are involved in this debate are not citizens of the West, but of Asian countries. The fact that individual liberty and freedom may have been championed in Western writings and even by some Western political leaders can scarcely compromise the claim to liberty and freedom that people in Asia may otherwise have. As a matter of fact, one can grumble, with reason, that the political leaders of Western countries take far too *little* interest in issues of freedom in the rest of the world. There is plenty of evidence that the Western governments have, by and large, tended to give priority to the interests of their own citizens engaged in commerce with the Asian countries and to the pressures generated by business groups to be on good terms with the ruling governments in Asia. It is not so much that there has been more bark than bite; there has in fact been very little barking either. What Chairman Mao had once described as a "paper tiger" has increasingly looked like a paper mouse.

But even if this had not been the case, and even if Western governments really had tried to promote political and civil rights in Asia, how could that possibly compromise the status of the rights of Asians? In this context, the idea of "human rights" has to be properly spelled out. In the most general form, the notion of human rights builds on our shared humanity. These rights are not derived from the citizenship of any country, or the membership of any nation, but taken as entitlements of every human being. They differ, thus, from constitutionally created rights guaranteed for specified people (such as, say, American or French citizens). For example, the human right of a person not to be tortured is independent of the country of which this person is a citizen and thus exists irrespective of what the government of that country—or any other—wants to do. A government can, of course, dispute a person's *legal* right not to be tortured, but that will not amount to disputing what must be seen as the person's *human* right not to be tortured.

Since the conception of human rights transcends local legislation and the citizenship of the person affected, it is not surprising that support for human rights can also come from anyone—whether or not she is a citizen of the same country as the person whose rights are threatened. A foreigner does not need the permission of a repressive government to try to help a person whose liberties are being violated. Indeed, in so far as human rights are seen as rights that any person has as a human being and not as a citizen of any particular country, the reach of the corresponding *duties* can also include any human being, irrespective of citizenship.

This basic recognition does not, of course, suggest that everyone must intervene constantly in protecting and helping others. That may be both ineffective and unsettling. There is no escape from the need to employ practical reason in this field, any more than in any other field of deliberate human action. I have discussed elsewhere the nature of the necessary scrutiny, including the assessment of rights and their consequences.[25]

Ubiquitous interventionism is not particularly fruitful or attractive within a given country, or across national boundaries. There is no obligation to roam the four corners of the earth in search of liberties to protect. The claim is only that the barriers of nationality and citizenship do not preclude people from taking legitimate interest in the rights of others and even from assuming some duties related to them. The moral and political examination that is central to determining how one should act applies across national boundaries and not merely within each realm.

A Concluding Remark

The so-called Asian values that are invoked to justify authoritarianism are not especially Asian in any significant sense. Nor is it easy to see how they could be made into an Asian cause against the West, by the mere force of rhetoric. The people whose rights are being disputed are Asians, and no matter what the West's guilt may be (there are many skeletons in many cupboards across the world), the rights of the Asians can scarcely be compromised on those grounds. The case for liberty and political rights turns ultimately on their basic importance and on their instrumental role. This case is as strong in Asia as it is elsewhere.

I have disputed the usefulness of a grand contrast between Asian and European values. There is a lot we can learn from studies of values in Asia and Europe, but they do not support or sustain the thesis of a grand dichotomy. Contemporary ideas of political and personal liberty and rights have taken their present form relatively recently, and it is hard to see them as "traditional" commitments of Western cultures. There are important antecedents of those commitments in the form of the advocacy of tolerance and individual freedom, but those antecedents can be found plentifully in Asian as well as Western cultures.

The recognition of diversity within different cultures is extremely important in the contemporary world, since we are constantly bombarded by oversimple generalizations about "Western civilization," "Asian values," "African cultures," and so on. These unfounded readings of history and civilization are not only intellectually shallow, they also add to the divisiveness of the world in which we live.

Authoritarian readings of Asian values that are increasingly being championed in some quarters do not survive scrutiny. The thesis of a grand dichotomy between Asian values and European values adds little to our comprehension, and much to the confusion about the normative basis of freedom and democracy.

NOTES

1. Quoted in W. S. Wong, "The Real World of Human Rights" (mimeographed, 1993).

2. Quoted in John F. Cooper, "Peking's Post-Tiananmen Foreign Policy: The Human Rights Factor," *Issues and Studies* 30 (October 1994), 69; see also Jack Donnelly, "Human Rights and Asian Values," paper presented at a workshop of the Carnegie Council's Human Rights Initiative, "Changing Conceptions of Human Rights in a Growing East Asia," in Hakone, Japan, June 23–25, 1995.

3. See, among other studies, Robert J. Barro and Jong-Wha Lee, "Losers and Winners in Economic Growth," Working Paper 4341, National Bureau of Economic Research (1993); Partha Dasgupta, *An Inquiry into Well-Being and Destitution* (Oxford: Clarendon Press, 1993); John Helliwell, "Empirical Linkages Between Democracy and Economic Growth," Working Paper 4066, National Bureau of Economic Research (1994); Surjit Bhalla, "Freedom and Economic Growth: A Vicious Circle?" presented at the Nobel Symposium in Uppsala on "Democracy's Victory and Crisis," August 1994; Adam Przeworski and Fernando Limongi, "Democracy and Development," presented at the Nobel Symposium in Uppsala cited above; Adam Przeworski et al., *Sustainable*

Democracy (New York: Cambridge University Press, 1995); Robert J. Barro, *Getting It Right: Markets and Choices in a Free Society* (Cambridge, Mass.: MIT Press, 1996).

4. On this see also my joint study with Jean Dreze, *Hunger and Public Action* (Oxford: Clarendon Press, 1989), Part III.

5. Amartya Sen, "Development: Which Way Now?" *Economic Journal* 93 (1983) and *Resources, Values and Development* (Cambridge: Harvard University Press, 1984, 1997); see also Dreze and Sen, *Hunger and Public Action.*

6. Although Ireland was a part of democratic Britain during its famines of the 1840s, the extent of political dominance of London over the Irish was so strong and the social distance so great (well illustrated by Edmund Spenser's severely unfriendly description of the Irish as early as the sixteenth century) that the English rule of Ireland was, for all practical purposes, a colonial rule. The separation and independence of Ireland later on simply confirmed the nature of the division.

7. Fareed Zakaria, "Culture Is Destiny: A Conversation with Lee Kuan Yew," *Foreign Affairs* 73 (March/April 1994), 113.

8. Isaiah Berlin, *Four Essays on Liberty* (Oxford: Oxford University Press, 1969), xl.

9. See Orlando Patterson, *Freedom,* Vol. I: *Freedom in the Making of Western Culture* (New York: Basic Books, 1991).

10. Simon Leys, *The Analects of Confucius* (New York: Norton, 1997).

11. Ibid., 14.22, 70.

12. Ibid., 14.3, 66.

13. Ibid., 13.18, 63.

14. Elias Canetti, *The Conscience of Words* (New York: Seabury Press, 1979); see also Leys, *The Analects of Confucius,* xxx–xxxii.

15. Translation in Vincent A. Smith, *Asoka* (Delhi: S. Chand, 1964), 170–71.

16. *Asokan Studies,* 34–35, edict XIII.

17. *Kautilya's Arthasastra,* trans. R. Shama Sastry, 8th ed. (Mysore: Mysore Printing and Publishing House, 1967), 47.

18. See R. P. Kangle, *The Kautilya Arthasastra,* Part II (Bombay: University of Bombay, 1972), chap. 13, sect. 65, pp. 235–39.

19. Translation from Vincent A. Smith, *Akbar: The Great Mogul* (Oxford: Clarendon Press, 1917), 257.

20. The exponents of contemporary Hindu politics in India often try to deny the tolerant nature of much of Moghul rule. That tolerance was, however, handsomely acknowledged by Hindu leaders of an earlier vintage. For example, Sri Aurobindo, who established the famous ashram in Pondicherry, specifically identified this aspect of the Moghul rule (*The Spirit and Form of Indian Polity* [Calcutta: Arya Publishing House, 1947] 86–89):

> The Mussulman domination ceased very rapidly to be a foreign rule. . . . The Mogul empire was a great and magnificent construction and an immense amount of political genius and talent was employed in its creation and maintenance. It was as splendid, powerful and beneficent and, it may be added, in spite of Aurangzeb's fanatical zeal, infinitely more liberal and tolerant in religion than any medieval or contemporary European kingdom or empire.

21. Percival Spear, ed., *The Oxford History of India,* 4th ed., trans. Vincent Smith (London: Oxford University Press, 1974), 412.

22. Ibid., 417–18.

23. Ainslie T. Embree, ed., *Alberuni's India,* trans. Edward C. Sachau (New York: Norton, 1971), Pt. I, Chap. I, p. 20.

24. *International Herald Tribune,* June 13, 1995, 4.

25. Amartya Sen, "Rights and Agency," *Philosophy and Public Affairs* 11 (1982); "Liberty and Social Choice," *Journal of Philosophy* 80 (January 1983); "Well-Being, Agency and Freedom: The Dewey Lectures 1984," *Journal of Philosophy* 82 (April 1985).

John Lewis Gaddis

On Moral Equivalency and Cold War History

For some strange reason, it occasionally happens that debates within that peculiar institution, the Oxford Union, reflect and perhaps even symbolize the preoccupations of an age. Recall the famous 1934 debate which resulted in a victory for the resolution that "this House will in no circumstances fight for King and Country." Whatever impression this may or may not have made on Adolf Hitler, it made an indelible one on an appalled young American who witnessed it, Dean Rusk, and he would draw on it for the rest of his life as the supreme example of irresponsibility in thinking about international relations—with consequences that would very much affect his own thinking about Ho Chi Minh.[1]

Or consider another lesser-known but no less interesting Oxford disputation, held precisely half a century later in 1984 between the great Marxist historian E. P. Thompson and the American secretary of defense Caspar Weinberger. These improbable contenders took on the issue: "Resolved, there is no moral difference between the foreign policies of the U.S. and the USSR." Thompson described the United States and the Soviet Union, during the debate, as "two terrorist states," with "born-again Christians on the one side and still-born Marxists on the other." "What is this quarrel about?" he demanded dramatically. "It is very simple," Weinberger responded, with remarkable calm under the circumstances. "It's all about freedom. Individual, personal, human freedom and whether we and our children will be allowed to exercise it."

Somewhat surprisingly, Weinberger won this debate, by a vote of 271 to 240, thereby astonishing the American embassy staff in London, which had urged him not to participate in it, and eliciting a congratulatory phone call early the next morning from Mrs. Thatcher herself.[2] That was a little over a decade ago—but look how far we've come.

The concern most often voiced these days is that the United States is too passive rather than too aggressive. There may well be more people in the world now who fear American weakness than who worry about American imperialism. Many Americans themselves welcome their country's diminished profile on the international stage, and see greater costs than benefits in continuing to try to be number one.

And of course our great erstwhile adversary the Soviet Union, morally equivalent or not, no longer even exists. Were the Oxford Union to restage such a debate today, several former officials of that government might eagerly participate, but for the purpose of condemning their own side. The general drift of the memoirs that have emerged from surviving Soviet Cold Warriors is not unlike that of Robert McNamara on the Vietnam War: "We were wrong, horribly wrong."[3]

Chinese historians these days take a similarly critical view of their country's policies under Mao, and certainly few East European scholars would defend the old regimes in that region. Nor would there be much sympathy within the Third World for earlier efforts there to follow the Soviet and Chinese examples.[4] Indeed, I would venture to say that the people now most likely to sympathize with E. P. Thompson's "moral equivalency" position—or at least a watered-down version of it—are some of my colleagues within the American academic community.

Controversies

Consider two issues that have suddenly made the writing and teaching of history a hot political issue. One is the controversy over the so-called "National History Standards," the other is the flap—there is no better word for it—over the Smithsonian Institution's abortive effort to mount a fiftieth anniversary exhibit on the decision to drop the atomic bomb.[5]

The National History Standards emerged from a federally funded commission that was to draw up guidelines for the teaching of history in the secondary schools. Drafted by prominent historians in all fields, these were meant to shape not only classroom instruction but also the textbooks and other teaching materials to be used in providing it. The intent was to bring secondary school instruction into line with the best and most advanced trends in scholarly historical research.

The atomic bomb exhibit grew out of the decision made some time ago to mount a display of the fuselage of the *Enola Gay* at the National Air and Space Museum, a branch of the Smithsonian in Washington. A carefully prepared set of texts and photographs was to accompany this exhibit, once again with a view to providing a context for this imposing historical artifact that would reflect current lines of scholarly research.

Both efforts misfired badly, it's now fair to say, in the sense that, far from generating a consensus on how to look at the past, they sparked controversies that went well beyond what those responsible for these projects ever imagined might happen.

The National Standards have attracted the ire of editorial writers, politicians, and talk-show hosts. In a rare display of near-unanimity, the United States Senate voted ninety-nine to one to condemn them—the nay vote was from a senator who thought the proposed condemnation not strong enough. The charge, fair or not, is that the National Standards have deliberately focused on what has been violent or unjust or depraved about the American experience, at the expense of most of what has been good about it. We are portrayed, or so the critics argue, as a nation of victims—and victimizers.

The *Enola Gay* controversy has fueled an equally vociferous debate featuring many of the same participants; joining them here, though, have been hordes of outraged veterans. The charge is that the curators at the Smithsonian focused on the horrors brought about by the decision to use the bomb as well as the possibility that it might not even have been needed to defeat the Japanese, but neglected what the Japanese themselves had done to start the war in the first place and what Americans at the time—both the policymakers and the troops about to storm the beaches—thought it was going to cost to force their surrender.

These two episodes have in common a tendency to treat the American experience—whether throughout the entire sweep of American history or with respect to the specific decision to use the bomb—in ways that reject American exceptionalism and tilt toward a kind of "moral equivalency." The American record, the National Standards imply, is about as bad as that of any other country; certainly the effect of the new guidelines is to shift the emphasis in teaching American history away from the idea of the United States serving as an example for the rest of the world. Or, at least, if we are to provide examples, they are henceforth to be of what to avoid.

The atomic bomb decision, the Smithsonian exhibit implied, was an act of vengeance, motivated by racism and by a determination to intimidate the Russians in the developing Cold War, rather than by any sincere belief that it might be necessary to end World War II. The suggestion is that we were at least as vicious as the Japanese in the way we fought the war, and that, having won it, we then proceeded to start another large and unnecessary conflict with the Soviet Union.

Now, there is certainly room for legitimate argument on these points; nor has there been any absence of it, even among historians, who have by no means unanimously supported either the National Standards or the Smithsonian curators. And surely there is a great deal to be said for taking a good hard look at all of the episodes in our past: the teaching of history is supposed to encourage the making of critical judgments. Smugness and self-congratulation are not what we should be about—especially since Americans are, by their nature, so notoriously good at smugness and self-congratulation.

But neither should we indulge in the questionable pleasures of self-flagellation. Coming to grips with our own history does not require that we emulate the example of those early Christian saints who wandered around in the desert or lived on top of tall poles, mortifying the body in the belief that only this would save the soul.

What the National Standards and the *Enola Gay* controversies have revealed, more clearly than any of us had previously realized, is the extent of the gap that now exists between scholarly research and writing on American history, on the one hand, and what the American public believes about its history, on the other. That is an interesting intellectual problem—and perhaps also a methodological problem—for historians.

But what is much more serious is the political problem, because the existence of this gap between scholarly and public perceptions is setting the principles of democracy and freedom of inquiry at odds with one another. The scholars are asking: What basis does anyone, whether inside or outside of government, have for challenging academic freedom, however unpopular the conclusions it produces? If *we* the professors say oppression is the dominant theme in American history, then that's what our kids should learn. The politicians, responding to their constituents, are asking: What obligation do *we* have to spend public funds to support research that undermines our most fundamental values and institutions? If our kids are taught to hold these in contempt, what future is there for them?

Or, to put it another way, the historians are saying, "Isn't it awful?" The people, through their representatives, are responding, "Compared to what?"

Cultural Transplantation

It is curious that this debate arose so soon after the Cold War ended, for some of the same scholars who condemn the oppressiveness of our culture at home have taken a rather different line in explaining how we won the Cold War. It was not so much the wisdom of our policies, they have insisted—it was the seductiveness of our life style. Marxism-Leninism just could not compete with blue jeans, rock music, and American television exports. We have become, according to this view, not just a city on a hill, but a multi-megawatt antenna, drowning most of the other signals out there.[6]

But isn't there a problem here? After all, nobody *forced* "I Love Lucy" or MTV or the Simpsons (take your pick, Bart or O.J.) on the rest of the world. There was always the option of switching the channel. If the American domestic example was as dreadful as the National History Standards suggest, why did it have so much appeal abroad, an appeal that went well beyond the pop-culture icons I've invoked here? Why did American culture, to say nothing of the American example in organizing politics or markets or the protection of human rights, spread as widely as it did during the second half of the twentieth century?

Think of it as a simple matter of comparative transplantation. For whatever reason, the American model took root more readily in other parts of the world than did that of its major Cold War adversary, the Soviet Union—this despite the fact that Marxism-Leninism was, from the start, an *internationalist* ideology that deliberately sought transplantation. Or think of transplantation in another sense, that of emigration. The United States remains one of the major countries of choice for those fleeing oppression in their own homelands. But victims normally seek to move away from, not toward, the sources of their victimization.

So there is an interesting clash between the argument that our culture is oppressive, on the one hand, and the claim that its attractiveness is what ended the Cold War, on the other. One cannot, without considerable strain, have it both ways.

Old Cold War History

This contradiction becomes all the more interesting in the light of what has been happening within the field of Cold War history since the Cold War came to an end. What used to be thought of as new approaches are suddenly showing their age, while what might recently have been regarded as old approaches have taken on a renewed vitality.[7]

Two decades ago, references to the "old" Cold War history would have called up images of the so-called "orthodox" interpretation, perhaps best exemplified in the works of such scholars as Herbert Feis, John Spanier, and Arthur Schlesinger, Jr., who tended to see that conflict much as American officials of the time did. It had been a challenge to the values and even the lives of free men everywhere, mounted through the use of a militantly expansionist world revolutionary ideology by a totalitarian regime different from that of Hitler only in its craftiness, its patience, and its sophistication in appealing to the downtrodden throughout the world.

Only a heroic Western response, led by reluctant Americans who would rather have been doing other things, managed to frustrate the Soviet design with such measures as the Truman Doctrine, the Marshall Plan, NATO, and the reaction to military aggression in Korea. Without it, these "orthodox" historians have argued, the world would have descended into a new dark age. The Americans came along at just the right time, stuck their finger in the dike, and then proceeded to rebuild the entire structure so that it held against the flood and thereby saved Western civilization. So much for the "orthodox" view.

A decade ago, references to the "old" Cold War history might well have added to the "orthodox" interpretation a totally different explanation of the coming of the Cold War, put forward by the so-called "revisionist" historians of the 1960s and early 1970s. Following in the tradition of William Appleman Williams, these scholars saw the United States itself as the source of whatever expansionist tendencies existed in the postwar world, for the simple reason that capitalism, by its very nature, requires access to markets, investment opportunities, and sources of raw materials. Alternative ways of organizing society were direct challenges and could not be allowed to succeed.

It followed from this—and was argued, with varying degrees of intensity, by historians like Gabriel Kolko, Walter LaFeber, Lloyd Gardner, and Thomas McCormick—that the Cold War arose from the efforts of the United States, accompanied by nervous but co-opted allies, to throttle, defang, or if all else failed at least buy out revolutions throughout the world. The interests of market capitalism and social justice, from this perspective, were thoroughly at odds with one another. So much for the "revisionist" view.

Today, I would further expand my definition of the "old" Cold War history to include several other explanations that gained prominence during the 1970s and became even more widespread during the 1980s. One of these would be post-revisionism, a well-intentioned but ill-defined effort to find common ground between the earlier "orthodox" and "revisionist" interpretations. A good deal of my own writing falls into this rather mushy category: the idea was that if only we could take the strongest elements of these two previous approaches, discard the weaker ones, and ground the whole thing as much as possible in whatever archives were available, then truth would emerge.[8]

Such differences in interpretation seem less significant now that the Cold War is over; indeed, what is interesting from today's perspective is how much they have in common. These shared features, I think, are going to cause a new generation of Cold War historians to regard all of these earlier interpretations as "old" Cold War history. They include:

(1) *Americocentrism:* Almost all of these accounts approached the Cold War from the perspective of the United States, its allies, or its clients. There was little sense of the Cold War as a rivalry in which there were *two* great centers of power, each interacting with the other; or in which less powerful states nonetheless carved out for themselves a certain amount of autonomy through their capacity to manipulate the superpowers.

To the extent that Americocentrists did see the Cold War as an international system, they tended to do so through a kind of billiard-ball model, borrowed from the so-called "realist" theories of international relations, in which collisions between states were important, but not their character. That brings us to another characteristic of the old Cold War history, which was:

(2) *Neglect of ideology:* Apart from some of the earliest "orthodox" Cold War histories written in the late 1940s and the early 1950s, surprisingly little attention was paid to the fact that one side in that conflict based its legitimacy upon a Marxist-Leninist authoritarian ideology, while the other espoused a looser but no less ideological vision grounded in democratic and capitalist values.

One reason for this neglect, I think, was the lingering legacy of McCarthyism within the American academic community. The excesses of the 1950s so traumatized us that, by the time I entered graduate school in the mid-1960s, to talk about the ideological roots of Soviet foreign policy was to sound a little like a member of the John Birch Society, if not Tail-Gunner Joe himself. Even in the field of Soviet studies, where ideology could hardly be dismissed, it tended to be explained as a rationalization for actions already decided upon rather than as a guide to action.[9]

Once again, the international relations theorists reinforced our thinking in this regard. Had it not been Hans Morgenthau himself who established that all nations, regardless of their domestic constitutional structure or their ideological predisposition, seek power? Had it not been Kenneth Waltz who dismissed as unscientific attempts to relate what he called "unit-level behavior"—where surely ideology would reside—to the workings of the international system?[10]

(3) *The absence (even in most orthodox histories) of a moral dimension:* Remember where realism came from in the first place. As conceived by Morgenthau, E. H. Carr, and George F. Kennan, it was a reaction against what the latter had called the "moralistic-legalistic" strain in the policies of the Western democracies that had taken hold with Woodrow Wilson, the Fourteen Points, and the League of Nations, and had so abysmally failed to prevent World War II.[11]

To be fair, the founding fathers of realism never entirely dismissed moral concerns. Morgenthau tried to find ways to integrate them into his theory; Kennan was certainly aware of them as a result of his exposure to Stalin's Russia; and another of those founding fathers was Reinhold Niebuhr, one of this century's most profound thinkers about the connection between morality and reality.

It is correct to say, though, that the realists regarded the arena of international relations as cold and cruel, a place where power relationships would dominate and even democratic states could not expect to apply the same standards of behavior that they did at home—that is, if they wished to survive. These realists themselves tended to be "moral relativists," if not explicitly believers in "moral equivalency," when it came to what the United States and its allies would have to do to survive in a hostile and power-dominated world.[12]

That quality of "moral relativism," and in some cases even "moral equivalency," certainly showed up in subsequent approaches to Cold War history. As a consequence, there was surprisingly little discussion within any of the major schools of the role of ideas in the Cold War—whether from an ideological or a moral point of view. Not, that is, until the summer of 1989, when Francis Fukuyama pointed out that the idea of democracy was about to end that conflict altogether, and all of history as well.[13]

Fukuyama, as it happened, was right about the Cold War but wrong about history. And it is to what I would call the "new" Cold War history—by which I mean the kind that is being written now, *after* the Cold War has come to an end—that I now want to turn. It is one in which ideas, ideologies, and morality are going to be central.

New Cold War History

It is hardly surprising that the end of a particular conflict should cause reassessments of it. To note this is not to fall into presentism so much as it is simply to acknowledge the inestimable advantage of knowing how things came out. Reaching the end of a historical process always elicits new insights into how it operated. That is why the end of the Cold War would have provided significant opportunities for a rethinking, and a rewriting, of Cold War history, even if we had no new sources with which to work.

But we do have new documents, memoirs, and oral histories, in ever increasing volume, from the former Soviet Union, the People's Republic of China, and Eastern Europe. A good indicator of how much exists is to compare the first *Bulletin* of the Woodrow Wilson Center's Cold War International History Project, which monitors these new materials, with the more recent ones. The first issue, published in the spring of 1992, came in at thirty-two pages. The sixth one, which appeared in early 1996, is almost three-hundred pages.

For decades, we wrote Cold War history pretty much in the way we used to look at the moon: we could see only one side of it. That told us a good deal and even gave us some basis for speculating about what the side that faced away from the earth might be like. But until the first lunar orbiters actually reached the other side and sent back photos of it, we didn't really know what was there.

These new archival sources give us, for the first time, a comparable ability to know what was on the "other side" during the Cold War. The release of these materials has by no means been a clear, consistent, or uncontroversial process, far from it. They are sure to raise at least as many questions as they answer. But that is not much different, again, from where things stood when we got the first view of the dark side of the moon. At least we know much better now what there is to argue about.

It's now clear that one of the things that will be worth arguing about is the topic with which I began: the question of "moral equivalency."

Body Counts

Let me provide some examples from the new sources that illustrate why it will be difficult to write and teach Cold War history without reference to moral issues. Let me also use these examples to advance a few suggestions about how we ought to go about making moral judgments in history in the first place.

Begin—pardon my gruesomeness—with body counts. Lionel Trilling once warned of the dangers of letting history become so dispassionate, so abstract, so concerned with the long view, that "the corpse[s] and the hacked limbs [come to seem] not so very terrible. . . . "[14] Interestingly, General George C. Marshall had a similar view. As he recalled of World War II: "I was very careful to send Mr. Roosevelt every few days a statement of our casualties. . . . You get hardened to these things and you have to be very careful to keep them always in the forefront of your mind."[15]

We have long considered that Hitler's crime of deliberately slaughtering six million Jews and other victims in the Holocaust put him beyond the pale of civilized society. These bodies bulk so large in our view of Hitler that they overshadow everything else we know or think important about him. As a consequence, no serious historian would argue that we could or should have attempted to negotiate with such a monster. There was no common ground—all you could do was to try to destroy him and the regime he created. These days the only differences among historians have to do with whether or not we accomplished that task as quickly and efficiently as possible.

Where does that leave us, though, with the new evidence we have about the victims of Stalin and Mao Zedong? One recent but reliable estimate suggests that Stalin's *domestic* victims alone—when one totals not only the figures for the purges but also for the collectivization of agriculture and the famine that resulted from it—numbered about twenty million dead. This does not count the additional acknowledged twenty-seven million Soviet citizens who died as a result of World War II.[16] But this is not the worst of it. Estimates of those who died in one single episode—the Chinese famine produced by Mao's ill-conceived Great Leap Forward from 1958 to 1961—now come to some thirty million, thereby qualifying the Chairman (whose image was once a popular adornment for t-shirts and dormitory wall posters in the West) as perhaps the greatest mass murderer of all time.[17]

Should that make a difference to us? We've long since agreed that it does with Hitler: the blood on his hands defines who he was and how he will be remembered. But what about Stalin and Mao? The dominant tendency in most of what has been written about the Cold War has been to treat them as more or less "normal" statesmen, and certainly many Cold War historians have made the case that we should have tried harder than we did to get along with them.[18]

But if you take the opposite line—that the blood on Stalin's and Mao's hands put them in the same league with Hitler—are you then prepared to say that we should never have collaborated with the Soviet Union to defeat Nazi Germany in World War II? Or that Richard Nixon should never have gone to Beijing? I have no easy answers to these questions; indeed, the more one thinks about them, the more difficult they become. But there are, I think, several things we as historians can do with this kind of information.

First, we must never ignore it. We should follow General Marshall's example and keep it in the forefront of our minds. Respect for the dead, if nothing else, requires that we not allow ourselves to become so hardened to this evidence that we take it for granted, or so naive that we try to sustain "moral equivalency" arguments in the face of it. The body count alone—the simplest and most elemental basis for making moral judgments in history—would seem to preclude that.

Second, we need to acknowledge that not only were there real bodies; there were also real consequences. Stalin's and Mao's atrocities, like Hitler's, had a profound impact on the societies in which they occurred, ultimately undermining the legitimacy of the regimes that perpetrated them. The fact that the Soviet Union no longer exists, and that China today is a very different kind of place from what it was in the Chairman's day, is to no small extent the result of their own policies and the enormous human cost they exacted.

Third, we need to take more seriously than we have the question of whether regimes that treat their own people this brutally are not likely to behave similarly toward the outside world. International relations theorists have shown quite convincingly that democratic regimes tend not to go to war with one another—that civil society at home tends to project itself onto the international scene. But what about the other side of the equation? What about authoritarian societies and the terror that sustains them? Are such states ever "normal" states, to be dealt with in normal ways?

Domestic Culture and External Behavior

That brings me to a second aspect of morality and Cold War history, which is the extent to which the *nature* of the regimes in question affected the evolution of that conflict. Let me focus here on just one case, drawn from the new information available to us. It has to do with what happened in Germany in 1945 and 1946 as the citizens of that defeated state confronted their respective occupiers.

It is now reasonably clear that what Stalin really wanted in Germany was both division *and* reunification: establishing a separate communist regime in eastern Germany would in time, be believed, provide a kind of magnet that would attract Germans in the western occupation zones without requiring the use of force—something the Russians could ill afford, given the exhaustion of their own country and the Americans' monopoly over the atomic bomb.[19]

Obviously, this is not what happened. Germans first voted with their feet—fleeing to the West in huge numbers to avoid the Red Army—and then at the ballot box in ways that frustrated all that Stalin had hoped for. But this outcome was not foreordained. There were large numbers of communist party members throughout Germany at the end of the war, and their prestige—because of their opposition to the Nazis—had never been higher. Why did the Germans so overwhelmingly welcome the Americans and their allies, and fear the Russians?

It has long been known that the Red Army behaved brutally toward German civilians in those parts of the country that it occupied. This contrasted strikingly with the treatment accorded the Germans in the American, British, and French zones. What we did not know, until recently, is that the problem of rape was much larger than once thought. Red Army soldiers, it now appears, raped as many as two million German women in 1945 and 1946.[20] There was no significant effort to stop this pattern of behavior or to discipline those who indulged in it. To this day, surviving Soviet officers tend to recall the phenomenon much as Stalin saw it at the time: troops that had risked their lives and survived deserved a little fun.[21]

Now, obviously rape in particular, and brutality in general, is always a problem when armies occupy the territory of defeated adversaries. Certainly Russian troops had good reason to hate the Germans, given what they had done inside the Soviet Union. But these semisanctioned mass rapes took place precisely during the period when Stalin was trying to win the support of German people, not just in the east but throughout the country. He even allowed elections to be held inside the Soviet zone in the fall of 1946, and suffered keen embarrassment when the Germans—the women in particular—voted overwhelmingly against the Soviet-supported candidates.[22]

The incidence of rape and brutality was so much greater on the Soviet than on the Western side that it played a major role in determining which way the Germans would tilt in the Cold War that was to come. It ensured a pro-Western orientation among all Germans from the very beginning of that conflict, which surely helps to explain why the West German regime was able to establish itself as a legitimate government and the East German regime never could. This pattern, in turn, replicated itself on a larger scale when the West Europeans *invited* the United States to organize the NATO alliance and include them within it. The Warsaw Pact, a Soviet creation *imposed* on Eastern Europe in reaction to NATO, operated on quite a different basis.[23]

What happened here was not so much a matter of deliberate policy as it was one of occupying armies reflecting their own domestic institutions, cultures, and standards of acceptable behavior. The rules of civil society implicit in democratic politics made the humanitarian treatment of defeated enemies seem natural to the Western allies. They didn't have to be ordered to do this—they just did it, and it didn't occur to them to do otherwise. Much the same thing happened, with equally important long-term results, in occupied Japan. But the Russian troops came out of a culture of brutality unparalleled in modern history. Given this background, it did not occur to many of them that there was anything wrong with brutalizing others. And it did not occur to their leaders to put a stop to the process, despite the fact that it lost them Germany.

In this instance, then, the existence of moral standards on one side and their absence on the other played a huge role in determining the course of events. Idealistic behavior turned out to have very realistic consequences. What this suggests is that, in thinking about moral issues in history, we would do well—in addition to counting bodies—to look carefully at what the people who actually had to confront these issues thought and did about them.

For when people vote with their feet they have ideas in their minds. But to understand these, we have to take seriously what *people at the time* believed, not just historians in retrospect. No historian looking at the religious practices of late antiquity, or at the medieval peasantry, or even at revolutions in America, France, or Russia, would quarrel with that proposition.

And yet, some of those same historians, when looking at the origins, the evolution, and the end of the Cold War—or for that matter at the gap between public and academic perceptions of the past today—take the view that it is the professionals who ought to tell the public what its memory of the past should be. Sometimes I think it wouldn't hurt for us as historians to indulge in a little self-scrutiny, to ask ourselves whether we are really treating the distant past and the recent past in exactly the same way.

The Bomb—and Alternatives

Finally, and in that regard, let me mention a third case in Cold War history where I think morality made a difference. It gets us back to the debate over the *Enola Gay,* for it has to do with the atomic bomb and its impact on the history of the world since 1945. And it raises yet another point about making moral judgments in history, which has to do with the need to consider alternatives to what actually took place.

The *Enola Gay* controversy focused narrowly on whether or not the United States did the right thing in dropping atomic bombs on Hiroshima and Nagasaki in August 1945. Implied in it, though, is a much larger issue: What are the moral implications of having been the *only* nation, so far, to use nuclear weapons against human targets? That is where the question of alternatives come in, and it does so in several different ways.

First, what would have been the alternative, within the immediate context of August 1945, to using the bomb? Even if Japan *was* on the verge of surrender at that point as a result of Soviet entry into the war, as some have suggested, would the number of lives required to bring about that capitulation have been less than the number expended in the two atomic bombings? The continued conventional bombing of Japanese cities, together with either a naval blockade or a ground invasion, could easily have cost as many lives—allied and Japanese—as the more than two hundred thousand taken in these two attacks and their aftereffects.

Second, would there have been a Cold War with the Soviet Union if the two atomic bombs had not been used? Were they the crucial determinant in bringing about that event? Although American officials certainly did have in mind the effect the bomb would produce on the Soviet Union, that was not the primary reason they dropped it. The very fact that these thoughts occurred to them suggests that the roots of the Cold War *predated* the atomic bombs. Where did ideas about the need to intimidate the Russians come from in the first place, if not from the prior behavior of the Russians in Central and Eastern Europe?

Third, would atomic bombs have been developed in the absence of the decision to use them in 1945? Is the United States therefore responsible for bringing atomic energy into the realm of military technology? The answer here is quite clear: several other nations were aware of the military potential of atomic energy and had launched programs to explore these possibilities during the war—the Soviet Union first among them.[24] There is no reason whatever to think that, in the absence of actual use in 1945, no such weapons would ever have been developed.

Fourth, would it have made a difference if the world had learned of the existence of atomic weapons by less violent means? If they had simply been tested and their existence then announced? Perhaps, but not necessarily in a desirable way. One advantage of military use was that the horror of atomic weapons fixed itself in people's minds at the moment they learned of their existence. Had an awareness of existence preceded an awareness of capabilities, it is not clear that the world—or the two Cold War superpowers—would have held these lethal instruments in such awe.

Fifth, would it have made a difference if another nation had developed atomic weapons first? Here it is worth pointing out the irony that the world's principal democracy wound up being the first nation to build—and the only nation to use—the world's most horrible weapon. Questions of human rights played a major role in determining this outcome, for many of the scientists who developed the bomb had come to the United States during the 1930s as refugees from Nazi Germany. It is also worth noting that, having used the bomb, the United States then handled its four years of actual monopoly—and perhaps a decade, altogether, of effective monopoly—with surprising restraint.

Why didn't the United States exploit its advantage to keep the Soviet Union from developing its own bomb? Or to avoid near-defeat in Korea? These are complicated questions, but one of the answers that comes up, when one looks at what American officials said to each other, is the conviction that a democracy could only use such a weapon as a last resort, and in self-defense.[25]

But that in turn raises another interesting question of comparative morality: would an authoritarian system—one based on an ideology that explicitly justified any means necessary to achieve its ends, one that employed terror as a method of government, and one as casual about the loss of human life as were Stalin's and Mao's—have shown similar restraint had it got the bomb first?

There is no way to answer any of these questions authoritatively, but posing them in these counterfactual terms is a useful exercise because it makes us see that history did not have to happen in the way that it did. There might have been better ways to have handled these situations. There might also have been worse ways.

Conclusion

All of this suggests, then, several things about the relationship of morality to the writing of Cold War history—or to any kind of history.

First, what people believe is at least as important as what they do. Historians have an obligation to make the imaginative leap from their own time to whatever age in the past they are writing about and try to figure out what was going on in the minds of those who lived then. It is critically important to take people from the past on their *own* terms and *only* after having done so to make judgments about them based upon our terms.

Second, it follows that ideas, ideologies, and moral frameworks become very significant. We have gone too far looking at the Cold War within a materialist framework devoid of moral content. This was, from the outset, a struggle for people's *minds* as well as for their bodies and their possessions. We are sure to understand it badly if we fail to take that fact into account.

Third, the history of the Cold War shows the gap between domestic and international spheres to have been less pronounced than the diplomatic historians or international relations theorists have led us to believe. Whether states were democratic or autocratic at home made an enormous difference in how they behaved in the world at large—and whether they prevailed, in the end.

Fourth, nobody today would claim that the *domestic* systems of the Western democracies and the Marxist-Leninist states were morally equivalent. The body count alone has ruled that out. But if the line between domestic and international behavior is indeterminate, then that would appear to make moral equivalency arguments with respect to foreign policy during the Cold War seem tenuous as well.

Fifth, what all of this suggests is that perhaps the Cold War really was, as Cap Weinberger explained to E. P. Thompson in that fabled year 1984, about individual freedom and the ability to pass it along to our kids. George Orwell, I believe, would not have disagreed.

But these conclusions, in turn, suggest the need for us as professional historians to rethink some of our academic approaches to this subject. We need to cultivate the art of critical celebration as well as condemnation: the idea of "criticism," as I understand it, involves the possibility for praise as well as for blame. We need to be able to cite, discuss, and explain those instances in which we did the right thing as well as those in which we did not. We need to avoid the pitfalls of *both* excessive self-congratulation *and* self-flagellation.

We need to stay in touch with what people outside our profession think. Professionalization can wall us off from some of the most important objects of our inquiry, opening up unhealthy gaps in the ways the academic world and the general public view the past.

We need to be careful about the methodological metaphors we keep in our minds. Too much of Cold War history was written as if its major contenders were indeed featureless billiard balls, whose internal composition and character didn't much matter. In retrospect, apples and oranges might have been the better metaphor: at least it would have allowed for irregularity, asymmetry, and the possibility of internal rot.

Finally, we may need to rediscover a very old idea: that there are such things as good and evil in history, and that part of our task as historians is not just to know them when we see them but to devise more explicit criteria for making such distinctions in the first place. If the history of our lamentable century has taught us anything at all, it ought to be how appalling the consequences can be when the moral constraints on human behavior, for whatever reason, drop away.

But this is an ancient truth, and surely we knew it, in our hearts, all along. Perhaps it is time we moved it back into our minds, as well as into the way in which we write, teach, and presumably still retain the capacity to learn from the field in which we work.

NOTES

1. Dean Rusk, *As I Saw It* (New York: Norton, 1990), 72–73.

2. Barton Gellman, "Weinberger Victorious in Oxford Debate," *Washington Post,* February 28, 1984. See also Caspar Weinberger, *Fighting for Peace: Seven Critical Years in the Pentagon* (New York: Warner Books, 1990), 169–70.

3. Robert S. McNamara, with Brian VanDeMark, *In Retrospect: The Tragedy and Lessons of Vietnam* (New York: Random House, 1995), xvi. For two examples of such Soviet memoirs, see Georgi Arbatov, *The System: An Insider's Life in Soviet Politics* (New York: Times Books, 1992); and Anatoly Dobrynin, *In Confidence: Moscow's Ambassador to America's Six Cold War Presidents (1962–1986)* (New York: Times Books, 1995).

4. The best single source for these new materials is the *Bulletin* of the Cold War International History Project at the Woodrow Wilson International Center for Scholars, Smithsonian Institution, indefatigably edited by James Hershberg.

5. Bibliographies on both of these controversies are already enormous. The most balanced coverage has probably appeared in the *Chronicle of Higher Education.*

6. This appeared to be the conclusion of a roundtable at the 1995 annual convention of the Society for Historians of American Foreign Relations on "Culture and Diplomacy," which featured Emily Rosenberg, Walter Hixson, Robert McMahon, and Jessica Gienow.

7. See, on this point, Douglas J. Macdonald, "Communist Bloc Expansion in the Early Cold War: Challenging Realism, Refuting Revisionism," *International Security* 20 (Winter 1995/96), 152–88.

8. A good recent review of Cold War historiography is Anders Stephanson, "The United States," in David Reynolds, ed., *The Origins of the Cold War in Europe: International Perspectives* (New Haven: Yale University Press, 1994), 23–52.

9. Martin Malia, *The Soviet Tragedy: A History of Socialism in Russia, 1917–1991* (New York: Free Press, 1994), strongly criticizes Soviet studies for neglecting the importance of ideology.

10. The classic texts, of course, are Hans J. Morgenthau, *Politics Among Nations: The Struggle for Power and Peace* (New York: Knopf, 1948), with five subsequent editions; and Kenneth N. Waltz, *Theory of International Politics* (New York: Random House, 1979).

11. See, in addition to Morgenthau, Edward Hallett Carr, *The Twenty Years' Crisis, 1919–1939: An Introduction to the Study of International Relations* (New York: St. Martin's Press, 1939); and George F. Kennan, *American Diplomacy: 1900–1950* (Chicago: University of Chicago Press, 1951).

12. For more on the moral relativists, see John Lewis Gaddis, *The United States and the End of the Cold War: Implications, Reconsiderations, Provocations* (New York: Oxford University Press, 1992), 55–57.

13. Francis Fukuyama, "The End of History?" *National Interest* 16 (Summer 1989), 3–18.

14. Quoted in Gertrude Himmelfarb, *On Looking into the Abyss: Untimely Thoughts on Culture and Society* (New York: Knopf, 1994), 117.

15. Quoted in Forrest C. Pogue, *George C. Marshall: Organizer of Victory* (New York: Viking, 1973), 316.

16. Malia, *Soviet Tragedy,* 263.

17. Basil Ashton, Kenneth Hill, Alan Piazza, and Robin Zeitz, "Famine in China, 1958–61," *Population and Development Review* 10 (December 1984), 613–45.

18. A recent example is Melvyn P. Leffler's justifiably prize-winning *A Preponderance of Power: National Security, the Truman Administration, and the Cold War* (Stanford: Stanford University Press, 1992).

19. R. C. Raack, "Stalin Plans His Post-War Germany," *Journal of Contemporary History* 28 (1993), 53–73 provides a useful overview of Stalin's plans.

20. Norman M. Naimark, *The Russians in Germany: A History of the Soviet Zone of Occupation, 1945–1949* (Cambridge: Harvard University Press, 1995), 69–140, is an eloquent and compelling account.

21. See the interviews with Red Army officers in part one of the recent British television series "Messengers From Moscow"; also Milovan Djilas, *Conversations with Stalin,* trans. Michael B. Petrovich (New York: Harcourt, Brace and World, 1962), 95.

22. Naimark, *Russians in Germany,* 120–21.

23. See, for this distinction, Geir Lundestad, "Empire by Invitation? The United States and Western Europe, 1945–1952," *Journal of Peace Research* 23 (September 1986), 263–77.

24. A point now made clear by David Holloway, *Stalin and the Bomb: The Soviet Union and Atomic Energy, 1939–1956* (New Haven: Yale University Press, 1994); and Richard Rhodes, *Dark Sun: The Making of the Hydrogen Bomb* (New York: Simon and Schuster, 1995).

25. See John Lewis Gaddis, *The Long Peace: Inquiries into the History of the Cold War* (New York: Oxford University Press, 1987), 142.

Part III: ISSUES

Augustus Richard Norton
Drawing the Line on Opprobrious Violence

Lyn S. Graybill
South Africa's Truth and Reconciliation Commission: Ethical and Theological Perspectives

Kristen Renwick Monroe
The Psychology of Genocide

Robert E. Goodin
International Ethics and the Environmental Crisis

Thomas Donaldson
Moral Minimums for Multinationals

David C. Hendrickson

The Ethics of Collective Security

In his *Abstract of the Abbé de Saint-Pierre's Project for Perpetual Peace,* Jean-Jacques Rousseau noted the elements of interdependence among the inhabitants of Europe that made it "a real society." The ease of communications, the rise of a community of knowledge and studies, the complicated ties of commerce that rendered each nation necessary to the others—all had produced in Europe "not merely, as in Asia and Africa, an ideal collection of people, who have nothing in common but a name, but a real society, which has its religion, morals, customs, and even its laws, from which none of the people composing it can separate without causing an immediate disturbance." Far from producing peace, however, the intimacy of their connections had only made their dissensions more fatal:

> To behold . . . the perpetual dissensions, depredations, usurpations, rebellions, wars, and murders, which are constantly ravaging this respectable abode of philosophers, this brilliant asylum of the arts and sciences; to reflect on the sublimity of our conversation and the meanness of our proceedings, on the humanity of our maxims and the cruelty of our actions, on the meekness of our religion and the horror of our persecutions, on a policy so wise in theory and so absurd in practice, on the beneficence of sovereigns and the misery of their people, on governments so mild and wars so destructive; we are at a loss to reconcile these strange contrarieties, while this pretended fraternity of European nations appears to be only a term of ridicule, serving ironically to express their reciprocal animosity.[1]

What Rousseau said of the old European system may also be said of the new world order. Instantaneous global communications (the "CNN effect"), the progressive codification of international law, the growth of international trade, and the newly found prominence of international organizations have all contributed to an unprecedented degree of interdependence among the nations of the world. As in Rousseau's time, however, interdependence is often a breeder of intractable conflict. More pointedly, we are caught up in "strange contrarieties" of our own and often have cause to reflect on the contrast between the humanity of our maxims and the cruelty of our actions, on policies that are wise in theory but absurd in practice. The new world order, confidently proclaimed by President Bush before and after the Gulf War, is normally invoked today as a form of ridicule, or at least of reproach. The end of the Cold War and the successful eviction of Iraq from Kuwait have not been accompanied by a more orderly international environment. Whether one looks at the civil war within Iraq, or the breakdown of Yugoslavia into savage fighting, or the appalling scenes of famine in the Horn of Africa, there is considerable evidence that we are as yet remote from the vision of a new world order proclaimed by the president.

In one respect, to be sure, much of the criticism directed against the president's vision of an orderly world moving steadily toward free institutions seems exaggerated. The Four Horsemen of the Apocalypse have not suddenly made an appearance in human history, making our own age unique in the horrors that it witnesses. Nor indeed is despotic government a recent innovation. What sets the present age apart from the past is, if anything, the belief that the twin ideals of a *pax universalis* and a world governed by liberal democratic regimes represent historical possibilities whose absence is a standing reproach to us. Wishing for something that never was, we appear fated to be disappointed by the gap between an idyllic vision and a depressing reality.

The collapse of the Soviet Union is responsible, above all else, for the resurgence of the hopes for a more democratic and peaceful world. If our most powerful adversary could collapse from its own inner contradictions, there was reason to hope that lesser despotisms might undergo the same process. For many in the West, and particularly in the United States, this development prompted the hope that increased pressure on despotic regimes might yield further successes. At the same time, the emergence of a Russian federation prepared to cooperate with its former adversaries in the UN Security Council made it seem equally plausible that the United Nations, freed from its Cold War stalemate, might succeed in realizing the vision of collective security that animated many of its initial architects.

These developments have produced an unprecedented situation in international society. They have persuaded many observers that we stand today at a critical juncture, one at which the promise of collective security, working through the mechanism of the United Nations, might at last be realized. Just as every discrete crisis during the Cold War came to be seen as symbolic of the larger contest between the United States and the Soviet Union, so every war and civil war today is seen as a test of the new order. Failure, whether in the Gulf, or Yugoslavia, or Cambodia—to name only the more prominent examples—is often portrayed as heralding the collapse of the new order, just as the spread of communism in any country, and by whatever means, was often seen during the Cold War as heralding the collapse of the old order. Global containment lives, but in a new guise: it is now the containment not of an identifiable adversary but of aggression itself, and it is to be organized not through traditional alliances but through an international organization representing the whole of the world community.

The Logic of Collective Security

Collective security as a device for the maintenance of international security is based on the assumption that states form a society, membership in which confers both rights and duties. The principal right each state enjoys is the ability to maintain its political independence and territorial integrity against external aggression; its principal duty is not only to refrain from aggression but also to aid the victims of aggression. Under collective security, war is seen, in Hans Kelsen's words, as either a delict or a sanction.[2] It is either an illegal act that violates the social order or an action of law enforcement that preserves that order.

An essential feature of a collective-security system is the conviction that peace is indivisible. "If history has taught us anything," Harry Truman declared in justifying American participation in the Korean War, "it is that aggression anywhere in the world is a threat to peace everywhere in the world."[3] George Bush gave expression to the same conviction, declaring in 1990 that "every act of aggression unpunished . . . strengthens the forces of chaos and lawlessness that, ultimately, threaten us all."[4]

If aggression is a crime against not only the immediate victim but also the entire foundation of international society, the clear implication is that states have not only a right but also a duty to respond to infractions of the law. There should be no neutrality before the aggressor and his victim. The fulfillment of duty, however, is not seen as requiring the sacrifice of self-interest. Though there may be an apparent conflict between the dictates of self-interest and the duty to international society, it is an apparent conflict only. The indivisibility of peace—the assumption that aggression will spread like a wildfire unless suppressed by the peace-loving members of the international community—indicates that the real choice is not between the duty to oneself and the duty to others but between the present dangers of involvement in the suppression of crime and the far worse future danger that will inevitably come about if aggressors learn that they can profit from their misdeeds.

The more states reason in this fashion, the more likely it is that collective security will constitute an effective system of international security. Collective security aims not at establishing a balance of power among states but at creating a preponderance of power against potential lawbreakers. The more states consult their immediate self-interest and decline effective participation in a collective-security system, by contrast, the more that system comes to resemble the system of alliances and spheres of influence it is meant to replace.

Indeed, the contrast between a system of collective security and a traditional statecraft is striking. Whereas the essence of a traditional statecraft is discrimination on the basis of power, interest, and circumstance, the essence of collective security is precisely the absence of discrimination on the basis of these same factors. To the former, it makes all the difference whether aggression is committed by a small or a great power. To the latter, this distinction is irrelevant. To the former, a state's geographic position must normally determine its response to aggression. To the latter, this too must be viewed as irrelevant: aggression is aggression, irrespective of the identity of the aggressor; the indivisibility of peace precludes a response determined by considerations of geography.

Collective security stands in sharp contrast with the system of international law that prevailed in the nineteenth century. Whereas nineteenth-century publicists conceded to states a right to resort to war and made no distinction between just and unjust causes in the resort to force, collective security pushes considerations of *jus ad bellum* to the forefront—a difference in approach that, as we shall see, has important implications for the status of the rules regulating the conduct of war. Whereas the nineteenth-century doctrines considered neutrality a highly valuable institution for the geographic limitation of armed conflict and prescribed an intricate set of rules for belligerents and neutrals intended to minimize the disruptions that war entailed for international society, collective security casts into moral disrepute the institution of neutrality and, if the UN Security Council so decides, makes neutrality illegal when an enforcement action under Chapter VII of the UN Charter is undertaken.

Whereas nineteenth-century doctrines considered particular

alliances as a normal and justifiable feature of international society, collective security must view alliances between particular states with alarm. Such particular alliances are either superfluous or dangerous: superfluous insofar as they provide a security guarantee to particular states that they already enjoy by virtue of their membership in the society of states, and dangerous insofar as they advertise the fact that those states participating in a particular community of states consider their own security of greater importance than the security of states generally. It is true that the Charter of the United Nations makes allowance for regional organizations to keep the peace. Nevertheless, there is the danger that such regional organizations will become substitutes for, rather than complements of, the system of universal security that the theory of collective security prescribes.

Given the importance that the theory of collective security places on the sovereign equality of states, one of the most striking features of the institutional mechanism by which that vision is to be effected today is the extraordinary role given to the great powers in the UN Security Council. There is little that is novel in the principle of a great-power directorate presiding over the peace and order of the world. That principle had been a foundation of the settlement following the Napoleonic wars in the early nineteenth century. Nor had it been absent from the plan of a new world order worked out at Versailles following World War I. Even so, the distinctive position accorded the great powers in the League Council pales when set alongside that accorded the victors of World War II by the UN Charter. The provisions of the Charter conferred on the great powers what amounted to an unlimited discretion in matters of peace and security in their role as permanent members of the Security Council, provided only that they remained united in outlook. Yet this extraordinary power vested in the great powers is difficult to reconcile with the egalitarian assumptions of collective-security theory. The real justification of this power is that without it the effectiveness of the organization would inevitably decline.

The effect of collective security on traditional ideas of sovereignty and intervention is not as clear as it might seem at first sight. In theory, collective security is erected on the foundation of respect for the political independence and territorial integrity of states and it consequently forbids intervention into the internal affairs of states. In practice, however, the distinction between what is internal and what is external tends to break down. In the first place, it seems rather arbitrary to restrict international concern to aggressive uses of force between states. It seems artificial to insist that an aggressive use of force across borders, such as Iraq's invasion of Kuwait, requires a massive display of countervailing power while at the same time holding that internal calamities that bring a much greater amount of human suffering, such as those resulting from civil war and drought in the Horn of Africa, cannot be addressed without obtaining the consent of the warring parties. Second, the distinction between civil conflicts and international conflicts is itself not wholly clear in particular circumstances. Nearly every civil conflict contains within itself the germ of an international dispute, since the warring parties normally represent distinct communities that can aspire to statehood of their own. If, as happened in Yugoslavia, the international community confers recognition on secessionist republics, a civil war becomes immediately transformed into an international conflict. More generally, if the international community concerns itself with preventing or settling ethnic conflicts, as many hold that it should do today, it will inevitably find itself regulating the treatment of minorities within existing states and thus involving itself ever more deeply in the most intimate details of internal governance. Finally, a collective-security action may itself give rise to consequences that generate a duty to intervene further into the affairs of the aggressor state. In the Gulf War, the relatively straightforward matter of Iraq's aggression against Kuwait could not be separated from the consequences of reversing it. Those consequences included the civil war that broke out in the aftermath of Desert Storm and, more generally, the humanitarian catastrophe that subsequently descended on Iraq as a cumulative result of war, civil conflict, and economic sanctions. In that instance, claims for further intervention arose because the war itself was plausibly seen as the proximate cause of the civil war, and it appeared inhumane and unjust to walk away from a disaster that was partly of our own making. For each of these reasons, the principle of concern underlying collective security is one that is difficult to reconcile with the principle of nonintervention, on which collective security is ostensibly based.

This is the third time in this century that collective security has appeared on the international horizon as a promising method for assuring international peace and security. It is perhaps no accident that it has risen to prominence each time at the conclusion of a major war (the Cold War being considered, in this context, as a worthy successor to the two world wars of this century). Yet there is little question that the version of collective security favored today is one that is substantially, and in some respects ironically, different from that which prevailed when the League of Nations was established. For Woodrow Wilson, the Covenant of the League was conceived as entailing the search for methods of international conflict resolution that would not continually raise the threat of force, as the nineteenth-century system had done. He placed almost exclusive reliance on the diplomatic and economic isolation of aggressor states; while not wholly dismissing the prospect that the obligations the United States would assume under the Covenant might raise the issue of force—a charge leveled by the opponents of the League in the Senate—Wilson continually reiterated that such occasions were most unlikely to arise. Today, the version of collective security now predominant is much more conscious of the likely necessity of using force to maintain international peace and security. If the emphasis is still placed upon deterrence and not on the potential breakdowns of the system requiring the actual employment of armed force in defense of law, it is nevertheless true that the economic and diplomatic isolation of aggressors on which Wilson relied is now generally considered insufficient to realize the vision of collective security. The contemporary system places a much greater degree of reliance on the necessity of a forceful counterpoise to aggression.

Common Concern and the Just War

The most common criticism directed against the idea of collective security is that it is inherently unworkable. States are, in the main, perfectly willing to pay lip service to the idea of collective security, but they are generally unwilling to make the tangible sacrifices that collective security requires, particularly regarding the commitment of military forces. Critics of collective security have characterized this obstacle in several ways, with some speaking of a conflict between interest and obligation and others of an inherent dispute between the suppliers and consumers of security. The basic objection, as Robert Osgood once observed, is that no "nation in its right mind is willing to subordinate its special security interests to a hypothetical general interest in maintaining a stable international order, especially if that subordination would impose a claim upon its armed forces."[5]

Though this objection, considered abstractly, does indeed have a great deal of force, it seems less than cogent in relation to the current constellation of international power. With the collapse of Soviet power, the United States has emerged, as is often proclaimed, as the world's only military superpower. Though it would be an exaggeration to claim that the international political system is now unipolar, there is no question that the United States possesses a capability of conducting interventions throughout the world and that its military strength is in a class of its own. So long as the United States understands its own interests to be closely bound up with the maintenance of world order—understood here as requiring universal adherence to the norm forbidding aggression—the prospect arises of a world in which the purposes of collective security could be achieved. Because of the critical importance of American leadership in securing this aim, this would not be an order of collective security in the sense that the champions of that system had always imagined. It has been made possible not because a true community of power has suddenly materialized where none existed before but because a hegemonic power has emerged where before there had been a balance of power. Still, if it was to develop and persist, such a hegemonically based order might well achieve the primary objective that collective security seeks.

As noted previously, the advocates of collective security insist that a commitment to the political independence and territorial integrity of other states flows from considerations of both moral duty and self-interest. The latter claim, however, rests upon a highly implausible reading of the likely consequences of aggression. Aggression anywhere is not necessarily a threat to peace everywhere. Peace is normally divisible, and conflicts, whatever their origin, are normally of merely local or regional significance. The primary exception to this rule arises when a great power threatens to dominate the entire states system. It was not unreasonable to find a connection during the Cold War between the successful aggression of a North Korea or a North Vietnam and the encouragement that might thereby have been given to the Soviet Union. Today, circumstances are much different. Insofar as the unanimity among the great powers required by collective security is possible today, the objectives that it seeks appear far less urgent. Indeed, one might even go further and claim that the easiest way to imperil American security interests is through a universal commitment to the territorial integrity and political independence of all states of the international system. Such a commitment is a sure road to war.

Although American security interests do not require the universal commitment that collective security demands, it can be argued more plausibly that there is a moral duty to make such a commitment. A state whose territory has been invaded and that has been robbed of its political independence by a foreign state may justifiably make an appeal for help. Outside parties clearly have a right to respond to such appeals, regardless of whether the concept of *jus ad bellum* is woven into the fabric of international law. The claim that outside parties also have a duty to respond to such appeals, however, is much more uncertain.

Perhaps the most important reason for skepticism in this matter is that an unlimited commitment to the security of other states may seriously conflict with the duties states owe to their own citizens. Insofar as this commitment requires that one's own soldiers be placed in harm's way, it stands in conflict with the duty of states not to cavalierly risk the lives of their own citizens. The commitment may be in tension with the principle of the democratic control of foreign policy; for if, as is sometimes contended, the authorization of the UN Security Council gives the president the right to commit American forces to battle even without congressional authorization, the commitment to collective security may succeed in nullifying the constitutional provision that gives to Congress the right to declare war. More generally, resources that are devoted to external purposes, however conceived, cannot be applied to internal needs, and these remain pressing even for a nation as wealthy as the United States. With substantial portions of our own population mired in poverty, living in cities where the minimum conditions of public order are barely satisfied, it is a morally defensible claim to insist that remedying such disorders is of higher priority than righting wrongs elsewhere in the world.

Because collective security is based on the community of states and not of individuals, its advocates can scarcely fail to recognize that such internal claims do have considerable weight. The value that collective security defends—sovereignty—is important because it stands as a shield behind which communities of people seek to realize their own destinies free from external interference. With one foot of the argument remaining, as it were, in the traditional world, where states are thought justified in giving priority to such internal concerns, the moral weight of the collective-security argument depends to a great degree on the ease with which it might be implemented. Yet it is doubtful that implementing collective security will in fact be easy, particularly for the power that must play the leading role in establishing and maintaining the system.

The idea that states are ethically justified in according primacy to the security and well-being of their own communities rests upon a principle that may be traced throughout a wide range of human transactions and institutions. Alexander Hamilton once identified its psychological basis in noting that "the human affections, like solar heat, lose their intensity, as they depart from the center; and become languid, in proportion to the expansion of the circle, on which they act." Thus, "we love our families, more than our neighbors: We love our neighbors, more than our countrymen in general."[6] So far, at least, as positive duties of aid are concerned, this psychological fact has ethical significance as well. Just as parents have far greater positive responsibilities for their own children than for children in general, so states are justified in according primacy to their own members. If this principle is accepted, it would also seem to follow that it is ethically legitimate to bring some states, but not others, within particular security communities, whether such communities go by the name of alliances or regional collective-security pacts. The United States has "special relationships" with a number of countries—Great Britain, Israel, perhaps Germany and Japan—that have arisen for complex reasons but that are nonetheless genuine and important. Yet if there is a duty to all, the duty we feel or the interest we have in protecting particular states is inevitably devalued.

Even if these considerations are put aside and a generalized duty to come to the aid of threatened states is acknowledged, there are still aspects of collective-security doctrine that are morally troubling. The propensity to view foreign conflicts as involving evil aggressors and innocent victims, which is an inherent feature of *jus ad bellum,* leads almost inexorably to a way of thinking that is at odds with other elements of just war doctrine, particularly that which governs the means the combatants may legitimately use even in a just cause. The progression is by now quite familiar. States resorting to force not only are aggressors but are led by thugs and villains, and journalists and politicians engage in a kind of terminological bidding war to paint the adversary in the darkest features imaginable. The emphasis that the advocates of collective security place on the deterrent effects of crushing aggression reinforces this tendency, for it makes every particular conflict part of a more general struggle against all aggressors and, indeed, against evil itself. This way of reasoning would seem almost inevitably to have the result of loosening the restraints that just-war doctrine imposes on the conduct of war. This is particularly true in relation to the requirement of proportionality—that is, the belief that there must be a rough relationship between the good secured and the evil inflicted in war. For if the good secured is nothing less than defeat of absolute evil, it seems almost a moral necessity to use any means necessary to achieve that end. Every war becomes a supreme emergency, which is to say, one in which the traditional rules may justifiably be dispensed with.

This way of reasoning also conflicts with the just war requirement that every effort be made to discriminate between combatants and noncombatants in the conduct of war. One need not assume, as was commonly done during World War II, that every member of the enemy nation is guilty for the requirement of discrimination to be breached. In practice, it is often very difficult to make these discriminations. However much it is repeated that it is not our intention to punish the people of an enemy nation, they inevitably seem to suffer grievously. In the Gulf War, the economic sanctions that were intended to deprive Saddam of his financial base had the most serious effect on children; military strikes at Iraq's electrical grid, intended to strike at Iraq's system of military communications, had an equally calamitous effect on those least able to bear it.

Collective punishments, though reprobated in theory, are accepted in practice and seem in fact almost inevitable. Bowing to the reality that it is frequently impossible to strike at the guilty without also harming the innocent, something odd happens to the humanitarian sentiments that normally accompany the response to aggression. Intense moral concern over two dozen Kuwaiti babies deprived of their incubators easily passes to moral indifference over a million Iraqi babies deprived of food and clean water. Though it is, of course, possible to reason ourselves out of responsibility for the suffering that might be indirectly attributable to a collective-security action, normally through dubious doctrines of double effect, there is still something disturbing about the ease with which it is done.

Collective security, at least as it was practiced during the Gulf War, also seems at odds with the just war requirement of last resort. It may eliminate the requirement altogether by assuming that the victimized state has already reached its last resort and that outsiders coming to its aid are justified in taking up arms immediately. Or it may insist that the peculiar dynamics of coalition politics severely limit the length of time for trying other options short of war. One of the most insistent arguments for Desert Storm was that the coalition was bound to fall apart, given sufficient time. Unless the United States went to war quickly, the opportunity for doing so would be lost. This argument may have substantially overstated the real time pressures for bringing the crisis to a rapid end, which were overwhelmingly domestic; at the same time, however, the prominence the argument had during the crisis that led to war serves as an ironic reminder that a commitment to collective security may precipitate, rather than delay, the onset of war.

The assumptions underlying the doctrine of collective security may also decrease the likelihood of reaching compromises that might lead to the peaceful resolution of disputes. The conviction that aggression is a crime leads directly to the view that under no circumstances may aggression succeed or even be seen to succeed. President Bush's formula for dealing with Iraq—"no negotiations, no compromises, no attempts at face-saving, and no rewards for aggression"—was a succinct, yet complete, expression of this attitude.[7] The logic of collective security virtually compels its advocates to ensure that an aggressor not only lose but lose spectacularly; it dictates that the criminal nation not only retreat but suffer a profound humiliation in the process; it forecloses negotiations (because they would confer respectability or equality on the enemy). The search for a peaceful resolution of the conflict comes to be regarded as a cowardly form of appeasement and thus constitutes a powerful impetus toward war.

Yet the war that is chosen may not be one that is capable of producing any kind of durable peace. For reasons that are not entirely clear, collective security may produce a kind of protracted stalemate. Partly this is due to the restriction on the means that intervening publics are likely to impose. Any kind of force commitment that risks being protracted or entailing substantial casualties is one from which Western publics instinctively turn away. Air power, in which the pain can be delivered from afar, thus becomes the favored military instrument. Yet air power, though indeed quite capable of sowing confusion and destruction in the enemy's ranks, cannot by itself produce a result that we would recognize as just. Its effects may instead resemble repeated blows against an anthill, killing many of the guilty ants but also producing anarchy. If the unwillingness to consider any compromises that are characteristic of collective-security doctrine is added to the restriction on means that the intervening powers will probably impose, collective security seems almost fated to produce protracted stalemates characterized by substantial amounts of intrastate violence and suffering, rather than the durable peace that it promises.

Two objections may be raised against these considerations. First, it may be claimed on behalf of collective security that the deterrent value of inflexible opposition to aggressors provides benefits that, though largely unseen, are nevertheless critical for the preservation of even a modicum of world order. And second, if the humanitarian effects of going to war weigh too heavily on the conscience, it makes the criteria for going to war so exacting that it becomes almost indistinguishable from pacifism.

Neither of these objections can be dismissed out of hand. The difficulty with the first, however, is that it requires making sacrificial victims of the unfortunates caught up in their own, normally tragic, circumstances. We cease being interested in nudging the parties in Yugoslavia's civil war to compromises that would end the fighting and instead become intent on making an example of the Serbs so that the rest of Eastern Europe and the former Soviet Union will not descend into chaos. This overweening emphasis on the bad precedent that would be set by compromises is a pernicious element in collective-security doctrine, and it is highly doubtful that the inflammation of conflicts to which it contributes is outweighed by the deterrent effects that it brings. Because states are not normally willing to fight unless vital interests are at stake, there will usually be a considerable degree of doubt that the coalition will spring into action; the coalition must therefore be willing to prove its bona fides every time. This is especially so if collective-security doctrine is wrong in its assumption that most conflicts arise because there is an evil aggressor and an innocent victim. If war normally arises through a more circuitous route, with both parties acting out of the conviction that justice is on their side, the deterrent effects of making examples out of evildoers are likely to be greatly overestimated. Most "aggressors" do not, in fact, see themselves as such. They do not generally have the consciousness of evil intent that collective security assumes they must have if they are to be deterred.

The difficulty with the second objection is that so much of what makes collective-security thinking attractive is its avowed adherence to the principles of justice. By acting in accordance with the dictates of collective security, we are asked to act in circumstances where our own vital security interests are not materially threatened; the real justification for acting is that in doing so we are performing a service to mankind by virtue of the protection afforded to innocents. If this is the case, however—if the real justification for collective security is to be found not in the appeal to interest but in the appeal to justice and humanity—we are all the more obliged to take seriously the real humanitarian costs and transgressions of *jus in bello* that military action may entail. There is considerable persuasiveness in the traditional realist argument that the violation of customary legal and moral standards may be countenanced in cases of necessity when, as Machiavelli said, "the safety of the state is in question." To countenance such transgressions in a philanthropic cause appears far less justifiable.

The commission of injustice on behalf of a just cause, to be sure, is not allowable under the just war theory to which advocates of collective security subscribe, and it is certainly the case that the philosophers and moralists who place the concept of aggression at the center of their theory do not also countenance violations of *jus in bello* save in exceptional circumstances ("supreme emergency").[8] To this it might be answered, however, that wars are not fought by philosophers and moralists, and that those who do fight them, and the people who support them, tend to be much less scrupulous regarding the means when they find themselves at war. In the court of public opinion, measures taken to reduce the risk to one's own combatants, even if they require the wholesale slaughter of enemy forces, are seen as wholly unobjectionable, and to raise an objection is deemed a sign of insufficient patriotism or deficient mental equipment. Even military actions that bring foreseeable harm to the civilian population of the enemy state are shrugged off as being part of the hard necessities of war, and a statesman who increased the risk to his own military forces to avoid such harm might well find himself indicted for having needlessly exposed his own soldiers. By postulating a duty to come to the aid of innocent states, collective security removes us from the self-interested world of political action, but we do not remain there for long. As Meinecke said: "Every influx of unpolitical motives into the province of pure conflicts of power and interest brings with it the danger that these motives will be misused and debased by the naturally stronger motives of mere profit, of *raison d'état*. The latter resembles some mud-colored stream that swiftly changes all the pure waters flowing into it into its own murky color."[9] Collective security tends strongly toward such a result in practice. We begin with outrage over the highly publicized atrocities committed by the enemy, and we end by bombing, and more bombing.

Conclusion

These reflections are not intended to suggest that multilateral approaches to "international peace and security" are a bad thing. The necessity of gathering a coalition together to meet any particular crisis provides a certain insurance that the intervening states are aiming for an approximation of the common good and not simply pursuing their selfish interests. The cooperation enjoined by multilateral action is also highly advantageous to international society insofar as it provides rewards to the great powers for cooperating, rather than quarreling, with one another. Since their quarrels are capable of doing the most damage, this must normally be accounted as a good thing.

Despite these considerations, it would be stretching matters to say that the mere existence of multilateralism is conclusive evidence of ethical or prudent action. The need to seek international legitimation may well serve as an excuse for not acting when acting is justifiable on either prudential or ethical grounds. This criticism was plausible during much of the Cold War; arguably, it was also well founded in the aftermath of the Gulf War, when the Bush administration pleaded the doctrine of nonintervention and the need to preserve the international consensus to justify its refusal to intervene in the Iraqi civil war. Conversely, multilateral action may in reality be the result not of a true meeting of the minds but, rather, of the power of a hegemonic state that others are afraid to offend. The prelude to the Gulf War can be seen in such a light, for there can be little doubt that many states had serious reservations over the course chosen by the United States but swallowed their doubts so as not to prejudice their relations with this country. A comparable phenomenon was at work in late 1991, when Britain and France, against their better instincts, went along with Germany's decision to recognize Croatia so as to preserve a unified European front in the immediate aftermath of the Maastricht negotiations. The urge to cooperate and to preserve a united front in negotiations may paradoxically give undue influence to the most unilateral member of a coalition, whose power is increased by virtue of its obstinacy.

One is thus tempted to conclude that multilateral action on behalf of illegitimate ends is no virtue and that unilateral action on behalf of legitimate ends is no vice. At a minimum, the existence of a multilateral imprimatur on an action is not conclusive evidence that it is free from objection on other grounds; conversely, the failure to obtain a multilateral imprimatur does not condemn an action that is otherwise legitimate.

This conclusion does not mean that we should not attempt to make the United Nations more effective, or otherwise cease to work through multilateral institutions. There are certain functions performed by the United Nations, such as the mediation activities contemplated in Chapter VI of the Charter or the provision of peacekeeping troops to uphold a negotiated settlement, that frequently cannot be performed, or performed as well, by any state or group of states acting alone. To this expression of outside concern and mutual aid there can be no substantial objection.

At the same time, however, there is the danger that the commitment to multilateralism will also be seen to imply a commitment to the distinctive method that collective security brings to the resolution of international conflict. That method carries with it a set of attributes that are highly questionable. It discourages the compromises that make possible the peaceful resolution of disputes and thus encourages the resort to war; it promotes a distorted vision of the causes of international violence by converting every particular conflict into a struggle between good and evil; and it encourages, by virtue of the inflated importance given to the ends it pursues, the loosening of the restraints imposed by just war doctrine on the conduct of war. Like the society of states described by Rousseau, the doctrine of collective security may be wise in theory, but it tends toward absurdity in practice. In practice, its most striking attribute is the contrast between the humanity of the maxims it ostensibly observes and the cruelty of the actions that it sanctions. A doctrine whose announced purpose is to create a *pax universalis* that will succeed in prohibiting war among nations has the paradoxical effect of exacerbating the level of violence in the particular wars to which its method is applied.

NOTES

1. Jean-Jacques Rousseau, *Abstract of the Abbé de Saint-Pierre's Project for Perpetual Peace* (1761), in Moorhead Wright, ed., *Theory and Practice of the Balance of Power, 1486–1914* (Totowa, N.J.: Rowman and Littlefield, 1975), 75.

2. Hans Kelsen, *Collective Security under International Law* (Washington, D.C.: Government Printing Office, 1957).

3. Address of April 11, 1951, excerpted in Thomas G. Paterson, ed., *Major Problems in American Foreign Policy*, vol. 2, *Since 1914* (Lexington, Mass.: D.C. Heath, 1989), 408.

4. President George Bush, "Remarks at a Fundraising Luncheon for Rep. Bill Grant," Sept. 6, 1990, *Weekly Compilation of Presidential Documents* 26, no. 36, p. 1331.

5. Robert E. Osgood, "Woodrow Wilson, Collective Security, and the Lessons of History," in Earl Latham, ed., *The Philosophy and Policies of Woodrow Wilson* (Chicago: University of Chicago Press, 1957), 190. See also Roland N. Stromberg, *Collective Security and American Foreign Policy: From the League of Nations to NATO* (New York: Praeger, 1963), 47; and Josef Joffe, "Collective Security and the Future of Europe: Failed Dreams and Dead Ends," *Survival* (Winter 1992), 39.

6. Cited in Gerald Stourzh, *Alexander Hamilton and the Idea of Republican Government* (Stanford: Stanford University Press, 1970), 81.

7. Statement by President George Bush, January 3, 1991, "Persian Gulf Crisis: Going the Extra Mile for Peace," *U.S. Department of State Dispatch* 2, no. 1, p. 1.

8. See Michael Walzer, *Just and Unjust Wars* (New York: Basic Books, 1977).

9. Friedrich Meinecke, *Machiavellism: The Doctrine of Raison D'Etat and Its Place in Modern History,* trans. Douglas Scott (New Haven: Yale University Press, 1957), 210.

Jack Donnelly

Post–Cold War Reflections on the Study of International Human Rights

The 1993 World Human Rights Conference in Vienna, only the second UN-sponsored global conference on human rights, provides an appropriate occasion to reflect on the state of international human-rights studies. The first global human-rights conference, held in Tehran in 1968, came on the heels of the Third World's rise to international prominence. The Tehran conference helped to initiate an era in which issues of economic, social, and cultural rights and development received steadily increasing attention in international human-rights discussions. The Vienna conference reflected the new international context characterized by the end of the Cold War and the global trend toward political liberalization and democratization. Substantively, the Vienna conference was perhaps most notable for its emphasis on the universality of international human rights—an emphasis, as I will argue below, that is reflected in the development of the academic human-rights literature as well.

Reflection on the state of the field also seems appropriate as the Clinton administration comes to the end of its first year in office. Human rights have not been an unusually prominent theme in Clinton's foreign policy. Nonetheless, human-rights issues have been pursued with some vigor in particular cases, such as Haiti and Bosnia. In fact, the Clinton administration seems to be the first in which human rights have become a relatively uncontroversial part of U.S. foreign policy, perhaps most notably in Central America. Even when human-rights concerns have been subordinated to other foreign-policy objectives over the past year, as in U.S. relations with China, decision making has been far less partisan, and there seems to be a more genuine sense of regret over the tradeoff. This deepening and maturing of the place of human rights in U.S. foreign policy, I will argue, can also be seen in the human-rights literature.

I must also admit to a much more personal motivation for reflecting on the state of the field. I am among the first generation of American scholars who have been able to make an academic career working on human rights. As a graduate student at Berkeley in the second half of the 1970s, human rights appeared to me to be both substantively important and professionally attractive. Prior to Jimmy Carter's election in 1976, the scholarly literature was remarkably sparse. There was a modest but steady stream of work in international law, stretching back into the 1940s, and a small body of work in the field of international organization that reached back even into the 1920s.[1] There were a few philosophical pieces, and even an occasional work on human rights and international relations, most notably Vernon Van Dyke's *Human Rights, The United States, and World Community* (1970).[2] But for a political scientist, it was a largely unexplored field that was not only of obvious substantive importance but also politically "hot."

I wrote most of my dissertation during the first flood of human-rights literature at the end of the Carter years. Since then, I have been a regular contributor to what is now a fairly substantial and increasingly mainstream literature. I thus write this review essay as a participant as well as an observer. While I trust that it stands on its own, I must say that it has provided me with a very welcome chance to reflect—I hope without too much self-indulgence—on the development of a field that has been my scholarly point of reference for my entire career.

Three issues have dominated the academic study of human rights in the United States over the past two decades, especially during the Carter and early Reagan years when the field came into its own: the proper place of human rights in international relations; the status of economic, social, and cultural rights; and the nature and force of arguments of cultural relativism. I will organize the bulk of this essay around these three issues, which together encompass perhaps the bulk of the human-rights literature outside the field of international law.[3] I will argue that in each case the old debates have largely been played out, but the underlying issues that motivated this early literature remain important and are appearing in new forms. In the final section I will address what I see as the most important new area of work in the field, namely, comparative human-rights studies.

Linking Human Rights and Foreign Policy

When Jimmy Carter became president in 1977, human rights were by no means an entirely new issue in international relations. The United Nations, especially its Commission on Human Rights, had regularly addressed human rights since 1946. The countries of the Council of Europe had participated in a scheme of regional human-rights monitoring and enforcement since the 1950s. The Conference on Security and Cooperation in Europe (CSCE) had linked human rights and international security in the Helsinki Final Act of 1973. And the U.S. Congress had in 1973 recommended, and in 1975 required, taking human rights explicitly into account in granting foreign aid.

Nonetheless, linking human rights and foreign policy was, in the mid-1970s, innovative and controversial. The United States had long employed the language of democracy and freedom. More often than not, though, this indirect approach to human rights took on an ideological, and peculiarly American, twist. The language of human rights was much more international—at home, Americans continued to prefer the language of constitutional and civil rights—and more clearly humanitarian or moral, rather than political or ideological.[4] Not surprisingly, Nixon, Kissinger, and Ford had strongly resisted the linkage of human rights and foreign policy (with the partial exception of the CSCE, where linkage served the obvious political objective of providing further grounds for attacking the Soviet Union). Even the European social democracies did not regularly make explicit reference to human rights in their foreign policies at this time. For example, the Netherlands, the first country to issue a white paper on the topic, did not explicitly make human rights an important part of its foreign policy until 1979.

The two most important books to appear initially were anthologies: Peter Brown and Douglas MacLean's *Human Rights and U.S. Foreign Policy* (1979) and Donald Kommers and Gil Loescher's *Human Rights and American Foreign Policy* (1979). These vague, almost generic, titles reflected both the lack of a previous literature—they could be used without any possibility of confusion with a prior work—and the very general nature of their concern with what was at the time still a rather innovative linkage.[5] Broad efforts to come to terms with the implications of Carter's new direction dominated the early discussions. *Human Rights Quarterly* (which began its life as *Universal Human Rights*), the most important scholarly journal in the field, devoted a major symposium in its very first issue (in 1979) to "Human Rights and U.S. Foreign Policy." The Foreign Policy Association devoted a headline series volume to the topic, and the United Nations Associations of both the United States and the United Kingdom commissioned studies.[6] And in perhaps the clearest indication of the penetration of human rights into the mainstream foreign-policy literature, *Foreign Affairs* published three articles on human rights and U.S. foreign policy in a period of two years (1978–80).[7]

This first burst of literature generally supported Carter's linkage of human rights and U.S. foreign policy. There were, however, two principal lines of criticism. The first was a realist critique of introducing moral concerns into foreign policy.[8] The second was a more political attack on the consequences of the Carter policy.

In an article that did much to earn her the position of U.S. ambassador to the United Nations, Jeane J. Kirkpatrick argued that the Carter human-rights policy had led the United States to attack and weaken important friends in the Third World and had deflected attention from the more important issue of the struggle against global communism.[9]

When the Reagan administration took office in 1981, a major change in policy appeared likely. For example, State Department staffers were ordered to refer to the Bureau of Human Rights and Humanitarian Affairs by the second, not the first, half of its name, and Secretary of State Alexander Haig publicly proclaimed that international terrorism would replace human rights as a priority concern of American foreign policy. The Reagan administration did reverse Carter's policy in a number of particular cases, especially in Central America and the Southern Cone of South America. In addition, the rhetoric of human rights in U.S. foreign policy did change dramatically. Nonetheless, during the 1980s human rights actually became more and more institutionalized in U.S. foreign policy, largely as a result of pressure from congressional Democrats and a variety of human-rights and liberal interest groups. Although the Reagan administration chafed at the restrictions represented, for example, by the congressionally mandated certifications of human-rights progress in El Salvador, in the end it was unable to remove human rights from the American foreign-policy agenda. And even under the highly ideological leadership of Elliott Abrams, the State Department's institutional infrastructure for human-rights reporting was strengthened and professionalized.

The thrust of the literature on human rights and U.S. foreign policy in the 1980s reflected a strong and remarkably clear unwillingness to follow the Reagan administration's attempted reorientation. Human-rights monitoring groups, such as Americas Watch and the Lawyers Committee for International Human Rights, produced a steady stream of increasingly professional studies of human-rights violations, especially in Central America. These groups also gave increasing attention to documenting—and condemning—the resistance of the Reagan administration to respond strongly and effectively to these violations.[10] And in tandem with the increasing institutionalization of human rights in U.S. foreign policy, the scholarly literature on human rights and foreign policy matured throughout the 1980s.

David Forsythe made a particularly significant contribution to the literature on human rights and U.S. foreign policy when he published the first textbook on the subject, *Human Rights and World Politics* (1983). This book was widely used by college teachers and went into a second edition in 1989. In a more scholarly vein, Forsythe also published an important book on the role of Congress in U.S. international human-rights policy, *Human Rights and U.S. Foreign Policy: Congress Reconsidered* (1988), which helped to counterbalance what had often been an excessive focus on the executive branch.[11]

Throughout the 1980s the number of scholars working on human rights and foreign policy grew, and their work gained increasing acceptance. In 1986, John Vincent published the second general international-relations text on human rights and an edited volume on human rights and foreign policy.[12] Major scholarly journals in political science and international relations began to accept human-rights pieces.[13] And perhaps most indicative of the penetration of human rights issues into the mainstream social-science literature, a lively debate has developed in the last few years over the quantitative evidence on the linkage of human rights and foreign aid in U.S. policy.[14]

In sharp contrast to ten or fifteen years ago, today the idea of pursuing human-rights concerns in foreign policy is relatively uncontroversial.[15] But one does not have to be remarkably cynical to suggest that the scholarly literature hasn't advanced very far beyond agreement on the legitimacy of the linkage. For example, there are remarkably few detailed empirical analyses of the policy process. Lars Schoultz's *Human Rights and United States Policy toward*

Latin America (1981) remains just about the only book-length study of U.S. international human-rights policy-making.[16] Forsythe's book on Congress has not been superseded. And only one major article has looked in detail at the bureaucratic apparatus of U.S. international human-rights policy.[17]

Even more surprising is the paucity of studies on particular international human-rights initiatives. Stephen Cohen and Roberta Cohen, respectively, published useful accounts of Carter's policy on security assistance and toward the Southern Cone.[18] Lisa Martin and Kathryn Sikkink recently published an interesting piece on U.S. human-rights policy toward Argentina and Guatemala in the 1970s.[19] A handful of similar studies exist. And, of course, a number of works have appeared on U.S. policy toward South Africa.[20] But after fifteen years of work, we simply do not have a substantial body of informed, detailed, empirical analyses of either the nature or the impact of U.S. international human-rights policy. And we know substantially less about the international human-rights policies of other countries.

In fact, an equally serious shortcoming of the literature on human rights and foreign policy is the lack of comparative work. Peter Baehr has published articles on Dutch policy. Cranford Pratt and Robert Matthews edited a fine volume on Canadian international human-rights policy. Jan Egeland produced an interesting comparative account of Norwegian and U.S. policy, emphasizing the differing constraints on, and opportunities available to, large and small powers. Rhoda Howard and I published a case study of U.S. and Canadian policy toward Nicaragua, emphasizing the difference between the more libertarian or minimalist social philosophy of the United States and the more social democratic orientation of Canadian society. And Kathryn Sikkink has recently published an important article, based on a much larger research project, that looks comparatively at the domestic roots of U.S. and European human-rights policies.[21] But except for a few other relatively isolated pieces, this is largely what is available, in English at least.[22]

Economic, Social, and Cultural Rights

A similar pattern of real but limited progress is apparent if we turn to the literature on the status of economic, social, and cultural rights, one of the most controversial theoretical issues of the late 1970s and early 1980s. The rather sparse theoretical literature on human rights prior to Carter was generally skeptical of economic, social, and cultural rights. Best known was Maurice Cranston's *What Are Human Rights?* which argued that purported economic, social, and cultural human rights in fact were impractical, of minor importance, and qualitatively different from true (civil and political) human rights.[23]

This line of argument has obvious affinities with the domestic political practice of the United States, where economic, social, and cultural rights (other than the right to property) do not enjoy the status of constitutional rights (the model that most Americans still use in thinking about human rights). It was restated in a strong and subtle form in an article by Hugo Adam Bedau in the Brown and MacLean anthology mentioned above. That same anthology, however, also featured an article by Henry Shue that, along with his book *Basic Rights,* published the following year, effectively demolished the categorical distinction between civil and political and economic, social, and cultural rights.[24]

Standard arguments against economic, social, and cultural rights draw heavily on a distinction between "negative" rights, which to be realized require only the forbearance of others, and "positive" rights, which require that others provide active support. Violating a negative right, it is argued, involves actively causing harm, a sin of commission. Violating a positive right, by contrast, involves only failing to provide assistance, a (presumably lesser) sin of omission. Shue showed that the distinction between negative and positive rights not only fails to match up with that between civil and political and economic, social, and cultural rights but that it has little moral significance.

For example, protection against torture, often seen as a quintessential negative right—the government must merely refrain from torturing people—in fact has a considerable positive component. In many countries, "simply" refraining from torturing people required major changes in law, administrative practice, and personnel. As Shue writes, "Any reductions in torture are much more likely to be matters of prevention rather than self-discipline, and therefore of powerful positive initiatives against torturers."[25] In all countries, realizing the right to protection against torture requires investigative and judicial institutions with strong positive powers. Furthermore, many civil and political rights are obviously not merely negative. What is the state to abstain from doing in order to realize the right to periodic and genuine elections under a system of universal and equal suffrage? Clearly the right to vote is a largely positive right. So is the right to trial by a jury of one's peers. It is something that can be claimed or demanded of the state, not merely a liberty that rests on state abstention. The same is true of the right to effective legal remedy for violations of fundamental rights.

Conversely, Shue argued that an apparently "positive" right such as the right to food could in many Third World countries be substantially better realized simply by "restraint" on the part of governments that have encouraged the production of cash crops for export at the expense of staple crops for local consumption. Furthermore, many economic, social, and cultural rights are just as negative as a number of classical civil and political rights. For example, the right to marry and found a family requires the state to abstain from interfering (although, of course, mere abstention may not be enough). It is no more "positive" than the right to choose and practice one's religion. The rights to participate in the cultural life of the community and to share in the benefits of science and technology are about as negative (or as positive) as the civil right to nondiscrimination.

All rights impose both negative duties to refrain from certain actions and positive duties to provide certain kinds of assistance. Whether a particular right is (relatively) "positive" or (relatively) "negative" is often more a matter of local social, economic, and political circumstances than anything else. And in any case, Shue showed that the categorical distinction between positive and negative rights, and violations involving acts of commission and acts of omission, has very little moral force.[26]

Consider a man stranded on a desert island without food or water. A passing sailor who came ashore but then left the man to die would be just as guilty of killing him as if he had strangled him.[27] Moral differences between rights rarely rest on the degree of activity or inactivity in typical violations. Therefore, priorities among rights must be established on substantive grounds.

Economic, social, and cultural rights stand up rather well to the test of substantive moral importance. Without certain minimum economic and social guarantees, a life of dignity is clearly impossible, especially in modern market economies. For example, the right to food is no less basic than the right to life. Even in the United States, the last major industrial country to take economic, social, and cultural rights seriously, there is growing recognition of the fundamental nature of the threats to personal dignity and security in the denial of the rights to work and to health care.

Shue's work did not entirely eliminate arguments against economic, social, and cultural rights. In particular, the Reagan administration and its supporters carried on a not entirely unsuccessful campaign to subordinate economic, social, and cultural rights (other than the right to private property) to civil and political rights in U.S. international human-rights policy. But these arguments increasingly came to be seen as fundamentally ideological.[28] For the most part, the literature on human rights dropped this categorical distinction.[29]

Basic Rights was one of those rare books that altered the way many people thought about and discussed an important issue. It also provided a model example of careful philosophical analysis applied thoughtfully and with powerful implications to policy questions of the greatest importance. In particular, Shue's argument that subsistence rights deserve no less priority than rights to liberty and security provided a powerful theoretical defense of the Carter administration's efforts to give greater emphasis to the satisfaction of basic needs in U.S. foreign aid and international human-rights policy. Even today, more than a decade after its publication, *Basic Rights* arguably remains the best single book ever written on international human rights. And most of what has been written since then on the philosophical basis of economic, social, and cultural rights is a footnote to Shue.

The implication of Shue's argument is that we must take much more seriously the often repeated notion that all internationally recognized human rights are "interdependent and indivisible." This is a theme that I have emphasized in my own work.[30] Differences certainly do exist between economic and social rights and civil and political rights. But there are no less important differences within each broad class of rights. And there are important similarities across these classes. For example, the right to life and the right to food can be seen as two different means to protect the same value. The right to work is a right to economic participation very similar to the right to political participation. The conventional distinction between civil and political rights and economic, social, and cultural rights—which is embedded not only in American discussions but in crucial international documents such as the International Human Rights Covenants—needs to be discarded. All human rights seek to protect human dignity, which is subject to a wide array of social, political, and economic threats that in complex, modern, industrial societies often cannot be sharply differentiated. Wherever the threat to, or denial of, an internationally recognized human right arises, it diminishes human dignity and reduces the value of other human rights.

During the Cold War, criticism of Soviet human-rights practices often included the reminder that a well-fed slave is still a slave. Parallel arguments from the other side of the ideological divide—a starving voter or churchgoer is still starving—also encapsulated an important truth. But such arguments, when made in one-sided, ideological ways, represented dangerous and misguided half-truths. In the 1980s the international human-rights literature managed to find a way to both capture and transcend these narrow insights and to begin to take seriously the interdependence and indivisibility of all internationally recognized human rights.

The human-rights literature of the last decade, however, has been disappointing in failing to go much beyond a general, theoretical recognition of the importance of economic, social, and cultural rights. In particular, very little has been written on the concrete issues of implementing economic, social, and cultural rights—even in the immense literature on social and economic development.

Much of the development literature does focus on the delivery of goods and services that have the consequence of implementing internationally recognized human rights. An explicit human-rights focus, however, is extraordinarily rare. This is unfortunate, because looking at development issues from the perspective of realizing or failing to realize internationally recognized human rights puts many issues in a fundamentally different light. This is particularly true in the case of market-oriented economic reforms, which for the past decade have been central policy concerns of most states. In part because of our failure to think of development in an explicit human rights perspective—that is, because of the failure of human-rights ideas to penetrate deeply into scholarly and policy discussions of development—we are today facing a new and, I believe, underappreciated threat to the idea of the interdependence and indivisibility of human rights.

In both the former Soviet bloc and the Third World, state economic planning is being abandoned in favor of market mechanisms. Often the desire for a greater market orientation is based locally, and often it arises from pressure from international financial institutions. But the manifest shortcomings of command economies should not blind us to the human-rights problems of markets or encourage us to slip into new ways of disparaging economic, social, and cultural rights.

Properly functioning markets are economically efficient: that is, with a given quantity of resources, they tend to produce a higher total quantity of goods and services. But markets are designed to respond to the interests and demands of those with "market power" (income, wealth, and information), not to human needs. Markets, at least when they operate properly, tend to produce more overall. They do not necessarily produce more *for* all. In fact, free markets typically produce gross inequalities in income, wealth, and living conditions.

The modern welfare state, a central institution of all contemporary industrial democracies, is the standard twentieth-century response to this moral failure of markets. Internationally recognized economic, social, and cultural rights provide the human-rights basis for these essential state interventions to correct some of the more debilitating inequities in market distributions of goods and services. Today, however, we face a real risk that in the understandable zeal to free economies from the constraints of inefficient state planning, the human rights of those least able to prosper in the market will be sacrificed to aggregate economic growth (efficiency).

In the development literature, the tension between growth and equity is a well-established theme. There are striking examples of countries that have managed to achieve both rapid growth and rapid implementation of economic and social rights, most notably Taiwan and Korea.[31] Whether this East Asian model is widely replicable is a matter of intense scholarly and policy debate. But whatever the case may be, the contemporary human-rights literature needs to address this issue in light of the fundamental principle of the interdependence and indivisibility of all human rights. At the very least, we must clearly face the full force of the pursuit of growth above all else: the human rights of some are being sacrificed to the interests of others in the present and, if everything works out as planned, the rights of others in the future.

During the Cold War era, the sacrifice of civil and political rights in both the Soviet bloc and the Third World was often justified in the name of realizing economic, social, and cultural rights.[32] One of the lessons we seem to have learned in the post–Cold War world is that repression typically does not lead to unusually good performance in economic, social, and cultural rights. But we must not stop at this particular affirmation of the interdependence of civil and political and economic, social, and cultural rights. We must remember that civil and political freedom does not by itself assure the enjoyment of economic, social, and cultural rights. And we must not lose sight of the fact that the "economic freedom" of the marketplace can be as devastating a threat to human rights as political repression.

This line of argument is clearly and deeply rooted in the conclusions reached in the human-rights literature of the 1980s. Whether scholars, policymakers, and human-rights advocates in the coming years will in fact move in this direction is by no means clear. Nonetheless, intellectually we are relatively well positioned. Fifteen years ago we lacked the normative consensus necessary to move decisively in this direction. Today, the conceptual tools are in place for such a constructive effort to deal with the contemporary threats to economic, social, and cultural rights presented by market inequities.

Cultural Relativism and Universal Human Rights

The debate over the status of economic, social, and cultural rights can also be seen as part of a substantially broader dispute over the universality of internationally recognized human rights. The Universal Declaration of Human Rights, the most important international statement of human-rights norms, explicitly proclaims itself to be a common standard of achievement for all nations and peoples. The standard form in which international human-rights instruments enumerate rights also stresses their universality: "All human beings . . ." "Every human being . . ." "Everyone has the right . . ." "No one shall . . ." This universality was implicitly challenged both by Western arguments against economic, social, and cultural rights and by Soviet bloc and Third World arguments for their priority. And in the human-rights literature of the 1980s, a lively debate raged over human rights and cultural relativism.[33]

Two questions lay at the heart of these debates. Is the concept of human rights Western in origin? Do the standards of the Universal Declaration and related international human-rights instruments bind all states in roughly the same way? All four possible combinations of answers were prominently advanced. A fairly substantial literature on non-Western conceptions of human rights emerged. Arguments were advanced that traditional societies in Africa, China, the Islamic world, and even Hindu India possessed indigenous conceptions of human rights.[34] One of the more exuberant proponents of this view went so far as to argue that "the concept of human rights can be traced to the origin of the human race itself."[35]

The alternative perspective was presented most forcefully by Rhoda Howard and me, both separately and in joint work. We argued that although all societies possess conceptions of human *dignity,* the idea of human rights—equal and inalienable rights held by each and every person and exercisable against society—emerged first in the modern West in response to the combined threats of modern markets and modern states. Many traditional societies, both in the West and elsewhere, possessed values and aspirations similar to those underlying internationally recognized human rights. They did not, however, attempt to realize those values and aspirations through the institution of human-rights policies.

Although some discussions confused issues of origins and contemporary applicability, these issues are, logically, entirely separable. In fact, both proponents and critics of the historical universality of human rights argued both for and against the contemporary normative universality of international human-rights standards.

Adamantia Pollis's "Liberal, Socialist, and Third World Perspectives on Human Rights" presented perhaps the classic version of the relativist argument of the 1970s and 1980s.[36] Pollis argued that in the contemporary world there are three "worlds" of human rights. The Western (First World) approach, it was argued, emphasizes civil and political rights and the right to private property. The "socialist" (Second World) approach emphasizes economic and social rights. The Third World approach emphasizes self-determination and economic development. Furthermore, both the socialist and the Third World conceptions are more group oriented, in contrast to the fundamental individualism of the Western approach.

Such arguments had an obvious political resonance during the Cold War. They also had a certain initial plausibility, given the radically different histories, social systems, and levels of development in these three "worlds." It is easy to understand the attractions of this position when it is linked to arguments that these contemporary approaches reflected or were rooted in locally developed conceptions of human rights. The three-worlds argument allowed a certain overarching universality to internationally recognized human rights, particularly in the long term. It also acknowledged a certain minimal cross-cultural and cross-ideological consensus on a relatively small subset of these rights. But it emphasized differences and considered fundamental divergences between human-rights practices in these three worlds to be entirely justifiable.

Again, Rhoda Howard and I were the principal exponents of the alternative view. We argued that internationally recognized human rights were not a menu from which one could choose but a comprehensive set of interdependent and indivisible rights that were generally binding on all contemporary states. In a world of modern states and modern markets, any plausible conception of human dignity could be protected only by something very much like the full list of human rights recognized in the Universal Declaration of Human Rights and the International Human Rights Covenants.[37] In our view, the three-worlds approach was largely a misguided capitulation to ideologically motivated arguments that sought to use the language of human rights to justify repression. And I can say with some satisfaction that events in the last few years seem to have confirmed this reading.

In the former Soviet bloc, citizens, given the opportunity, demanded their civil and political rights in country after country. Civil and political rights, far from being a superfluous bourgeois luxury, seem to be viewed by Central and Eastern Europeans no less than Western Europeans, as essential to a life of dignity. Likewise, the wave of liberalizations and democratizations throughout the Third World in the past decade suggests that the so-called Third World conception of human rights has little basis in local aspirations or understandings. As in the former Soviet bloc, ordinary citizens in country after country have found internationally recognized civil and political rights essential to protecting themselves against repressive economic and political elites. When given the chance, they have in effect declared that the sacrifices they have made in the name of development, self-determination, or national security have most often been imposed on them by force, and that their resistance has been denied through systematic violations of civil and political rights.

One of the more heartening results of the Vienna conference was the repudiation of Chinese efforts to revive the relativist position. Despite lingering fears of Western neocolonialism and a continuing preoccupation with the task of development in the former Soviet bloc and the Third World, the resolutions adopted at Vienna generally reflect a commitment to the true universality and interdependence of internationally recognized human rights.

But just as I warned against the dangers of a post–Cold War overreaction in the case of markets, we need to be careful to avoid excessive rigidity in our approach to international human rights. This is particularly true for the United States, where there remains a strong (although diminishing) strand of post–Cold War triumphalism. Not just with respect to overreliance on markets but more generally as well, we must be careful that the universality of human rights is not turned into a device for attempting to replicate the United States in other parts of the world. In particular, we must strive to avoid reproducing the worst elements of what Pollis characterized as the "Western" approach to human rights.

The reality of Western practice over the past half century has been quite different from Pollis's caricature of civil and political rights plus private property. In Western Europe, economic and social rights are generally well guaranteed. Social democracy is much closer to the norm than libertarianism. Even in the United States, which has by far the worst record on economic and social rights of the major developed countries, a fairly extensive welfare state exists. For all their antistatist and free-market rhetoric, even Ronald Reagan and Margaret Thatcher supported a large and extensive welfare state. And internationally recognized human rights require such protections.

No less important is a recognition that relativist arguments, although often overdrawn in the human-rights discussions of the 1980s, do rest on important (if limited) insights. Political histories, cultural legacies, economic conditions, and human-rights problems do differ not only among the First, Second, and Third Worlds but within each world as well. In the practical work of implementing universal human rights, this needs to be kept in mind. Internationally recognized human rights provide general direction. They do not provide a plan of implementation that can be applied mechanically, irrespective of political, economic, and cultural diversity.

For example, a country's historical development must be taken into account in assessing a government's human-rights practices. What should be accepted as, for now, adequate protection of the person's rights to liberty and security will vary quite considerably between, say, Sweden and Somalia. These rights are not less important or less desired in Somalia. If anything, the opposite is true. Nor should such an argument be used to justify failing to press whatever government ultimately emerges in Somalia not only to meet minimal international human-rights standards but also to make steady and substantial progress toward a more comprehensive and effective implementation of the full range of internationally recognized human rights. Nonetheless, we cannot ignore the fact that what can be achieved, by both national action and international cooperation, is in significant measure conditioned by existing practices and resources, which vary dramatically with time and place.[38]

The other important insight of relativist arguments is to draw our attention to the problems of expressing universal human-rights standards in terms that respect and respond to indigenous cultural traditions. In the earlier debate over non-Western conceptions of human rights, an important subtext often seemed to revolve around dispensing credit to those societies that developed the notion of human rights, or blame to those that did not. But if human-rights ideas in fact developed in seventeenth-century Europe in response to the threats of modern markets and modern states, the West is at least as much to be blamed for creating a need for human rights, which capitalist international trade and imperialism spread throughout the world. And societies—including premodern Western societies—that did not develop notions of human rights can hardly be blamed for pursuing conceptions of human dignity that emerged out of the conditions they faced, rather than pursuing those that rested on unexperienced threats to human dignity. If we can dispense with such silly considerations of praise and blame, we can begin to come to terms with the real problems of cultural diversity.

Modern states and markets are a universal feature of life in all countries of the world. But they have penetrated different countries to different degrees and in different ways. Whether one laments, tolerates, or celebrates cultural diversity, it is an international fact of life that must be grappled with in the implementation of universal human rights. Without giving in to the excesses of the "Third World" approach of the 1980s, we must recognize that unless internationally recognized human rights can be presented in ways that are consistent with local traditions, their impact and influence is likely to be significantly diminished. Without abandoning the notion of the universality of human rights, we must recognize that in different countries and regions, different cultural barriers to their implementation may require differing national and international implementation strategies.

For example, even though discrimination against women is a nearly universal feature of almost all past and present human societies, the forms it takes vary substantially from place to place. For example, where fundamentalist religions dominate—whether the fundamentalism is Muslim, Christian, Jewish, or Hindu—the character of the domination typically differs. And there are differences between these various types of fundamentalism as well. Unless we take into account the particular character of historically and culturally rooted resistances to implementing internationally recognized human rights, we may actually harm, rather than aid, the cause of universality. In any case, without cultural sensitivity, the impact of our efforts is likely to be diminished.

In this regard, the recent work of Abdullahi Ahmed An-Na'im deserves special attention. An-Na'im attempts to develop areas of cross-cultural consensus on internationally recognized human rights, based on traditional values in cultures that have not historically recognized such rights.[39] The goal is cross-cultural consensus not because it shares the credit or somehow validates the norms but because consensus eases implementation—especially once we recognize that human rights (understood as equal and inalienable rights held by every person against society) are not indigenous to most cultural traditions.

Conclusion: The Need for Empirical and Comparative Analysis

Running through the assessments with which I concluded each of the preceding sections has been an argument that the human-rights literature of the past fifteen years has been seriously lacking in detailed empirical analyses of even the most discussed issues. Overarching conceptual issues have been fairly thoroughly discussed, and some clear theoretical progress (or at least development) is evident. But there has been a striking and surprisingly consistent inattention to the particularities of implementation. We still do not know much about the details of international human-rights policies or their impact. We have little handle on the difficult problem of implementing economic, social, and cultural rights. And we are, at best, only beginning to understand the ways in which cultural diversity impedes implementing universal human rights.

One source of these empirical shortcomings is the rather shallow penetration of human rights into established social-science disciplines. Political scientists and interdisciplinary specialists in international relations today readily accept work on human rights that fifteen years ago probably would have been seen as at best peripheral to the central concerns of the field. Nonetheless, most work on international human rights still is done by people who specialize in human rights, rather than by people who have other interests within their discipline that lead them to pursue human-rights questions. Those of us who work on international human-rights issues may get more respect, and fewer strange looks, today than fifteen years ago. But we get very little in the way of help from our colleagues in the disciplinary mainstream. And there still are not enough of us to get the needed work done.

One way of ameliorating this situation would be to show greater care in selecting the topics we choose to work on. One of the oddities of the field is that it has been dominated by students of international law and international relations. Philosophy and political theory are the other areas where we can see a sizable and fairly coherent body of work. Yet just about everyone involved agrees that the principal causes of both respect for and violation of human rights are national, not international.

Those of us who by training are internationalists, rather than students of national or comparative politics, are unlikely to be willing to retrain ourselves, even if we were able. The same is true of philosophers and political theorists. The work we do remains, at its best, interesting and important. We need more of it, and we can do even better. But what the field needs most is a steady decline in the proportion of people studying human rights from the perspective of international law and international relations.

The most glaring shortcoming of the current human-rights literature, in my view, is its almost total failure to penetrate the fields of comparative politics, sociology, and development studies. Numerous scholars in these fields do work that is clearly relevant to human rights. Many even have an active concern with international human rights in their nonprofessional lives. Yet they rarely frame their research in human-rights terms.[40]

I am not unaware of the irony of advocating *de-emphasizing* philosophical and international work in a journal on ethics and international affairs. Nonetheless, the struggle for human rights will be won or lost at the national level. Unless we begin to study such struggles, we will neither understand the most important issues nor be able to make the most effective possible contribution to the realization of internationally recognized human rights.

NOTES

1. For fairly representative surveys of the state of the literature at this time, see Asbjorn Eide and August Schou, eds., *International Protection of Human Rights, Nobel Symposium* 7 (Stockholm: Almquist and Wiksell, 1968); and Moses Moskowitz, *The Politics and Dynamics of Human Rights* (Dobbs Ferry, N.Y.: Oceana, 1968). See also Ernst B. Haas, *Human Rights and International Action: The Case of Freedom of Association* (Stanford: Stanford University Press, 1970); and C. Wilfred Jenks, *Social Justice in the Law of Nations* (New York: Oxford University Press, 1970).

2. Vernon Van Dyke, *Human Rights, the United States, and World Community* (New York: Oxford University Press, 1970). Philosophical pieces would include, for example, H. L. A. Hart, "Are There Any Natural Rights?" *Philosophical Review* 64 (1955), 175–91; Maurice Cranston, *What Are Human Rights?* (New York: Basic Books, 1964); D. D. Raphael, ed., *Political Theory and the Rights of Man* (Bloomington: University of Indiana Press, 1967); and Joel Feinberg, "The Nature and Value of Rights," *Journal of Value Inquiry* 4 (1970), reprinted in *Rights, Justice, and the Bounds of Liberty* (Princeton: Princeton University Press, 1980).

3. The international legal literature, however, still makes up the major part of the scholarly literature on human rights. For better or worse, I have neither the space nor the inclination to address it here. Perhaps the best introductory overview is Hurst Hannum, ed., *Guide to International Human Rights Practice,* 2nd ed. (Philadelphia: University of Pennsylvania Press, 1992). The other major, although significantly overlapping, omission is the literature on international and regional human-rights organizations. For summary overviews, see Jack Donnelly, *International Human Rights* (Boulder: Westview Press, 1993), chap. 4; David P. Forsythe, "The Politics of Efficacy: The United Nations and Human Rights," in Lawrence Finkelstein, ed., *Politics in the United Nations System* (Durham: Duke University Press, 1988); and Burns H. Weston, Robin Ann Lukes, and Kelly M. Hnatt, "Regional Human Rights Regimes: A Comparison and Appraisal," in Richard Pierre Claude and Burns H. Weston, eds., *Human Rights in the World Community* (Philadelphia: University of Pennsylvania Press, 1989).

4. One still valuable article from this time that addresses some of these differences is Louis Henkin, "Rights: American and Human,"

Columbia Law Review 79 (1979), 405–25. On American exceptionalism in the area of human rights more generally, see David P. Forsythe, *The Internationalization of Human Rights* (Lexington, Mass.: Lexington Books, 1991).

5. Peter G. Brown and Douglas MacLean, eds., *Human Rights and U.S. Foreign Policy: Principles and Applications* (Lexington, Mass.: Lexington Books, 1979); Donald P. Kommers and Gil Loescher, eds., *Human Rights and American Foreign Policy* (Notre Dame: University of Notre Dame Press, 1979).

6. Charles Frankel, "Human Rights and Foreign Policy," *Headline Series* 241 (New York: Foreign Policy Association, 1978); Paul R. Newberg, ed., *The Politics of Human Rights* (New York: New York University Press, 1980); Evan Luard, *Human Rights and Foreign Policy* (Elmsford, N.Y.: Pergamon Press, 1981).

7. Sandy Vogelgesang, "What Price Principle? U.S. Policy on Human Rights," *Foreign Affairs* 56 (Spring 1978), 819–41; Arthur J. Schlesinger, "Human Rights and the American Tradition," *Foreign Affairs* 57 (1979), 503–26; William F. Buckley, Jr., "Human Rights and Foreign Policy: A Proposal," *Foreign Affairs* 58 (Spring 1980), 775–96.

8. See, e.g., Hans J. Morgenthau, *Human Rights and Foreign Policy* (New York: Council on Religion and International Affairs, 1979); and Henry A. Kissinger, "Continuity and Change in American Foreign Policy," in Abdul Aziz Said, ed., *Human Rights and World Order* (New York: Praeger Publishers, 1978).

9. Jeane J. Kirkpatrick, "Dictatorships and Double Standards," *Commentary* 69 (November 1979), 34–45.

10. See, for example, Americas Watch, Helsinki Watch, and Lawyers' Committee for International Human Rights, *Failure: The Reagan Administration's Human Rights Policy in 1983* (New York: Americas Watch, 1984); Americas Watch Committee and the American Civil Liberties Union, *As BAD As Ever: A Report on Human Rights in El Salvador* (New York: Americas Watch, 1984); Americas Watch, *Human Rights in Nicaragua: Reagan, Rhetoric, and Reality* (New York: Americas Watch, 1985); Cynthia Brown, ed., *With Friends Like These: The Americas Watch Report on Human Rights and U.S. Policy in Latin America* (New York: Pantheon Books, 1985); Americas Watch, Helsinki Watch, and Lawyers' Committee for International Human Rights, *". . . in the Face of Cruelty": The Reagan Administration's Human Rights Record in 1984* (New York: Americas Watch, 1985); The Watch Committees and Lawyers' Committee for

Human Rights, *The Reagan Administration's Record on Human Rights in 1986* (New York: Americas Watch, 1987).

11. David P. Forsythe, *Human Rights and World Politics* (Lincoln: University of Nebraska Press, 1983), and *Human Rights and U.S. Foreign Policy: Congress Reconsidered* (Gainesville: University of Florida Press, 1988).

12. R. J. Vincent, *Human Rights and International Relations* (Cambridge: Cambridge University Press, 1986).

13. For example, in 1981 and 1982 I published articles in *International Organization, American Political Science Review,* and *World Politics.*

14. See, for example, David Carleton and Michael Stohl, "The Foreign Policy of Human Rights: Rhetoric and Reality from Jimmy Carter to Ronald Reagan," *Human Rights Quarterly* 7 (May 1985), 205–29; David L. Cingranelli and Thomas E. Pasquarello, "Human Rights Practices and the Distribution of U.S. Foreign Aid to Latin American Countries," *American Journal of Political Science* 29 (August 1985), 539–63; David Carleton and Michael Stohl, "The Role of Human Rights in Foreign Assistance," *American Journal of Political Science* 31 (November 1987), 1002–18; James M. McCormick and Neil Mitchell, "Is U.S. Aid Really Linked to Human Rights in Latin America?" *American Journal of Political Science* 32 (February 1988), 231–39; Steven C. Poe, "Human Rights and U.S. Foreign Aid: A Review of Quantitative Studies and Suggestions for Future Research," *Human Rights Quarterly* 12 (August 1990), 499–512; and Stephen C. Poe, "Human Rights and Economic Aid Allocation under Ronald Reagan and Jimmy Carter," *American Journal of Political Science* 36 (February 1992), 147–67.

15. The one significant exception is a continuing realist uneasiness. For one of the best short statements focusing on the issue of morality and foreign policy in general, see George F. Kennan, "Morality and Foreign Policy," *Foreign Affairs* 64 (Winter 1985–86).

16. Lars Schoultz, *Human Rights and United States Policy toward Latin America* (Princeton: Princeton University Press, 1981).

17. Edwin S. Maynard, "The Bureaucracy and the Implementation of U.S. Human Rights Policy," *Human Rights Quarterly* 11 (May 1989), 175–248.

18. Roberta Cohen, "Human Rights Diplomacy: The Carter Administration and the Southern Cone," *Human Rights Quarterly* 4 (May 1982), 212–42; Stephen B. Cohen, "Conditioning U.S. Security Assistance on Human Rights Practices," *American Journal of International Law* 76 (April 1982), 246–79.

19. Lisa L. Martin and Kathryn Sikkink, "U.S. Policy and Human Rights in Argentina and Guatemala, 1973–1980," in Peter Evans, Harold Jacobson, and Robert Putnam, eds., *Double-Edged Diplomacy: International Bargaining and Domestic Politics* (Berkeley: University of California Press, 1993).

20. On South Africa, see especially Christopher Coker, *The United States and South Africa* (Durham: Duke University Press, 1986).

21. The best books on human rights in the foreign policy of countries other than the United States are Robert O. Matthews and Cranford Pratt, eds., *Human Rights in Canadian Foreign Policy* (Kingston and Montreal: McGill-Queen's University Press, 1988); Jan Egeland, *Impotent Superpower—Potent Small State: Potentialities and Limitations of Human Rights Objectives in the Foreign Policies of the United States and Norway* (Oslo: Norwegian University Press [distributed by Oxford University Press], 1988); and David Gillies, "Between Ethics and Interests: Human Rights in the North-South Relations of Canada, the Netherlands, and Norway" (Ph.D. Dissertation, McGill University, July 1992). On aid policies more generally, see Olav Stokke, ed., *Western Middle Powers and Global Poverty: The Determinants of the Aid Policies of Canada, Denmark, the Netherlands, Norway, and Sweden* (Stockholm: Almquist & Wiksell International, 1989). See also the concluding sections of chapter 5 of Donnelly, *International Human Rights.* Other useful sources include Peter R. Baehr, "Concern for Development Aid and Fundamental Human Rights: The Dilemma as Faced by the Netherlands," *Human Rights Quarterly* 4 (February 1982), 39–52; Peter R. Baehr, "Human Rights, Development, and Dutch Foreign Policy: The Role of an Advisory Committee," in David P. Forsythe, ed., *Human Rights and Development: International Views* (London: Macmillan, 1989); Irving Brecher, *Human Rights, Development, and Foreign Policy: Canadian Perspectives* (Halifax, N.S.: Institute for Research on Public Policy, 1989); Rhoda E. Howard and Jack Donnelly, "Confronting Revolution in Nicaragua: U.S. and Canadian Responses" (New York: Carnegie Council on Ethics and International Affairs, 1990); and Kathryn Sikkink, "The Power of Principled Ideas: Human Rights Policies in the United States and Western Europe," in Judith Goldstein and Robert O. Keohane, eds., *Ideas and Foreign Policy: Beliefs, Institutions, and Political Change* (Ithaca: Cornell University Press, 1993).

22. See, for example, Wolfgang Heinz, "The Federal Republic of Germany: Human Rights and Development," in Forsythe, ed., *Human Rights and Development: International Views.*

23. Maurice Cranston, *What Are Human Rights?* (New York: Basic Books, 1964; London: The Bodley Head, 1973). For a shorter, article-length version of this argument, see Cranston, "Are There Any Human Rights?" *Daedalus* 112 (Fall 1983), 1–18. For a somewhat more sophisticated version of an argument leading to the same conclusion but focusing on the character of rights as valid claims, see Feinberg, "The Nature and Value of Rights."

24. Hugo Adam Bedau, "Human Rights and Foreign Assistance Programs," and Henry Shue, "Rights in the Light of Duties," in Brown and MacLean, eds., *Human Rights and U.S. Foreign Policy;* Henry Shue, *Basic Rights: Subsistence, Affluence, and U.S. Foreign Policy* (Princeton: Princeton University Press, 1980).

25. Shue, "Rights in the Light of Duties," 70.

26. Shue, *Basic Rights,* 41–46, 51–60.

27. Shue, "Rights in the Light of Duties," 72–75.

28. This is particularly clear in the common defense of the right to property by critics of economic, social, and cultural rights. A right to property is clearly an *economic* right, not a civil and political right—if control over wealth and the means of production is not an economic right, it is hard to imagine any economic rights at all—and a rather extravagant economic right at that. Furthermore, the standard defenses of a right to property also support other economic and social rights. For example, rights to work and to social insurance no less than a right to private property provide a sphere of personal economic security.

29. The principal exception, which ironically linked the Reagan administration and its enemies in the Soviet bloc, was the literature on the so-called socialist conception of human rights, discussed below.

30. See especially Jack Donnelly, *Universal Human Rights* (Ithaca: Cornell University Press, 1989), chap. 2.

31. For a discussion of arguments over development-rights trade-offs, with special attention to Korea, see Donnelly, *Universal Human Rights,* chaps. 9 and 10.

32. For a critical discussion of such arguments, see Donnelly, *Universal Human Rights,* chap. 9, and, more briefly, the section below.

33. The reader should be warned that I was a central participant in these debates. What follows, then, is not an entirely impartial account, although I believe that it is accurate and fair.

34. There are several useful readers that deal entirely or principally with issues of cultural relativism. I list them here in chronological order of publication: UNESCO, *Human Rights: Comments and Interpretations* (London: Allan Wingate, 1949); Adamantia Pollis and Peter Schwab, eds., *Human Rights: Cultural and Ideological Perspectives* (New York: Praeger Publishers, 1980); Kenneth W. Thompson, ed., *The Moral Imperatives of Human Rights: A World Survey* (Washington, D.C.: University Press of America, 1980); Claude E. Welch, Jr., and Virginia A. Leary, eds., *Asian Perspectives on Human Rights* (Boulder: Westview Press, 1990); Jan Berting et al., eds., *Human Rights in a Pluralist World: Individuals and Collectivities* (Westport, Conn.: Meckler, 1990); Francis M. Deng, Abdullahi Ahmed An-Na'im, eds., *Human Rights in Africa: Cross-Cultural Perspectives* (Washington, D.C.: The Brookings Institution, 1990); Abdullahi Ahmed An-Na'im, ed., *Human Rights in Cross-Cultural Perspectives: A Quest for Consensus* (Philadelphia: University of Pennsylvania Press, 1991). Alison Dundes Renteln has presented perhaps the most radical relativist account; see "The Unanswered Challenge of Relativism and the Consequences of Human Rights," *Human Rights Quarterly* 7 (November 1985), 514–40, and *International Human Rights: Universalism versus Relativism* (Newbury Park, Calif.: Sage Publications, 1990).

35. Yougindra Khushalani, "Human Rights in Asia and Africa," *Human Rights Law Journal* 4 (1983), 403–42, at 404. Compare Adamantia Pollis and Peter Schwab, "Human Rights: A Western Construct with Limited Applicability," in Pollis and Schwab, eds., *Human Rights,* xiv, 15.

36. In Peter Schwab and Adamantia Pollis, eds., *Toward a Human Rights Framework* (New York: Praeger Publishers, 1982). A revised version appears in Richard Claude and Burns Weston, eds., *Human Rights in the World Community,* 2nd ed. (Philadelphia: University of Pennsylvania Press, 1992).

37. Rhoda E. Howard and Jack Donnelly, "Human Rights, Human Dignity, and Political Regimes," *American Political Science Review* 80 (September 1986), 801–17. More generally, see Donnelly, *Universal Human Rights,* chaps. 3–8. For a more detailed version of Howard's arguments focusing on concrete problems in Africa, see her *Human Rights in Commonwealth Africa* (Totowa, N.J.: Rowman and Littlefield, 1986), especially chap. 2; "Evaluating Human Rights in Africa: Some Problems of Implicit Comparisons," *Human Rights Quarterly* 6 (May 1984), 160–79; and "Women's Rights in English-Speaking sub-Saharan Africa," in Claude E. Welch, Jr., and Ronald I. Meltzer, eds., *Human Rights and Development in Africa* (Albany: State University of New York Press, 1984), which includes a balanced, brief discussion of the issue of female genital operations.

38. For a good example of such an argument applied to Africa, see Howard, "Evaluating Human Rights in Africa."

39. See his contributions in An-Na'im, ed., *Human Rights in Cross-Cultural Perspectives: A Quest for Consensus,* and An-Na'im and Deng, eds., *Human Rights in Africa: Cross-Cultural Perspectives.* For a particular application to a difficult case, see "Religious Minorities Under Islamic Law and the Limits of Cultural Relativism," *Human Rights Quarterly* 9 (February 1987), 1–18.

40. There are, of course, exceptions, perhaps most notably Rhoda Howard, a sociologist who has made human rights the center of her research for the past decade. Nonetheless, a perusal of the shelves of the human-rights sections of any good library will show a striking pattern: considerable scholarly work on theoretical and international issues, with the vast majority of country-specific, national-level studies being descriptive reports by international human-rights NGOs.

Michael J. Smith*

Humanitarian Intervention: An Overview of the Ethical Issues

The capacity to focus on the issue of humanitarian intervention represents what Joel Rosenthal has noted as the maturation of the field of ethics and international affairs.[1] If nothing else, the debate surrounding this vexed issue has demonstrated that we have left behind the so-called oxymoron problem: there is no reason now to be defensive about bracketing the terms "ethics" and "international relations." One can hardly talk about Bosnia, Rwanda, Haiti, Somalia, or any cases of possible outside intervention, without recognizing from the very beginning that ethical dilemmas abound in the way we define our goals, our interests, and the means we use to pursue them. Even Samuel P. Huntington, not usually known to be a moralist, has asserted that "it is morally unjustifiable and politically indefensible that members of the [U.S.] armed forces should be killed to prevent Somalis from killing one another."[2] Whether or not one agrees with that assertion (I do not), one may note that Professor Huntington speaks in terms of moral justification and regards his view of morality to be, in effect, self-evidently true. Thus even archrealists invoke morality in urging their preferred policies.

The discussion in this essay proceeds in three unequal stages. First, I present a brief and oversimple sketch of the objective and

*This essay is adapted from opening presentations given to the Carnegie Council's Faculty Institutes in 1996 and 1997. I have tried to retain the informal flavor of the discussion. The essay draws substantially from a joint work-in-progress with Professor Stanley Hoffmann of Harvard University.

subjective changes in the broader milieu of international relations as they relate to humanitarian intervention. Second, and more substantially, I survey and analyze the arguments justifying or opposing the notion of humanitarian intervention from realist and liberal perspectives. Finally, I offer the beginnings of my own argument and consider the enormous difficulties of undertaking humanitarian intervention with any degree of effectiveness and consistency.

The Milieu

A New International Setting

What are some of the salient changes in the contemporary international system? Perhaps symptomatic of our current confusion is the absence of consensus even on what to call this new system. Is it unipolar? Balance-of-power? A globalized economic system and regional security system? The new world order? We agree only on the term "post-Cold War" and on the idea that we have no exact model for the kind of international system in which we find ourselves. The notion of unipolarity is not terribly helpful: the apparent single "pole," the United States, has shown singular reluctance to exert its military power, and functionally and economically the international system can hardly be described as unipolar. So, while apparently appealing, unipolarity doesn't work.

Realist analysts may struggle to find some sort of balance-of-power analogue, but this too is not terribly useful. Power is not fungible in the way that many realists following E. H. Carr have treated it, and much of contemporary international relations involves the intersection of the traditional realm of security and the modern arena of economic interdependence. But even theorists who emphasize the elusiveness of power or who have reclassified kinds of power have not as yet articulated a crystallized conception of the contemporary system.[3] In general, we continue to look for ways in which the contemporary system may or may not be like the balance-of-power system of the nineteenth century, to identify what features of the Cold War system it still has, and to seek other historical models, but it is clear that we are in a system with many aspects we have never before encountered. Although nuclear weapons have not gone away, they no longer structure the international competition. We now have contending successor states within the former Soviet empire in the midst of profound political and economic transformations—transformations as yet incomplete and poorly understood. At the same time, a truly global economy now means that events in the stock markets of Seoul, Bangkok, or Hong Kong reverberate distortedly on Wall Street. In short, the model of billiard ball states combining and colliding in ways beloved of diplomatic history textbooks (and some realists) has given way to a kaleidoscope of factors including nationalism, ethnicity, and religion, as well as security and economics.

Perhaps our understanding of the international system was always over simplified: states were never billiard balls impermeable to transnational norms, influences, and activities. But the simplifications were defensible as a way to abstract the underlying logic of a system based on discrete sovereign states. Now, with the operational sovereignty of states systemically eroded, we know that no simple model encapsulates the complex reality of contemporary international relations.

If we shift our focus to the level of state actors, we may note some broad trends that at the same time undermine and affirm the idea of national sovereignty as the constituent principle of international society. Consider first the widely noted phenomenon of so-called failed or failing states, which are breaking down as a result of their inability to establish legitimacy with any degree of certainty. In addition, there are states, like Rwanda and Burundi, or Algeria, in which conflicts appear to be endemic or imminent or both. Such conflicts seem now to have greater salience.[4]

Finally, there is the phenomenon of so-called dangerous states: states that may, like Libya or North Korea, challenge the basic tenets of the society of states; states that for various reasons seek to bring attention to themselves through outrageous actions. Such states, because of the danger they pose for other states, may indeed make intervention necessary. For example, it is certainly an open question as to whether we should tolerate the overt acquisition of nuclear weapons by North Korea. When it invaded Kuwait, Iraq provided an occasion for a traditional collective security intervention of the sort envisaged by the framers of the League of Nations Covenant and the UN Charter. As I write this essay, Saddam Hussein's refusal to allow UN inspectors unfettered access to potential weapons sites in Iraq has triggered an international crisis. By the time it appears, we may well have seen another U.S.-led military action against Iraq.

Then there are still cases of old-fashioned aggression, and it is not inconceivable that a state might simply attack another state or help itself to another bit of territory. How dangerous are such renegade states, and what ought we do about them? The overt acquisition of territory or goods by dangerous states will continue to provide a worry for those trying to enforce some version of international order. Together, all these factors at the state level seem to guarantee that we shall have no shortage of occasions for intervention.

A New Climate of Opinion

Thus the objective setting of the international system is not settled, and it is perhaps emblematic of this that we still refer to it as the post–Cold War system. And subjectively, on the issue of humanitarian intervention, we have seen a change even in the brief post–Cold War period in the prevalent attitude toward this issue. For a brief time, from about 1991 to 1993, there existed a sort of Dudley Do-Right euphoria, a sense that we could solve many problems throughout the world just by the use of goodwill and the dispatching of peacekeepers wherever they might be necessary. Thomas Franck characterized the time as an "exciting moment" in which we could begin to intervene on behalf of democratic legitimacy—to create democratically legitimate states everywhere.[5] There was indeed a large increase in the number of humanitarian operations.[6] Since 1993, and the perceived American debacle in Somalia, the attitude toward humanitarian intervention, especially in the United States, has become decidedly more cautious. The most immediate effect of this caution, of course, was the inaction (and worse) of the international community in the face of the conflict between the Hutus and Tutsis in Rwanda. Since then the brutal war in Bosnia, the absence of any international action in the conflict in Chechnya, and a kind of collective sense of shame at the failure of the international community to prevent or arrest the slaughter of tens of thousands of innocent civilians in Rwanda have all created a new climate of wariness about the whole issue of humanitarian intervention. The puzzled and ineffectual international response to the recurring massacres of villagers in Algeria reflects this same uncertainty.

Moreover, there was always a debate about whether humanitarian intervention is legal under international law. In an incisive review of the issue, Tom Farer concludes: "States will still have to choose between compliance with formal prohibitions [against intervention] and response to urgent moral appeals." Because international law is both "thinly institutionalized" and constantly evolving in ways that reflect emerging normative ideas, an appeal to the law itself cannot solve the underlying moral issues raised by humanitarian intervention.[7]

But such normative consensus is yet to emerge. Even sociologically, the events that may lead to humanitarian intervention are far from clear. Morally, substantively, the issues are deeply controversial. Is humanitarian intervention a rescue operation, a quick in and quick out, leaving the basic norms of sovereignty intact, or is it, rather, an attempt to address the underlying causes of the conflict and even to create the conditions for democracy? If the latter, then the model of going in and getting out quickly is obviously not appropriate. Even Michael Walzer, often criticized for the "statist" character of his theory in *Just and Unjust Wars*, has recently amended his rules for intervention. He now argues that there is an obligation to make sure the conditions that require the intervention in the first place do not simply resume once you leave.[8]

In terms of the subjective environment, there is some question as to whether or not international intervention for humanitarian causes is even moral. Both in the literature and in the pronouncements of leaders and actions of states, there is still a great deal of doubt and suspicion of unauthorized, unilateral intervention. This obviously reflects traditional international law and the traditional rules of a society of states. Recently, the United States has sought to gain multilateral authorization even for its unilateral actions, as was the case in Haiti and, to some extent, even in the Persian Gulf War. As Walzer suggests, there may still be situations in which autonomous unilateral intervention for humanitarian purposes is ethically justified, and certainly from the military point of view the formidable problems of command and control may be simplified when intervention is autonomous and unilateral.[9] But in general it seems that the old norms of sovereignty and nonintervention are still persuasive for states—at least in their official and quasi-official pronouncements.

What about collective intervention? Traditional international law has been hostile not only to unilateral intervention in domestic affairs but also to collective, coercive action, except in cases of threats to peace, breaches of peace, and overt aggression. The founding fathers of international law have always treated the concept as suspect. The most striking recent development has been some "creative exegesis" (Farer's phrase) on the part of international lawyers as exemplified in the willingness in the Security Council to broaden the traditional definition of threats to peace as a justification for intervention.[10] Was the intervention for the Kurds the application of a new principle of humanitarian intervention on behalf of oppressed minorities? Or was it a simple extension of a classical collective security operation against Iraq? Would it even have occurred if Iraq had not invaded Kuwait? The question is not entirely rhetorical, but almost. The relief action certainly did not recognize a right of Kurdish self-determination, as the United Nations has proclaimed its respect for Iraqi territorial integrity.

Many of the recent collective interventions in weak states have occurred at the formal request of the state concerned or of all parties involved. In its attempt to restore democracy in Haiti (and of course acting mainly by approving U.S. intervention), the Organization of American States (OAS) moved into new territory by justifying collective intervention. Other UN interventions have mainly concerned emergency relief for violations of minority rights, the monitoring of elections, or more traditional-style peacekeeping missions. When the United Nations monitored elections in Nicaragua, the operation was explicitly connected to the Central American peace process rather than to concern for democracy per se or human rights. Whether Somalia and Cambodia will be exceptions or the first in a series of temporary takeovers of failed states will depend on the lessons being drawn from those two operations. So far the United Nations has resisted endorsing a general doctrine, proceeding, as is its wont, case by case. This means that the normative scene is still rather cloudy, and the extent to which we have moved beyond traditional norms is dubious. Even the definition of what constitutes threats to peace is ambiguous. Must an egregious violation of human rights that constitutes a "threat to peace" have an inescapable impact on interstate relations? Or are some violations in themselves, and virtually by definition, threats to peace? The "creative interpretation of its constitutional obligation to maintain peace and security" undertaken by the Security Council cannot by itself solve these ambiguities.[11] If all violations are defined as threats to peace, then the Security Council, in principle, could intervene in the affairs of any state; but if only violations that threaten interstate peace count, then many egregious violations (as, say, in Tibet or East Timor) could go unaddressed.

To summarize the relevance of the changes in the international milieu for humanitarian intervention: First, there is a lack of leadership and clear direction at the top of the system, either among the major states or in the institutions themselves. Former UN secretary-general Boutros Boutros-Ghali was probably out a little too far in front of the member states in his "Agenda for Peace"; his successor now labors to keep the organization financially afloat, especially in the face of U.S. recalcitrance about its debt. The activist phase of interventions, at least in official pronouncements, has receded. Second, there will continue to be occasions for humanitarian interventions, and we will continue to be faced with dilemmas of rescue, peacekeeping, and peace making, to list the problems in ascending order of difficulty. Third, there is no real consensus on when or how to intervene in these conflicts or on who should do so. And fourth, it is also fair to say that such enthusiasm as may have existed for these types of operations from 1991 to 1993 seems by now to have evaporated.

A remark by David Rieff in a recent essay that Western states favor humanitarian intervention seems now to be singularly inapposite.[12] The United States is not about to embark on broad Wilsonian crusades. The two most recent instances of our intervention, in Haiti and Bosnia, were undertaken with evident reluctance. The title of the rather dyspeptic monograph written in 1978 by Ernst Haas, *Global Evangelism Rides Again*, now seems almost quaint.[13] As we close out the 1990s, global evangelism at best limps along, led by a motley if erudite array of philosophers and human-rights advocates. More typical is the remark of the freshman Republican member of Congress who, responding to President Clinton's belated speech justifying the Bosnian intervention, said she did not see any reason why we should be sending "our boys" to a country about which we know nothing to stop the fighting there.[14] It is doubtful that she knew how closely she was echoing Neville Chamberlain.

So what does this say? It tells us that we are unlikely to find guidance from leaders, either of major states or of institutions. International lawyers will continue to debate whether or not interventions are legal, and the prescriptions from the political scientists will remain murky. Where does this leave us? These are serious ethical problems that cannot be ignored, and ethicists must be willing to tread where lawyers and politicians fear to go. Thus, on to the arguments about humanitarian intervention itself.

Humanitarian Intervention

A provocative challenge to the very terms of the debate comes from Rieff, who says that in effect humanitarian intervention is just a sop to the Western conscience and that the rich nations are using it as a way to avoid dealing with the chronic and serious issues of poverty and misgovernment in Third World states.[15] This is a legitimate point, but I take it to be a kind of *cri de coeur* of a committed journalist who has seen some of the worst humanitarian disasters of the decade. The insight, or warning, should act only as the beginning, and not the end, of an argument. Extraordinary and excruciating dilemmas are raised by some of the situations we observe across the world, but throwing up one's hands at the horror of it all or raining down curses on all the world does not help us to address them.

There are various ways to characterize and categorize the positions in the debate, but I have no wish to impose a complicated taxonomy here. Stanley Hoffmann—and more recently Michael Doyle—divides the theoretical approaches to the issue into realist, Marxist, and liberal varieties.[16] One might also divide the theorists into statists, or people who look at states as the source of values, and cosmopolitans. This is the old distinction made famous some time ago by Hedley Bull in *The Anarchical Society*, where he discussed statist and universalist cosmopolitan conceptions of justice.[17] Today, however, the real debate is taking place mainly between realists and liberals.

Realist Arguments

As I have outlined elsewhere, realists, whether they reside in academia or in the military, are traditionally hostile to any intervention that is justified for allegedly ethical reasons.[18] They claim, in general, that there is a self-delusory quality to all ethical justifications regarding state actions. That is a larger argument, which I have tried to address elsewhere.[19] But how does this argument play out when it comes to humanitarian intervention? Realists say two things that are partly incompatible. One is that states only act when it is in their interest to do so and that therefore when they engage in a humanitarian intervention they are really pursuing some other agenda. They may just be worried about prestige or image on the "soft" end of the interest calculus. Or they may have some actual "hard" interests involved, interests that are convenient to subsume under the category of "humanitarian." In any case, say realists, when states intervene for allegedly humanitarian reasons they do not seek disinterestedly to do the right thing; they have "real" interests at stake. However, there is also a kind of political assertion that is slightly incompatible with this one. It says that interventions work and are supported politically only when they are closely connected to real interests. But if the first assertion were true, then the second would not apply: states would act *only* when their interests were really engaged. Apparently states sometimes really do act in spite of the fact that their so-called national interests are not engaged to the degree that realists think they ought to be.

In addition to these not-quite-compatible empirical assertions about why states act, realists also make what amounts to an ethical argument that states are necessarily self-interested creatures and are, by definition, unable to act in other than self-interested ways.

To expect them to do so—to support genuinely humanitarian action—is to engage in self-delusion, error, and hypocrisy. Thus the best, indeed most ethical, thing to do is to hold on to a more concrete definition of interests and leave humanitarian interventions to *Médicins sans Frontières*. Humanitarian intervention, therefore, is in a sense a chimera, or, as in Rieff's account, a sop to our collective conscience. Moreover, humanitarian crusades dilute the national purpose, say realists: Only when we recognize the inevitably self-interested character of all our policies can we think clearly about our interests. Realists developed this argument most fully in their opposition to the U.S. intervention in Vietnam. People tend to forget that some of the earliest opponents of that intervention, which was by no means humanitarian, were realists like Hans Morgenthau, George Kennan, and Reinhold Niebuhr, all of whom thought that Vietnam was not a core American interest and that we were vainly seeking to project our anticommunism in ways quite inappropriate to the local conditions.

There is, nevertheless, a quasi-realist case for humanitarian intervention that some have made, and that is to define interests in terms of what Arnold Wolfers called "milieu goals."[20] That is, there is a realist case for structuring a more orderly international system and paying attention to the requirements of leadership by a great power. Realist arguments on behalf of intervention may even invoke credibility ("No one will take us seriously as a great power if we allow this to occur"). If the United States is to be believed about anything it is to do, the argument goes, it cannot allow a group of thugs in Haiti to thumb its nose at everything it says. This is an interesting redeployment of an argument originally made in a very different context. We heard it during the intervention in Vietnam, and we hear it recurringly in debates about how many nuclear weapons we need for what. The argument rests on a broad definition of national interest.

In addressing national interest, one can perhaps distinguish between imperatives and preferences, but even defining what is imperative to a state involves deploying ethical preferences.[21] The classical arguments, again, are made by Wolfers: even "survival" must be defined according to moral values. Consider the different choices made by Czechoslovakia in 1938 and Poland in 1939, when faced with Hitler's demands. The Czech and Polish leaders, like Marshal Pétain and General de Gaulle in the France of 1940, defined "survival of the state" quite differently. Even the apparently starkest imperatives are not straightforward or objective. In the middle of the Vietnam War, Bruce Russett wrote *No Clear and Present Danger*, which for many was an annoying little book. It was annoying because it challenged settled beliefs about World War II, but it was also useful in that Russett showed that it is possible to make the case that there was no clear and present danger to the United States in 1941 and that we did not really need to fight the war the way we did. He argues that we could very well have survived without fighting the Germans or the Japanese. The point here is not to agree with that position but rather to note that values are built into the very notion of what constitutes an imperative. Russett showed that imperatives, even the apparently most obvious ones like resisting Nazi Germany and Tojo's Japan, are not self-evident. They are, in the prevailing jargon, "constructed." And therefore, when one is talking about humanitarian intervention, it is not necessarily helpful to distinguish between imperatives and preferences.

The key questions are, what constitutes an integrated definition of national interest, and what value should be placed on having an international system that acts to prevent the sort of brutal behavior we have been observing in the 1990s? These questions of course lead into order as a justification for intervention. There is a component of morality to order, after all, as well as a quasi-moral notion that imputes to great powers a responsibility to ensure a relatively orderly international system. The realist route to humanitarian intervention thus involves a conception of international society that requires us to define what constitutes acceptable behavior within it. Although this is founded on classical, "statist" values, it still provides a means of justifying humanitarian intervention. Thus one need not be a dewy-eyed idealist to think that there are times when humanitarian intervention can be justified on grounds that are fairly traditional and well connected to definitions of interest.

Liberal Arguments

Whereas liberals have traditionally valued self-determination, community, and shared history, as seen in Walzer's work, there is also within liberalism a more universalist conception of human rights in which sovereignty is a subsidiary and conditional value. Self-determination, after all, has been among the most abused of liberal values. Indeed Amir Pasic has shown in an essay on Bosnia how the liberal value of self-determination can and is used to create what he calls a "negative normative reality" that leads to acts of genocide and ethnic cleansing.[22] A deep fault line of liberal theory runs along the question of how a given community defines itself, what means it can use, what legitimate goals it can pursue to establish its conception of freedom and autonomy, and to what extent outsiders are legitimately a party to these conflicts when they get nasty. Most famously perhaps, and most familiarly, J. S. Mill and Walzer following him have asserted both the virtue and the necessity of Mill's argument of the "arduous struggle of self-help" as the way for a community to achieve freedom and autonomy. This sets the bar rather high, even for humanitarian intervention.

At the noninterventionist end of the liberal spectrum, we find again two sorts of claims—one ethical and one prudential. The ethical claim of the noninterventionists places high value on community in itself, on a notion of shared history—what Walzer calls the "thick" values in his 1995 book *Thick and Thin.*[23] These values are to be respected almost prima facie by outsiders. There is also an ethical component to the historical/empirical claim that unless freedom is "earned" by a people, it will not survive and endure. But what if "earning" communal autonomy and freedom means ethnic cleansing? And, if so, what does that imply for the rest of the international community in terms of its rights and/or obligations to intervene?

Related to the claim about community is a claim about the legitimating function of domestic political processes—apparently almost any domestic political process. In a perhaps unguarded passage in *The Anarchical Society*, Bull wrote that to the extent that the words of a despot are authenticated by a political process, one ought to weigh them more heavily than the pronouncements of, say, Bertrand Russell, Buckminster Fuller, or Norman Cousins (in perhaps descending order of profundity), none of whose pronouncements has been authenticated by any sort of process at all. The political claim is that, unlike individuals, at least spokesmen for states, even authoritarian states, have passed through some political process.

At the same time there may be an unconscious arrogance in assuming that the most extreme leader in a community is necessarily the "right" spokesperson for that community's aspirations. This is a point made well by the late political theorist Judith Shklar in her powerful essay "The Liberalism of Fear."[24] By what right is Radovan Karadzic accepted as the authoritative spokesperson of the Bosnian Serbs? It is not clear who has consulted the ordinary people there. Does Pat Robertson speak for all white, evangelical Christians? Or Louis Farrakhan for African Americans as a group? There is a tendency in an argument that privileges states and domestic political processes, however rudimentary, to overvalue the most extreme leader and to reward the people least supportive of peaceful accommodation. The so-called Parliament of Bosnian Serbs came into being solely at the behest of Karadzic and his supporters; its actions in the midst of the diplomacy to end the war in Bosnia conferred no conceivable legitimacy.

These ethical and practical arguments for nonintervention slide almost imperceptibly into prudential claims about order. A prudential concern for order tells us that we cannot license intervention everywhere to everyone who is of a mind to intervene. It would be a recipe for disaster in the international milieu. Not every violation can justify intervention. Pierre Laberge cites a play by Molière in which a wife is suffering a beating at the hands of her husband. To the surprise of a well-meaning stranger who tries to intervene, the wife rudely rejects the offer of help. She tells him to mind his own business, that she and her husband will work out their problems.[25] Noninterventionist liberals make a similar claim: people should be left alone to work out their own governance.

What about the interventionist end of the liberal spectrum? Franck has written that in the light of recent orgies of genocide, Mill's position on the arduous struggle of self-help is a posture of insufferable insouciance.[26] Indeed, if one looks at what occurred even in a success story, South Africa, it is clear that success was the product of more than self-help. A combination of external sanctions and sustained action on the part of the international community sought to convince white South Africans that apartheid was deeply unacceptable, that South Africa would have to abandon it and grant full citizenship rights to the black majority if it were ever to join the international community of states as a fully acceptable member. This external pressure aided the undoubtedly more potent internal developments that ultimately led the remarkably peaceful transformation to occur. Intervention, after all, can involve more (or less) than sending troops. In the case of South Africa, it involved sustained sanctions at almost every level of international interaction. And many of these sanctions were the product of grassroots activism in the democratic states that were also trading partners, or sporting competitors, of the South African state.

In his deservedly standard treatment of the issue in *Just and Unjust Wars*, Walzer sought to avoid the extreme non- or interventionist positions. Since the book's publication in 1977, people on both sides of the debate have tried to claim him as an ally because his legalist paradigm rests on a tension between the statist and cosmopolitan positions. The book recognizes the pull of one side of an argument even when it lands on the other side. In effect, Walzer tries to ground the legalist paradigm of the rights of states in the rights of individuals—because the rights of states rest on the rights of individuals. But at the same time, states as members of international society are by definition entitled to presumptive legitimacy. The first reading of the rule is that we as outsiders must assume that another state is legitimate unless it has proved otherwise by actions that we cannot ignore. Walzer revises the absolute rule of nonintervention only when the absence of "fit" between people and regime is radically apparent. He cites interventions in civil wars involving secessionist movements; interventions to balance prior interventions; and—here is our focus—interventions to rescue peoples threatened by massacre, enslavement, and (in "The Politics of Rescue") by large-scale expulsion.

Walzer conceives of humanitarian intervention as a kind of international analogue to domestic law enforcement. Governments that engage in acts that allow us to intervene for humanitarian purposes are in effect criminal governments. Those who initiate massacres lose their right to participate in the normal, and even normally violent, processes of domestic self-determination. Governments and armies engaged in wholesale massacres of individuals are readily identifiable as criminal. Hence, humanitarian intervention comes closer than any other kind of intervention to what we commonly regard in domestic society as police work. But can one intervene unilaterally to stop an outlaw? Walzer prefers a collective action, but it seems that he does not insist on it. His discussion conceives of international humanitarian intervention as a rescue operation in which the intervenor goes in and then comes out. In "The Politics of Rescue," Walzer expresses willingness to allow members of the international community to stay a little longer, to move from what Hoffmann calls rescue to the restoration of peace.[27] He does not directly treat the murderous conflicts in failed states or the systematic terrorization of a population by another seeking its own version of self-determination, as in Bosnia. The model is still one of states acting as states to punish a particularly egregious member of the society of states. So the values of community, shared history, and culture—in general, the "thick" values—trump the universalist values of human rights, at least in Walzer's account.

A Liberalism of Human Rights

I would like to sketch very briefly a version of liberalism that, at least ethically, makes the value of sovereignty subordinate to human rights claims.[28] This version rests on a view of liberalism that seeks to value both the universal and the communitarian aspects of the political doctrine. Most communitarian critiques of liberalism fail to recognize the extent to which liberals value community and how liberalism itself embodies a conception of the good. Such critiques take aim at the priority given to rights and try to show how this comes at the expense of the common good. But, in fact, liberalism does work to establish conditions in which individuals will be able to fulfill themselves and their projects, their vision of the good, while respecting the personality and personhood of the projects of others. This means that there are liberal virtues—tolerance is an important one—and also that there are limits to so-called liberal neutrality. At bottom, liberalism seeks to establish a form of social life free of moral coercion even in circumstances of deep social disagreement. A liberal polity is therefore fully entitled to place limits on projects that would impose moral coercion and hamper the ability of individuals to define and pursue their own idea of the good. The goal of a liberal political society is individual autonomy in a community of tolerance. Political society can be regarded as a combined product of history, with its vast share of accidents, upheavals, and manipulations, and of human choice. Thus it is both willed and historical.

And very often, as we know from many studies, it is the sort of shared history that is sometimes invented, or re-created, by poets, philosophers, and the like.

Whatever its origins, the moral standing of a society rests on its ability to respect and to protect the rights of its members and on their consent, explicit or implicit, to its rules and institutions. Both the nation, which we define as a group that provides individuals with a sense of social identity and transcends other secular and often religious cleavages, and the state, which we define as a set of institutions that aims at providing individuals in a certain territory with order and a variety of resources, derive their moral standing and their rights from the will and the rights of the individuals that compose the nation and over whom the state rules. Political life is, as a whole, a ceaseless process of accommodation among the rights and duties of individuals within a nation, those of a national group, and those of the state. But here we would join forces with the broader liberal worldview. Neither the group nor the nation nor the state can be seen as possessing inherent rights. The rights they claim derive from individuals. When they define their rights and duties in a way that tramples the basic rights of individuals they forfeit their legitimacy. This version of liberalism recognizes that persons are social beings and that society, therefore, cannot be seen only as protector of private lives and activities from anarchy. Individuals often want to come together to achieve common purposes, to carry on grand designs, to build a common civil culture—sounding all the usual communitarian hymns. Political society is not simply a market for free private enterprise. From a moral point of view we look at social groupings formed by persons as derivative and constructed and as drawing their legitimacy from the will and consent of these persons. Thus in international relations we treat the notion of the morality of states with suspicion. At the same time, we recognize that cosmopolitanism, however desirable it may be as a political goal, does not yet correspond to the choice of the great majority of states or individuals. But we would still insist that community is not a value that trumps all others.

In this conception of liberalism, then, the justification for state sovereignty cannot rest on its own presumptive legitimacy. Instead it must be derived from the individuals whose rights are to be protected from foreign oppression or intrusion and from their right to a safe, "sovereign" framework in which they can enforce their autonomy and pursue their interests. It follows, then, that a state that is oppressive and violates the autonomy and integrity of its subjects forfeits its moral claim to full sovereignty. Thus, a liberal ethics of world order subordinates the principle of state sovereignty to the recognition and respect of human rights. And when an illiberal state is attacked by another one, the defense and integrity of its independence against aggression must be accompanied by an international effort to improve its own human rights record. Steps have been taken for the international protection of human rights that move slowly and haltingly toward this goal. Here, obviously, we have in mind Kuwait. The principle of an individual's right to moral autonomy, or to put it differently, to the human rights enshrined in the Universal Declaration on Human Rights, should be recognized as the highest principle of world order, ethically speaking, with state sovereignty as a circumscribed and conditional norm.

What does this mean for humanitarian intervention? The answer is complex. We have still to maintain and even raise barriers to illegitimate intervention, define the areas, conditions, and procedures for legitimate ones, pay particular attention to both sets of cases and the special problems raised by coercion, particularly military coercion, and proceed as much as possible on a broad basis of consent. What does this mean in practice? I think we must maintain our suspicion of unilateral intervention, because it always contains a component of self-interest, and unilateral intervention risks almost by definition violating the autonomy of the target. Unilateral intervention should thus be presumptively illegitimate, but the presumption can be overridden. Would it have been wrong for the United States to act in Haiti even if it did not have OAS sanction? The point is arguable, but I believe that humanitarian intervention would nevertheless have been justifiable. A blanket requirement for multilateral approval or participation in a case of potential humanitarian intervention may have the unfortunate effect of ensuring that nothing is done. One could certainly argue that Rwanda was a case of "Well, I'll do it if you do it," with nobody willing to take the first step. Meanwhile, tens, even hundreds, of thousands of people were killed in a brutal, low-tech, and rather time-consuming way, largely by machetes. It is quite clear to most people who have studied this case that a modest deployment of international troops placed early and decisively could have prevented a large number of deaths. Because of cases like this, it does not seem reasonable to rule out unilateral action. At the same time, a collective process serves as a check on an individual state's tendency to intervene for self-interested purposes.

When could one intervene collectively? I think that we could build on the emerging consensus on threats to peace, breaches of peace, and acts of aggression—the traditional causes that allow us to intervene in interstate conflict. In domestic affairs the equivalent causes would be domestic policies and practices capable of leading to serious threats to peace, and in cases of egregious violations of human rights—even if those violations occurred entirely within the borders of a given state. A genocide is no less "a common threat to humanity"—the characterization of former UN secretary-general Boutros-Ghali—if it occurs within borders than if it crosses them. The basic principle that should guide international intervention is this: Individual state sovereignty can be overridden whenever the behavior of the state even within its own territory threatens the existence of elementary human rights abroad and whenever the protection of the basic human rights of its citizens can be assured only from the outside.

State sovereignty, in short, is a contingent value: its observance depends upon the actions of the state that invokes it. Members of the international community are not obliged to "respect the sovereignty" of a state that egregiously violates human rights. Why "egregiously"? The sad answer is that the world presents a far too rich array of human rights violations that might justify outside intervention. We must choose among the evils we seek to end. For much of the world, for example, capital punishment violates human rights. Yet few disinterested observers would urge or welcome the forcible landing of an international military force to prevent Virginia's next execution. However one regards capital punishment after due process of law, it cannot compare with the scale of violations that occurred in Rwanda or in the Cambodia of Pol Pot. As one analyst has observed, we currently possess "neither the capabilities nor the willingness to right all wrongs, even the relatively small number of wrongs that are deemed to warrant international action."[29] But as President Clinton put it in his speech justifying the NATO action in Bosnia: "We cannot stop all war for all time. But we can stop some wars. . . . There are times and places when our leadership can make the difference between peace and war."[30] Some judgment about the scale of evil, and about the capacity we have to end it, must be made.

This process of judgment should, in my view, be multinational. For all the flaws of the United Nations, it does provide a forum for international debate and for the emergence of consensus. And, as I have suggested, if taken as a general but not rigid rule of thumb, an insistence upon collective, multilateral intervention or, as in Haiti, collectively approved unilateral action can correct for self-interested interventions that are draped in a thin cloak of humanitarianism. At the same time, it may be necessary for a state to declare its intention to act on its own; if the cause is truly just, this very declaration may make collective action more possible. And the intervention may still be just even if its motives are mixed: the examples of India's intervention in the former East

Pakistan and of Tanzania's in the Uganda of Idi Amin are often cited as unilateral interventions that nevertheless ended humanitarian disasters.[31]

What about the problem of consistency? Does the fact that we can do little, if anything, about human rights violations in Tibet have implications for what can be done about human rights violations in Haiti or East Timor? Alas, it seems obvious that there simply won't be consistency, but what does that mean ethically? Is it more ethical to say that since I cannot do everything everywhere consistently I should do nothing? My own view is that the fact that one cannot do everything everywhere does not mean that one should not try to do anything anywhere.

A first stab at setting priorities for action might be to suggest humanitarian interventions where the threats to peace for neighboring states are indeed the greatest. One could also come up with a list that sets the potential costs of the intervention against what might actually be achieved. In short, we could seek to adapt the traditional criteria of the just war tradition to cases of humanitarian intervention. But this does require that we develop the means and capacities for acting in these ways.

I am not sympathetic to those who think that we must reserve our military for a single purpose lest it lose, so to speak, its "purity of essence," to quote a famous (movie) general.[32] It is not inconceivable to me that we can have dual-purpose military organizations. People can be trained to do more than one thing. We do have to address more seriously collective capacities. We have stopped talking about the UN standing force, and the Clinton administration has stopped trying to build up the collective capacities of the United Nations, apparently because the issue is regraded as a political loser. Nevertheless, there seems to me to be a clear ethical imperative to begin to develop means that are capable of addressing some of the problems that we have been seeing.

But as always in ethical arguments, ought implies can. It is clear that weighing in on the human rights side implies a willingness to intervene far more extensively than we are currently willing to do; and there are significant costs and dangers attached to this willingness. On the other hand, weighing in heavily on the side of traditional sovereignty and nonintervention entails a willingness to turn a blind eye to many outrages in the world. We could say, "Well, it is a pity that people are killing each other and it's true that there is something that we could do about it relatively easily, but it is actually occurring within a state so it's not our business." Surely one of the lessons of the Holocaust is that we should not allow this to occur again. And one of the benefits of the end of the Cold War is that we can now begin to address questions of endemic injustice and human suffering in ways that were not possible when the United States and the Soviet Union were worried about blowing each other up.

There remain formidable worries about the consistency and effectiveness of humanitarian intervention. But one has to begin working those out by deciding how much one is willing to overlook for the sake of sovereign independence. To claim that sovereignty is subsidiary to human rights is not to say that sovereignty is negligible or automatically weaker. Rather, claims to sovereignty are subsidiary in that they do not automatically trump other compelling claims. There may be times when prudence suggests doing something less, but I regard it still as a moral imperative to prevent or mitigate evil when one has the capacity to do so. Thus as an ethical imperative, the issue of humanitarian intervention demands our deepest attention and response.

NOTES

1. Joel H. Rosenthal, ed., *Ethics and International Affairs: A Reader* (Washington, D.C.: Georgetown University Press, 1995), introduction.

2. Samuel P. Huntington, "New Contingencies, Old Roles," *Joint Forces Quarterly*, no. 2 (Autumn 1992), 338.

3. See Joseph S. Nye, *Bound to Lead: The Changing Nature of American Power* (New York: Basic Books, 1990), or, much earlier, Stanley Hoffmann, "Notes on the Elusiveness of Modern Power," *International Journal* 30 (Spring 1975), 183–206.

4. An exhaustive analysis of such conflicts can be found in Ted Robert Gurr, *Minorities at Risk: A Global View of Ethnopolitical Conflicts* (Washington, D.C.: U.S. Institute of Peace Press, 1993). An alarmist, journalistic account is offered by Robert D. Kaplan, *The Ends of the Earth: A Journey at the Dawn of the 21st Century* (New York: Random House, 1996).

5. Thomas M. Franck, "The Emerging Right to Democratic Governance," *American Journal of International Law* 86 (January 1992), 46–91.

6. For an excellent summary of these operations, see the appendix prepared by Robert C. Johansen and Kurt Mills in Stanley Hoffmann, *The Ethics and Politics of Humanitarian Intervention* (Notre Dame, Ind.: University of Notre Dame Press, 1996), 101–15.

7. Tom J. Farer, "A Paradigm of Legitimate Intervention," in Lori Fisler Damrosch, ed., *Enforcing Restraint: Collective Intervention in Internal Conflicts* (New York: Council on Foreign Relations Press, 1993), 341.

8. Michael Walzer, "The Politics of Rescue," *Dissent* (Winter 1995), 41.

9. Michael Walzer, *Just and Unjust Wars* (New York: Basic Books, 1977), ch. 6.

10. Farer, "A Paradigm of Legitimate Intervention," 320, 330. On the "founding fathers," see J. L. Brierly, *The Law of Nations*, 6th ed. (New York: Oxford University Press, 1963), 403 ff., and Richard B. Lillich, ed., *Humanitarian Intervention and the United Nations* (Charlottesville: University Press of Virginia, 1973).

11. Farer, "A Paradigm of Legitimate Intervention," 330.

12. David Rieff, "The Lessons of Bosnia: Morality and Power," *World Policy Journal* (Spring 1995), 76–88.

13. Ernst B. Haas, *Global Evangelism Rides Again*, Institute of International Studies Policy Paper, no. 5 (Berkeley: University of California, 1978).

14. Quoted in the *New York Times*, November 28, 1995, A15.

15. Rieff, "The Lessons of Bosnia."

16. Hoffmann, "Notes on the Elusiveness of Modern Power" and Michael Doyle, *Ways of War and Peace* (New York: W. W. Norton, 1997).

17. Hedley Bull, *The Anarchical Society* (New York: Columbia University Press, 1977).

18. Michael J. Smith, "Ethics and Intervention," *Ethics and International Affairs* 3 (1989).

19. Michael J. Smith, *Realist Thought from Weber to Kissinger* (Baton Rouge: Louisiana State University Press, 1987).

20. See Arnold Wolfers, "Statesmanship and Moral Choice," in his *Discord and Collaboration* (Baltimore: Johns Hopkins Press, 1962).

21. Stanley Hoffmann, "Politics and Ethics of Military Intervention," *Survival* 37 (Winter 1995–96), 29–51; Wolfers, "Statesmanship and Moral Choice."

22. Amir Pasic, "Ethics and Reality: The Hard Case of Bosnia," paper presented at the International Studies Association meeting, San Diego, Calif., April 1996.

23. Michael Walzer, *Thick and Thin: Moral Argument at Home and Abroad* (Notre Dame, Ind.: University of Notre Dame Press, 1995).

24. Judith N. Shklar, "The Liberalism of Fear," in Nancy Rosenblum, ed., *Liberalism and the Moral Life* (Cambridge, Mass.: Harvard University Press, 1989), 21–38.

25. Pierre Laberge, "Humanitarian Intervention: Three Ethical Positions," *Ethics and International Affairs* 9 (1995).

26. Franck, "The Emerging Right to Democratic Self-Governance."

27. Hoffmann, "Politics and Ethics of Military Intervention," 34–46.

28. The following passage draws on a manuscript in progress written with Stanley Hoffmann; hence the change to the first-person plural pronoun.

29. Franck, "The Emerging Right to Democratic Self-Governance."

30. President Clinton quoted in the *New York Times*, November 28, 1995, A12.

31. See Walzer, *Just and Unjust Wars*, 102–10.

32. I refer to the character in Stanley Kubrick's *Dr. Strangelove*, General Jack D. Ripper.

Amir Pasic and Thomas G. Weiss

The Politics of Rescue: Yugoslavia's Wars and the Humanitarian Impulse[1]

The humanitarian impulse is remarkably prevalent in the post–Cold War world. Whether or not we have actually entered "the age of humanitarian emergencies" is open to debate,[2] but the dramatic increase in the number of humanitarian interventions since 1991 has been widely noted, as has sobriety after debacles or disappointments in Somalia and elsewhere.[3] Humanitarianism as an expression of concern for the victims of armed conflict and political disorder has traditionally been spearheaded by nonstate actors. That states themselves have begun to include humanitarianism in their policy architectures is evidence of the extent to which this orientation has become a prominent feature of both contemporary transnational civil society and interstate relations.[4] The notion of rescue is also emerging in the philosophical and policy literature.[5]

There is, however, a dramatic downside to what might otherwise be considered a positive moral development at the international level. Rushing to rescue victims based on a visceral reaction to their suffering may, depending on the circumstances, be a palliative or, even worse, counterproductive. A poor basis for policy, it builds erroneously on the metaphor of saving a drowning stranger and distorts the context surrounding humanitarian efforts. It seems to initiate a new relationship with distant peoples who are suddenly of concern to us because they are subject to unacceptable suffering. At the same time, this link is exceptional and limited only to the duration of a particular rescue effort. It does not alter significantly the relationship between the rescuers and the rescued.

The multiple ties that bind rescuers and victims long before the onset of a complex emergency, and throughout its evolution, are ignored. In particular, rescue does not capture sufficiently the absence of secure ground in war zones to which to bring imperiled victims. Furthermore those in danger are not as foreign, unknown, and unconnected to us as often is implied by the rescue metaphor. Before, during, and after complex emergencies rescuers and victims are related through many relationships that their representatives conduct in economic, diplomatic, and cultural domains.

States have always intervened in one another's affairs. Justifications and rationalizations for incursions across sovereign boundaries have included past grievances and the protection of co-religionists or nationals.[6] Remarkably, interventions along with other less invasive but more routine human rights intrusions into domestic affairs are now being justified in terms of humanitarian concerns.[7] National interests and other justifications have not disappeared, nor will they, but they have acquired a definite humanitarian flavor.

Moreover, the humanitarian impulse is not limited to the most obvious agents: protectors, aid deliverers, peacekeepers, and journalists.[8] It has also seeped into foreign ministries and security agendas as heads of states proclaim the virtues of "doing the right thing," despite the usual warnings that moral sentiments should not guide the ship of state.[9]

Indeed, pundits and professors use that nebulous term, "the international community," as a stock concept to analyze contemporary world politics, increasingly with the implication that there is a moral obligation to act even if there is no consensus about the requirement to do so.[10] Furthermore, a focus on multilateral military endeavors with humanitarian justifications is becoming a standard feature of strategic, operational, and doctrinal discourse in the United States military and the North Atlantic Treaty

Organization (NATO).[11] In the process, humanitarians from both the United Nations and nongovernmental organizations (NGOs) are being recognized as natural partners in what the British military first labeled "operations other than war," now the preferred term in most militaries.[12]

Given the surge in humanitarian intervention and its impact on foreign policy, it is imperative to examine its limitations. This essay explores the ethical challenges presented by the emergency mode of humanitarianism in war zones. One example is the former Yugoslavia, where the United Nations High Commissioner for Refugees (UNHCR) was designated the lead agency by the UN secretary-general and orchestrated rescue operations in Europe's largest involuntary displacements since the Second World War.[13] The UNHCR's relative success in bringing assistance to four million victims in the Balkans reflected a principled extension of the organization's charge to take care of refugees; that is, people who have no state to protect them.

At the same time, the experience of the refugee agency in this instance demonstrates the limits of rescue. The Balkans benefited from a substantial resource abundance vis-à-vis the rest of the world, and the international community is unlikely to devote such ample material resources and political attention to other complex emergencies. In 1995 the former Yugoslavia received more than 100 percent of estimated aid requirements—as it had in previous years—which contrasted with less than 50 percent received by Angola, Sudan, Somalia, Afghanistan, Iraq, Sierra Leone, and others.[14]

However, rescue served also as a substitute for robust diplomatic and military engagement and prolonged the need for assistance. Moreover, as former U.S. assistant secretary of state Richard Holbrooke has pointed out, "the damage that Bosnia did to the UN was incalculable."[15] As long as something was being done to assuage the suffering, international leadership could declare that it had a policy for dealing with the former Yugoslavia. The means available amounted to what the former UN senior political adviser characterized as "trying to hold back the tide with a spoon."[16] The outpouring of help was manipulated by those political authorities who did not share humanitarian goals, thus damaging the long-term interests of endangered populations and the quest for peace and stability. Aid was diverted, access to civilians was denied in order to extort resources and recognition of territorial claims, and the multilateral humanitarian presence became a pawn in the capricious maneuvers of irresponsible demagogues whose policies would ultimately exacerbate the difficulties that the region would have in rehabilitating itself when peace finally came.[17] The delivery of relief settled into a bizarre pattern, sustaining civilians who were being manipulated by leaders whose primary political resource was their capacity to threaten civilians and even humanitarians. Simultaneously, scores of opinion leaders in the West and in the Islamic world agonized over the rescue effort and its meaning for the moral identities of all of us who were witnessing the tragedy.[18]

Although it seeks to moderate the ugly realities of international politics, rescue—even with the exceptional level of commitment it received in the former Yugoslavia—in actuality adds new ethical dilemmas to international politics. Perhaps the foremost of these dilemmas regards the proportionality of needs and the affirmation that life is as precious in one part of the globe as another. Thus, the "privileged position" of Yugoslavia's victims should trouble us as much as the failure of a policy based on such an extensive expenditure of resources.

Rescue affects the political lives and identities not simply of victims but of the rescuers as well. It reveals a troubled and unsettled link to sovereignty, which separates humanity into integral units, each pursuing a distinctive way of life. Does rescue seek to establish a new kind of "revolutionary" humanitarian relationship among peoples or is it "restorative," seeking to rebuild the capacity of endangered populations to continue their distinctive way of life under state authority as before the crisis? The former option would establish a transcendent moral link among human beings as such, thus overriding or at least going beyond sovereignty; the latter would seek to restore the autonomy of suffering populations within a self-contained polity, thus sustaining traditional sovereignty.

On the one hand, revolutionary humanitarianism makes rescuers self-conscious participants in a "foreign" political community, thus rearranging the boundaries of the political space occupied by victims. Restorative humanitarianism, on the other hand, accepts the necessity of tolerating blatant abuses of rights because relief efforts are fundamentally directed toward reestablishing the endangered population's autonomy with as little outside political involvement as possible. Rescue is thus a radically ambiguous principle, persisting incoherently between revolutionary and restorative humanitarianism. Although these two points are at either end of a continuum, with many gradations between them, they are not merely heuristic devices to amuse analysts. They are principled choices that circumscribe policy options. The fundamental purpose of this essay is to explore the normative tension between them, hoping to understand better why rescue founders.

We begin with an overview of apolitical attempts to rescue the "wretched of the earth," during which both outside aid personnel and victims are implicated in the politics of rescue. Then, by focusing on the UNHCR and its attempt to deal with displacement from Yugoslavia's wars, we discern the shortcomings of any episode of rescue and the implicit principles that could guide future rescue missions. This serves as background for a discussion of the ambiguity of humanitarianism—a principle that can be used either to buttress sovereignty or to challenge it. Whether one opts for the more conservative (restorative) or, alternatively, the more radical (revolutionary) vision, the Yugoslav cause suggests the limits of humanitarianism.

The Politics of Rescue

Distinctions between humanitarian and political concerns are instructive, reflecting the difference between the goals of rescue and of stability. In spite of the initial lofty rhetoric of the post–Cold War world, the various members of the international community are becoming aware of the necessity for more reflection and fewer automatic responses to humanitarian tragedies. Removing superpower rivalry clearly has been insufficient for the international humanitarian system to move from the pursuit of rescue to the institution of political order.[19]

There are inevitable tradeoffs between the two goals. To pursue rescue is to seek the immediate and unconditional alleviation of human suffering. To institute political order is to seek to create and sustain viable social institutions that will prevent the need for subsequent rescue efforts. Political strategies to create an enduring sociopolitical order will sometimes require reining in the impulse to save lives and alleviate the suffering of noncombatants with all available means.[20] In the prescient prose of Alain Destexhe, the former secretary-general of Doctors Without Borders:

> All over the world, there is unprecedented enthusiasm for humanitarian work. It is far from certain that this is always in the victims' best interests. . . . In dealing with countries in ongoing wars of a local nature, humanitarian aid has acquired a near-monopoly of morality and international action. It is this monopoly that we seek to denounce. Humanitarian action is noble when coupled with political action and justice. Without them, it is doomed to failure and especially in the emergencies covered by the media, becomes little more than a play thing of international politics, a conscience-solving gimmick.[21]

To complicate matters, the use of the term "peace" as a synonym for "stability" is philosophically loaded. Decolonization, for example, showed that everything cannot be sacrificed at the altar of peace, and that not all political orders are worth preserving no matter how apparently stable. We confront the age-old tensions between order and justice. There are situations in which it would be justifiable to increase suffering and create disorder for the purpose of fashioning a more equitable and sustainable political order in the long run. It is, of course, by no means obvious when we may justifiably calculate the costs and benefits of such endeavors.

In fact, conflicts between order and justice have been temporarily obscured by a superficial consensus about the values of democratization and liberalization. Orderly, just, and peaceful liberal democracies and their mutual relations do not necessarily provide guidance for states going through the potentially destabilizing transition to democracy, where violence may become a favored option.[22] Also, the normative guidelines are even less clear for a conflict that has become about whom to include or exclude from membership in a state. When the bounds of a state and its identity are contested, it is also not clear *for whom* there should be order and justice.

What makes the problems of rescue, order, and justice stand out so vividly is the conventional wisdom regarding the impulse—some, for example the International Committee of the Red Cross (ICRC), would say "imperative"—of rescue even in cases where de jure sovereignty presents a prima facie legal prohibition.[23] Most humanitarian endeavors without the consent of a state take place in areas of turmoil supposedly governed by failed or collapsed states.[24] That sovereignty should be subordinated to the demand for rescue from calamity is less problematic than the moral and operational implications of actually assuming responsibility for those rescued. The subordination of sovereignty, even if it is only in situations where effective political authority is absent, still implies an obligation to assume a longer-term perspective, a commitment to the sustainability and health of a society rather then merely to one episode of rescue. Without such a commitment, rescue can become self-defeating.

No matter how intense and heroic an intervention to deliver food, resettle people, or even eliminate an irresponsible tyrant or an armed threat, such an intervention is only a start. A simple declaration that sovereignty presents no bar to our intervention against intolerable suffering only begins to expose obligations across borders.[25] We do not know how the decentralized international humanitarian system might work to maintain order after an intervention. Nor do we possess normative criteria to trigger interventions and guide them so that there is more consistency, or perhaps less selectivity, in unleashing the humanitarian impulse.[26] The dilemmas of humanitarian challenges—in particular the reality of unanticipated negative consequences resulting from well-meaning but counterproductive humanitarianism—are thus truly unsettling.[27]

Ideas move people figuratively and can also serve to displace them literally, especially as manipulated by Serbian and Croatian politicians to justify ethnic cleansing. And in situations where people are not threatened at gun point, fear can move them whether or not it is ultimately warranted. In the Yugoslav context, ethnic identity became a potent guiding principle even for those national and international actors who most wanted to stop hostilities and were appalled by the disappearance of a multiethnic society. As Susan Woodward writes of the September 1992 peace conference in the Hague, convened under the auspices of the European Community: "No pro-Yugoslav parties were represented in the formulation, nor were the representatives of non-ethnic parties, the civilian population, or the many civic groups mobilizing against nationally exclusive states and war consulted."[28] Genocidal extermination, forced migration to achieve ethnic purity, and national animosity did not fester in a vacuum. They were clearly and faithfully reported and legitimated by the actions of humanitarians, governments, and the media even before violent hostilities commenced.

The overarching lesson to be extracted from the lot of war victims in the former Yugoslavia is the extent to which humanitarianism and politics are inextricably intertwined. The policy response thus should not be to try to keep the two as separate as possible, but rather to understand how they should be addressed simultaneously. Those who support the apolitical approach of separating the two advocate keeping the issue of who makes decisions about the distribution of aid to those at risk their own affair. As such, humanitarians can only provide relief to those in need, making whatever compromises are required. Aid providers typically respond viscerally to massive human suffering. As such, immediate and direct access to civilian victims becomes an absolute priority. Issues of sustainable order, much less its quality, appear so distant that even thinking about them detracts from the immediacy of the lifesaving tasks at hand. Thus, humanitarianism becomes the emergency-response mechanism of the sovereign state system, seeking to restore the viability of sovereign compartments that have temporarily become irresponsible and dysfunctional, as revealed by the gross suffering that they contain. Mitigating the suffering begins to restore the viability of the sovereign container.

That outside intervention can save lives and reduce suffering without advancing anyone's political agenda is at best an outmoded notion. Long championed by the ICRC and many other humanitarians, this notion is increasingly viewed by critics as naive and wrong. Humanitarian efforts have never really been neutral; there is no such thing as "pure" humanitarianism because the distribution of aid always has political ramifications. As former U.S. secretary of state for African affairs Chester A. Crocker reminded us in commenting upon the November 1996 crisis in Zaire, "intervention (just like nonintervention) is an inherently political action with inescapable political consequences."[29]

Even without military forces, humanitarian efforts are profoundly political; and unless they are carefully designed, they can actually exacerbate conflicts.[30] If done properly, civilian humanitarian efforts, and certainly ones supported by the use of military forces, should alter the balance of power in favor of victims. Decisions to remain on the sidelines can be considered a form of intervention in that by failing to help the oppressed, humanitarians comply with the oppressors. This latter view, championed especially by Doctors Without Borders (Médecins Sans Frontières [MSF]), has been gaining ground in the debate with the more traditional view espoused by the ICRC.

Those of us who support the more calculating and political approach recognize that virtually all humanitarian agencies, even the 125-year-old ICRC, are necessarily involved in political calculations and have had to compromise in many post–Cold War efforts.[31] For example, the ICRC, in spite of its principles, relied upon armed escorts, including the infamous "technicals" in Somalia, because sometimes only such private mini-armies or gangs can secure access and protect humanitarians in areas of turmoil. By actually diverting a portion of aid as bribes to those who control infrastructure, or giving in to extortion, humanitarian efforts are already deeply involved in political affairs.[32] As United Nations high commissioner Sadako Ogata has stated, ignoring the political consequences of humanitarianism is not an option: "Mass displacement of the most cruel kind imaginable has become a conscious objective of thc combatants in many armed conflicts. Humanitarian assistance is used as a weapon of war."[33]

An incident in Bosnia can serve as a particularly poignant illustration of how politicized humanitarian efforts have become despite their purveyors' fervent desire to remain neutral and impartial. At the beginning of 1993, the United Nations was unable to convince the Bosnian Serbs to let humanitarian convoys through to besieged towns in eastern Bosnia where people faced imminent starvation. Radovan Karadzic, the Bosnian Serb president who was subsequently indicted for war crimes, offered to guarantee "humanitarian corridors" of safe passage to the Muslims of Gorazde, Srebrenica, and Zepa, provided that they remove themselves from their besieged towns and thus from their islands in territory occupied by Bosnian Serbs. Responding with indignation to what they saw as a proposal for an abandonment of political commitment to eastern Bosnia and ethnic cleansing under humanitarian auspices, the Bosnian government banned all aid deliveries to Sarajevo with the intention of goading the United Nations into a more aggressive stance vis-à-vis the Bosnian Serbs. Viewing this as blackmail and a clear indication that the warring parties were unwilling to respect internationally sanctioned procedures, Ogata suspended all relief in Serb-held Bosnia and ordered staff to withdraw from Sarajevo. On the next day, February 19, then-UN secretary-general Boutros Boutros-Ghali reversed Ogata's decision.

This incident illustrates the degree to which humanitarian endeavors can become part of the local political landscape, especially when they help to change the demographic composition of an area in an ethnically charged war over territory. Even though Karadzic's plan for eliciting humanitarian endorsement for ethnic cleansing was not accepted, on many occasions well-meaning humanitarians have greased the wheels of ethnic resettlement. This has been especially the case, understandably, when the apparent alternative was the death of civilians.

Ethnic cleansing is an utter abomination. At the same time, accepting Karadzic's offer had a strong allure. It might have been sensible, especially because the alternative would have been unmentionably worse for the endangered people as a result of the West's unwillingness to use adequate military force. We now know that Srebrenica and Zepa were overrun by Bosnian Serbs in the summer of 1995, and that the flight of tens of thousands from the area led to mayhem and murder, including a massacre in Srebrenica under the watch of Dutch UN soldiers.[34] Our humanitarian impulse would have us turn back the clock and accept Karadzic's "humanitarian corridor."

Yet, this perspective and calculation are incomplete because Srebrenica's citizens would not have been the only victims of Karadzic's proposal. The movement out of the enclaves in eastern Bosnia would also have changed the strategic situation dramatically by creating what the Serbs had long sought—an ethnically homogenous swath of territory bordering on Serbia itself. The delicate balance on the ground, however fragile, maintained by the various actors would have been altered.

The moral justification for order is conservative, reflecting fears that tampering with established procedures could bring about an even worse state of affairs. While the rejection of Karadzic's proposal seems to have embraced the argument regarding the need to preserve the strategic order, it also went beyond to considerations of justice and morality in that the welfare of other potential victims, especially in Sarajevo and other so-called safe areas, was part of the policy calculation.

Sometimes the need to preserve order does not dominate. We are often confident that improvements can be made without risking chaos, and we even judge that dramatic changes are imperative. In such situations, the long-term collective good may require a sacrifice of the short-term interests of a group. Although the Bosnian government and the United Nations did not have to sacrifice themselves, they did face the almost certain prospect of institutional failure if all of eastern Bosnia turned into killing fields. They could not bow to Karadzic even though he seemed to have the capacity to realize his implied threats. In the case of Karadzic's corridors, governmental and intergovernmental officials went beyond the knee-jerk reaction characteristic of restorative humanitarianism. They ignored the injunction against political involvement to become thoroughly enmeshed in the political fate of threatened populations.

There are many moral facets in judging appropriate responses to Karadzic, but ultimately the justifiable rejection of his proposal involved a political judgment by both the United Nations and the Bosnian government that overrode the normal and visceral impulse to do anything in order to rescue the Muslims of eastern Bosnia. There was a greater value to be gained by not rushing to succor victims. There was also the outright rejection of the manner in which Karadzic's proposal was framed. His implied threat that aid would not be allowed was met with a momentary stiffening of

NATO resolve. His proposal made him even more of a pariah because its consequences were beyond what was considered imaginable abuse even by the deteriorating standards of behavior in the Balkans.

It took some time for the United Nations and the West to realize that negotiating with Karadzic was not fruitful, even if the failure to negotiate was at loggerheads with the humanitarian impulse. Can we generalize about the unspoken, yet pragmatic, political judgments that rejected Karadzic as a partner? Can we find a systematic way to consider relevant factors? Are there ways to analyze conflicts and leaders more quickly and directly so that we do not waste so many lives and resources in the process of blundering our way into situations where help is counterproductive?

A logical starting place would be to spell out political and ethical principles that might guide, and occasionally constrain, the humanitarian impulse. An unusual case of principled adaptation can be seen from the UNHCR's experience in the former Yugoslavia.

Rescuing the Displaced from Yugoslavia's Wars

Humanitarian action requires effective management of inevitable political pressures rather than maintenance of the myth that humanitarianism and politics occupy separate spheres. In the former Yugoslavia, the UNHCR's performance illustrated the most that can be expected even from the most successful rescue effort.

What was especially vital to the UNHCR's leadership was the expansion of its guiding mission to include not just the right of asylum and the protection of refugees but also assistance for all those with a well-founded fear of persecution. From its inception, the refugee agency has operated in the interstices of sovereignty, catering to the one right in the pantheon of human rights that is both national and international.[35] In the process of expanding its mandate to cover internally displaced persons (IDPs) and even those who were not displaced but whose lives were endangered, the UNHCR extended the legitimate purview of international organizations, although the debate will continue as to whether states have consented to this extension or been unable to mount an effective protest.[36]

Whom should humanitarians rescue? Here it is instructive to adopt and extend the definition of displacement. "Refugees" in the sense discussed here are no longer only those persons who have crossed the border of a sovereign state with a legitimate fear of persecution, as they were defined by the 1951 Convention on the Status of Refugees. They also include those who have not crossed state boundaries and thus are not entitled to special treatment by host states.[37] Most are confined to the states of which they are citizens or nationals. Furthermore, in war zones like Bosnia and Croatia, many of the neediest victims are not physically removed from their homes at all; rather the economic and social conditions necessary for survival are removed from them, just as they are for involuntary migrants. Displacement broadly defined to include all the victims of war is the most appropriate focus of rescue. It encompasses all those who do not have a polity or a state to which they can appeal and through which they might alter their condition without outside assistance.

In the former Yugoslavia, involuntary migration was not a side effect of armed conflict; it was an explicit war aim. The theme of forceful displacement was mixed with vituperative rhetoric, and this volatile combination preceded the actual uprooting of groups and individuals. Being a Muslim or a Serb in the "wrong" suburb of Sarajevo or a Muslim or a Croat in Mostar or a Serb or a Croat in Vukovar meant being "in the wrong place." The idea spread that each ethnic group had exclusive rights to certain geographic areas, and that these physical spaces could not be shared. This sentiment then accompanied political developments which situated ethnic or national groups within legal jurisdictions that they or their leaders found unacceptable.[38]

People were aware that they found themselves in the wrong political space before they were physically displaced from it. The political process—which reconstructed relations between people and their places of residence as well as made an issue of "who" would govern, rather than "how"—eliminated the basic trust that allows politics to proceed without violence. For too many people, even those who did not suffer physical displacement, fear and hatred dominated as they were excluded from a common social and political space because of their ethnic backgrounds.

The former Yugoslavia's proximity to Western Europe and the relative socioeconomic privilege of its populations distinguish this case from most other complex emergencies. Geopolitical position had consequences for a variety of issues ranging from military logistics and journalistic coverage to emigrant destinations and humanitarian access. Distances, logistics, the literacy of the populations, and available infrastructure were obstacles only because they were affected by the political conflict. Unlike other complex emergencies, there was no shortage of material resources; like others, however, political will was certainly absent.

Another atypical characteristic of Yugoslavia's wars was the prevalence and salience of international security organizations as actors, including the European Community (now Union), NATO, the Conference (now Organization) on Security and Cooperation in Europe, and the Western European Union. Although their impact was limited—and some observers would argue counterproductive—such a formidable array of politically powerful and resource-rich actors is unusual in current war zones. A comparable range and depth of involvement by the West or other powerful military actors in other future cases of displacement would be hard to imagine.

The substantial military presence meant that the UNHCR, as lead agency for the first time in the midst of armed conflict, was obliged to innovate with military liaison and personnel. Officers borrowed from Western armed forces were temporarily based at

UNHCR headquarters to help plan the airlift and manage large numbers of new recruits in the field who had no previous military experience. Subsequently, a recently retired military officer was engaged as an advisor to the high commissioner, and the UNHCR published a manual for staff who were working side by side with outside military forces.[39] Nonetheless, these organizational innovations and formidable military capabilities proved largely beside the point until there was political will to use them to stop the carnage in tandem with a Croatian-Bosnian military offensive in August-September 1995.

Most important, with the urging and financial backing of a host of donors, the UNHCR succored all casualties of Yugoslavia's wars, whatever their juridical status or physical location—a sharp departure from its traditional mandate and previous reluctance to pursue this task with the energy and enthusiasm required. As demonstrated by the data in the following table, "populations of concern" to the refugee agency included all the casualties of Yugoslavia's wars, 85 percent of whom fell outside the mandate of the refugee agency. The UNHCR helped everyone who needed help.

From the beginning, the UNHCR has expanded its protection and assistance activities. Begun as a temporary institution with a restricted scope for refugees after the Second World War, it became permanent under the 1951 Convention on the Status of Refugees, and global under the 1967 protocol. A concern for IDPs has emerged in the 1990s, though it has not been codified. The organizing principle is protecting and assisting people who require refuge in the broadest sense—those who do not have access to a state's protection and are vulnerable to persecution.

The UNHCR has been struggling to square its mandate, which is confined to refugees, with the stark reality that other persons involuntarily displaced by wars are "refugees in all but name," while still others live in "refugee-like conditions." With civil wars on the increase in the 1990s, IDPs began to outnumber refugees

Year-end Statistics, Populations of Concern to the UNHCR, 1991–1995

Date		*1991*	*1992*	*1993*	*1994*	*1995*
UNHCR assistance						
Bosnia-Herzegovina	Refugees	..	..	0	0	0
	IDPs*	..	..	1,290,000	1,282,600	1,097,800
	War victims	..	..	1,450,000	1,456,700	1,442,800
	Total	0	810,000	2,740,000	2,739,300	2,540,600
Croatia	Refugees	..	..	280,000	183,600	188,600
	IDPs*	..	..	344,000	307,000	198,700
	War victims	..	..	176,000	0	60,000
	Total	0	648,000	800,000	490,600	447,300
FYROM	Refugees	..	..	15,000	14,900	9,000
	IDPs*	..	..	0	0	0
	War victims	..	..	12,000	0	0
	Total	0	32,000	27,000	14,900	9,000

Continued

Yug. FR	Refugees	..	..	479,100	195,500	650,000
	IDPs*	..	..	0	0	700
	War victims	..	..	150,000	0	0
	Total	500	516,500	629,100	195,500	650,700
Slovenia	Refugees	..	..	45,000	29,200	22,300
	IDPs*	..	..	0	0	0
	War victims	..	..	0	0	0
	Total	0	47,000	45,000	29,200	22,300
Total	**Refugees**	**..**	**..**	**819,100**	**423,200**	**869,900**
	IDPs*	**..**	**..**	**1,634,000**	**1,589,600**	**1,297,200**
	War victims	**..**	**..**	**1,788,000**	**1,456,700**	**1,502,800**
	Total	**500**	**2,053,500**	**4,241,100**	**3,469,500**	**3,669,900**

* IDPs = internally displaced persons

in many crises and eventually worldwide. The UN secretary-general and donors increasingly asked the UNHCR to assume responsibility for assisting and protecting both refugees and IDPs. UN high commissioner for refugees Ogata commissioned a study to spell out a "comprehensive approach to coerced human displacement."[40]

The UNHCR truly acted as the "lead agency" in the former Yugoslavia; in UN jargon, it was in the humanitarian driver's seat. It played a role that a growing number of observers see as vital: a "UN Humanitarian Organization for Casualties of War." With the blessing of donors, the UNHCR moved away from its usual statistical preoccupation with categorizing refugees—as distinct from other civilians in need—and ceased to restrict assistance and protection efforts to those victims who had crossed an international boundary. The UNHCR seized responsibility where the leaders of the former Yugoslavia had failed dismally. This is not to say that the UNHCR's activities were without problems. It is rather the enterprising interpretation of its mission along with competent implementation in difficult circumstances that needs to be emphasized.[41] Accompanied by the lack of international political will, however, helping victims was clearly insufficient.

Humanitarianism and Sovereignty

Observers of and participants in humanitarian endeavors in the former Yugoslavia see these efforts as reweaving a tattered social fabric. They work to reconstitute a society in disrepair whose rescue was as successful as any such effort is ever likely to be. But this approach avoids confronting sovereignty—the principle that upholds the autonomy of populations and their polities. Humanitarian practice points us toward the ambiguity of the principles that regulate the crossing of lines demarcating autonomous societies, cultures, and nations as well as the states that represent and protect them. In normal times these sovereign boundary lines are indispensable. In the words of Article 2(7), "nothing contained in the present Charter shall authorize the United Nations to intervene in matters which are essentially within the domestic jurisdiction of any state." When the fabric of a community has been shredded, seeking that community's consent for aid is problematic; its weakened condition does not allow it to respond as it might in less trying times.[42]

Often overlooked in discussions about when humanitarian intervention is justified is the fact that even forceful intrusions do not necessarily challenge the principle of autonomy, but rather may seek to bolster what outside soldiers are violating temporarily, for the sake of restoring it. This is because there are temporarily no viable institutions to exercise or express the autonomy that is presumed to be present. Humanitarianism is not exclusively a cosmopolitan effort to unite all humanity at the expense of the autonomy of political communities encapsulated by sovereign states. The humanitarian impulse is triggered precisely in circumstances in which the autonomous continuation of a population under minimal standards of human dignity is jeopardized. The UNHCR's efforts in pre-Dayton Yugoslavia can be usefully viewed as a response to the condition of displacement broadly understood, whereby people had no ground on which to stand, no place in which to exercise their autonomy.

The essential question then becomes not one of respecting it, but rather one of understanding the nature of the processes through which outside humanitarians participate in reweaving an unraveled autonomy. Are humanitarians restoring the autonomy of the people whom they rush to rescue or are they participating in a more revolutionary process through which they are establishing a lasting link with the endangered population, contravening the habit of moral separation reflected by sovereignty? A direct examination of this question should help clarify the difficulties in defining the exact role of the humanitarian impulse in contemporary world politics.

The activation of the humanitarian impulse shines a new light on the boundaries that once preserved the integrity of a polity and its dignity as an independent culture. We suddenly recognize the salience of boundaries that in normal times are taken for granted. Populations "over there" are no longer primarily an autonomous strand of the global fabric; they become humans in inhuman distress. Is the goal to restore autonomy along pre-emergency lines or to reweave a cloth so that it will be better able to withstand future crises, something that implies a deeper intrusion into the political lives of the distressed population?

Before considering the justification for each alternative, it would be useful to delineate the relationship between humanitarianism and sovereignty. The original overriding concern of the former—best exemplified by the venerable ICRC and international humanitarian law—was to limit the most destructive and indiscriminate consequences of armed conflicts among sovereign states and a few aspects of civil war.[43] If there were questions regarding the status of the belligerents and their links to populations for whom they claimed to be fighting, their control over such populations and a fixed territory provided a reliable guideline to the domain of their responsibilities.[44] Outsiders would adjust their relations to a particular conflict or complex emergency by recognizing a specific government or authority as reflective of legitimate sovereignty. Today, the humanitarian impulse often responds to situations in which there are no integral polities—no viable unities of government, people, and territory to serve as candidates for sovereignty.

With the agents of outside assistance as the saintly executors of a universal moral sense, the humanitarian impulse collapses the barriers that normally separate Americans and Swedes from Bosnians and Rwandans. The moral barriers between "us" and "them" dissolve as we encounter naked humanity and are exposed to misery that is no longer mediated by social differences and distance. No culture, custom, religion, or ethnicity ever justifies the suffering that befalls individuals in a complex emergency. Individuals just like us, possibly huddling together in families or family-like groups, await assistance from those to whom they have established a direct link of common humanity by virtue of having fallen out of the social and cultural web that had made them closer to one another than they were to us. Now, as humanitarian subjects they are equally close to all of us.

The recent unleashing of the humanitarian impulse reveals the extent to which sovereignty is no longer sacrosanct.[45] When the suffering of entire populations overwhelms their capacity to fend for themselves, we sometimes bound over the barriers of sovereignty because the victims are no longer strangers. Their threatened existence connects them intimately to us through their ineffable humanity. Differences of culture, nation, ethnicity, and religion are no longer a concern because they will persist only in diminished form, if at all, should their carriers perish. In such times, distressed humanity is "over here," unadorned by social artifice and shorn of its differences and exoticism.

Nonetheless, the shibboleth of sovereignty remains key when decision makers contemplate humanitarian intervention. Sovereignty should be examined dispassionately; we should not delude ourselves into thinking that it is a natural fact.[46] It is not an insurmountable mountain. As a conceptual shorthand, sovereignty summarizes a series of other moral considerations.[47]

Sovereignty promises and protects much that is valuable.[48] It is meant to preserve autonomy, in the same way that we mean to preserve the independence of our communities, workplace, and family life in domestic politics. In particular, we expect and insist that others, especially the state, respect our separateness and autonomy. In international affairs, sovereignty delineates the units of survival and the boundaries of identity. But it is not only for the protection of people who want to preserve their distinctiveness. Humanity benefits from knowledge—no matter how limited—about the variety of potential modes of human existence and association. But sovereignty also remains frustrating for humanitarians because it divides peoples by protecting their diversity. Sovereignty establishes a moral distance and provides no guide when the autonomy that it so absolutely enshrines collapses or is used to justify intolerable abuse.

Humanitarianism can thus be viewed as a principle that indirectly links human beings, recognizing the fallen barrier of sovereignty in order to resurrect it. In its reformist, restorative guise, humanitarianism is not an end in itself, but a means for reestablishing the sovereign separateness of target populations. Humanitarian responses to the failures of sovereign divisions can be compared to the emergence of social work in domestic polities. The progress of capitalism and modernization inevitably generates victims whose suffering demands mitigation, and social workers help people regain their autonomy.[49]

The comparison of humanitarian efforts to social work is apt because of the contrast with conventional notions of foreign policy practice.[50] Mortally endangered populations lose their diplomatic voice because no one in particular is authorized to speak or act on their behalf.[51] In spite of their broad mandates, various intergovernmental and nongovernmental humanitarian organizations inevitably seek to negotiate with authoritative representatives, but there is no indigenous sovereign to assume responsibility. And the relationship of other sovereigns to the endangered population is not clear. Conventional recognition does little to alleviate the suffering that indigenous aspirants to sovereignty are usually unprepared or unwilling to address. Humanitarianism, then, helps reconstitute a moral community so that it may once again function as an autonomous member of international society, permitting us to return to and reinforce the habits of moral separation that undergird the international society of sovereigns.

Diplomacy rests on a process of competition, be it cooperative or conflictive, through which agents of sovereign populations occasionally gather to conduct business and reaffirm the distinctiveness of the peoples for whom they speak. In the humanitarian context, there is no sovereign to speak for the destitute. Those mortally endangered have lost the capacity to assert their separate identities, and they require outside humanitarian attention because the vessel that carried them has run aground. Foreign ministers and heads of state have seen their role in the emergence of humanitarianism as an effort to simultaneously save the drowning wretches and rebuild their vessel—to relocate them in the ship of state that carried them prior to the onset of disaster. That the person at the helm may be a war criminal who has offended humanity itself is frequently attributed to the unavoidable realities of world politics. Certainly the more privileged sovereigns may come to the conclusion that social work is not their business, and that there is virtually no national interest to be pursued or protected in complex emergencies.

If that is to be the case, we should recognize and acknowledge the nature of such decisions, being careful not to delude ourselves into thinking that to resist the humanitarian impulse is simply to realize that there are limits to what can be done in the uncertain and insecure international realm. Such decisions also question the limits of our identities and what we think of ourselves.[52]

When humanitarians rush to rescue, sovereignty fades. Moral barriers crumble as the suffering of now-intimate others authorizes assistance and insists upon access to victims. The invocation of boundaries that preserve diversity and pluralism becomes a weak excuse for not acting according to our moral sense, which says that we cannot stand apart from naked humanity. We may choose to reinforce our side of the fence of sovereignty once we get tired and discouraged or when the demands on limited resources for multiple rescues exceeds the supply. But that is a peculiar choice that requires justification. The appeal to sovereignty diminishes in moral weight during complex emergencies because endangered populations cannot assure their own survival, which obviously is the precondition for their continued dignity. This line of argument is further complicated because the benefits of rescue are often difficult to ascertain. One dilemma is a heightened dependence that distorts and displaces indigenous survival mechanisms,[53] which has led one analyst to a new bottom line: "do no harm."[54]

The humanitarian impulse is a reflection of a universal moral sense that sovereignty does not bar our concern for strangers in distress. The expansion of humanitarian efforts in the post–Cold War era indicates that sovereignty is waning, though not necessarily irreversibly. At the same time, those whose powers, prerogatives, and privileges may be threatened by humanitarian action routinely invoke sovereignty as a barrier and point to the supposed weakness of the obligation flowing from the direct connection to distressed humanity.

Humanity, however, is not a category for which we have prepared our political concepts, despite the seeming internationalization of human rights and humanitarian discourse.[55] Hannah Arendt, who drew on her own experience of displacement, discussed "the terror of the idea of humanity" and the existential burden that it placed on fellow humans.[56] Indeed, the history of the stateless and of refugees is a prominent theme in the twentieth century as states jockey to adjust the precise distributions of populations for whom they would assume responsibility. Through Hannah Arendt we can appreciate the challenge displaced populations represent to the decision makers of sovereign states.

One of the great tribulations in the twentieth century is statelessness, which Arendt equated with rightlessness. For her the exercise of rights that was fundamental to the human condition was not a question of moral philosophy or legal doctrine but a matter of political action. The horror of displacement was the condition of not being engaged in the political construction of one's life. She looked to a politics across state domains as an alternative to the arbitrary decisions of states to include or exclude portions of humanity. And this mode of politics was to be built by and around precisely those people who had no state to call their own.

Rescue in complex emergencies is problematic because it is triggered precisely when the autonomy of a society is in jeopardy. To return to our original metaphor, we seek to bring the drowning person back to a beach whose sands shift continually and which is occupied by deadly armed combatants who hamper relief efforts and often menace victims and aid personnel as well. Such rescue efforts attempt to return the endangered populations to a *status quo ante*. The central paradox of rescue thus is that it seeks to restore a social order that has failed to protect its members from natural or man-made deprivations. Triggering the humanitarian impulse, social collapse leads to justifications for the rush of aid, relief, and crisis diplomacy. It is then, at best, short-sighted to restore any social order that will be autonomous only to the extent that outsiders will have politically disengaged themselves.

The case of the former Yugoslavia illustrates that while we may want to do the right thing, the right thing to do is not always obvious, although we have often deceived ourselves into embracing a simplistic idea of rescue as an absolute good. This concept implies that one is going to pull drowning strangers from a turbulent sea and restore them to firm ground, whereupon they will be able to continue a dignified life as the same strangers who they were before the peril. In spite of the reluctance to utter the "N-word"—nationbuilding—after Vietnam and Somalia, we hope to restore populations to conditions in which they will be able to sustain themselves and remain a self-contained entity "foreign" to us and separated by the legal and moral boundary of state sovereignty.

What happens when the need for rescue becomes episodic and almost routinized? Interventions closely modeled after Good Samaritan rescue often seem to require repetition—for example, Liberia, the Sudan, and Rwanda. In the last few years the term "exit strategy," which provides a deadline for disengagement and not a criterion of success, has entered the humanitarian lexicon. However, future rescue efforts almost become assured in such cases, as experiences in Somalia and Haiti suggest. The exit of outsiders is simply not an adequate test for the autonomy of the target, if that is to be our concern. As UN high commissioner for refugees Ogata has stated, time and patience are required because "there is certainly no such thing as a humanitarian surgical strike."[57]

We have not yet thought through what it will mean to move beyond the ineffective and sporadic conscience-salving variety of rescue whose main motivation is the removal of horrific images from our television screens and newspapers.[58] Populations in danger require sustained commitments that are different from the current approach of rescue.

Institutionalizing such a sustained humanitarianism is problematic because it would establish a direct moral link to "foreigners" and a lasting responsibility toward them. Moreover, we could not easily extricate ourselves, contrary to George Kennan's argument with respect to the U.S. role in today's humanitarian interventions. He has proposed that the United States return to the kind of policy promoted by John Quincy Adams, whereby we would help not by actually getting involved, but by concentrating on perfecting our own polity and allowing it to serve as an example for others:

> The interventions in which we are now engaged or committed represent serious responsibilities. Any abrupt withdrawal from them would be a violation of these responsibilities. . . . Only when we have succeeded in extracting ourselves from the existing ones with dignity and honor will the question of further interventions present itself to us in the way it did to Mr. Adams.[59]

Kennan implies a responsibility to ourselves and to those whom we seek to help, but the nature of this responsibility is unclear. Removing the official agents of states from the territory of a failed sovereign makes matters appear simpler for those who have the capacity to help, but it does nothing to clarify the inevitable continuation of relations among different populations and their representatives, which relations are neither terminated nor simplified by outside military and diplomatic engagement or disengagement.

To see sovereignty as an unquestioned idea that aims to preserve the good of a plurality of nations, societies, and cultures seeking to survive on their own is to evade responsibilities that attach to already existing relations among societies. At present, we are trapped between two principles: one that asks us to restore sovereignty and one that tells us to embrace the long-term transnational responsibilities that emerge from the pursuit of humanitarianism as an end in itself.

Conclusion

Bridging the normative gap between restorative and revolutionary humanitarianism—between actions that seek to rebuild state sovereignty and those that seek to transcend it—is a central foreign policy challenge. Groping to go beyond rescue—having learned, often painfully, about its limitations—is the priority agenda item for humanitarians, be they scholars or practitioners. We cannot rely on sovereignty to take care of itself, nor are we certain how to control the humanitarian impulse that causes us to rush in to rescue those who can no longer look to a sovereign to assure their survival. Rescue is misleading in that it fails to acknowledge the possibly irreparable disorder which preceded the crisis that motivated the rescue. Moreover, rescue fails to recognize the moral implications of humanitarian connections across borders.

The UNHCR's experience in the former Yugoslavia exemplified its role as an institution located at the interstices of sovereignty. It was designed to help the community of states manage the people who fled beyond the borders of certain states, relocating them in appropriate sovereign jurisdictions. With the emergence of internal displacement as a global problem and its direct, violent politicization in the case of the former Yugoslavia, the UNHCR extended the principle of caring for refugees to encompass all victims. Its legitimacy rested on its charge to assist all those without refuge, whatever their physical location or juridical status. However limited its discretion as an agent of member states, the UNHCR and the humanitarian community that it led sought to rescue endangered populations where neither indigenous nor outside political authorities took their responsibilities to these populations seriously.

Although the UNHCR extended itself admirably as rescue coordinator in the former Yugoslavia, it was not in a position to challenge the political problems that caused the suffering in the first place and, in fact, allowed it to continue.[60] The management of the conflict almost exclusively through the politics of rescue also served to delay and perhaps eclipse consideration of the mutual obligations of the rescuers and the rescued beyond the immediacy of the emergency phase. The final outcome of the Dayton process is far from clear as of this writing, but the international community, with the United States at the helm, seems intent on restoring minimally sustainable sovereign boundaries as a prelude to an eventual disengagement of outside military forces.[61]

The people of the former Yugoslavia were rescued under the restorative principle of humanitarianism. We should realize the limits of humanitarianism inherent in the politics of rescue; otherwise we can do additional injustice by not considering the political relationships that accompany the humanitarian impulse. Thus, it is not so much the separation of humanitarianism and politics that presents a challenge for the future as it is the conscious analysis and management of the tensions between them. From a global perspective, dilemmas attending the scarcity of resources and the burgeoning demands for rescue can be compared to triage in medical emergencies.[62] Decisions regarding who gets prior attention and scarce medical resources are based on a stock of medical knowledge and a corpus of medical ethics supported by well-worn practice. In the rapidly changing field of politically conscious humanitarian engagement, however, we have only begun to digest the profound implications of "humanitarian war"[63] and the inherent limits of multilateral military efforts.[64] There is no return to the apparent clarity and simplicity of the decades when Cold War politics persuaded us too easily that who was worth rescuing and who was not depended upon ideological or geopolitical affiliations.

We can continue to assume the appropriateness and applicability of an apolitical and automatic response to earthquakes or other natural disasters. Although these too will have political implications, they will be relatively minor in comparison with the straightforward charge to alleviate suffering. Complex humanitarian emergencies, however, are different. They often overwhelm not just short-term but also longer-term local coping capacities, as well as the coping capacities of the international humanitarian system. It is necessary to contemplate the need, rationale, and consequences of lending helping hands in such circumstances. Developments that bring about deterioration in the human condition, cause international outrage, and catalyze responses are also part of the social fabric that outside assistance is supposed to mend. Humanitarians must proceed into this maelstrom with care, reflecting before responding rather than acting impulsively. They must recognize that they are not simply mending a rent fabric, but also participating in the process through which it is being repaired.

The rescue model of intervention implies discrete acts of assistance that seek to restore a person or a group of persons to a position of autonomy. The person in need is a stranger, a fellow human with whom we share little besides our common humanity. When we help, we also enlarge and dignify ourselves. Our humanity becomes more expansive and encompassing. The relationship between the rescuer and the rescued is based on a simple occurrence. Nothing significant changes in the relations between the strangers—except perhaps a warm afterglow of common affection—because isolated acts of kindness are not integrated into an ongoing relationship.

But this image misrepresents the mutual involvement of the agents of the international humanitarian system and the peoples of the former Yugoslavia. Thus, rescue provides no guidance or justification for the politics that it is supposed to guide. This was clear from 1991 to 1995, and it also is evident from the implementation of the Dayton agreements. Bosnia's displaced people—those who were rescued and promised the choice of returning to their homes—continue to complicate what might otherwise have been a symbolically multiethnic state divided along orderly ethnic lines.[65] It is in our vacillating commitment to the promise made that we again see the inadequacy of rescue as a guiding principle.

If we are unable or unwilling to provide a clear justification for the political action that we undertake in response to the humanitarian impulse, we should at least be honest and skeptical about our own kindness.

NOTES

1. This essay draws on the authors' study of human displacement in the former Yugoslavia. See Weiss and Pasic, "Dealing With Displacement and Suffering from Yugoslavia's Wars: Conceptual and Operational Issues," in Francis M. Deng and Roberta Cohen, eds., *Masses in Flight* (Washington, D.C.: Brookings Institution, forthcoming). The authors would like to thank Jarat Chopra for his comments and Béla Hovy for his help in generating statistics.

2. Raimo Vayrenen, *The Age of Humanitarian Emergencies* (Helsinki: World Institute for Development Economics Research, June 1996), draft working paper.

3. See Samuel M. Makinda, "Sovereignty and International Security," *Global Governance* 2 (May–August 1996), 149–68, and Thomas G. Weiss, "Military-Civilian Humanitarianism: The 'Age of Innocence' Is Over," *International Peacekeeping* 2 (Summer 1995), 157–74.

4. Paul Wapner, "Politics Beyond the State: Environmental Activism and World Civic Politics," *World Politics* 47 (April 1995), 311–40, and Kelly Kate Pease and David P. Forsythe, "Human Rights, Humanitarian Intervention, and World Politics," *Human Rights Quarterly* 15 (1993), 290–314.

5. See a special issue on "Rescue—The Paradoxes of Virtue," *Social Research* 62 (Spring 1995), especially Michael Walzer's "The Politics of Rescue," 53–66. See also David Rieff, "The Humanitarian Trap," *World Policy Journal* 12 (Winter 1994–95, 1–11).

6. See Stephen Krasner, "Sovereignty and Intervention" in Gene Lyons and Michael Mastanduno, eds., *Beyond Westphalia? State Sovereignty* *and International Intervention* (Baltimore: Johns Hopkins University Press, 1995), 228–49, and Hedley Bull, ed., *Intervention in World Politics* (New York: Oxford University Press, 1984).

7. Complete bibliographic information and its interpretation are found in Oliver Famsbotham and Tom Woodhouse, *Humanitarian Intervention in Contemporary Conflict* (Cambridge: Polity Press, 1996). See also John Harriss, ed., *The Politics of Humanitarian Intervention* (London: Pinter, 1995); James Mayall, ed., *The New Interventionism: United Nations Experience in Cambodia, Former Yugoslavia, and Somalia* (New York: Cambridge University Press, 1996); and Jan Nederveen Pieterse, ed., *World Orders in the Making: Humanitarian Intervention and Beyond* (London: Macmillan, forthcoming).

8. See Larry Minear and Thomas G. Weiss, *Mercy Under Fire: War and the Global Humanitarian Community* (Boulder: Westview Press, 1995), and *Humanitarian Politics* (New York: Foreign Policy Association, 1995).

9. Bill Clinton, "Why Bosnia Matters to America," *Newsweek* 126, November 13, 1995, 55.

10. Here it is interesting to note the alteration in the French literature from *devoir* (or duty) to *droit* (right). See Bernard Kouchner and Mario Bettati, *Le devoir d'ingérence: Peut-on les laisser mourir?* (Paris: Denoël, 1987), and Mario Bettati, *Le droit d'ingérence: Mutation de l'ordre international* (Paris: Odile Jacob, 1996).

11. Department of State, *Clinton Administration's Policy on Reforming Multilateral Peace Operations* (Pub. 1061, Bureau of IO Affairs, May 1994), which explicates a presidential directive known as PDD-25. See also Chris Seiple, *The U.S. Military/NGO Relationships in Humanitarian Interventions* (U.S. Army War College Peacekeeping Institute: Center for Strategic Leadership, 1996); Com. Richard R. Beardsworth, Com. Richard V. Kikla, Lt. Col. Philip F. Shutler, and Col. Guy C. Swan, *Strengthening Coordination Mechanisms Between NGOs and the U.S. Military at the Theater/Country Level During Complex Humanitarian Emergencies*, draft, March 1996, from Harvard University's National Security Program; and Kenneth Allard, *Somalia Operations: Lessons Learned* (Washington, D.C.: National Defense University Press, 1995). For a critical perspective proposing that preparation for and engagement in peace operations diminish the military's preparedness, see Colonel Charles J. Dunlap, "The Last American Warrior: Non-traditional Missions and the Decline of the U.S. Armed Forces," *The Fletcher Forum for World Affairs* 18 (Winter/Spring 1994), 65–82.

12. See R. M. Connaughton, *Military Support and Protection for*

Humanitarian Assistance: Rwanda, April–December 1994 (Camberly, Surrey, U.K.: Strategic and Combat Studies Institute, 1996), 18, p. 71. See also Hugo Slim, "The Stretcher and the Drum: Civil-Military Relations in Peace Support Operations," paper presented in Pretoria, South Africa, March 13–14, 1996.

13. See Thomas G. Weiss and Amir Pasic, "Reinventing UNHCR: Enterprising Humanitarians in the Former Yugoslavia, 1991–1995," *Global Governance 3* (January–March 1997), 41–57.

14. United States Mission to the United Nations, *Global Humanitarian Emergencies, 1996*, document dated February 1996, p. 24. The periods vary slightly, and there may be some needs and some disbursements not reflected in the data. The accuracy of the broad comparative data and the privileged position of the former Yugoslavia, however, are clear.

15. Quoted by Alison Mitchell, "Clinton's About-Face," *New York Times*, September 24, 1996, A8.

16. Cedric Thornberry, "Saving the War Crimes Tribunal," *Foreign Policy* 104 (Fall 1996), 72–85, quote at 75.

17. For an elaboration of the foundational role played by neutrality and impartiality at the core of the identity and mission of the International Committee of the Red Cross and the Red Cross and Red Crescent Movement, see Denise Plattner, "ICRC Neutrality and Neutrality in Humanitarian Assistance," *International Review of the Red Cross* 36 (March–April 1996), 161–79. Clearly, our discussion assumes that humanitarianism cannot be apolitical and that the dilemma at hand revolves around the principled relation between humanitarianism and sovereignty.

18. For example, see Rabia Ali and Lawrence Lifschultz, eds., *Why Bosnia? Writings on the Balkan War* (Stony Creek, Conn.: Pamphleteer's Press, 1993).

19. For a review of the limits of the post–Cold War ambitions of humanitarian intervention, see Stephen John Stedman, "The New Interventionists," *Foreign Affairs* 72 (Winter 1993), 1–16. For a normative argument in the opposite direction, see Nigel Rodley, ed., *To Loose the Bonds of Wickedness: International Intervention in Defence of Human Rights* (London: Brassey's, 1992).

20. The most controversial analysis is Rakiya Omaar and Alex de Waal, *Humanitarianism Unbound? Current Dilemmas Facing Multi-Mandate Relief Operations in Political Emergencies* (London: African Rights, 1994), Discussion Paper No. 5. There is also a rapidly growing literature on the political dimensions of humanitarian action and peacekeeping. See, for example, Jarat Chopra, "The Space of Peace-Maintenance," *Political Geography* 15 (March–April 1996), 335–57, and Antonio Donini, *The Policies of Mercy: UN Coordination in Afghanistan, Mozambique, and Rwanda* (Providence: Thomas J. Watson Jr. Institute for International Studies, 1996), Occasional Paper No. 22.

21. Alain Destexhe, "Foreword," in François Jean, ed., *Populations in Danger 1995* (London: Médecins Sans Frontières, 1995), 13–14.

22. For a recent infusion of sobriety, see Ed Mansfield and Jack Snyder, "Democratization and the Danger of War," *International Security* 20 (Summer 1995), 5–38. A less technical version can be found in *Foreign Affairs* 74 (May–June 1995), 79–97. For a general argument regarding the priority of order over justice, see Hedley Bull, *The Anarchical Society* (New York: Columbia University Press, 1977).

23. For collections of essays, see Marianne Heiberg, ed., *Subduing Sovereignty: Sovereignty and the Right to Intervene* (New York: St. Martin's Press, 1994); Lyons and Mastanduno, eds., *Beyond Westphalia?*; and Paul A. Winters, ed., *Interventionism: Current Controversies* (San Diego: Greenhaven Press, 1995).

24. See Gerald B. Helman and Steven R. Ratner, "Saving Failed States," *Foreign Policy* 89 (Winter 1992–93), 3–20, and I. William Zartman, ed., *Collapsed States: The Disintegration and Restoration of Legitimate Authority* (Boulder: Lynne Rienner, 1995).

25. See Stanley Hoffmann, *Duties Beyond Borders: On the Limits and Possibilities of Ethical International Politics* (Syracuse: Syracuse University Press, 1981).

26. For a brief overview of the political obstacles that marred the humanitarian mission in Bosnia, see Mark Prutsalis, "Humanitarian Aid: Too Little, Too Late," in Ben Cohen and George Stamkoski, eds., *With No Peace to Keep: United Nations Peacekeeping and the War in the Former Yugoslavia* (London: Grainpress Ltd., 1995), 77–85.

27. One analytical effort to understand this phenomenon is Thomas G. Weiss and Cindy Collins, *Humanitarian Challenges and Intervention: World Politics and the Dilemmas of Help* (Boulder: Westview, 1996).

28. Susan Woodward, "Redrawing Borders in a Period of Systemic Transition," in Milton Esman and Shibley Telhami, eds., *International Organization and Ethnic Conflict* (Ithaca: Cornell University Press, 1995), 213.

29. Chester A. Crocker, "All Aid Is Political," *New York Times*, November 21, 1996, A29.

30. See John Prendergast, *Frontline Diplomacy: Humanitarian Aid and Conflict in Africa* (Boulder: Lynne Rienner, 1996); and Michael Maren, *The Road to Hell: The Ravaging Effects of Foreign Aid and International Charity* (New York: Free Press, 1997).

31. For discussions of the ICRC's principles and approaches, see David P. Forsythe, *Humanitarian Politics* (Baltimore: Johns Hopkins University Press, 1977), and James A. Joyce, *Red Cross International and the Strategy for Peace* (New York: Oceana, 1959).

32. See the discussion of the use of relief resources to feed soldiers and as bribes for safe passage in Åge Eknes, "The United Nations' Predicament in the Former Yugoslavia," in Thomas G. Weiss, ed., *The United Nations and Civil Wars* (Boulder: Lynne Rienner, 1995), 109–26. In mid-1994, he wrote: "The accusation that the United Nation has indirectly legitimized ethnic cleansing and territorial aggression does not bite as much today—not because it is less true but because it has become a fact of life" (p. 124). For a discussion of the possible manipulation of aid agencies by belligerents, see Gayle E. Smith, "Relief Operations and Military Strategy," in Thomas G. Weiss and Larry Minear, eds., *Humanitarianism Across Borders: Sustaining Civilians in Times of War* (Boulder: Lynne Rienner, 1993), 97–116.

33. Quoted by Christopher S. Wren, "Resettling Refugees: U.N. Facing New Burden," *New York Times*, November 24, 1995, A15.

34. See O. van der Wind, *Report Based on the Debriefing on Srebrenica* (Assen: Netherlands Ministry of Defence, October 4, 1995).

35. Ernst Tugendhat, "The Moral Dilemma in the Rescue of Refugees," *Social Research* 62 (Spring 1995), 127–41.

36. For a discussion of migration as a multifaceted security issue, see Michael S. Teitelbaum and Myron Weiner, eds., *Threatened Peoples, Threatened Borders: World Migration and U.S. Foreign Policy* (New York: Norton, 1995), and Myron Weiner, ed., *International Migration and Security* (Boulder: Westview, 1993).

37. For an overview of the issues raised by the secretary-general on internally displaced persons, see Francis M. Deng, *Protecting the Dispossessed: A Challenge for the International Community* (Washington, D.C.: The Brookings Institution, 1993). See also Roberta Cohen and Jacques Cuénod, *Improving Institutional Arrangements for the Internally Displaced* (Washington, D.C.: Brookings Institution, October 1995), and Francis M. Deng, "Dealing with the Displaced: A Challenge to the International Community," *Global Governance* 1 (Winter 1995), 45–58.

38. See Bogdan Denitch, *Ethnic Nationalism: The Tragic Death of Yugoslavia* (Minneapolis: University of Minnesota Press, 1994), 173–85; Norman Cigar, *Genocide in Bosnia: The Policy of "Ethnic Cleansing"* (College Station: Texas A&M Press, 1995), 22–37; V. P. Gagnon, "Ethnic Nationalism and International Conflict: The Case of Serbia," *International Security* 19 (Winter 1994/95), 130–66; Branka Magas, *The Destruction of Yugoslavia: Tracking the Breakup 1980–92* (London: Verso, 1993); Slavko Curuvija and Ivan Torov, "The March to War (1980–1990)," in Jasminka Udovicki and James Ridgeway, eds., *Yugoslavia's Ethnic Nightmare: The Inside Story of Europe's Unfolding Ordeal* (Chicago: Lawrence Hill Books, 1995); Misha Glenny, *The Fall of Yugoslavia: The Third Balkan War* (New York: Penguin, 1992); Susan Woodward, *Balkan Tragedy: Chaos and Dissolution after the Cold War* (Washington, D.C.: Brookings Institution, 1995); and Richard H. Ullman, ed., *The World and Yugoslavia's Wars* (New York: Council on Foreign Relations, 1996).

39. See *A UNHCR Handbook for the Military on Humanitarian Operations* (Geneva: UNHCR, January 1995).

40. Office of the United Nations High Commissioner for Refugees, Division of International Protection, *UNHCR's Operational Experience with Internally Displaced Persons* (Geneva: UNHCR, September 1994).

41. See Alex Cunliffe and Michael Pugh, "The UNHCR as Lead Agency in the Former Yugoslavia," *Journal of Humanitarian Assistance* (April 1, 1996), http://131.111.106.147/Articles/A011.htm.

42. For an explication of the need to have consent and preserve "the autonomy of the 'target,' " see Michael Joseph Smith, "Ethics and Intervention," *Ethics & International Affairs* 3 (1989), 1–26.

43. See Geoffrey Best, *Humanity in Warfare* (New York: Columbia University Press, 1980); Sheldon M. Cohen, *Arms and Judgment: Law, Morality, and the Conduct of Warfare in the Twentieth Century* (Boulder: Westview, 1989); and Hilaire McCoubrey and Nigel D. White, *International Law and Armed Conflict* (Aldershot, U.K.: Dartmouth, 1992).

44. The classic text is Hersch Lauterpacht, *Recognition in International Law* (Cambridge, U.K.: Cambridge University Press, 1947). See also James Crawford, *The Creation of States in International Law* (New York: Oxford University Press, 1979).

45. See Jarat Chopra and Thomas G. Weiss, "Sovereignty Is No Longer Sacrosanct," *Ethics & International Affairs* 6 (1992), 95–117.

46. See Thomas Biersteker and Cynthia Weber, eds., *State Sovereignty as Social Construct* (New York: Cambridge University Press, 1996).

47. Indeed, when scholars defend the principle of nonintervention, they elucidate the positive aspect of sovereignty. See, for example, Michael Walzer, "The Moral Standing of States: A Response to Four Critics," in Charles Beitz et al., eds., *International Ethics: A Philosophy and Public Affairs Reader* (Princeton: Princeton University Press, 1985), 217–37.

48. See Terry Nardin, *Law, Morality, and the Relations of States* (Princeton: Princeton University Press, 1983).

49. See, for example, June Axinn and Herman Levin, *Social Welfare: A History of the American Response to Need* (New York: Longman, 1992).

50. See Michael Mandelbaum, "Foreign Policy as Social Work," *Foreign Affairs* 75 (January–February 1996), 1–16.

51. For a discussion about living up to the responsibilities of sovereignty with particular reference to IDPs, see Francis M. Deng, "Frontiers of Sovereignty," *Leiden Journal of International Law* 8 (1995), 249–86.

52. For a psychological description of the processes that lead to international human rights advocacy and the concern for those outside one's own domestic polity, see Todd E. Jennings, "The Developmental Dialectic of International Human Rights Advocacy," *Political Psychology* 17 (March 1996), 77–95.

53. See John Prendergast and Colin Scott, *Aid with Integrity: Avoiding the Potential of Humanitarian Aid to Sustain Conflict; A Strategy for USAID/BHR/OFDA in Complex Emergencies*, draft manuscript (Washington, D.C.: Center of Concern, March 1996).

54. Mary B. Anderson, *Do No Harm: Supporting Local Capacities for Peace through Aid* (Cambridge, Mass.: Collaborative for Development Action, 1996).

55. See David P. Forsythe, *The Internationalization of Human Rights* (Lexington, Mass.: Lexington Books, 1991); Jack Donnelly, *Universal Human Rights* (Ithaca: Cornell University Press, 1989); and Jonathan I. Charney, "Universal International Law," *American Journal of International Law* 87 (October 1993), 529–51.

56. See Hannah Arendt, "Peace or Armistice in the Near East," in Ron Feldman, ed., *The Jew as Pariah* (New York: Grove Press, 1978), 193–224. See also Jeffery C. Isaac, "A New Guarantee on Earth," *American Political Science Review* 90 (March 1996), 61–73.

57. Sadako Ogata, "Opening Address," in *Healing the Wounds: Refugees, Reconstruction and Reconciliation* (New York: International Peace Academy, 1996), 5.

58. For discussions of this phenomenon, see Robert I. Rotberg and Thomas G. Weiss, eds., *From Massacres to Genocide: The Media, Public Policy, and Humanitarian Crises* (Washington, D.C.: Brookings Institution, 1996); Larry Minear, Colin Scott, and Thomas G. Weiss, *The News Media, Civil War, and Humanitarian Action* (Boulder: Lynne Rienner, 1996); Edward Girardet, ed., *Somalia, Rwanda, and Beyond: The Role of the International Media in Wars and Humanitarian Crises*, Crosslines Special Report 1 (Dublin: Crosslines Communications Ltd., 1995); Johanna Newman, *Lights, Camera, War* (New York: St. Martin's, 1996); and Nik Gowing, *Real-Time Television Coverage of Armed Conflicts and Diplomatic Crises* (Cambridge, Mass.: Harvard Shorenstein Center, 1994).

59. George Kennan, "On American Principles," *Foreign Affairs* 74 (March/April 1995), 116–26, quote at 124.

60. See Thomas G. Weiss, "Collective Spinelessness: U.N. Actions in the Former Yugoslavia," in Ullman, ed., *The World and Yugoslavia's Wars*, 59–96.

61. The role of the International Criminal Tribunal for the Former Yugoslavia as an agent of the international community in the reconciliation process may imply a more lasting commitment to the peoples who were rescued. See Madeleine K. Albright, "Bosnia in Light of the Holocaust: War Crimes Tribunals," *U.S. Department of State Dispatch* 5 (April 18, 1994), 209–12. For a more skeptical view, see Thornberry, "Save the War Crimes Tribunal."

62. Thomas G. Weiss, "Triage: Humanitarian Intervention in a New Era," *World Policy Journal* 11, (Spring 1994), 1–10.

63. See Adam Roberts, "Humanitarian War: Military Intervention and Human Rights," *International Affairs* 69 (1993), 429–49.

64. For a straightforward realist perspective, see John J. Mearsheimer, "The False Promise of International Institutions," *International Security* (Winter 1994–95), 5–49.

65. See "Pursuing Balkan Peace," OMRI *Special Report* 1 (November 12, 1996).

Andrew Natsios

NGOs and the Humanitarian Impulse: Some Have It Right

The article by Amir Pasic and Thomas G. Weiss on the politics of complex humanitarian emergencies presents a useful, though incomplete, framework for thinking through some of the issues confronting policymakers in responding to these crises. The article is both interesting in itself and reflective of the broader shift of academic opinion on the subject of politics in complex emergencies. Thomas Weiss has been perhaps the most thoughtful academic proponent of the school of intervention, which argues that relief responses must be separated from the politics of the conflict—that is, that humanitarian relief should be a neutral intervention to save lives and reduce human suffering, not to advance any political agenda. His conversion to the Doctors Without Borders school of intervention, which insists on the righting of injustices, is an indication that the advocates of neutrality are losing ground in the debate.

Pasic and Weiss have rescued relief managers from our own naiveté and from a certain arrogance that infects too many of us. The unanticipated pernicious consequences of relief interventions have become a source of some consternation to more self-critical NGO, ICRC, and UN managers. Relief efforts are profoundly political, and can exacerbate conflict unless carefully designed. When the economy of a country in civil war collapses, and it inevitably does, humanitarian relief programs become the principal generator of gross national product and creator of jobs and wealth. That these humanitarian programs represent substantial political power to aid recipients, local elites, and combatants alike should not come as any surprise, nor should it be surprising that the stakeholders in the conflict will aggressively attempt to manipulate relief aid to serve their own political and military objectives. We cannot claim to be above the political fray in distributing neutral relief to suffering people when the suffering people are sharing the relief commodities they receive with their husbands and sons who are doing the fighting or, more troubling still, when the relief never gets to the intended recipients but becomes booty for a local warlord instead.

Relief efforts, when unmatched by political, diplomatic, and security interventions to deal with the conflict itself, can be a palliative—a safe way for policymakers to show concern and yet avoid making difficult decisions. This was too long the case in Bosnia.

Having said all this, I don't think the authors have thoroughly presented the schools of thought in the humanitarian community on the question of first principles—of what animates humanitarian interventions. They use the curious concept of rescue as a framework for reflecting on what they describe as the two approaches to the question of preeminent objectives: restorative and revolutionary humanitarianism. Restorative rescue is custodial in nature—that is, it only seeks to reduce the death rate and alleviate suffering without regard to politics.

The authors present a more expansive definition of rescue that "establish[es] a new kind of 'revolutionary' relationship among peoples"—that is, between rescuer and victim, superseding sovereignty. This revolutionary humanitarianism, as the authors describe it, establishes a permanent duty for long-term assistance between the rescuer and the victim to ensure that the injustices that initially caused the conflict do not return. This seems to be to be a new-age recasting of the principles underlying the Geneva Conventions and other international conventions on human rights (on genocide, for example). These conventions are based on ancient principles of natural law, or, to use a more modern phrase, moral law, which implicitly supersedes the sovereignty of the nation-state. Moral law is based on the notion that human life has value and ought to be protected against egregious abuse. Realizing that this principle in application presents many moral dilemmas, philosophers and theologians since St. Augustine have struggled to reconcile our moral duty to the individual with our moral duty to the greater society: Do we protect one person at any cost, endangering the entire society over the long term? That some countries sometimes violate the human rights of their own populations or that other countries do not come to the aid of those people whose right to life is being violated, say in a genocide, does not change the fact that the moral law exists. The authors seem to substitute some new humanitarian relational principle among people across national boundaries for this ancient principle of moral law.

Pasic and Weiss properly argue that there is an inherent conflict between order and justice as determining objectives in complex emergencies like the one in Bosnia. It is not clear whether these two terms refer to the economic, humanitarian, political, or security interventions in a society. Much of what humanitarian agencies did in Bosnia during the war was in fact custodial—they sought neither justice nor order. Both the relief and the security measures were designed to keep people alive, with the presumptive hope that either the war would burn itself out or a diplomatic settlement would be reached. As far as I can tell, until the Dayton Accords, few of the outside intervenors—humanitarian, diplomatic, or military—actively sought to restore prewar Bosnia or Yugoslavia or even to restore people to permanent self-sufficiency.

The authors seem to argue that justice should be a preeminent value in humanitarian intervention. We should remember, however, that justice is a complex and ambiguous term. Much current conflict arises from the threat one group feels from another or the *perceived* injustices of one ethnic or religious group against another, with a heavy emphasis on the word "perceived," because the injustices may be illusory or exaggerated. Does justice necessarily require that the ambition for national self-determination of every ethnic group in the world be realized, given that this ambition motivates a great number of conflicts? Is the conflict in Canada over an independent Quebec really about injustice? Some social orders with high degrees of relative injustice are nevertheless stable; the societies do work.

Justice is not necessarily the answer to, nor is injustice always the cause of, conflict. And even when injustice clearly is the source of a conflict, it is dangerous to presume that we can rearrange the affairs of a highly unstable society torn apart by war to eliminate this injustice. Even when brilliant relief programming, skillful diplomacy, and disciplined military force are brought to bear, imposed settlements are usually precarious. The Dayton Accords, however artfully drawn, essentially sanction ethnic cleansing: they are hardly just, but they do appear to have ended the war. If the objective of this school of humanitarian intervention is ending injustice, even if only the most egregious injustice, we may be in business a very long time given human nature. This does not mean we should ignore injustice, only that we should understand its inherent pervasiveness and adjust our aims accordingly, working to make societies functional enough to solve their own problems peacefully over the longer term.

Pasic and Weiss associate the ICRC with what they call restorative rescue. In doing so, they miss an important subtlety in the agency's position. The ICRC, which of all relief agencies has the most refined doctrine on intervention, affirms the proposition that certain human rights defined in the Geneva Conventions transcend considerations of sovereignty. The agency does not dispute the need for reform, even revolutionary reform, in an unjust society. Rather, it argues that its relief and protection efforts during a conflict should not be contingent upon or advance this reform. While it does some rehabilitation work in conflicts, its efforts are on the whole more custodial, and though it may hope for a political settlement, its only aim is to protect those who are suffering while conflict rages. Some international relief agencies have adopted the ICRC custodial view of humanitarian intervention by default—that is, not by informed decision but because they have not considered the alternatives. They try to do good without understanding that short-term good can cause great long-term harm, given the operation of the principle of unintended consequences. While I share the doubts of Pasic and Weiss on the viability of rescue as defined by the ICRC, I do feel they should be fair to the ICRC in describing its doctrine.

Because restorative rescue fails to deal with root causes, ignores local political dynamics, and may, in some cases, extend conflict, while revolutionary rescue is far too ambitious and seems to establish new duties which may prove more mischievous than helpful, I generally reject both notions as first principles in intervention. I say "generally," however, because each crisis is quite different, and there are a few which do require custodial or revolutionary intervention. In some conflicts the aggressor and the victim may trade places several times. Clearly for much of the Bosnian civil war, the Serbs were the aggressors, but toward the end of the conflict the Croatian offensive turned the Serbian civilian population into victims. Because of the intractability or murkiness of some crises, the custodial approach is the only viable option for outside agencies. In some crises there are no serious options or the ones available fail. In others the atrocities are so terrible and the suffering so great that only revolutionary rescue will suffice. In general the less intrusive, the less revolutionary, and the more incremental the outside intervention, the more likely it will be to succeed in both the short and long terms.

If revolutionary rescue is flawed and restorative rescue too narrow, what other alternatives might there be? Humanitarian intervention should be directed toward the protection of innocent life over the short term and the reestablishment of a minimal level of self-sufficiency over the long term: the ultimate objective should be to strengthen the social and economic order to the point where the society can function without outside interventions. If that can only happen with a political settlement, then a political settlement should be added to the objectives, but political settlements, like national governments, are not absolutely essential. Witness Somalia, a country where there is no national government but where there is also no large-scale loss of life. Nation-building and justice are usually unobtainable objectives in the immediate aftermath of complex emergencies. More modest objectives are in order.

Morton Winston

An Emergency Response System for the International Community: Commentary on "The Politics of Rescue"

The international system created after the Second World War through the United Nations Charter and the North Atlantic Treaty Organization was designed to preserve the peace by permitting international intervention to thwart cross-border aggression. But the present international system left unresolved the question of what responsibilities the members of the international community have concerning armed conflicts, systematic human rights violations, mass killings, genocides, and politicides which take place within the borders of sovereign nation-states. Until this question is resolved, civil wars will go on undeterred, massive human rights violations will continue, perpetrators of crimes against humanity will go unpunished, and the international community will respond fitfully and unpredictably to the complex humanitarian emergencies.

The debate about whether or not international law permits intervention in the affairs of sovereign states during complex humanitarian emergencies should give way to the recognition that there is a collective responsibility of states to rescue and bring relief to those populations placed at risk by such events. The time has come for the international community to begin to think seriously about creating the international equivalent of a "911" number that can be dialed when complex humanitarian emergencies occur and which will call forth a regular, predictable, and competent response dependent upon the nature of the emergency. In some cases, such as natural disasters, traditional humanitarian relief operations will work. In complex emergencies resulting from armed conflict, however, a security or military component, and a human rights monitoring and policing component will often be necessary to augment the efforts of the medical and relief workers sent to the area.

Although such rescue operations will continue to be necessary for the foreseeable future, rescue should be seen as just one among many intervention strategies available to international actors; and one that should be used only when all else has failed. Early warning and prevention are preferable to rescue of course. But when rescues prove necessary, a sustained commitment to peace and nation-building must continue afterward to prevent those nations from slipping back into the chaos that created the need for the international community to respond in the first place.

The present danger is that the political ambiguities and difficulties of rescue will lead to neoisolationism and the abandonment of vulnerable peoples. Humanitarian and relief organizations, as well as the militaries of several nations, have learned some bitter lessons in the past several years concerning the dangers inherent in rescuing vulnerable populations caught in complex humanitarian emergencies. The rule of neutrality under which relief and humanitarian nongovernmental organizations have operated in the past has been shown by Somalia, Bosnia, and Rwanda to be naive and sometimes counterproductive. Humanitarian intervention is never really neutral since it inevitably alters in some way the existing balance of power on the ground. Done properly, humanitarian rescue should alter the balance of power in favor of the most vulnerable members of the population: internally displaced persons, refugees, and civilian noncombatants. By coming to the aid of the displaced and the vulnerable, rescuers necessarily make themselves the enemies of their victims' oppressors. Likewise, by failing to intervene on behalf of the oppressed, the international community aids the oppressors who often depend on a weak international response.

As Pasic and Weiss note, the United Nations High Commissioner for Refugees (UNHCR) has in the past few years taken a leading role in redefining international responsibilities in rescue situations. By operationally treating internally displaced persons in the former Yugoslavia as refugees in the strict sense, it has created a presumption that the humanitarian claims of vulnerable populations supersede those of sovereignty. But Pasic and Weiss note that doing so creates a moral ambiguity. "Are humanitarians restoring the autonomy of the people whom they rush to rescue," they ask, "or are they participating in a more revolutionary process through which they are establishing a lasting link with the endangered population, contravening the habit of moral separation reflected by sovereignty?" They imply the answer is yes to both these questions.

The system of sovereign nation-states represents a conventional division of moral labor not unlike that found within particular civil societies in which individuals are regarded as autonomous moral agents capable of protecting their own interests through self-help. This conventional assumption breaks down when individuals lose their capacity to make decisions independently or when they lose their capacity to effectively protect their own interests. In such cases, the authority and responsibility normally accorded to individuals devolves to socially designated surrogate decision-makers and caregivers who are enjoined to act in the incapacitated persons' best interests.

A comparable system on the international level would recognize that states can become so dysfunctional that the normal assumptions of national self-determination and self-help no longer apply. In such situations, authority and responsibility should devolve upon the international community and, in particular, upon specially designed international institutions that can function to protect the vital interests of populations that under normal circumstances would be the responsibility of their own governments. These interests include provision of food and shelter, medical services, organization and facilitation of movement, policing, justice, and so forth.

The goal of international intervention would be to restore the capacity of the society in crisis to provide these social goods for itself. Rescuers should naturally wish to restore failed or failing states to full sovereignty and autonomy, for that is the necessary condition of their being able to reciprocate the favor at some time in the future. In this way the cooperating moral community is extended across borders.

But what are we to say when the "patient state" does not respond to our ministrations and slips further into chaos and anarchy? On the other hand, what can realistically be done when the offending state is so powerful that the international community cannot intervene without provoking a wider destabilizing conflict?

Here the analogy between dysfunctional individuals and failing nations breaks down since we can still rescue *persons* who are citizens of dysfunctional states by removing them to the territories of other states. Rescue has two strategies: to rescue peoples in their own countries by assisting failing or failed states to rebuild themselves, and to grant individuals asylum as refugees in second countries. While the former is generally preferable, the latter must also be used when no other means can be found to spare innocent people from persecution, oppression, and death. In either case, the relationship between the rescuer and the rescued only appears to change: the rescued persons become "us," or, more correctly, we recognize, at last, that they always were.

Only when international actors accept their responsibilities to provide both kinds of rescue will we be able to say that we have a global moral community. The real dilemma facing the international system is not the one Pasic and Weiss identify between restorative and revolutionary conceptions of rescue. It is the harder dilemma between acting on the humanitarian impulse (and so extending the bounds of the moral community) or not acting on it (or acting only on national self-interest narrowly conceived), and so continuing to tolerate a "state of nature" in which vulnerable members of global civil society are left to fend for themselves without benefit of international assistance in times of crisis).

That this same dilemma hobbles domestic programs for the poor and vulnerable within American society does not auger well for America's commitment to international humanitarianism. Yet without American leadership, the community of nations appears unable to act decisively in the global arena. This impasse can be overcome by agreeing on a regular method of cost- and burden-sharing among the donor countries, and by adequately funding international institutions such as the UNHCR and a volunteer interventionary military force under the control of a reformed and expanded Security Council.[1]

It is folly to suppose that nongovernmental organizations acting alone could ever have the necessary resources for carrying out the sort of intervention called for in complex humanitarian emergencies. Moreover, it is clearly unfair to vulnerable peoples to continue with a de facto system in which the United States participates in humanitarian interventions only when it deems doing so to be in its national self-interest. Thus, the next major phase in the evolution of the international system must involve the creation of a cooperative and multilateral equivalent of the "911" response with no single nation bearing all the risks and costs or being in a position to call all the shots.

NOTE

1. For a carefully worked out proposal of this kind see Carl Kaysen and George Rathjens, *Peace Operations by the United Nations: The Case for a Volunteer UN Military Force* (Cambridge, Mass.: Committee on International Security Studies, American Academy of Arts and Sciences, 1996).

Alain Destexhe

Holding Humanitarianism Hostage: The Politics of Rescue

In 1941, during the Second World War, the cities of Greece suffered terrible scarcity as a result of the war and German seizure for Nazi troops in North Africa. Two hundred thousand Greeks perished during the winter of 1941–42. Subjected to Allied blockades, the country was unable to receive assistance. For Winston Churchill, the English prime minister, "total war" against the Nazis justified blockading food to occupied Allied countries. The moral dilemma this posed was quickly dismissed in the name of victory against the forces of evil: the quicker the victory, the sooner it would be possible to alleviate suffering. In the concept of total war, political concerns take precedence over humanitarian ones.

In Bosnia, as Amir Pasic and Thomas G. Weiss have shown, the humanitarian approach prevailed over the political, at least until the NATO air strikes of September 1995 that led to the Dayton Accords. Humanitarian intervention turned against the very victims it was supposed to help, seeing these victims not as human beings but as organisms to be fed, even against their will. The Bosnian leaders made it known that if they had to choose between humanitarian aid and the possibility of arming themselves through the lifting of the embargo, they preferred the second alternative. But the international community decided for them that they should be fed but not armed. Worse, with the laudable intention of protecting the people, the humanitarians accelerated the process of ethnic cleansing—a windfall for its perpetrators. And with their humanitarian mandate, the blue helmets of the

United Nations soon became an excuse for the international community—which did not want to risk putting its troops in danger—to refuse military action against Serbian forces.

From this point of view, the United Nations High Commissioner for Refugees found itself in an untenable position. Asked to embody international political resignation by coordinating the distribution of aid, the agency was quick to see the absurdity of a situation that, despite its own objections, led it to comply with ethnic cleansing and its originators, Karadzic and Mladic. When High Commissioner Ogata decided to interrupt the activities of the UNHCR, this absurdity was revealed in full. Nevertheless, UN secretary-general Boutros Boutros-Ghali decided to proceed, and ordered the revival of the operations. This day marked a sinister turning point in the conflict; it signed, as it were, the death certificate of the political approach. Not until the summer of 1995, with the fall of Srebrenica, did the principal Western countries understand that the humanitarian approach had led to an impasse.

As Pasic and Weiss affirm, the problem is not so much a strict separation between humanitarianism and politics as it is the relationship between the two. With the exception of natural disasters, humanitarian action is always deployed on political battlefields. The victims are not just individuals in need of help. They are members of a community who want to play a role in shaping their own future. Content to focus on the obvious—the situation of physical distress—the humanitarian is guided solely by concern for humanity and too often fails to consider the importance of political solidarity. The French writer Albert Camus articulated the tension this creates when he affirmed that "human solidarity is founded on the movement of revolt. Thus we can rightfully say *that any* revolt that allows itself to destroy this solidarity by this very fact loses the name of revolt and consents to murder."

In Bosnia, where a perverse conception of the humanitarian triumphed over the political, the international community has long clearly chosen consenting to murder over solidarity. This implies making a choice—choosing between very different political projects, at least at the beginning of the conflict. On one hand, there was the Serbian plan, an authoritarian "fascist" plan, which depended on a single party and the exclusion of all non-Serbs; on the other, there was the Bosnian government's plan, which was based on the coexistence of communities, pluralism, and respect for individual rights within the framework of a democracy. Certainly, this distinction was increasingly blurred, notably after the Croatian attack on Mostar and with the progressive radicalization of the Bosnian government. But these things were themselves, in part, the consequence of the interminable prolongation of the conflict, made possible by the strictly humanitarian approach of the international community. The same type of threat or deterrent that was finally put in place in September 1995—the air strikes that led to the Dayton Accords—would probably have stopped the conflict as early as the summer of 1992. The humanitarian approach led to three years of useless suffering and the definitive partition of Bosnia on an "ethnic basis."

Max Weber first made the formulation that politics by necessity divides ethics in two, into an ethics of conviction and an ethics of responsibility. If cynicism thrives on the creation of an abyss that separates moral realism from political realism, another modern form of cynicism consists of accepting the ethics of the humanitarian as the new conscience of the political. On this point one cannot agree more with the authors.

David R. Mapel

When Is It Right to Rescue? A Response to Pasic and Weiss

In their article, Amir Pasic and Thomas G. Weiss offer a number of important lessons about the limitations of humanitarian intervention. Alain Destexhe, Andrew Natsios, and Morton Winston add to those lessons in helpful ways. But neither Pasic and Weiss nor their commentators pose some of the moral issues raised by humanitarian intervention precisely enough. As a result, we miss some of the complexities involved in deciding how—and whether—to rescue endangered populations.

Let me begin with the central lesson emphasized by Pasic and Weiss: namely, that humanitarian intervention can never be politically neutral. Although we ignore this lesson at our peril—as Bosnia and Somalia illustrate—it can be overdrawn. Certainly, absolute political neutrality is an impossibility. Particularly in "failed states" marked by intense civil conflict, relief aid almost inevitably becomes a basis for local political power. And certainly if aid agencies cannot avoid effectively taking sides in a local political struggle, then Pasic and Weiss are right that relief agencies should at least take sides consciously and deliberately. But from that the fact that some kind of political role is inevitable, it does not follow that humanitarian agencies should choose to play a more active political role than necessary. As Andrew Natsios points out with respect to the policy of the International Committee of the Red Cross, for example, it is not inherently a sign of naivete or bad faith to choose to pursue an intervention aimed primarily at the immediate relief of suffering while hoping that a political conflict will eventually reveal possibilities for reestablishing order that are not yet apparent. As Natsios suggests, as long as we are aware of the political implications of humanitarian policies, we may sometimes deliberately and rightly decide that the best thing is to aim at the relief of suffering while leaving the active pursuit of political issues to others. In retrospect, such a policy was probably the right one to pursue in Somalia, despite our clear failure at "nation-building." By contrast, in Zaire, policies aimed primarily at the relief of suffering seem to have produced horribly counterproductive results, enabling increasingly serious guerrilla raids into Rwanda from the relief camps and finally provoking the recent war which has driven most of the refugees back across the border. The general lesson, then, is that there is no general lesson to be drawn from the impossibility of maintaining absolute political neutrality, beyond that of the necessity of making much more conscious decisions about one's political role. In other words, whether a relief agency or intervening state should pursue a more or less expansive political agenda would seem to depend almost entirely upon the circumstances of the particular case.

How, then, should we frame the sorts of choices forced onto us by the unavoidably political nature of humanitarian intervention? Following Natsios, we can distinguish between three types of humanitarian intervention: "custodial," aimed primarily at the immediate relief of suffering; "restorative," aimed primarily at the restoration of a minimal political order; and "revolutionary," aimed at the achievement of justice. Pasic and Weiss are not as clear in distinguishing these three types of intervention as they might be (nor is Natsios, who first distinguishes custodial and restorative intervention, then runs them together again). Once we have clearly distinguished the goals of each type of intervention, the question posed by Pasic and Weiss is whether we should generally favor one over the others.

Initially, Pasic and Weiss observe that there may be a trade-off between the relief of suffering and the achievement of minimal political stability. They then observe that the goal of stability may also be traded off against a third objective, justice: "There are situations in which it would be justifiable to increase suffering and create disorder for the purpose of fashioning a more equitable and sustainable political order in the long run." They do not emphasize, however, that there may also be situations in which it would be justifiable to increase (or at least settle for) injustice for the sake of achieving stability and relieving suffering. In other words, it may sometimes be for the best, all things considered, to accept some injustice for the sake of peace. In the case of the former Yugoslavia, for example, the Bosnians preferred the goal of justice to the goals of order and the relief of suffering—that is, they wanted to arm themselves through lifting the embargo, even if that meant prolonging the war and foregoing humanitarian aid. In his commentary, Alain Destexhe disapprovingly observes that the international community decided this matter for the Bosnians and against their will by keeping the embargo in place. Destexhe echoes the other writers in emphasizing that political goals may be more important than the immediate relief of suffering, and certainly the international community may have made the wrong trade-offs in this particular case. Nevertheless, it should also be emphasized that the international community should not simply accept the priorities of any party—even one with justice on its side—without making its own decisions about the relative priority of relieving suffering, establishing order, and securing justice. Outsiders must make such decisions or fail in their own responsibilities.

In general, Pasic and Weiss seem to prefer humanitarian intervention that aims at a "revolutionary" rebuilding of disordered political communities so that they will be better able to withstand future crises. They are less sanguine about intervention that aims at a "restorative" rebuilding of communal autonomy along pre-emergency lines. The logic of their argument in favor of revolutionary intervention is sometimes difficult to follow, however. For example, they assert that "the subordination of sovereignty, even if it is only in situations where effective political authority is absent, still implies an obligation to assume a longer-term perspective, a commitment to the sustainability and health of a society rather than merely to one episode of rescue." This assertion is difficult to accept without serious qualifications, for two reasons.

First, in situations where there is little or no effective authority, one would think that the decision to subordinate de jure sovereignty is not a very serious matter. In these cases, there is little real authority left to worry about. Taking over some of the functions of political authority in a failed state, for example, is certainly not the same kind of challenge to sovereignty as choosing to intervene against functioning authority for the sake of preventing human rights abuses.

Second, whether a long-term obligation to help an endangered population is "implied" by a decision to subordinate the de jure sovereignty of a failed state would appear to depend primarily upon the intentions and promises of those who choose to intervene, not upon the mere fact of their intervention. If the intentions of an intervening state are not made clear, or if "mission creep" forces a change in the initial aims of an intervention, then an intervening state may become responsible for having encouraged unreasonable expectations among the local parties. But no long-term obligation is implied by the mere fact of a state choosing to intervene to alleviate immediate suffering, particularly if the intervening state disavows any such long-term obligation from the outset. Presumably, the question of how politically involved we should become depends to some extent on how far the social fabric has already unraveled. If everything has come apart, then an intervention may have to be rather politically intrusive in order to achieve even a minimal set of objectives. Nevertheless, this "if/then" proposition only establishes what is required if we are to intervene effectively over the long haul; it does not establish that we have an obligation to intervene in the first place.

At this point, we begin to reach a deeper set of questions. Pasic and Weiss complain that rescue "does not alter significantly the relationship between rescuers and rescued." But why should it? Why should we be involved in rescue at all, and why are we obligated to go beyond rescue to form a deeper set of relationships? Sometimes Pasic and Weiss appear to suggest that our obligation to help those in peril stems directly from a universal moral duty of aid between individuals. This universal moral sense of duty collapses the boundaries of sovereignty, and indeed would seem to lead in the direction of challenging even normal exercises of sovereignty when they involve the violation of human rights. At other times, however, Pasic and Weiss seem to suggest that it is only a prior collapse of sovereignty that allows us to act. In other words, as long as sovereignty is functioning, it should be respected. In general, Pasic and Weiss are never clear about the relative weight they place on human rights versus sovereignty. However, their view of why we should attempt to rescue endangered populations when sovereignty does collapse boils down to the answer, "because we are all human beings."

It has always been problematic whether this is a sufficient basis for claiming that others have a duty to intervene. But the real problem here is not, as Pasic and Weiss assert, that "a deeper responsibility is evaded by seeing sovereignty as an unquestioned idea." Rather, the deeper problem is that the nature and scope of moral responsibility is itself a very difficult and controversial matter. Thus, everyone believes we are morally responsible for the harm we intend (although even here matters are more complex, since we usually distinguish between intending harm and intending wrongful harm). Most people also believe we are morally responsible for at least some of the harm that we cause, although exactly how far moral responsibility and causal responsibility go hand in hand is also a problematical issue. Aside from some utilitarians, few people have ever thought that we are morally at fault for every serious harm in the world we fail to prevent, although again we are no doubt responsible for some allowings as well as some doings. (Here it is appropriate to note that Morton Winston's assertion that in omitting to intervene, one also acts, suggests an implausibly broad assignment of moral responsibility.)

In trying to decide whether one has an obligation to intervene, then, difficult issues are raised about the scope of moral responsibility, and a number of additional considerations need to be taken into account. In particular, it is relevant to consider the magnitude of the harm to be prevented; the costs to ourselves and others of preventing the harm (calculated both in terms of competing special moral obligations to family, friends, country, and allies, and in terms of prudential interests); the relative claims of others in distress; whether we are causally responsible for the suffering of others by virtue of any previous economic and political ties; and much else besides. Few of these considerations are raised in "The Politics of Rescue" or in the commentaries, although Pasic and Weiss do say that we need to pay attention to "the multiple ties that bind rescuers and victims long before the outset of a complex emergency." Instead, the focus of their discussion is largely on sovereignty as an obstacle to intervention. This is of course an important issue, but I think the hardest moral issues raised by humanitarian intervention lie elsewhere.

Only when we have taken these other considerations into account does it make sense to consider the issues raised by Pasic and Weiss—namely, whether rescue will prove counterproductive and/or be used as an excuse for failing to undertake more demanding long-term diplomatic, military, and economic commitments. Of course, Pasic and Weiss are perfectly correct that once an intervention is launched, we may acquire new and potentially much more lasting obligations (particularly if the limited nature of the commitment is not made clear at the beginning). But this is yet another reason for being extremely careful in specifying what one intends to accomplish in intervening and how far one is prepared to see it out. In this light, it seems preferable to think in terms of a right rather than a duty of humanitarian intervention, although this may be a somewhat less cosmopolitan and more statist way of approaching the issue of intervention than Pasic and Weiss apparently wish to endorse.

Nevertheless, Pasic and Weiss are certainly correct that humanitarian intervention forces us to reconsider the normal way in which we understand our moral identities. Among the commentators, Morton Winston addresses this issue directly. Pasic and Weiss note that "the international community" is "a nebulous term" and Winston agrees. He argues that our real choice is not whether to launch restorative or revolutionary interventions but whether to begin to create a real international moral community or instead withdraw into isolationism. One step toward such a moral community might be through the creation of a standing, volunteer UN military force designed to undertake humanitarian interventions. I am a bit dubious about Winston's view that the motivation for the creation of such a force is that rich nations, and particularly the United States, want poor nations to be able to reciprocate on some future day. I also doubt that the choice of whether to work toward such a community is as simple as choosing between moral duty and national interest. Nevertheless, Winston is probably right that at least some of the current resistance to humanitarian intervention could be overcome by a UN force run according to regular methods of cost- and burden-sharing.

The major stumbling block to the UN proposal, however, is international disagreement about the nature of justice. As Natsios points out, Pasic and Weiss seem to believe that justice should be the preeminent value in international affairs, but they do not sufficiently emphasize the highly controversial nature of justice. Here Natsios puts his finger on the fundamental difficulty: a complex emergency may have multiple sources that are murky and intractable, and aggressors and victims may frequently swap places. Frequently, there are also partially valid claims of justice (or of having suffered injustice) on both sides of civil conflict. Pasic and

Weiss also make the important point that when the identity and boundaries of a state are themselves contested, it is sometimes unclear for whom there should be order and/or justice. What all of this suggests is that Winston's advice to "always take the side of the oppressed" may prove too simple to lead to any clear consensus about the objectives of humanitarian intervention. But such a consensus must be in place, at least with respect to the major international players, before any UN military force can be used quickly and effectively. This is not to say that the idea of a standing volunteer UN military force is a bad one, but only that it can also be easily oversold. It is no substitute for a long-term international commitment to the political and economic rebuilding of states torn apart by civil conflict. The international community does not seem ready to undertake a universal commitment to this sort of reconstruction any time soon.

Augustus Richard Norton*

Drawing the Line on Opprobrious Violence

A detailed excursus into moral philosophy is hardly required to convince most members of the human race that the intentional slaughter of innocent people is morally indefensible. No cause, no matter how just, and no national interest, no matter how elegantly or passionately formulated, justifies the purposeful murder of innocents merely to punctuate a claim or to deliver a lesson. There is no room for moral relativism on this point. Such tactics are absolutely evil and cannot be viewed otherwise. The time has come for the international community to delegitimize absolutely this form of political violence.

For all of the justified indignation that terrorism arouses, it is altogether remarkable that the quest for a definition of terrorism has bedeviled diplomats and international lawyers. In fact, there is no internationally accepted definition of terrorism. The standard practice has been to proceed inductively, criminalizing specific

*This article is a revised version of a paper delivered at a faculty institute on "Teaching Ethics and International Affairs," sponsored by the Carnegie Council on Ethics and International Affairs (New York) at Yale University, June 11–17, 1989.

The author would like to thank Russ Howard, Deanna J. Lampros-Norton, and Robin Wright for their critical readings of the manuscript. They each provided some very useful comments and insights. The views expressed are naturally those of the author and should not be construed to represent necessarily the positions of the Carnegie Council or the U.S. Military Academy.

acts such as air piracy, attacks on diplomats, or the theft of nuclear materials, rather than attempt to define terrorism as an offense.

The perpetrators of abhorrent acts of violence appropriately earn opprobrium, whether what they do is called terrorism or not. As the deluge of published pages on the subject testifies, no matter how precisely we strive to define terrorism, there is a zone of ambiguity where terrorism fades into political violence and warfare. This is why some observers even believe the term may be beyond repair. As John Murphy observes in a new book, some legal experts would prefer, if it were possible, to drop the term entirely.[1] Often, conventional and adequately descriptive terms, such as hijacking, kidnapping, and murder, suffice.

Yet there is merit in solidifying a consensus on those acts of violence that are simply impermissible; this will be impossible, however, unless a parsimonious definition of terrorism is adopted. The central premise of this article is that there are some forms of terrorism that raise no arguments: they are morally obnoxious, pure and simple. The murder of innocents, the "tool of those who reject the norms and values of civilized people everywhere," is despicable by any humane standard, no matter what name is used to describe it, and it is precisely these acts that richly deserve to be labeled terrorism.[2] Patent examples would include the anonymous car bomb exploded on a crowded shopping street in Beirut, random shooting in the Rome and Vienna airport departure lounges, the destruction of Pan Am 103, or the wholesale slaughter of patients in a Mozambican hospital.

In point of fact, the problem with much of the commentary and thinking about terrorism is precisely that statesmen and scholars too readily accept the shopworn cliche that "one man's terrorist is another man's freedom fighter." If the term "terrorist" is used with the care and consistency urged here, one man's terrorist is simply another man's terrorist.

Even warfare has a framework of moral rules. Although these rules will necessarily fail to make warfare anything less than horrific, without them war would be even more horrendous. Noncombatant immunity is a basic principle of the laws of warfare. As a minimum standard, what is impermissible in war—specifically and especially the intentional targeting of civilians—should be impermissible outside of the war zone.

The clear delineation of an ethical boundary separating clearly objectionable forms of violence from other acts of violence is not only morally compelling but of practical utility as well, and as Stanley Hoffmann has noted, "necessity is the mother of morality."[3] In a complex, increasingly intertwined world, the minimal expectation must be that people can travel without fear of being blown up or raked by machine-gun fire.

There is little difficulty in agreeing on the protected status of civilian air transport, or civilian facilities at airports or rail stations, where the potential victims are literally innocents who have had the misfortune of stepping into harm's way. Hence, there is broad agreement in international law that acts such as skyjacking are in nearly all conceivable instances impermissible. Other clear-cut cases include attacks upon children, the elderly, and, usually, women. The intentional targeting of innocent noncombatant civilians—whether they are found in encampments, villages, towns, cities, or airports—is simply morally objectionable, and such wanton acts deserve universal condemnation.

Defining Terrorism

Academics have been struggling with the definition of terrorism for years. Acts that one state denounces may be—and often are—justified by another. Some authorities stress the illegality of terrorism; legality is, however, a sticky point (and, unfortunately, often an irrelevant one in the international arena).[4] The laws of a state, taken as a whole, may be morally commendable or morally reprehensible. To argue that an act is unlawful (a factual statement) is not the same as arguing that it is illegitimate (a normative conclusion). Paul Wilkinson, one of the more careful thinkers on this subject, distinguishes between those political systems where citizens may effectively voice their demands and those in which categories of citizens are disenfranchised. In the first category of states, political violence is both illegal and illegitimate because the enfranchised citizen need not resort to violence to be heard and to enjoy the protection of the state. By contrast, in the second category of states—those that are deaf to their citizens and residents—violence may be justifiable and legitimate even though it is deemed illegal.[5]

Although many "official" definitions have been proffered, one developed by the United States Department of State comes closest to capturing terrorism in most of its possible dimensions. The definition is particularly meritorious because it does not exclude states as sponsors or perpetrators of terrorism: "Terrorism is the threat or use of violence for political purposes by individuals or groups, whether acting for, or in opposition to, established governmental authority, when such actions are intended to influence a target group wider than the immediate victim or victims."[6] The defect of this definition is that it does not clearly separate or delineate political violence from terrorism. In short, the very breadth and ambiguity of the definition ensures controversy, not consensus.

As defined above, the tactic of terrorism may be employed in a variety of contexts, including widely sanctioned struggles as well as regional conflicts. For instance, the right of a people to resist foreign occupation is widely, if somewhat erratically, upheld. Few observers outside the Soviet Union described the Afghan resistance fighters as terrorists, even though some of their attacks were decried as terrorism by the USSR. So long as the Afghan mujahedin directed their efforts against the Soviet presence in Afghanistan, right was literally on their side. By the same token, though agreement is less general, especially in the United States, the resistance by the Lebanese to the continuing Israeli occupation of a portion of southern Lebanon would be similarly sanctioned, despite Israel's penchant for describing those who attack its soldiers and client militiamen as terrorists.

When the Afghans or the Lebanese resistance forces, however, broaden their campaigns to encompass protected categories of noncombatants, their actions tend to lose their privileged status. Whatever our politics, we can readily distinguish between attacks on soldiers occupying foreign lands and attacks on persons in universally accepted protected categories, such as children or, more broadly, noncombatants.

Thus, in general it makes more sense to concentrate on the moral legitimacy of the means rather than on the technical legality of the ends. It is also sensible to attempt to focus on categories of objectionable acts that may be clearly distinguished from general political violence. Clearly, legal character notwithstanding, there is a big difference between an attack on a police station and an attack on a crowded shopping street.

In this essay the focus is upon the deliberate, unjustifiable, and random uses of violence for political ends against protected groups.[7] This is a functional and unpolemical approach that has the merit of parsimony and universality. (This narrow perspective merely helps us to deal effectively with the problem on an appropriate ethical level; it does not excuse actions that fall outside of the definition. There are still names for the other acts.) The perpetrators may be states, agents of states, or individuals acting independently. The qualifying condition is that their actions constitute—in the eyes of the world—uniquely abhorrent and morally objectionable attacks upon noncombatants.

Admittedly, the international system is biased in favor of the state (the alternative, at present, would be chaos), and states can often get away with heinous activities that nonstate actors would not even contemplate. But the fact that less can be done directly about the behavior of a state—particularly when it is acting within its own borders—by no means precludes a moral indictment, which often has more weight than may be presumed. Even, and perhaps especially, the most autocratic and ruthless governments are preoccupied with their image. Of course condemnation is a sword that can swing both ways. Thoughtful scholars like Raymond Aron describe the Anglo-American carpet bombing of Germany in World War II as terrorism precisely because it was, by design, indiscriminate.

Multilateral Dialogue

Unilateral responses to terrorism—though viscerally satisfying—often undermine multilateral cooperation, which, in the long run, may be more effective in dampening the incentives for people to resort to opprobrious forms of violence.

Throughout the 1980s the relationship between the United States and the Soviet Union was marred by the trading of charges and countercharges in which one side accused the other of supporting, promoting, or carrying out acts of terrorism. Moscow's support for Third World revolutionary movements that engaged in a range of violent activities was used by the United States to indict the Soviet Union for supporting terrorism. Washington's support for a variety of governments that used violence to suppress and eliminate political opponents was seen as supporting a form of state terrorism. But as Moscow grew increasingly skeptical of its revolutionary clients (and of the Third World in general), Washington came to appreciate the fact that states like Libya, Syria, and Iran were the real state sponsors of terrorism and that the USSR, at worst, provided only very indirect support for terrorists.

These developments, coupled with the extraordinary changes in Soviet foreign policy under Mikhail Gorbachev, created a fertile opportunity for the two superpowers to find common ground for a dialogue on the problem of terrorism. In January 1989, an unofficial U.S.-USSR exchange involving scholars, former officials, and lawyers began in Moscow and was followed by a September meeting at the RAND Corporation in California. Significantly, both sides proceeded from the implicit view that there are some forms of violence that are simply beyond the moral pale. Thus, rather than stressing their marginal disagreements, the two sides rightly focused on the real core of the problem.

Encouraged by the success of these private meetings, the two governments have begun a series of official exchanges. If the unofficial sessions, which will continue in 1990, are any guide, it is quite possible that the two governments will reach agreement on a range of practical steps, including:

- Exchanges of intelligence data
- Cooperation in early warning measures
- Steps to dissuade clients from using terrorist tactics
- Cooperative steps to buttress international law, including the promulgation of a convention to make the deliberate targeting of civilians an international crime

If the dialogue continues to develop productively, as now seems likely, the dynamics of the exchange will necessarily induce a growing reluctance to lend support to groups or states continuing to pursue their aims through the use of opprobrious violence. This implication of the dialogue may be more important than any concrete bilateral measures springing from it. Each side should reasonably expect that its interlocutor's clients will risk losing material and diplomatic support should they persist in using terrorism.

Equally important, the superpowers' progress could well help to foster a growing multilateral consensus on the need to prevent opprobrious acts of terrorism. One obvious setting for multilateral discussions is the Council of Europe, but the United Nations, which is enjoying a rejuvenation, should not be foreclosed as an appropriate forum either.

When the United Nations was created forty-five years ago, it was thought that it would function as a mechanism of collective security. Cold War bipolarity rendered collective security impossible. But now that the organization, especially the Security Council, is beginning to function as a more collegial body, the potential for enforcement measures no longer seems an idealistic pipe dream. Enforcement actions to deter, disrupt, or punish perpetrators of morally obnoxious forms of violence probably represent a clear textbook case for Security Council cooperation. Granted, permanent members' veto powers would inhibit a range of direct military actions against relatively powerful states like Iran, but steps to counter extremist organizations resembling gangs less than states will not necessarily be precluded in the 1990s.[8]

A key tenet of the extant protocols on aerial hijacking, the theft of nuclear materials, and attacks on protected persons (such as diplomats) is that the state apprehending the perpetrators will either prosecute them or extradite them for prosecution. Two different factors have robbed this tenet of full effectiveness: divergent views of a given act of violence and a not unreasonable concern that convicting and jailing perpetrators will only be a magnet for further attacks to free them and to punish the government responsible for their incarceration.

The first factor will not be fully erased in the foreseeable future. Some acts will continue to be viewed as political in nature and therefore exculpatory. The case of assassination is illustrative. Though assassination is certainly murder, there are many instances in which natural law and positive law conflict, thus assuring some assassins a safe haven in many countries. Other crimes, such as the hijacking of ships and planes, are increasingly unlikely to be viewed sympathetically, regardless of the circumstances or the motives of the perpetrators. On the whole, progress toward drawing the line on opprobrious violence will further diminish the likelihood that perpetrators will escape punishment.

The second factor, the fear that the prosecuting state will only invite terrorist attacks so long as it holds a terrorist in its prison, may be mitigated by the creation of an international jail administered by the United Nations. This type of facility would not only symbolize international resolve to punish terrorists; it might ease the dilemma of states that find themselves holding terrorists. A related step, which has already been recommended by some legal experts, would be the creation of an international criminal court, which could be a major contribution to world order.

The Need for Dispassionate Analysis

Admittedly, terrorism is neither the most important nor the most dangerous problem facing civilized society, but there can be little argument about the extent to which terrorism has continued to capture the attention of audiences and government officials around the globe. Terrorism both compels attention and inspires fear. As Raymond Aron wrote, its "lack of discrimination helps spread fear, for if no one in particular is a target, no one can be safe."[9] (How many readers of this essay have—following a deadly episode of aerial piracy—at least contemplated changing an upcoming flight or switching to a "safer" air carrier?)

The fact that terrorism, which physically touches very few people, has maintained its grip on the public's consciousness is a macabre tribute to the nature of the phenomenon. Indeed, it is easy to minimize the threat of terrorism, especially in contrast to risks more common in everyday life, such as traffic accidents, lightning, and even falls in the bathtub. Yet terrorism does cut a wide emotional swath, even if the physical dangers are often more apparent than real.

For democracies, which are especially, but by no means uniquely, vulnerable, the risk of overreaction may be more dangerous than the threat itself. In this regard, the penchant of many "experts" to exaggerate and misconstrue the threat of terrorism is at best mischievous and at worst repugnant. Some of the writing on terrorism, especially in the United States and the United Kingdom, is more akin to special pleading and downright deception than dispassionate and objective analysis. Books and articles are filled with unsubstantiated claims that confound independent confirmation and play to public opinion rather than to accuracy. Scholarly studies are not immune to this charge, and some of them are particularly egregious examples. The field seems to beg for exploitation, and one is sometimes prone to conclude that the entrepreneurs of terrorism studies are more numerous than the terrorists themselves.

Although there is no magic antidote to bad writing or muddled thinking on terrorism, there is much to be said for a clearheaded approach to the problem, especially if governments are to avoid falling in their own slippery language.

Paul Bremer, former U.S. Department of State ambassador-at-large for counterterrorism, observes, "The word 'terrorism' in current literature is freely used to describe any violent political activity with which the writer happens to disagree, and thus the word is robbed of its meaning."[10] How true! Ambassador Bremer then goes on to reject the label of terrorism when affixed to the U.S.-supported contras in Nicaragua, as though it were inconceivable that Washington could lend support to people who would actually commit terrorism.

The point, of course, is that "terrorism" is a marvelous epithet with which to bludgeon or tar one's enemies. But the moral indictment inherent in the term is debased if it is used only to label acts of which we disapprove, while turning a blind eye to equally contemptible acts carried out by friends or allies for congenial goals. Used in this way, "terrorism" simply becomes a rubric for all forms of opposition violence.

The priests of the ten-second sound bite, in tacit alliance with policymakers impatient with details and analysis, have intoned "international terrorism" so frequently that sensible scholarship sometimes seems a mere heretical whisper. But like monolithic communism in the 1950s, the bugbear of "international terrorism" in the 1980s does not stand up well to close inspection. As many academics and government experts have long known, terrorism is not simply a cabalistic international phenomenon uniquely targeted against the free societies of the West. The phenomenon of terror-violence is neither unique to the present era nor practiced only by one's enemies. It is certainly not monopolized by one or another ethnic, ideological, or religious group.

Terrorism's Double Edge

Nineteenth-century examples notwithstanding, modern terrorists do not proudly don the label "terrorist." In fact, much of the writing by terrorists is precisely for the purpose of claiming that they are not the "real terrorists" and that what they are doing is therefore justified. But the tactic and the vocation of terrorism are unjustifiable not only on moral grounds but also on practical grounds. Terrorism is patently counterproductive. Rather than weakening the resolve of the target population, terrorists supply the argument (and all too often the methods) for their own eradication. The reaction in Europe and the United States to the downing of Pan Am 103 is illustrative. If nothing else, the destruction of Pan Am 103 has stiffened the resolve in many corners to catch the perpetrators and prevent a repeat performance.

Terrorism has a contagious effect. As Adam Roberts reminds us in a fine article, legitimate counterterrorism campaigns all too often end literally as counter*terrorism*.[11] This is an observation as well as a cautionary note. Terrorism breeds contempt for limits and inspires imitation. Consider the following pairings, each representing a case in which terrorism has inspired imitative acts of terrorism:

- Israeli Jew and Palestinian Arab
- Greek Cypriot and Turkish Cypriot
- Catholic and Protestant in Northern Ireland

Terrorism may be the product of popular struggles, but it is hardly a substitute for it. Indeed, all too often the use of terrorism stereotypes a community and inflicts heavy societal costs. Rather than enhancing international support for a community's claims, it corrodes sympathy and support. Consider the heavy moral baggage the Palestinian Arabs must lug around as a result of past outrages. The Israeli view of the Palestine Liberation Organization (PLO) as a terrorist organization is not, as some Palestinians unfortunately still presume, merely a negotiating tactic or a negotiating scheme but the response of a population faced with attacks that have no moral limits. Conversely, the *intifada,* a popular revolt with clear moral limits, has not yet erased the visceral fears of the Israeli public. (It is not too far afield to wonder how long it will take to erase the memory of the brutal Israeli response to the *intifada;* these problems seem to come in pairs.)

The case of the Shia Muslims in Lebanon, who certainly represent an array of legitimate demands, is particularly striking. The Shia have found themselves stigmatized as a result of the despicable actions of some members of their community. Not surprisingly, there is good evidence to indicate that many Shia have come to resent the kidnapping of foreigners, sometimes on the admirable stance of moral principle but often simply out of pragmatism. It is no joy to be seen in the eyes of the world as a potential terrorist.

Conclusion

An ethical response to terrorism begins with the recognition that all states share an interest in protecting the political and social environment, just as the whole world shares an interest in preserving the quality of the physical environment. States that sponsor opprobrious violence usually disclaim their sponsorship not just because of the risk of retaliation but to avoid censure. The weight of that censure must be increased. In this regard, the now gestating U.S.-Soviet dialogue is very promising, especially if it will provide a platform for a more encompassing multilateral discussion.

The exploration of the world that lies beyond the boundaries of the Cold War is only just beginning. This is a moment to applaud and encourage the peaceful transformations that are under way in Eastern Europe. But this is also a propitious period to prepare against the worst. Although the 1990s may hold marvelous new opportunities for people everywhere to savor the elixir of freedom, familiar demons may also lurk ahead. In Europe, revived nationalistic and ethnic sentiments come in train with old grievances, which might well spark violent irredentist campaigns aiming to repair old tears in Europe's political geography. Terrorism may well be the vehicle that some will choose to draw attention to their demands or to strike fear in the hearts of opponents. Thus, as we embark on the last decade of a violence-ridden century, the time is ripe for concerted international action to disable terrorism ethically by underlining the notion that certain acts of violence are wrong and will not be tolerated, period.

NOTES

1. See John Murphy, *State Support of International Terrorism: Legal, Political, and Economic Dimensions* (Boulder: Westview Press; London: Mansell Publishing, 1989), 3.

2. The quotation is from Deputy Secretary of State John C. Whitehead in an address before the Brookings Institution Conference on Terrorism, Washington, D.C., December 10, 1986.

3. Stanley Hoffmann, *The Political Ethics of International Relations* (the seventh Morgenthau Memorial Lecture on Ethics & Foreign Policy) (New York: Carnegie Council on Ethics and International Affairs, 1988), 17.

4. On the illegality of terrorism, see, for example, the *Public Report of the Vice President's Task Force on Combatting Terrorism* (Washington, D.C.: February 1986), 1, where it is argued that terrorism is the "*unlawful use* or threat of violence against persons or property to further political or social objectives. It is generally intended to intimidate or coerce a government, individuals, or groups to modify their behavior or policies [emphasis provided]."

5. Paul Wilkinson, *Terrorism and the Liberal State* (New York: John Wiley & Sons, 1977). Also see Oleg Zinam, "Terrorism and Violence in the Light of Discontent and Frustration," in Marius H. Livingston, ed., *International Terrorism in the Contemporary World* (Westport, Conn.: Greenwood Press, 1978), 240–65.

6. United States Department of State, *Patterns of International Terrorism 1982* (Washington, D.C.: 1983).

7. This perspective, though developed independently, is close to that of Michael Walzer, who argues that terrorism's method is "the random murder of innocent people. Randomness is the crucial feature of terrorist activity." *Just and Unjust Wars: A Moral Argument with Historical Illustrations* (New York: Basic Books, 1977), 197.

8. See Augustus Richard Norton and Thomas G. Weiss, *Soldiers with a Difference: The Rediscovery of UN Peacekeeping* (New York: Foreign Policy Association, Headline Series, 1990).

9. Raymond Aron, *Peace and War: A Theory of International Relations* (Garden City, N.Y.: Anchor Books, 1973), 153.

10. L. Paul Bremer, III, book review, *Parameters* 19 (June 1989), 102–3.

11. Adam Roberts, "Ethics, Terrorism, and Counter-Terrorism," *Journal of Terrorism and Political Violence* 1 (January 1989), 62.

Lyn S. Graybill*

South Africa's Truth and Reconciliation Commission: Ethical and Theological Perspectives

How do governments deal with human rights violations committed by former regimes? South Africa's solution has been to set up the Truth and Reconciliation Commission (TRC), which offers amnesty to perpetrators who tell the truth about the past and disclose their deeds to the victims; the goal is the reconciliation of former enemies. While the TRC has a clear political focus, it is at its heart a deeply theological and ethical initiative. At times, however, it appears that ethics and theology are at cross-purposes, that justice is less important than Christian mercy; this viewpoint springs from a narrow understanding of what constitutes justice. Does offering amnesty to perpetrators and forgiving enemies deny the victims justice? Or does the TRC embody a "different kind of justice," as one commentator recently suggested? In this overview of the TRC—its establishment, procedures, and principles—special attention is given to the ethical and theological arguments for this unique approach.

*Support for this research was provided by the National Endowment for the Humanities, the Virginia Foundation for the Humanities, and the Carter G. Woodson Institute.

The Move Toward Reconciliation

Nelson Mandela: The Great Reconciler

The Truth and Reconciliation Commission is one manifestation of the impulse that has motivated South Africa since Nelson Mandela's election in 1994. Indeed, Mandela set the example of reconciliation by displaying no rancor or bitterness toward his former oppressors, despite his 27-year imprisonment. In a postelection celebration on May 2, 1994, in Johannesburg, he set the tone for the incoming government: "Let us stretch out our hands to those who have beaten us and say to them that we are all South Africans. . . . Now is the time to heal the old wounds and to build a new South Africa."[1]

Later, as host of a luncheon for the wives of former South African prime ministers, presidents, and liberation movement leaders, Mandela again acted as reconciler by including Tiene Vorster and Elize Botha, wives of former prime ministers John Vorster and P. W. Botha. And when Betsie Verwoerd, widow of Hendrik Verwoerd, the so-called architect of apartheid, politely declined to join the spouses of the other heads of state at the luncheon but offered a pro forma "drop-in-for-tea-when-you're-in-the-area" invitation, South Africa's first black president traveled to the white enclave of Orania in the isolated Karoo region to pay his respects to the 94-year-old grande dame. Nelson Mandela's understanding of the power of symbolic acts of reconciliation surpasses that of the canniest religious leaders, and his insight into the capacity of grace to transform people and nations puts most theologians to shame.[2]

The Rush to Portray the Past

Inspired perhaps by Mandela's example, South Africans have shown an extraordinary willingness to confront the past in an effort to bring about reconciliation. The transformation of museums is proceeding apace, with representations of the apartheid era taking center stage. The new Museum Africa in Johannesburg is a permanent apartheid museum, and museums in Durban, Pretoria, and Robben Island (where Mandela served out his sentence) display documents, instruments of torture, and other artifacts of the apartheid era.

Also notable is the zeal with which South Africans have approached the rewriting of history texts. Immediately after the 1994 elections, the government asked for a review of the curriculum to purge all elements of racism and to change the way the history of the resistance was portrayed. In pre-1994 texts apartheid was described as the nation's crowning achievement, and no mention of the African National Congress (ANC) or Mandela was allowed in the syllabus. A widely used textbook mentioned only three black politicians, two of whom were government collaborators. Blacks had effectively been written out of history. Publishers were quick to provide textbooks that recover the previously hidden histories of the majority population. In short, South Africa is in the forefront of nations that are seeking "ways of educating their citizens to their guilty as well as their proud pasts."[3]

The Work of the TRC

Just 15 months after South Africa held its first all-race elections in April 1994, it promulgated the Promotion of National Unity and Reconciliation Act authorizing the TRC. The 17-member commission, headed by Nobel laureate Bishop Desmond Tutu, was given a two-year mandate to hold hearings on allegations of human rights abuses committed from March 1, 1960, through December 6, 1993, the date of the adoption of the interim constitution.[4] Parliament extended the cutoff date to May 10, 1994, the date of Mandela's inauguration, to enable victims and perpetrators of human rights abuses committed after December 1993 to approach the commission. The TRC is divided into three committees: the Committee on Human Rights Violations (HRV), the Committee on Amnesty, and the Committee on Reparations and Rehabilitation.

Although it was planned that the three committees would hold hearings simultaneously around the country during the two years of operation, the Committee on Human Rights Violations took center stage in 1996. It is entrusted to hear victims' stories in order to establish whether gross violations of human rights occurred. A gross human rights violation is defined as the "violation of human rights through the killing, abduction, torture, or severe ill treatment of any person . . . which emanated from conflicts of the past . . . and the commission of which was advised, planned, directed, commanded, or ordered by any person acting with a political motive."[5]

The Committee on Amnesty—originally made up of seven members, then enlarged to thirteen and later nineteen to deal with the heavy workload—takes applications from those seeking amnesty for "acts associated with political objectives." This committee decides which applicants meet the "political objective" qualification: to be "political," an act must have been committed by a member or supporter of a "publicly known political organization or liberation movement" or by an employee of the state, acting either "in furtherance of a political struggle (including both acts by or against the state and acts by one political organization or liberation movement against another) or with the object of countering or otherwise resisting the said struggle." The act must have been committed "in the course and scope of his or her duties and within the scope of his or her express or implied authority."[6]

The role of the commission's third committee, the Committee on Reparations and Rehabilitation, is to decide how each victim should be compensated and make recommendations to the president "in an endeavor to restore the human and civil dignity of such victim."[7]

Religion and the TRC

Church people were instrumental in prompting the government to establish a truth commission, and a good number of the commissioners come from the faith community.[8] The TRC's chair and deputy chair, Desmond Tutu and Alex Boraine, are, respectively, a former archbishop in the Anglican Church and a former president of the Methodist Church of Southern Africa. The heavy representation of church people is not surprising. South Africa is a country that is "Christian" in a sense that would be unrecognizable to Americans. Theological discourse on political matters is taken seriously, and, not surprisingly, the principles under which the TRC operates are heavily influenced by Christian theology and ethics.

The hearings resemble a church service more than a judiciary proceeding, with Bishop Tutu dressed in his purple clerical robes and clearly operating as a religious figure. Some South Africans regard Tutu as the perfect person to oversee the process because of his Christian compassion and moral stature as an activist bishop. Others criticize him for the religious atmosphere he has brought to the hearings and for his tearful outbursts, which have led some detractors to term the TRC the "Kleenex Commission."

Many people find the Christian atmosphere and discourse of the TRC distasteful. Secular academics criticize the very framing of the issue in terms of repentance and forgiveness, which they see as uniquely Christian concepts that are alienating to South Africans who do not come from this faith perspective. Not only academics but some victims as well have complained about "the imposition of a Christian morality of forgiveness."[9] One letter writer to the weekly *Mail & Guardian* expressed this common complaint: "I understand how Desmond Tutu identifies reconciliation with forgiveness. I don't, because I'm not a Christian and I think it grossly immoral to forgive that which is unforgivable."[10] A mother of a victim explains: "It is easy for Mandela and Tutu to forgive . . . they lead vindicated lives. In my life nothing, not a single thing, has changed since my son was burnt by barbarians . . . nothing. Therefore, I cannot forgive."[11]

While some critics find the Christian framework and verbiage unacceptable, for many South Africans—77 percent of whom identify themselves as Christians—the Biblical language resonates. Christianity was manipulated by the National Party, which argued that Afrikaners were God's elect in southern Africa and that separate development was God's will and plan.[12] Christianity was also used by the resistance leaders to justify the struggle against apartheid, serving as an ethical critique of apartheid, a source of righteous anger that inspired action, and a wellspring of confidence in eventual victory.[13] Given the importance of Christianity in South Africa, it is not surprising that the framework under which the TRC operates is heavily influenced by Christian thought and tradition. The Christian church from its beginning has been concerned with truth, reconciliation, confession, guilt, and forgiveness—issues with which the TRC now grapples.[14]

Reconcilation

Christianity is not alone in viewing truth and confession as preconditions of reconciliation; all the great religions sound these themes. Furthermore, most religious traditions place reconciliation above "justice." In traditional African thought, the emphasis is on restoring evildoers to the community rather than on punishing them. The term *ubuntu*, which derives from the Xhosa expression *Umuntu ngumuntu ngabanye bantu* (People are people through other people), conveys the view that an environment of right relationships is one in which people are able to recognize that their humanity is inextricably bound up in others' humanity. *Ubuntu* emphasizes the priority of "restorative" as opposed to "retributive" justice. Tutu's description of *ubuntu* is enlightening:

> *Ubuntu* says I am human only because you are human. If I undermine your humanity I dehumanize myself. You must do

> what you can to maintain this great harmony, which is perpetually undermined by resentment, anger, desire for vengeance. That's why African jurisprudence is restorative rather than retributive.[15]

The universality of reconciliation in the major religious and philosophical traditions suggests that the truth and reconciliation process upon which South Africa has embarked may serve as a guide for other countries dealing with a divisive past or the aftermath of ethnic bloodletting.

Recognizing the centrality of reconciliation to all religious traditions, Tutu has called on all faith communities to contribute to the TRC process. In response to his call, an interfaith service at St. George's Cathedral in Cape Town was held as a prelude to the work of the TRC. Commissioners received a candle and an olive branch, symbols of the quest for truth and peace, and were blessed by Jewish, Christian, Buddhist, Muslim, and traditional African religious leaders as they stood in a semicircle with their lighted candles. Tutu, on the first day of hearings, appealed to the different communities of faith to uphold the commission "in fervent prayer and intercession" and acknowledged that a great deal would depend on the "spirituality of the commissioners." He urged all houses of worship to make available their resources to provide counseling and corporate confessions.[16] He has also emphasized the need to reach deep into the "spiritual wells of our different religious traditions" to address the challenge of healing and nation building, while pointing out that those who stand in the Christian tradition have "a special responsibility" because of the way that Christian theological resources were used to promote apartheid in the past.[17]

Storytelling

Storytelling is central to many faiths and an integral part of African tradition. The narrative element has made the HRV hearings compelling. "While the importance of narrative has been a central issue in much contemporary theology and ethics, this theory is rarely demonstrated with as much power as it is in the TRC hearings," assert theologians H. Russel Botman and Robin Petersen.[18] Encouraged to tell their stories of pain and suffering in their own way, victims routinely use overtly Christian terminology and Biblical allusions to describe what happened to them and how they dealt with their loss.

It is important that victims be allowed to tell their stories; survivors often feel misunderstood and ignored, their sacrifice unacknowledged, their pain unrecognized, and their identity destroyed. Theologian Robert Shreiter writes that individuals cannot survive without a narrative of identity. Oppressors attempt through torture and coercion to substitute another narrative so that people will acquiesce in their subjugation. If they succeed in suppressing the original narrative, the lie will be accepted as truth. Only by overcoming the narrative of the lie and embracing a redeeming narrative can victims overcome suffering.[19] South Africa's Black Consciousness Movement of the 1960s and 1970s stressed the point that blacks, through daily intimidation and subjugation, had internalized a sense of inferiority and accepted the inferior status preached to them by whites. Even though, over the years, counter-ideologies arose to combat the false ideology of Afrikanerdom, it is a near-universal phenomenon that victims blame themselves. Constitutional Court Judge Albie Sachs, a survivor of a car bomb attack, commented on the importance of storytelling in the process of identity reclamation, saying, "We need to feel that basically we did right, that we did not deserve what was inflicted upon us. This gives us a sense of rightness to the world, not just to us but to the future."[20]

Psychology tells us that suppressing stories leads to stress, depression, and anxiety; sharing stories in a supportive setting leads to healing. Through the TRC, "people who have nurtured their subjugated stories in the confines of their hearts and hearths—

offstage—now have an opportunity to articulate and own their stories on stage. What was hidden is now becoming public."[21]

Theologians Gerald West and James Cochrane have written of the need for "dangerous memories" and "subjugated knowledges" to be aroused, recovered, and expressed. Without expression, memories that are sufficiently intense will engender not only personal but also social brokenness. War may result.[22] These stories, then, have significance not only for victims but for perpetrators and bystanders as well. Botman notes, "Every time [we] hear the stories, the contemporary miracle happens; the deaf begin to hear!"[23]

Storytelling is significant because it is a way for victims, perpetrators, and bystanders to construct a common memory of the past. In *The Story of Our Life*, H. Richard Niebuhr writes: "Where common memory is lacking, where people do not share in the same past, there can be no real community, and where community is to be formed common memory must be created."[24] The TRC offers the opportunity to participate in each other's humanity in story form.

The authors of *Reconciliation through Truth* argue that through the stories emanating from the TRC, South Africans are facing unwelcome truths in order to "harmonize incommensurable world views" so that conflicts and differences stand "at least within a single universe of comprehensibility."[25] Boraine insists that South Africans need a "common memory to remind us what our society was like and of the dark era we have passed through."[26] Reconciliation requires that there be some general agreement between both sides as to the wrongs committed. The danger exists that if perpetrators do not come forward, an essential part of that larger narrative will remain untold.

Remembering the Past

The National Party has been wary of the TRC's effort to uncover the past, arguing in effect that South Africa should let bygones be bygones. Former president F. W. de Klerk has urged South Africans not to look backward, insisting that national unity requires moving forward. But remembering the past is central to the Christian faith. Both the Old and New Testaments speak of redemptive memory. "Remember when you were slaves in Egypt" is a constant Old Testament refrain. "Do this in remembrance of me" are words said at each eucharist. To paraphrase Donald Shriver, forgiveness begins with a remembering, a moral judgment of wrong, injustice, and injury. Shriver argues that the Christian injunction is not to "forgive and forget" but to "remember and forgive."[27] H. Richard Niebuhr reminds us, "We cannot become integrated parts . . . until we each remember our whole past, with its sins . . . and appropriate each other's past."[28] Karl Barth called the Christian confession of faith an exercise in name giving.[29] In order to give a name, to be in agreement, to concur, to admit the other is right, those parts of the past of which one is unaware, for whatever reason (including denial and self-deception), must be made known. For instance, listening to narratives of pain, the perpetrator is invited to share the victim's experience of the truth and make it his own, making confession possible.

Forgiveness and Repentance

Ideally in the TRC confessional process, perpetrators repent their sins and victims offer forgiveness, leading to reconciliation between individuals and ultimately of the nation at large. Tutu understands and encourages this process and has implored perpetrators to apologize publicly and accept the forgiveness he believes would be forthcoming from victims. However, the act authorizing the TRC grants amnesty in exchange for full disclosure—remorse is not a requirement. Should victims be expected to forgive perpetrators who have not apologized? One view is that forgiveness is two-sided, requiring not only mercy on the part of the persecuted but repentance on the side of the oppressor. Beyers Naude, head of the former Christian Institute and one of the leading Afrikaners to oppose apartheid, says, "In some incredible way God has sown the seeds of a gracious attitude, of the spirit of *ubuntu*, in the hearts and minds of the whole African community." He adds, "As far as I know, none of the leaders of the National Party ever said they were sorry about the system they created."[30]

De Klerk has resisted apologizing for actions of the previous National Party government. He does not believe that apartheid was inherently wrong and attributes no evil intent to its architects. His reforms were motivated by the belief that apartheid had simply failed to work out.[31] During his first presentation before the TRC, de Klerk, speaking for the National Party, denied that he or his cabinet planned murders, tortures, or assassinations of opponents.[32] He added that, while accepting responsibility for political decisions taken when it was governing, the National Party could not be held accountable for such unauthorized actions as cold-blooded murder, as they were not mandated by the policy of his government but committed by "maverick elements." In the National Party's second submission, de Klerk insisted that he was as shocked as anyone on hearing of such acts committed by a "handful of operatives" in the police and military and could not accept that the government's policies gave security forces a "license to kill." When presented with a document that showed he was present at a cabinet meeting in 1986 when a decision was made to create a security force that would "eliminate" the state's enemies, de Klerk denied that "eliminate" meant to kill, a statement the TRC commissioners did not find credible.[33]

P. W. Botha has refused to take part in any way in the TRC proceedings. After defying three subpoenas to tell what he knows about the State Security Council—an organization set up during his presidency that has been implicated in masterminding the killing, torturing, and detaining of thousands of blacks—the 81-year-old former president is being prosecuted for contempt. On the opening day of his trial, Botha told reporters, "I only apologize for my sins before God."[34]

Some believe that de Klerk and Botha may have ruined chances for reconciliation by refusing to respond to the politics of grace offered by the TRC. According to Michael Lapsley, former pastor to the ANC in exile and now chaplain for the Trauma Center for the Victims of Violence and Torture, "The perpetrators have the audacity to tell the victims 'it is your job to forgive and forget' while at the same time refusing to acknowledge that they have been party to evil."[35]

Since none of the former government's leaders has yet responded to Tutu's call for public apologies, is reconciliation possible? The South African theologians who penned the *Kairos Document* following the state of emergency in 1985 argued that without true repentance, it is *not*. For these theologians, reconciliation can only *follow* repentance by whites and a clear commitment by them to fundamental change.[36] Critics of the TRC process point out that whereas remorse is not a condition of amnesty, it would be taken into consideration in any routine court case. In their view the TRC's "reconciliation" is a code word for the one-sided forgiveness of perpetrators by victims.

The reality is that victims cannot be compelled to forgive any more than perpetrators can be forced to repent. It is clear that Tutu yearns for forgiveness and repentance to happen, but nothing in the legislation requires it. One cannot realistically expect all victims to forgive readily even when asked to do so. When Dirk Coetzee turned to the families of his victims at his amnesty hearing and asked their forgiveness, Charity Kondile's legal representative read her client's statement: "You said that you would like to meet Mrs. Kondile and look her in the eye. She asked me to tell you that she feels it is an honor . . . you do not deserve. If you are really sorry, you would stand trial for the deeds you did."[37] Perpetrators have not always expressed remorse, nor have victims always found it in their hearts to forgive them. Former Methodist bishop Peter Storey does not view the lack of contrition of many amnesty applicants as problematic, arguing that forced repentance would devalue those moments of apparently genuine repentance that do occur.[38] Whether amnesty applicants are remorseful or not, at the very least disclosure means acknowledging the truth about what happened.

Both Sides Are Guilty

The TRC operates from the Christian paradigm of original sin. No one has clean hands, although there are of course degrees of guilt. Dietrich Bonhoeffer, a German Christian involved in an assassination attempt on Hitler's life, recognized that he would be committing a sin and would need to be forgiven. Bonhoeffer accepted that he could not merely claim that the Nazi regime's evil justified what he was doing.[39] According to the doctrine of original sin, all are implicated in its web and, as Christians, are required to confess their sins. Thus, when appearing before the TRC, both sides—oppressors and oppressed—must disclose violations of human rights to be eligible for amnesty.

That no moral distinction is made between the violence used to maintain an unjust system and the violence employed to oppose it has been one of the major criticisms of the commission. To compare the limited excesses of the ANC, a liberation movement fighting for freedom, to the colossal atrocities committed by an illegitimate government in aid of shoring up white supremacy is tantamount to ignoring the distinction between the size of a flea and an elephant, argues Michael Lapsley, whose hands were blown off by a letter bomb.[40]

Because the ANC believes its struggle was a moral one against an apartheid system condemned worldwide as a "crime against humanity," it initially urged its members not to seek amnesty. ANC Secretary-General Cheryl Carolus argued, "We believe that every single act we engaged in was morally justified."[41] However, Tutu threatened to resign from the TRC if the ANC tried to exempt itself from the provisions of the legislation requiring all individuals involved in gross human rights abuses to apply for amnesty in order to avoid prosecution. After its differences with the TRC were ironed out, the ANC said it would no longer discourage its members from applying.

Although the ANC is adamant that it fought a "just war," a basic tenet of just war theory distinguishes between justice of war (*jus ad bello*) and justice in war (*jus in bello*). It does not follow that if the cause is just, the rules of justice in war—such as the rule that noncombatants not be killed—can be ignored. Tutu insists that the Committee on Amnesty is not concerned with the morality of a politically motivated offense, only with whether the applicant could be held criminally or civilly liable for his actions. Tutu's thinking was echoed by Boraine, who said, "No matter how just the cause may be, if there are violations of human rights, the liberation movements must accept responsibility for them."[42]

Speaking for the ANC at its party submission, Deputy President Thabo Mbeki, while denying that it was official ANC policy to attack civilians or to "necklace" government collaborators, admitted that "excesses" had occurred in the ANC exile camps, including the execution of 34 cadres in Angola accused of mutiny, murder, and rape.[43] In its second party submission in May 1997, the ANC was more forthright, admitting to having assassinated informers who betrayed the struggle, committed violations of women's human rights (including rape), set up township self-defense units in the early 1990s, and bombed companies involved in worker disputes.[44] The ANC also accepted responsibility for the 1983 bombing of the South African Air Force headquarters in Pretoria, an attack that killed civilians.[45] Political analyst Tom Lodge says of the party hearings that more has come out about the behavior of the liberation movements than about the government of the day, as the National Party will admit to little.[46]

Background information from political parties will be supplemented by reports submitted by historians, journalists, and others to help the research department of the TRC prepare a comprehensive report on the violations of this period. Even if individuals have failed to come forward to confess and political parties have offered less than full disclosure, it is hoped that at least some questions may be answered by the research and investigative units.

No Innocent Bystanders?

Lapsley says there are three kinds of stories to tell: "What was done to me; what I did; and what I didn't do."[47] In the Christian tradition each person is responsible for the way society conducts itself, and the faithful take upon themselves the guilt for sins that they did not necessarily commit. It follows that, although most white South Africans did not engage in acts of torture or murder, they are nonetheless guilty.

The TRC may have particular significance for the many white South Africans who insist they do not know much of what was done in their name. An ANC member of Parliament, Willie Hofmeyr, believes that there may be a number of white people who are genuinely sorry for what happened during the apartheid era and who would welcome the opportunity to come to terms with their consciences.[48] As University of Cape Town Professor Mahmood Mamdani explains, in South Africa there may have been few actual perpetrators but there were many beneficiaries.[49] One view of the TRC is that due to its very nature, ordinary whites get off the hook. Because the hearings focus on atrocious crimes of torture and murder, usually at the hands of police, it is easy for ordinary white people to think, "Well, I never did anything like that. I have nothing to apologize for."

The TRC ignores the massive denial of human rights experienced by millions of ordinary people—the violence of pass laws, group areas, and forced removals. The hearings, then, warn police against torturing people but say nothing about the injustice of allowing people to be poor or exploited or pushed around. To counter this objection and to move beyond demonizing a few torturers toward implicating all of society, the TRC set up special hearings—outside the purview of the regular work of the three committees—on the role of the media, the medical profession, and the judiciary. Other hearings followed on the role of business and the faith community, suggesting that reconciliation is envisaged not just between victims and perpetrators, but between victims and beneficiaries as well. Charles Villa-Vicencio, the TRC's research director, explains: "We are trying to enable South Africans of all levels to acknowledge their guilt. There are different levels, but the bystander is still part of it."[50] In an effort to draw in the population at large, the TRC in December 1997 established a register of reconciliation that members of the public can sign to express their regret at failing to prevent human rights violations and to pledge their commitment to a future South Africa in which human rights abuses will not take place.

Does Denial Mean Failure?

Do the denials by de Klerk that the National Party ever authorized human rights violations of political opponents or fueled black-on-black violence (between ANC and Inkatha Freedom Party supporters) signify that the TRC has been unsuccessful? Psychologist Sean Kaliski argues that even when denials come from the highest levels, they are a positive step, akin to the initial step in the emotional stages terminally ill patients experience: denial, rage, bargaining, depression, and finally, acceptance. About white Afrikaners, Kaliski says: "If you personalize it: a very proud person who is publicly exposed for being a scoundrel will almost never respond with humility and contrition; they will almost always respond with anger and outrage." He adds that he would be concerned if whites were too quick to integrate information that overturns their whole world. "It will take decades, maybe generations, for people to assimilate the truths of this country's past. But there will be no grand release—every individual will have to devise his or her own personal method of coming to terms with what happened."[51]

The TRC has made it possible for all South Africans to hear something of what happened during the dark years of apartheid. Political scientist Andre du Toit asserts: "In whatever way they may still be interpreted or explained, the sheer number and gravity of political atrocities in our recent past can no longer be doubted or ignored. This is already a historical achievement for the TRC."[52]

Restitution

To be meaningful, confession and repentance must be followed by restitution. "Apologies set the record straight; restitution sets out to make a new record," writes Shriver.[53] Tutu explains: "Those who have wronged must be ready to make what amends they can. They must be ready to make restitution and reparation. If I have stolen your pen, I can't really be contrite when I say, 'Please forgive me,' if at the same time I still keep your pen. If I am truly repentant, then I will demonstrate this genuine repentance by returning your pen."[54]

How to compensate people who have suffered is problematic. Early thinking on reparations was that they would necessarily take symbolic form, for the simple reason that there would not be enough money to compensate all victims of abuses. In the TRC's interim report Tutu expressed amazement at "how modest people's expectations of reparations have often been—a tombstone, the renaming of a school, a bursary for the surviving children."[55]

At a national workshop of the TRC's Reparations and Rehabilitation Committee, Commissioner Wendy Orr said that South Africa was obliged to provide victims with fair and adequate compensation, not token amounts of money.[56]

In October 1997, the Reparations and Rehabilitation Committee announced its final policy proposal, which it will submit to Parliament as part of the TRC's final report in July 1998. It proposed that in addition to symbolic reparations, which will help communities to commemorate "the pain and victories of the past,"[57] each identified victim receive an individual reparation grant for a period of six years, with a minimum payment of 17,000 rand per year. Victims having many dependants or living in rural areas will be offered 23,000 rand a year.[58] Only those who came forward to the commission with written submissions by December 15, 1997, are eligible for reparations.

Church Response to the TRC

Despite the light that Christian theology sheds on the proceedings, church response to the TRC has been minimal. Formal responses came early on from the Research Institute on Christianity in South Africa at the University of Cape Town, the theological faculty at the University of the Western Cape, and church leaders from the South African Council of Churches (SACC). But support from denominations and individual churches has been weak. Etienne de Villiers, professor of ethics at the University of Pretoria, makes the point that the TRC can only function successfully if the Dutch Reformed Church and other Afrikaner churches lend it their support: "If the political parties of the Afrikaner, the Afrikaans newspapers, and, in particular, the Afrikaans churches withdraw their support and encourage Afrikaners to refuse any co-operation with the TRC, the TRC will surely not succeed in its objectives."[59] Yet most white churches—especially Afrikaner ones—have not been involved in the process.

The Salvation Army and the Apostolic Faith Mission (AFM) were the first national church bodies to make official submissions to the TRC. The Salvation Army admitted that during the apartheid years it had chosen to remain silent, "a sin of omission which we deeply regret."[60] The AFM confessed that it had failed in its duty to question the system and pledged to become a more faithful watchdog to ensure that history would never be repeated.[61]

Finally, in November 1997, more churches responded to the TRC's invitation for a special public hearing of the faith communities. Operating the hearing in East London, Tutu announced that no church in South Africa could claim a perfect record of opposing apartheid and all would have to confess to shortcomings.[62] Over three days confessions came from Christian denominations as well as from Jewish, Muslim, and Hindu communities, who in varying degrees apologized for not having done enough to oppose the government's policies.

The most self-critical submission came from the South African Council of Churches—the umbrella group of mainline churches formed in 1967 and once headed by Tutu. Though the SACC was the most activist church organization in its opposition to apartheid, for which it was often a target of police raids and harassment, it nevertheless expressed some regrets. Its general secretary, Brigalia Bam, said to the commission, "The SACC did not do enough to seek out the victims of apartheid, but relied, in the main, for people to come to it for assistance and aid."[63]

On the final day of hearings the Dutch Reformed Church (DRC), the denomination closely linked to the National Party and popularly called the "National Party at Prayer," presented its long-awaited submission. Tutu thanked the DRC for its presence: "I am so glad that you have seen the light. To have you on our side is a tremendous thing, and we give thanks to God. We are glad you are part of the process of healing in our land."[64] The DRC's submission was a disappointment, however, for the DRC moderator, Freek Swanepoel, said little about the past and how the DRC's teachings lent credibility to apartheid. He focused instead on the present need for reconciliation. Ironically (though not surprisingly), the denomination that was most explicit in the theological justification for apartheid and support of the National Party's policies was the church body that could find the least for which to apologize.

Amnesty

It is in fact the renunciation of punishment—the amnesty provision—that is the most controversial aspect of the TRC. Many in the human rights community are disappointed with the decision to offer immunity from prosecution. Human Rights Watch says it is opposed in principle to the granting of indemnity, maintaining that governments have a duty under international law to prosecute those guilty of gross violations of human rights.[65] Human Rights Watch's position overstates the case, as international law contains few specific regulations dealing with prosecutions.[66] It is more accurate to say that international law *permits* prosecution, but as Daan Bronkhorst points out, it is more the exception than the rule to prosecute those who have committed serious human rights abuses.[67] Lapsley, the former pastor of the ANC in exile, joined others in the human rights community who opposed the decision to offer immunity from prosecution. "No trials means no justice," he said.[68] A group of victims and victims' families, including the widow of Steve Biko, fought unsuccessfully to have the section of the Promotion of National Unity and Reconciliation Act that allows amnesty with no prospect of future criminal or civil trials deemed unconstitutional.

As the May 10, 1997, deadline to apply for amnesty approached, applications were submitted in unprecedented numbers, bringing the tally to 7,700. One last-minute submission was the 1,000-page application of Eugene de Kock—the jailed former police commander of Vlakplaas, the notorious base near Pretoria that was the center of the government's death squad operations—who had been convicted of 87 charges of murder. Another last-minute applicant was Piet Koornhof, a former National Party cabinet minister, who called his amnesty application a "symbolic act of asking for forgiveness." Applying for amnesty, he said, "is a sign of feeling intensely sorry."[69] Koornhof is only the second National Party cabinet member, following former law and order minister Adriaan Vlok, to file for amnesty.

Notably absent were applications from Botha and de Klerk, former deputy minister Magnus Malan (who spent the day on the golf course), and the Inkatha Freedom Party's leader, Mongosuthu Buthelezi, who said he would not apply because he never killed anyone or ordered anyone killed.[70] Missing also were applications from former members of the South African Defense Forces.

While some of the "foot soldiers" of the old regime (especially police) have come forward, few senior officials, including politicians and generals who had ultimate responsibility for implementing apartheid, have applied. Many senior officials continue to play a prominent role in the new South Africa and may be betting that the present government lacks the will to prosecute.

The day after the amnesty deadline, which had been extended once again to September 30, 1997, Justice Minister Dullah Omar stated that attorneys general would be duty bound to prosecute perpetrators of apartheid-era crimes who had not applied to the TRC for amnesty if sufficient evidence to prosecute were found.[71] Omar's statement may be some consolation to critics of amnesty who have seen it as an obsequious attempt at white appeasement and have called for prosecution.

Retribution

In the view of some theologians, the TRC is wrong to offer amnesty to perpetrators since what is needed is punitive, retributive justice without which reconciliation is impossible. Addressing the pent-up anger of victims requires nothing short of a court of law. Willa Boesak argues that whites do not expect blacks to succumb to bitterness or anger and that in fact this "unnatural

. . . patience or reasonableness" is not Christian in origin as thought but a distorted ethos of submissiveness. The wrath of the marginalized reflects the wrath of God, and the evildoer must be punished, according to Boesak. He draws a distinction between *wraak* (revenge, vengefulness, blind destructive fury, vindictiveness) and *vergeldig* (recompense, requital, retribution, reward). The distinction is between subjective and objective punishment, the latter finding its fulfillment in a court of justice where the civil authorities became God's rightful avengers.[72]

Wolfram Kistner rejoins that there are two theological approaches to reconciliation and justice. The classical approach (Boesak's theology of retribution) says the offender has to be punished to make atonement. Kistner suggests that whether or not to punish an offender should be determined by considering the best means of promoting healing and reconciliation in the life of the offender and the victim. This approach offers a basis for renouncing punishment as long as such a renunciation serves the purposes of reconciliation by reintegrating offenders into the society and healing victims.[73]

The Court Route versus the TRC Route

It is not certain that a Nuremberg-type legal prosecution would necessarily have ensured more justice for the victims than the TRC process provides. To equate pure justice with the court route and something vastly inferior with the TRC route is to create a false dichotomy.

First, in a court setting witnesses would not have had the advantage of telling their stories in their own way but would have been subjected to hostile cross-examination by the defendants' attorneys. It would have been an adversarial situation for them rather than the "user-friendly" forum the TRC provides.[74] Second, hard evidence, much of which has been destroyed, would be required to convict. The burden of proof in a court trial would be beyond reasonable doubt; inevitably, many perpetrators would maintain their innocence and get off scot-free. In the TRC setting, on the other hand, a perpetrator may get amnesty, but at least there is an accounting of what happened—often all the victims want anyway.

In fact, there is concern that a platform for victims to tell their stories is the most the TRC can offer, and that even then the truth will not come out. Perpetrators have been hesitant to come forward, and many of those who did apply for amnesty were sometimes less than completely honest. One high-profile case involving Biko's killers points to the limited success of the TRC's Committee on Amnesty in uncovering the entire truth. The five amnesty applicants denied that they intended to kill Biko in police custody, calling his death the result of an accident that occurred when he hit his head against a wall following a scuffle with his interrogators. Their testimony disappointed many, who didn't believe it.[75] The amnesty committee has not acted on this case yet, but if it finds the applicants' accounts unsatisfactory, it can deny them pardons and the attorney general may prosecute them.

Establishing the identities and pinpointing the deeds of everyone responsible for various violations may be only somewhat successful. However, even if the TRC becomes primarily a forum for victims to share their stories, it will have provided a worthwhile service for those who were previously voiceless, restoring the dignity of which they were robbed. This would not have happened in a courtroom. Nor would victims have had the psychological counselors Tutu has provided for them before, during, and after their testimony. The TRC forum puts the victim—not the perpetrator—center stage.

An Imperfect Solution

Defenders of amnesty point out that it was a necessary political compromise. The National Party demanded that its supporters be indemnified from criminal prosecutions through an amnesty agreement. Omar, one of the ANC negotiators, explained:

> The amnesty clause in our interim constitution is the result of political negotiations. . . . Without that amnesty provision, there would have been no political settlement. It was the one issue that stood in the way of democratic elections . . . and we had to concede that the amnesty problem would be dealt with after the elections.[76]

Without the guarantee of amnesty the National Party would have walked out of negotiations altogether.

Nuremberg-type trials, with their emphasis on absolute justice, are only possible where there is a clear military victory. This was not the case in South Africa; the ANC did not ride victorious into Pretoria on tanks but rather came to power through a negotiated settlement. ANC member of Parliament Willie Hoffmeyr says:

> We had to accept very early on that we would not get complete justice. . . . We could have chosen the revolution and overthrow route, but we chose the negotiations route, and that means having to live and work with and rebuild the country together with people who have treated us very badly in the past and against whom we have very strong feelings.[77]

The 1993 interim constitution's postamble, "National Unity and Reconciliation," became the basis for the Promotion of National Unity and Reconciliation Act passed by the Government of National Unity in 1995. Although the National Party favored a blanket amnesty, the ANC insisted on conditional amnesty—amnesty offered to perpetrators on an individual basis in exchange for full disclosure.[78]

The politics of compromise may be at odds with a strict notion of justice, but that does not deny the TRC's ethical basis. Peter Storey characterizes the TRC as offering a "different kind of justice" than one that metes out harsh punishment.[79] Tutu poses the options available: "justice with ashes" against "amnesty with the possibility of continuing survival for all of us." Without the compromise on amnesty, the bitter conflict between the government and the resistance movements undoubtedly would have continued, with many more human rights violations and deaths. Tutu explains: "It's realpolitik, this forgiveness thing. It's not just something in the realm of religion or the spiritual. If justice is your last word, you've had it. You've got to go beyond it."[80]

Conclusion

Though flawed and subject to criticism, the Truth and Reconciliation Commission marks an important stage in the process of coming to understand the past. First and foremost, the TRC's findings will have significance for the victims. Despite the willingness to forgive and the apparent absence of hate and vengefulness on the part of many of the formerly oppressed, Richard Goldstone, South African Constitutional Court judge and chief prosecutor of Bosnian and Rwandan war crimes says, "There is a deep, deep hurt and pain in the hearts of many of our compatriots."[81] One witness, blinded from a police bullet, conveyed the potential healing power of the hearings when he stated after testifying: "Now I have been given my eyes back."[82]

But are apartheid's willing beneficiaries—the majority white population—being transformed by the process? The *Mail & Guardian* reported in February 1997 that as a result of complaints by white radio listeners who objected to hearing TRC-related stories, such reports are now broadcast at non-prime-time hours, after 8 PM, "when most of the farmers are no longer listening." Also, few whites are believed to be watching television journalist Max du Preez's weekly "TRC: Special Report," the highest-rated public affairs broadcast thanks to its one million black viewers. The whites "don't want to deal with the truth," explains investigative journalist Jacques Pauw.[83] But whether willingly or not, the past is being confronted and a new social memory for South Africa is being created. Interpretations of the past that were previously suppressed are now being legitimized.

Is the TRC perfect? Not by any means. It was a compromise between the morally ideal and the politically possible. As Reinhold Niebuhr reminds us, neither perfect love nor perfect justice is fully attainable in political communities, and society's best solution can only be an "approximation of brotherhood under the conditions of sin."[84] If justice depends on groups' agreeing on a tolerable solution to inevitable conflict, the TRC meets that requirement. The TRC may lead, if not to perfect reconciliation, then at least to the possibility of coexistence in this once deeply divided society. Nations moving through democratic transitions may find a workable model in South Africa's ethical, yet pragmatic, experiment in dealing with the past.

NOTES

1. John Battersby, "South Africa Takes Final Steps Toward Long-Sought Democracy," *Christian Science Monitor*, May 4, 1994, 1.

2. Robin Petersen, "The Politics of Grace and the Truth and Reconciliation Commission," in H. Russel Botman and Robin Petersen, eds., *To Remember and to Heal: Theological and Psychological Reflections on Truth and Reconciliation* (Cape Town, Pretoria, and Johannesburg: Human & Rousseau, 1996), 59.

3. Donald Shriver, *An Ethic for Enemies: Forgiveness in Politics* (New York: Oxford University Press, 1995), 229.

4. The seventeen commissioners (including Bishop Tutu) were nominated by a representative panel appointed by President Mandela, which solicited applicants from all walks of life and held public hearings on the selections. Members—seven blacks, two coloreds, two Indians, and six whites—range from a Pan-Africanist Congress member on the left to a Freedom Front member on the right. Membership has since been augmented to give further gender and ethnic balance and to be broadly representative.

5. *Promotion of National Unity and Reconciliation Act*, no. 34 (1995).

6. Ibid.

7. Ibid.

8. Roughly one-third come from the church, one-third from the health and mental health professions, and one-third from the legal system.

9. Statement by Marius Schoon, whose wife and daughter were murdered by the explosion of a parcel bomb that was sent to them in Angola. Cited in Charles Villa-Vicencio, "The Road to Reconciliation," *Sojourners* 26 (May/June 1997), 36.

10. Harold Strachan, Letter to Editor, *Mail & Guardian*, July 25, 1997.

11. Antjie Krog, "The Parable of the Bicycle," *Mail & Guardian*, February 6–13, 1997.

12. See T. Dunbar Moodie, *The Rise of Afrikanerdom: Power, Apartheid and the Afrikaner Civil Religion* (Berkeley: University of California Press, 1975); William A. de Klerk, *The Puritans in Africa: The History of Afrikanerdom* (London: Rex Collings, 1975); and J. Alton Templin, *Ideology on a Frontier: The Theological Foundation of Afrikaner Nationalism, 1652–1910* (Westport, Conn.: Greenwood Press, 1984).

13. See Lyn S. Graybill, *Religion and Resistance Politics in South Africa* (Westport, Conn.: Praeger, 1995).

14. Dirkie Smit, "Confession-Guilt-Truth-and-Forgiveness in the Christian Tradition," in *To Remember and to Heal*, 96.

15. Mark Gevisser, "The Ultimate Test of Faith," *Mail & Guardian*, April 12, 1996.

16. TRC Press Release, "Archbishop Desmond Tutu's Address to the First Gathering of the Truth and Reconciliation Commission," December 16, 1995.

17. Desmond Tutu, foreword, *To Remember and to Heal*, 8.

18. H. Russel Botman and Robin Petersen, introduction, *To Remember and to Heal*, 12.

19. Robert Shreiter, *Reconciliation: Mission and Ministry in a Changing Social Order* (Maryknoll, N.Y.: Orbis, 1992), 34–35.

20. Cited in Terry Dowdall, "Psychological Aspects of the Truth and Reconciliation Commission," in *To Remember and to Heal*, 35.

21. Gerald West, "Don't Stand on My Story: The Truth and Reconciliation Commission, Intellectuals, Genre, and Identity," *Journal of Theology for Southern Africa* 98 (July 1997), 6.

22. James Cochrane and Gerald West, "War, Remembrance and Reconstruction," *Journal of Theology for Southern Africa* 84 (September 1993), 25.

23. H. Russel Botman, "Narrative Challenges in a Situation of Transition," in *To Remember and to Heal*, 39.

24. H. Richard Niebuhr, cited in Smit, "Confession-Guilt-Truth-and-Forgiveness," 98.

25. Cadre Asmal, Louise Asmal, and Ronald Suresh Roberts, *Reconciliation through Truth* (Cape Town and Johannesburg: David Philip Publishers, 1996), 46.

26. "Reaction Strengthens Against Secrecy Compromise on Truth Commission," *SouthScan* 9 (December 9, 1994).

27. Shriver, *An Ethic for Enemies*, 7.

28. H. Richard Niebuhr, cited in Smit, "Confession-Guilt-Truth-and-Forgiveness," 100.

29. Karl Barth, cited in "Confession-Guilt-Truth-and-Forgiveness," 102.

30. "South Africa: The Spirit of Reconciliation," *Sojourners* 23 (July 1994), 9.

31. David Ottaway, *Chained Together* (New York: Times Books, 1993), 62.

32. South African Press Association (SAPA), "FW Apologises for Apartheid but Denies Sanctioning Assassinations," August 21, 1996.

33. Transcript of the National Party Recall in Cape Town, May 14, 1997.

34. Lynne Duke, "South Africa's Botha Offers No Apologies," *Washington Post*, January 24, 1998.

35. Eddie Koch, "The Truth and Reconciliation Commission," *Mail & Guardian*, May 19–25, 1995.

36. Institute for Contextual Theology, *Kairos Document: The Challenge to the Churches* (Grand Rapids, Mich.: William B. Eerdmans, 1986), 11.

37. Krog, "The Parable of the Bicycle."

38. Peter Storey, "A Different Kind of Justice: Truth and Reconciliation in South Africa," *The Christian Century* 114 (September 10–17, 1997), 793.

39. Dietrich Bonhoeffer, *Life Together* (London: SCM, 1983).

40. Alex Boraine, *Dealing with the Past: Truth and Reconciliation in South Africa*, ed. Janet Levy and Ronel Scheffer (Cape Town: Institute for Democracy in South Africa, 1994), 29.

41. SAPA, "TRC Members Not Morally Neutral: Tutu," March 7, 1997.

42. Ibid.

43. Transcript of the ANC Statement to the TRC, August 22, 1996.

44. Transcript of the ANC Party Political Recall in Cape Town, May 12–13, 1997.

45. The ANC insisted, however, that the attack did not contradict its policy to avoid civilian casualties, faulting instead the government for placing strategic installations in high-density civilian areas.

46. Eddie Koch, "Military Third Force Walks Free," *Mail & Guardian*, May 16–22, 1997.

47. "Tears, Fears, and Hope: Healing the Memories in South Africa," *Southern Africa* 7 (January/February 1997), 1.

48. Eddie Koch and Gaye Davis, "Firing Up the Truth Machine," *Mail & Guardian*, July 26–August 3, 1995.

49. Krog, "The Parable of the Bicycle."

50. Tina Rosenberg, "Recovering from Apartheid," *New Yorker* 72 (November 18, 1996), 95.

51. Antjie Krog, "Unto the Third or Fourth Generations," *Mail & Guardian*, June 13–19, 1997.

52. Andre du Toit, "No Rest Without the Wicked," *Indicator* 14 (Summer 1997), 9.

53. Shriver, *An Ethic for Enemies*, 224.

54. Desmond Tutu, "We Forgive You," in, John Allen, ed., *The Rainbow People of God: The Making of a Peaceful Revolution* (New York: Doubleday, 1994), 222.

55. TRC's First Interim Report (June 1996).

56. SAPA, "Billions Needed for Victims of Apartheid Rights Abuses," April 3, 1997.

57. "Reparation and Rehabilitation," *Truth Talk* 3 (November 1997), 1.

58. TRC Press Release, "Introductory Notes to the Presentation of the Truth and Reconciliation Commission's Proposed Reparation and Rehabilitation Policies," October 23, 1997. (In U.S. dollars, the total payment over six years would be approximately $21,000 to $28,000 for those receiving the larger grant.) The average payment (R 21,700) is based on the average annual income of a South African household. The Reparation and Rehabilitation Committee considered but rejected using the poverty line of R 15,000 for the average payment because it would condemn victims to a life of near poverty. "TRC Proposes Grants," *Truth Talk* 3 (November 1997), 2.

59. Etienne de Villiers, "The Challenge to the Afrikaans Churches," in *To Remember and to Heal*, 151.

60. SAPA, "Salvation Army Tells TRC It Regrets Silence During Apartheid Years," June 3, 1997.

61. SAPA, "AFM Failed Duty, TRC Told," August 4, 1997.

62. SAPA, "SA Churches Must Confess to Shortcomings, Says Tutu," November 17, 1997.

63. SAPA, "SA Churches Were Not United Against Apartheid, SACC Tells TRC," November 17, 1997.

64. SAPA, "TRC Focuses on Reconciliation in TRC Submission," November 19, 1997.

65. South Africa: Threats to a New Democracy," *Human Rights Watch/Africa*, May 7, 1995.

66. The Nuremberg Principles of the 1945–46 military tribunal against the Nazi war criminals asserted that crimes against humanity could be tried in an international court because they offended humanity itself. The Genocide Convention of 1948 (Article 4) makes genocide a punishable crime. The Apartheid Convention of 1973 classifies apartheid as a crime against humanity and provides for prosecution in a court of law in one of the states involved or in an international criminal tribunal. The Convention against Torture of 1985 requires that states submit cases to the competent authorities for prosecution but does not require that actual prosecution take place. The Fourth Geneva Convention (Article 146) states that parties shall bring persons alleged to have committed serious breaches before its own courts or hand them over to another high contracting party.

67. Daan Bronkhorst, *Truth and Reconciliation: Obstacles and Opportunities for Human Rights* (Amsterdam: Amnesty International Dutch Section, 1995), 91.

68. Koch, "The Truth and Reconciliation Commission."

69. SAPA, "7700 Amnesty Applications Received by Midnight Deadline Saturday," May 10, 1997.

70. SAPA, "Amnesty Committee Faces Monumental Task," May 11, 1997.

71. Since the constitutional amendment extending the amnesty cutoff date from December 6, 1993, to May 10, 1994, had only become law in late August 1997, it was believed that some perpetrators might have decided not to submit their applications until they were sure that Parliament would approve this extension.

72. Willa Boesak, "Truth, Justice and Reconciliation," in *To Remember and to Heal*, 65–69.

73. Wolfram Kistner, "The Biblical Understanding of Reconciliation," in *To Remember and to Heal*, 89.

74. Although the commissioners are working under time constraints and attempt to hear ten to twelve witnesses a day, their efforts to get witnesses to stick to their presubmitted testimony, not to get off track, and to tell only what is relevant often fail. Even when told to start at a certain point, the witnesses invariably say they will start somewhere else in the story—much earlier—and then do!

75. Alex Russell, "We Didn't Intend to Kill Biko," *Daily Telegraph*, September 11, 1997.

76. Dullah Omar, "Opening Address," reporting to the Truth Commission conference, Johannesburg: March 1–2, 1996.

77. Mark Gevisser, "Can South Africa Face Its Past?" *Nation*, June 26, 1995, 920–21.

78. In November 1997, the Amnesty Committee granted what appeared to be "blanket" amnesty to 37 ANC leaders (including Deputy President Thabo Mbeki) who in their applications accepted "collective responsibility" for acts committed by their members on behalf of the ANC. The decision was roundly criticized because it contravened the requirement of the Promotion of National Unity and Reconciliation Act for full disclosure on an individual basis. The TRC has asked the High Court to rule on its validity.

79. Storey, "A Different Kind of Justice," 788.

80. Gevisser, "The Ultimate Test of Faith."

81. Gevisser, "Can South Africa Face Its Past?" 919.

82. SAPA, "Blinded Man Forgives Soldier Who Shot Him, TRC Hears," August 5, 1996.

83. Claudia Braude, "Media Should Get the Truth Out," *Mail & Guardian*, February 7–13, 1997.

84. Reinhold Niebuhr, *The Nature and Destiny of Man*, vol. 2, *Human Destiny* (New York: Charles Scribner's Sons, 1964), 254.

Kristen Renwick Monroe

Review Essay: The Psychology of Genocide[1]

Final Solutions: Biology, Prejudice, and Genocide, Richard M. Lerner (Pennsylvania State University Press, 1992), 238 pp., $25.00 cloth.

Genocide Watch, Helen Fein, ed., (Yale University Press, 1992), 204 pp., $25.00 cloth.

Ordinary Men: Reserve Police Battalion 101 and the Final Solution in Poland, Christopher Browning (Aaron Asher/HarperCollins, 1992), 256 pp., $12.00 paper.

Survivors: An Oral History of the Armenian Genocide, Donald E. Miller and Lorna Touryan Miller (University of California Press, 1993), 242 pp., $25.00 cloth.

The Path to Genocide: Essays on Launching the Final Solution, Christopher R. Browning (Cambridge University Press, 1993), 191 pp., $44.95 cloth, $11.95 paper.

Why Genocide? The Armenian and Jewish Experiences in Perspective, Florence Mazian (Iowa State University Press, 1990), 291 pp., $29.95 cloth.

What causes genocide? Two explanations are frequently offered. The first stresses group disparities in political-economic situations and the desire of a dominant group to use its power to obtain better living conditions, more land, and the material wealth held by an ethnic minority. Such explanations offer reasons the mind can comprehend; they suggest a glimmer of rationality, a kernel of sense underlying the pathology of a renegotiation of the political-economic balance gone tragically awry. In contrast to such rational explanations, we find genocide explained through ancient hatreds festering in the body politic, hatreds that remain inherently unresolvable through moderate forms of political negotiation because of their primordial force and passion. Both explanations, however, stumble on one striking fact: similar disputes and political-economic disparities exist elsewhere and are resolved without resort to genocidal brutality.[2] Young girls systematically gang-raped, babies murdered before their mothers' eyes, old men made to dig their own graves before being shot—these are not the usual fare of politics, even in politics with deep ethnic, social, economic, racial, and religious cleavages. In the face of genocide, then, we experience a helplessness that is intellectual as well as personal and political.

In this review essay I attempt to understand the political psychology of genocide. To do so, I first define genocide and then discuss its prerequisites, precipitating factors, and facilitating conditions. I next turn to an empirical examination of the first mass genocide of the twentieth century, the Turkish massacre of the Armenians, and then to the act of ethnic cleansing and genocide most familiar to the world, the Nazi attempt to destroy the Jews during World War II. An examination of memoirs by the architects of genocide and of legal testimony by men who actually committed genocidal massacres suggests that genocide occurs when existing ethnic differences are overlain by specific situational factors (primarily economic distress and political instability) and then further combined with a critical cognitive perception of one's neighbors as "the other." This initial psychological distancing from former friends and fellow citizens facilitates an eventual process of dehumanization of "the other"—a cognitive perception that is the match that lights the tinder of genocidal violence. Only when friends and fellow citizens are dehumanized does the unimaginable become possible.

What Is Genocide? How Widespread Is It?

A combination of the Greek word *genos* for race or tribe and the Latin word *cide* for killing, genocide refers to the deliberate and systematic destruction of people, not because of individual acts or culpability but because of their birth in a national, ethnic, racial, or religious group.[3] Although precise definitions vary, most conceptualizations of genocide concentrate on three related categories: (1) physical genocide, involving the death or crippling injury of members of specific groups, (2) biological genocide, which restricts the births of group members, and (3) cultural genocide, often referred to as ethnocide and entailing the destruction of the specific character of the group through forced exile; destruction of books, monuments, and objects of historic, religious, and artistic value; the forced transfer of children; and prohibition of the national language.[4] Genocide is defined more formally by Article II of the United Nations Convention on the Prevention and Punishment of the Crime of Genocide:[5]

> [G]enocide means any of the following acts committed with intent to destroy, in whole or in part, a nation, ethnical, racial, or religious group, as such: (a) killing members of the group; (b) causing serious bodily or mental harm to members of the group; (c) deliberately inflicting on the group conditions of life calculated to bring about its physical destruction in whole or in part; (d) imposing measures intended to prevent births within the group; (e) forcibly transferring children of the group to another group.[6]

How widespread is genocide? While the term itself dates only from the 1930s, the practice of murdering entire populations is ancient. The biblical Hebrews practiced it, as did most other early people. In more recent history, the English eliminated the native population of Tasmania in seventy-three years, and the Dutch who settled the Cape of Good Hope treated the native blacks and bushmen as "dangerous vermin" on a par with wild animals. Helen Fein's edited volume documents the extent to which genocide has continued in the post–World War II period: in Africa against tribal groups in Burundi, Rwanda, and Uganda; against Indian groups in Brazil and Paraguay; in Cambodia by the Khmer Rouge in the 1970s; in Sri Lanka against the Tamil separatists during the 1980s; in the Indian subcontinent during the 1940s, and again during the creation of Bangladesh in the early 1970s.[7] And today genocide continues in Bosnia.

Given its long history, it may be significant that the term "genocide" was not coined until the twentieth century. Is it because twentieth-century genocides have so exceeded past outrages that we now require a specific word for what was once accepted as an inevitable part of life? Or, more optimistically, has the world finally attained a level of civilization sufficient to consider this kind of mass murder unacceptable?

Prerequisites, Precipitating Factors, and Facilitating Conditions

If we accept that genocide goes beyond the normal realm of political disputes and cannot be dismissed as mere ignorance or mass hysteria, what accounts for it? Certain background conditions appear as virtual prerequisites of genocide. Genocide most commonly occurs in a pluralist society in which diverse racial, ethnic, and/or religious groups experience persistent and pervasive cleavages.[8] These cleavages may exist in many different spheres, from institutionalized inequality in political incorporation to more informal socioeconomic inequalities.[9] Genocide is greatly facilitated when such long-standing inequalities in political participation overlap accentuated economic and social cleavages and when there is a history of conflict between the groups.[10]

Unstable political conditions that threaten the social order compound the effects of these preconditions. Wars and revolution are particularly powerful triggers for genocide; this is especially true when they bring geographic and psychological dislocations. A government that is losing battles grasps greedily for scapegoats, as amply illustrated by Hitler's treatment of both the Jews and the democratically elected politicians who supposedly stabbed Germany in the back at Versailles. Beyond this, a modernizing minority may be politically linked to an enemy of the host state. This was the case for the Armenians, who had close ties to Armenian communities in Russia.[11] Fear of a Russian entrance into World War I against the Turks (a fear that was, in fact, realized) was a relevant consideration for both the Turkish elite and locals, who overreacted to frightening images of Russians massacring their people and taking their land. In the case of the Jews, the ancient stereotype of Jews as cosmopolitan elites who feel no loyalty to the homeland was prevalent throughout much of Europe, and Nazi propaganda fanned this prejudice shamelessly.

Economic downturn also prompts genocide. The economic distress of the Depression combined with the threat to the Ottoman empire during World War I and the crippling of Germany after World War I provided the backdrop for the particular genocides considered here. (The disintegration of communism in the former Yugoslavia and the general economic deterioration in the states of the former USSR provide both contemporary examples and concern about future unrest in this geographic region.)

Psychologically, both a scapegoat and a victim are needed to explain the disintegration of the old economic, political, and social order and to justify the beginning of the new. The stereotypes of wealthy, cosmopolitan Jews and affluent Armenian merchants provided handy scapegoats; the good German people and the noble Turkish peasants filled the useful role of victims. This may explain the power of genocide at both the local level and at the level of more sophisticated political leadership; both elite and masses respond to threats to their economic situation, political power, and way of life. The political elite may do so in a more cynical and calculating way while the followers—the ones who actually perform the genocidal acts—are moved out of their own personal frustration and hostility as much as in response to orders.

Finally, secrecy helps. Genocide is frequently carried out under conditions that discourage intervention by the outside world. The tight control of information exercised by the Nazis and the difficulties in communication in the hills of Anatolia during the early twentieth century greatly facilitated genocide. Indeed, to this day the Turkish government has never fully admitted to the Armenian massacre.[12]

Stage 1 of Genocide: Psychological Preconditions

What critical psychological factors trigger genocide? There must be an intentional identification of a particular group for destruction, and these individuals must differ in some way from the majority population. Most frequently these differences are in ethnicity, race, or religion, and are reflected in distinct communal dissimilarities.[13] The perpetrators of the genocide usually claim—and indeed frequently believe—that individuals within the victimized group represent a threat to the majority population because they do not share characteristics in harmony with the majority's goals and values.[14] This is very important. It means an individual German, for example, cannot be Jewish and still have the same desires for Germany as non-Jewish Germans do.[15] Allegiances and goals are thus ascriptive and flow inevitably from birth. This sets genocide apart from other conflicts in which allegiances can shift and opponents can be converted.

Because it is state-sanctioned, if not state-induced, genocide also requires a legitimizing principle or ideology to justify the scale of human destruction. For the unfortunate Armenians, the ideology was pan-Turkism; for the Jews, anti-Semitism and the myth of Aryan superiority. Ironically, then, genocide is related to the persecuting group's search for group meaning, identity, and power.[16] Collective violence on such an extensive scale must make reference to a myth or theory in order to justify killing people not because of their own acts but simply because they fit into a particular category by virtue of their birth.

Ironically, the doctrine of biological determinism serves as a justification for genocide and genocide is frequently equated with a holy crusade to free the body politic of diseased tissue. Thus genocide becomes a scientific prevention of contamination by agents of "racial pollution" who are viewed as parasites and bacteria causing sickness, deterioration, and death in the host peoples they supposedly infect. The mass murder of a people is thus justified through a twisted logic in which it becomes necessary to prevent the members of a biologically degenerate group from destroying a biologically superior one.[17] What is at stake is the very existence of the in-group; in the Alice-in-Wonderland world of genocide, mass murder becomes an act of survival, in which even the most draconian measures are justified.

This bizarre double-think exists at all levels of society. Richard M. Lerner devotes a chapter of *Final Solutions* to the Nazi activities of Nobel Prize winner Konrad Lorenz and quotes other respected scholars who were Nazis. The following quote from Paul de Lagarde (1927–91), a prominent professor of Asian studies and an important figure in the German anti-Semitism movement, is but one example.

> One would need a heart as hard as crocodile hide not to feel sorry for the poor exploited Germans and . . . not to hate the Jews and despise those who—out of humanity!—defend these Jews or who are too cowardly to trample this usurious vermin to death. With trichinae and bacilli one does not negotiate, nor are trichinae and bacilli to be educated; they are exterminated as quickly and thoroughly as possible. (p. 28)

This passage illustrates that—although it is comforting to attribute such rhetoric to backward people, crippled by the lack of education and poverty—the linkages among biology, prejudice, and genocide existed among even the most respected academic, political, and social circles in the nineteenth and early twentieth centuries.[18] Both Lerner and, to a lesser degree, Christopher Browning in *The Path to Genocide,* make clear the degree to which the Nazi genocide in particular was not an aberration imposed on an otherwise civilized German nation by a small group of socially marginal fanatics. Lerner writes:

> This mystical or transcendental vision of the genetic superiority of the German *Volk* was not born in the mind of Adolf Hitler or in the propaganda of Joseph Goebbels. Quite the contrary, the Nazis adopted a tradition in German biological and medical science which placed within the genes of the German *Volk* the basis of the salvation of humanity, a salvation made necessary because of the threat of genetic pollution posed by miscegenation with genes from subhuman or nonhuman populations. (p. 23)

The Armenian and Jewish Genocides

The outlines of the Holocaust are too well known to require historical summary. I note only that two of the books reviewed here make particularly valuable contributions to the debate over the causes of the Holocaust. Lerner finds its origins in the connection between biology and prejudice. He traces the road from nineteenth century Social Darwinism of the Monist League and the eugenics movement to the racist writings of Haeckel and Lagarde to Hitler and Hess. Browning's *Path to Genocide* focuses on the Nazis' Jewish policies from 1939 to 1942, describing in detail how the Nazis moved from a resettlement policy advocated by Himmler—whereby Jews would be resettled to the Lublin reservation and then, of all places, to the island of Madagascar. In outlining how these policies gave way to the gas chamber, Browning seeks a broader perspective than Lerner, attempting to evaluate the historical debates between those who stress the underlying impersonal causes of the Holocaust (as Lerner does) and those who focus on the role of Hitler. Browning himself seems to argue that while Hitler's role was far from predetermined, it was central in the process leading to the mass murders.[19] *The Path to Genocide* is particularly strong in summarizing and evaluating the various historical debates over the Holocaust, such as the debate between the intentionalists and the functionalists and the debate over whether the Holocaust was a calculated attempt to solve the population problem in newly conquered lands or a policy carried out in spite of its economic irrationality.[20]

The Armenian massacres are less well known and require more factual description. Historic Armenia (often referred to as Greater Armenia) covered 100,000 square miles clustered around Mount Ararat, the supposed resting place of Noah's Ark, in what is now northeastern Turkey. It included parts of what are currently the republics of Armenia, Azerbaijan, and Georgia and extended south toward Iran and Iraq and west toward Turkey.

The Armenians' geographic fortune was their curse: they were located at the intersection of East and West. While this provided a rich cultural life and excellent trade and commerce, it also invited frequent invasions. Like the Jews, the Armenians clung to their language and their religion. (Armenians are Christians and proudly claim to be the first nation to accept Christianity.) They had an intense sense of national identity and strong cultural taboos against intermarriage with Muslims.

The Armenians needed these taboos to prevent assimilation, for they have been a subject people for most of their history. Since the sixteenth century they had been ruled by Ottoman Turks as a semiautonomous *millet* in a multinational empire.[21] This semiautonomy provided the Armenians both with freedom to practice their religion and with relative independence in their civil affairs; nonetheless, they were second-class citizens. As Lorna and Donald Miller explain in *Survivors:*

> [T]hey did not have the same legal rights as Turks, and they were subject to special taxes, which were often extortionary. Equally important, Armenians were viewed as *gavurs* (infidels) which, particularly at a local level, meant that they were often thought to have less human worth than Muslims.

Armenian peasants constituted the single largest group of Armenians in the Ottoman empire and were highly visible in banking, business, finance, and trade. Like the Jews in Germany, the Armenians thus enjoyed an economic presence that was disproportionate to their actual numbers.

The Armenian situation was precarious as the twentieth century opened. Although there had been some emigration after the smaller massacres of 1894–99 and 1909, more than two million Armenians still lived in Turkey in 1915. As the Ottoman empire began to crumble from within, a group called the Young Turks turned to the ideology of pan-Turkism to find a new vision of their empire, an empire to unite all Turkic peoples from Constantinople to central Asia. At first, hostility against the Armenians consisted of relatively minor pogroms. (I use "minor" as a comparative term—as many as some fifteen to twenty thousand people were killed in the pogroms of 1909.) But in 1913, an extreme nationalist group took power, bringing with it three of the Young Turks who were the architects of the genocidal policy that would be responsible for the deaths of half the Armenian population in Turkey: Enver Pasha (minister of war), Talaat Pasha (minister of internal affairs), and Jemal Pasha (minister of the navy). These men provided the virtual dictatorship that usually accompanies genocide.

Specific policy changes began after November 2, 1913, when Turkey entered World War I on the side of Germany and the Central Powers against Britain, France, and Russia. The Turks offered the Armenians a deal whereby for their wartime cooperation they would be rewarded with land in Russia after the victory of the Central Powers. Fearful of fighting fellow Armenians living within Russian borders, the Armenians refused, opting instead for neutrality. They were conscripted anyway, and a quarter of a million Armenian men were sent to serve in the Turkish army. With rare exceptions, all went and fought loyally.

Despite this, the Young Turks felt betrayed and argued that the Armenians would side with the Russian army if it entered Turkish soil during the fighting. What transpired next has never been fully acknowledged by the Turkish government, and in both *Survivors* and *Why Genocide?* the authors take great pains to document their claims about specific incidents in the genocide.[22] It appears that it was during this time (late 1914 and 1915) that a centralized plan of genocide was developed. This was possible, as suggested in *Survivors,* for three reasons: (1) Although most Armenian men were already drafted and serving loyally in the Turkish army, Armenian soldiers were disarmed early in 1915 and then put into labor battalions where they were poorly fed and clothed. Those who did not die of exhaustion and malnutrition were eventually shot after being forced to dig their own graves. (2) All Armenian guns were confiscated.[23] These guns were then photographed and presented as evidence of Armenian insurrection. This propaganda justified future ill-treatment.[24] The disarmament also eliminated any opportunity for effective resistance. (3) Local Armenian authorities were told to report to government headquarters where they were imprisoned without trial. Many were tortured; most were eventually shot. The poor communications in the hills of Anatolia apparently facilitated this procedure. Historic records suggest the victims never knew why they were asked to report to the central authorities and had no knowledge of the fate of fellow officials who had received similar summonses.

On April 8, 1915, Armenians from Zeitun were deported. On April 24, the day now commemorated by Armenians in remembrance of the genocide, Armenian intellectuals and religious and political leaders in Constantinople were arrested. This was followed by the deportation of the local populations.

Late in May 1915, the Temporary Law of Deportation was enacted. The Millers write that this emergency order authorized "the deportation of persons who might be guilty of treason or espionage or who could be justifiably removed for military purposes" (p. 42). The order did not specifically single out the Armenians; in this it differed from the Nazi promulgations later in the century. But the order did effectively clear the way for the deportation of the entire Armenian population. The only exceptions were Armenians living in Constantinople and Smyrna, those with specific military skills, those who converted to Islam, and those rescued and hidden by their Turkish, Greek, or Kurdish neighbors.[25] (The latter category usually consisted of children who were used as servants or converted, adopted, and raised as Turks.)

The usual procedure was to deport entire villages, allowing only a few days for people to gather together their food and belongings. Armenian homes were initially sealed but were later looted or turned over to Turks. On the day appointed for departure, gendarmes ordered people to assemble into a caravan whose members then set off walking, carrying whatever they could. As the caravans reached the city limits, men were usually separated, had their hands tied, and were led away from their families. The survivors of these marches (usually women and children) then heard shots. The gendarmes returned alone and ordered the march to resume. No one was allowed to return to bury loved ones.

The deportation routes were circuitous, rough, and isolated. The Armenians rarely received food or drink. Turks were not allowed to assist deportees, and those who did risked imprisonment. During World War II the Nazis used similar tactics. They shot gentiles who helped Jews and, as the war neared its end, evacuated concentration camp survivors via death marches designed to destroy the human evidence of their genocide. According to the Millers:

> The actual butchering of [Armenian] deportees was often left to members of the "Special Organization." Created by an order of the Ministries of Justice and the Interior, these units were made up of criminals and murderers who had been released from prison in the Ottoman Empire . . . [and were] led by

> officers from the Ottoman War Academy. . . . These men were heartless, butchering deportees in ravines and on narrow mountain passes, raping women, and stealing what few possessions they still carried. Kurdish tribal groups were similarly encouraged to raid caravans. The gendarmes who were supposed to "protect" the caravans either disappeared during these attacks or joined in the assault.[26] (pp. 43–44)

Armenian survivors report murders of the most sadistic nature: burning people alive, cutting off women's breasts and nipples, decapitating people with pruning instruments, and ripping open stomachs of pregnant women. In addition to this, many deportees perished from malnutrition.[27] Starvation is a cheap tool of genocide, and anyone who reads the Millers' descriptions of Armenian children eating grass or picking grains out of animal manure will never again lightly use the phrase "starving Armenians."[28] Although less sophisticated than the Nazis' later efforts, the deportations were an effective way to achieve genocide for, in addition to those starved and killed outright, tens of thousands died from exposure, disease, dehydration, and exhaustion. Although figures vary, the general estimate is that 1.5 million perished between 1915 and 1923.[29] It seems widely accepted that approximately half the Armenian population of Turkey died and that this constituted one-third of the total population of Armenians in the world.

After the genocide and the collapse of czarist Russia, there was a brief attempt to resurrect the Armenian political cause. On May 28, 1918, the independent Republic of Armenia was proclaimed. (This included the Armenians who had always lived in Russia plus nearly 300,000 refugees from Turkey.) The fledgling state was ill-fated, however, and in 1920 the republic accepted the protection of the Bolsheviks against the Turks, thus becoming integrated into the USSR. Once the Soviet empire dissolved, Armenia reappeared. On September 23, 1991, Armenia declared its independence from the Soviet Union and once again proclaimed the existence of the Republic of Armenia. For Armenian patriots, however, the story still lacks a happy ending since recently Armenians have been brutally massacred by Azerbaijanis in Sumgait and Baku and the region remains plagued with fighting, blockades, and political uncertainty.

Stage 2: Shifts in Perception of Self in Relation to Others

What occurs in the minds of people who construct and perform genocide? The books reviewed here offer a variety of evidence, from historical documentation about bureaucrats and doctors who participated in medical exterminations to "prevent disease" to legal testimony by policemen who performed genocidal mass murder. Taken as a whole, this evidence suggests that genocide occurs when there is a critical psychological shift in the genocidalist's self-image in relation to others.[30] To briefly illustrate this psychology, let me refer to one memoir from an architect of the Armenian massacre and then turn to Browning's compelling analysis of legal testimony from men who massacred Polish Jews.

Talaat Pasha provided some insight into the psychology of genocide in a manuscript written after he fled Constantinople at the end of World War I. This manuscript was made public by Talaat's wife after Talaat was assassinated for his part in the genocide. Unlike others, Talaat does not deny that the Armenian deportations occurred. But he treats the Armenians as subhuman and blames the victims for their own deaths. In particular, he claims the Armenians collaborated with the Russians, leaving the Turks no other recourse than to quell the uprising. The genocide was thus justified as a "preventive measure."[31] The Millers write:

> [H]e distances himself from the abuses by blaming the Armenians for the necessity of deporting them, implying that any

> atrocities that occurred in the process of deportation were carried out by fanatical local Turks who were pursuing personal vendettas, and he excuses himself from punishing these Turks because it would have been politically divisive. (p. 91)

Talaat's memoirs are sketchy, and memoirs are always somewhat self-serving. Nonetheless, Henry Morgenthau, the American ambassador to Turkey during this period, confirms that Talaat expressed the beliefs that the Armenians had enriched themselves at the Turks' expense and wanted to dominate the Turks, establish a separate state, and openly encourage Turkish enemies. Whether Talaat sincerely believed this or was merely spouting propaganda to justify his acts cannot be ascertained.

The limited information on the psychology of genocide that appears in Talaat's memoirs is supported by more complete evidence in *Ordinary Men,* Browning's analysis of legal testimony taken from Germans in a reserve order police battalion during World War II. This evidence is particularly valuable because it comes from the men involved in the mass murder at the heart of the Holocaust—the period from March 1942 to February 1943.[32] This testimony paints a fascinating portrait of the psychology of genocide, and I shall concentrate the rest of my discussion on it.

Browning's masterful analysis draws on legal interrogations, taken in the 1960s by the Office of the State Prosecutor in Hamburg, of 210 men who served in Reserve Order Police Battalion 101. These police units, composed primarily of men judged too old to fight in the war, were charged with keeping the peace in the German-occupied territories, mostly to the east. Much of their activity, however, consisted of rounding up, killing, and deporting Jews to concentration camps. Over 260 deportation trains took German, Austrian, and Czech Jews directly to the ghettos and death camps in Poland and Russia; virtually all of these trains were guarded by order police. While much about guilt and responsibility during the Holocaust is unascertainable, at least one point is abundantly clear: the men in these units knew exactly what they were doing to the Jews.

The interrogations Browning presents and analyzes focus on a unit of five hundred men who were directly responsible for the deaths of at least 38,000 Jews and who put another 45,000 on trains to concentration camps. Although there is no evidence that Battalion 101 was atypical, it was—surprisingly—one of the few reserve police units ever investigated by authorities. The legal evidence from the interrogations of this unit thus provides a unique, albeit horrific, opportunity to understand those who kill innocent strangers, not bureaucratically and at a distance, but face to face. Browning writes:

> These men were not desk murderers who could take refuge in distance, routine, and bureaucratic euphemisms that veiled the reality of mass murder. These men saw their victims face to face. . . . No one participating in the events described . . . could have had the slightest doubt about what he was involved in, namely a mass murder program to exterminate the Jews. (p. 36)

The men of Battalion 101 are particularly interesting for several reasons. As Browning's title suggests, they are so very ordinary, so like other individuals in their society. To the extent that they differed from the rest of German society, they tended to come from the lower orders. The majority of these men thus came from a social class that was anti-Nazi in its political culture, with communist, socialist, and/or labor-union sympathies. The men in this particular unit came mostly from Hamburg, one of the cities least sympathetic to the Nazis. They were old enough at the time of the war—most were above 35—that their formative years occurred in the pre-Nazi era. Any general ethical belief systems thus were well-established before the Nazis came to power. Finally, and most remarkably, much of the testimony focuses on the unit's first genocidal action in the Polish town of Jozefow where the commanding officer offered the men the extraordinary option of not taking part in the action. All of this suggests that situational factors, in addition to the men's background characteristics and socialization, made them unlikely recruits for Nazi mass murder.

What actually happened at this first genocide at Jozefow, and how did the men themselves explain what they did there? The unit's assignment was to round up the 1,800 Jews living in Jozefow, separate the able-bodied men for work detail, and take the rest of the villagers to the forest for execution.

How the men responded to their assignment is instructive. While some said they avoided shooting infants, and all but two later denied having shot old men, only twelve of the five hundred chose to be excused from the duty. This seems surprising given the conspicuous absence of the commanding officer, Major Trapp, when the executions took place. Furthermore, Trapp's men knew Trapp was upset by the detail he had been assigned. He was heard to say, "Oh, God, why did I have to be given these orders. . . . [S]uch jobs don't suit me" (p. 58). Other men remember Trapp weeping like a child. He was later heard to confide to his driver, "If this Jewish business is ever avenged on earth, then have mercy on us Germans" (p. 58). Despite this, most of the men and all of the other officers complied with the orders without protest and with little expression of chagrin. Only one officer refused to take part, saying he would "in no case participate in such an action, in which defenseless women and children are shot" (p. 56). He received another assignment but no punishment.[33]

This pattern shifted only slightly on the second day, when the orderly executions of women and children were carried out after the able-bodied Jewish men had been taken for work details. As the day wore on, however, a few more men asked to be relieved. Two policemen "pleaded that they too were fathers with children and could not continue" (p. 62). At first they were refused, but after a midday break they were sent back to their barracks. Some other men who had not originally requested release from service took evasive action and shot past their victims or spent their time searching homes. Again, no reprisals were taken against any of these men. One man testified:

> It was in no way the case that those who did not want to or could not carry out the shooting of human beings with their own hands could not keep themselves out of this task. No strict control was being carried out here. I therefore remained by the arriving trucks and kept myself busy at the arrival point. . . . [O]ne or another of my comrades noticed that I was not going to the executions to fire away at the victims. They showered me with remarks such as "shithead" and "weakling" to express their disgust. But I suffered no consequences for my actions. I must mention here that I was not the only one who kept himself out of participating in the executions. (pp. 65–66)

Realizing that the executions in the forest were going too slowly, some men began to grumble that the job would not be completed that day (p. 63). Men in the third platoon were called in; they too were offered the chance to report out of duty. No one chose this offer initially, although a few men later opted out. Browning estimates that in all, between 10 and 20 percent of the five hundred men reported out of the assigned detail at Jozefow.

After the Jozefow massacre, Battalion 101 was less involved in direct killing, concentrating instead on rounding up Jews to send to concentration camps. This distance between themselves and their victims made their jobs easier.

The men of Battalion 101 became more hardened and callous as the killings became less visible. One man even brought his pregnant bride to watch him perform during a roundup. "Out of sight was truly out of mind" (p. 90). Those men who had earlier asked to be excused from killing duties tended to become more isolated and separate from the rest of the battalion. One of the men who had asked to be excused commented, "No one ever approached me concerning these operations [the so-called Jew hunts]. For these actions the officers took 'men' with them, and in their eyes I was no 'man'" (p. 129). But these men were never punished or assigned to firing squads.[34]

The last major action for Battalion 101 was the *Erntefest* (Harvest Festival) massacre in Lublin in November 1943. There were 42,000 Jews in the Lublin district and the *Erntefest* killed more people than the infamous Babi Yar massacre.[35] Browning estimates that after *Erntefest,* the men of Battalion 101 had participated in the direct shooting of at least 38,000 Jews and physically placed 45,000 on trains to concentration camps, mainly Treblinka. This means that fewer than five hundred men were responsible for the deaths of at least 83,000 Jews.

As the war turned against Germany, Battalion 101 increasingly fought armed partisans and enemy soldiers. Major Trapp returned to Germany early in 1944 and was followed in turn by most of his men. Ironically, the only serious repercussions from Battalion 101's wartime actions occurred when one of the policemen in this unit was denounced by his estranged wife; this policeman, in turn, named three others: his sergeant, Major Trapp, and Lieutenant Buchmann, Trapp's adjutant and the only man to immediately and consistently protest the battalion's actions. These four men were extradited to Poland in 1947 and had a one-day trial in Siedlce. All four defendants were found guilty. Both the policeman denounced by his wife and Trapp were executed in December 1944; the sergeant was sentenced to three years in prison and Buchmann to eight. But the trial focused on the reprisal shooting of seventy-eight Poles in Talcyn. The actions toward the Jews were never mentioned. And not one of the SS officers involved in the actions of Battalion 101 was ever punished for wartime actions.

Further investigations of this unit did not take place until the 1960s. Between 1962 and 1967, 210 men from the battalion were interrogated. Fourteen were indicted, and all were found guilty. Of these, six were given no sentence at the judge's discretion. The rest received short sentences, usually five to eight years, and these were later reduced. Of all the reserve order police battalions that operated during the Third Reich, Battalion 101 was one of the few even investigated.[36]

Cognitive Perceptions and Genocide

What can we make of the evidence concerning the psychology of genocide presented in Browning's disturbing legal testimony and in the secondary sources scattered throughout the other books reviewed here? These are only two instances of genocide, and in both cases the data has inherent limitations. Memoirs are self-serving, interrogation testimony given after many years can be distorted by psychological defense mechanisms, and the victims' childhood memories of searingly traumatic events hardly provide reliable historical evidence. Nonetheless, these two examples are in keeping with other instances of genocide for which we have first-hand testimony, and I believe we can, with great care, draw some general conclusions, as Browning, in particular, does extremely well. The most striking of these conclusions is that dehumanization is a constant psychological component of genocide.

Browning notes that in their testimony, descriptions of Jews by the men of Battalion 101 varied significantly. The Nazi stereotype of twenty-five years earlier still surfaced when the men spoke of the Jews, using words like "dirty, unkempt, and less clean," when comparing them to the Poles (p. 152). "Although, for the most part the Jews remained an anonymous collective in the German accounts," Browning notes two exceptions (p. 153). When a Jew was German, the policemen would often remember the Jew's hometown. And Jews who worked in the kitchen took on a personal identity for the men.[37]

How did the men themselves explain their actions when queried about them in the 1960s? Why did the men follow orders, even when their commanding officer told them the assignment was "frightfully unpleasant," refused to take part in the executions himself, explicitly offered them the option of dropping out of the assignment, and meted out no punishment to those who eventually did opt out or took evasive actions?

The first surprise, as Browning notes, is that anti-Semitism was never offered as an explanation; remarkably, the interrogators did not raise it when questioning the men some twenty years later. Browning links this to their perceptions of the Jews:

> What is clear is that the men's concern for their standing in the eyes of their comrades was not matched by any sense of human ties with their victims. The Jews stood outside their circle of human obligation and responsibility. (p. 73)

After this astonishing omission, we find that the men's explanations fall into five categories. The first was cowardice. "Who would have 'dared', one policeman declared emphatically, to 'lose face' before the assembled troops?" (p. 72)[38]

Another explanation is lack of choice. Browning writes:

> Most of the interrogated policemen denied that they had any choice. Faced with the testimony of others, many did not contest that Trapp had made the offer [to opt out of the assigned duty] but claimed that they had not heard that part of the speech or could not remember it. A few policemen made the attempt to confront the question of choice but failed to find the words. It was a different time and place, as if they had been on another political planet, and the political values and vocabulary of the 1960s were useless in explaining the situation in which they had found themselves in 1942. (p. 72)

Third, we find a kind of twisted compassion, the idea that the men were putting people out of their misery. (This idea is also expressed by doctors and bureaucrats who dealt with Jews in the Polish ghettoes and claiming it was more merciful to shoot the Jews than to let them starve slowly.) Such a view is predicated on the assumption that the Jews were going to die anyway and thus shooting them would not alter their fate. Browning offers a chilling quote from a thirty-five-year-old steel worker from Bremerhaven:

> I made the effort, and it was possible for me, to shoot only children. It so happened that the mothers led the children by the hand. My neighbor then shot the mother and I shot the child that belonged to her, because I reasoned with myself that after all without its mother, the child could not live any longer. It was supposed to be, so to speak, soothing to my conscience to release children unable to live without their mothers. (p. 73)

Fourth, although ethical or political principles were seldom offered as a reason for asking to be excused, something that may border on this category does occur: sheer physical revulsion and extreme distaste for the messiness of the task. One explanation is typical: "The shooters were gruesomely besmirched with blood, brains, and bone splinters. It hung on their clothing" (p. 65). Browning notes that this physical revulsion might well have originated in humane instincts and that strange instances of pity did occur. The emphasis on the distasteful aspects of the job for the individual performing it, however, would seem to remove this consideration from the realm of traditional ethics, and certainly from any political opposition to the task.

Finally, in his conclusion, Browning offers another explanation, one that I believe constitutes a critical component in the psychology of genocide: dehumanization and distancing. Browning dismisses the literature that attributes wartime atrocities to the frenzy of battle since this was no battle.[39] But there was indeed distancing. What provided this distancing mechanism?

It is very clear from Browning's account that for the men of Battalion 101 the killing was neither impersonal nor bureaucratic. Hannah Arendt's explanation of the banality of evil thus cannot apply, for these men killed face to face. Let me be very clear about this. I am not discounting the general value of Arendt's explanation. The men found it vastly easier to put Jews on transports and send them to their death that way than to murder them themselves. But since they did perform face-to-face murders, some additional explanation seems necessary to fully explain the men's ability to distance themselves from their victims.[40]

Browning considers, and rejects, some of the traditional explanations found in the literature, such as geographic origin or social background.

> By geographical origin, and social background, the men of Reserve Police Battalion 101 were least likely to be considered apt material out of which to mold future mass killers. On the basis of these criteria, the rank and file—middle-aged, mostly working class, from Hamburg—did not represent special selection or even random selection but for all practical purposes negative selection for the task at hand. (p. 164)

Browning also considers and rejects the argument that a disproportionately high number of these men might have been party members and therefore that any process of political self-selection occurred. He further rejects John Steiner's argument of a sleeper effect—the idea that personality characteristics lie dormant until particular conditions awaken them. (Steiner argues that this is what occurred with the SS men he studied.)[41] Browning seems to agree more with Zygmunt Baumann who argues that most of us are capable of great cruelty and fall into the roles society assigns us. The exception is the rare individual who resists such assignment and pursues ethical action, even in opposition to the authorities. Browning also considers Theodor Adorno's argument on authoritarianism and Stanley Milgram's work on obedience to authority—not obedience out of fear of immediate reprisal but rather obedience at a more general level of deference and arising out of long-term socialization. Browning discounts this explanation for the men of

Battalion 101, however, both because these men were socialized in the pre-Nazi period and because their immediate superior, Trapp, was not a stern authority figure. (The men even referred to him as Papa Trapp.) Florence Mazian offers a sociological explanation for genocide, based on Smelser's hostile outburst theory, to explain why genocide (as opposed to more traditional and certainly preferable solutions) emerges in situations of extreme strain. Her explanation, which attempts to delineate the conditions that increase the likelihood of genocide and establish a theoretical framework for its analysis, goes under the rather dreadful name of "value-added process." It stresses "the creation of 'outsiders,' internal strife, powerful leadership with territorial ambitions, destructive uses of communication, the organization of destruction, and the failure of multidimensional levels of social control" (p. 3). While Mazian's theory is unconvincing as a whole, if we combine its emphasis on the creation of outsiders with that part of the Milgram experiments that Browning does find relevant to the actions of the men in Battalion 101, we begin to make some progress in understanding the key psychological factor in the distancing that is critical for genocide: the idea that psychological or emotional connection to a victim affects one's willingness to participate in inhumane behavior toward that person.

In a process replicated in other genocides, the Nazis changed the way people looked at the Jews. In telling them of their first assignment, for example, Browning reports that Trapp mentioned that "the Jews had instigated the American boycott that had damaged Germany" and that "in Germany, bombs were falling on women and children" (p. 2). Furthermore, Trapp continued, the Jews in the village of Jozefow were working with the partisans. Beyond this, the policemen had undergone extensive ideological indoctrination, receiving many lectures on the importance of keeping the Aryan blood pure. They heard regular lectures (daily or every other day) interpreting current events from a Nazi perspective. In all of this, the German *Volk* (people) and *Blutsgemeinschaft* (blood community) were critical; both were depicted as facing a constant struggle for survival, ordained by nature, against the weaker peoples who would contaminate them with their racially impure blood. The effect of this on the men in Battalion 101 was summed up in a surreal understatement by Lieutenant Drucker: "Under the influence of the times, my attitude to the Jews was marked by a certain aversion" (p. 182). Browning writes:

> [T]he men of Reserve Police Battalion 101, like the rest of German society, were immersed in a deluge of racist and anti-Semitic propaganda. Furthermore, the order police provided for indoctrination both in basic training and as an ongoing practice within each unit. Such incessant propagandizing must have had a considerable effect in reinforcing general notions of Germanic racial superiority and "a certain aversion" toward the Jews. (p. 184)

Browning does not, however, believe that this general propaganda was sufficient to prepare the men for the killing at Jozefow. He argues that something more had to occur. While Browning does not label them as such, his critical factors are what I would call identity and group ties. By refusing to shoot, a man left the dirty work to his comrades. Refusal therefore constituted an asocial act toward one's fellows. It also left the defecting policeman open to ostracism and rejection, a significant factor for men living in a hostile occupied country, with only their comrades to provide support and social contact. Refusing to shoot also constituted a moral statement that what the others were doing was wrong; hence, Browning argues, men who refused to shoot couched their refusal in terms of being too weak, not too humane, to kill (p. 185). Such a stance implied no criticism of the others, but rather reinforced the dominant ethos of toughness that the unit so carefully cultivated. Browning concludes:

> Pervasive racism and the resulting exclusion of the Jewish victims from any common ground with the perpetrators made

> it all the easier for the majority of the policemen to conform to the norms of their immediate community (the battalion) and their society at large (Nazi Germany). Here the years of anti-Semitism . . . dovetailed with the polarizing effects of war. The dichotomy of racially superior Germans and racially inferior Jews, central to Nazi ideology, could easily merge with the image of a beleaguered Germany surrounded by warring enemies. . . . Nothing helped the Nazis to wage a race war so much as the war itself. In wartime, when it was all too usual to exclude the enemy from the community of human obligation, it was also all too easy to subsume the Jews into the "image of the enemy," or *Feindbild*. (p. 186)

The Importance of Perceptions and the Dehumanization of the Other

What do the Armenian massacres and the Holocaust suggest about a psychology of genocide? Genocide seems to require a particular congruence of negatives. Long-standing ethnic differences must be politicized in a certain manner. Wars, revolutions, or breakdowns in regimes often lead to the search for a scapegoat for economic distress and political inequalities. Innocuous differences between members of the scapegoated minority group and the majority then come to be seen as threatening to the lifestyle of the dominant political culture. An ideology is next developed to justify the displacement and killing of members of this ethnic minority, not for individual deeds but simply because of their membership in the victimized group. Finally, secrecy helps; certainly genocide occurs more easily when it can be hidden, denied, or minimized.

The match that lights the fire of genocidal violence is cognitive and perceptual, a critical shift in how members of the minority are viewed and how the genocidalists view themselves in relation to members of the victimized group. This perception draws on the genocidalists' feelings of being wronged or mistreated by the minority and ironically shifts the responsibility for the genocide onto its victims. The genocide is thus viewed as a way of redressing long-standing wrongs. All these factors are evident in varying degrees in the two instances of genocide considered here.

In all of this, the final critical psychological factor is the dehumanization of the "other," which contributes immeasurably to the psychological distancing that facilitates the killing. The importance of dehumanization was poignantly pointed out to me in my own work on altruism by a man on the other side of the moral equation, a German Czech named Otto Springer who resisted the Nazi genocide and was arrested and sent to a concentration camp for rescuing Jews.

> I was always intrigued by the question: How could seemingly normal people become killers? Once I got an interesting answer. In a [concentration] camp in Upper Silesia, I asked one of our guards, pointing at the big gun in his holster, "Did you ever use that to kill?"
>
> He replied, "Once I had to shoot six Jews. I did not like it, but when you get such an order, you have to be hard." And then after a while he added, "You know, they were not human anymore." *That* was the key: dehumanization. You first call your victim names and take away his dignity. You restrict his nourishment and he loses his physical ability and sometimes some of his moral values. You take away soap and water and then say the Jew stinks. And then you take their human dignity further away by putting them in situations where they even will do such things which are criminal. And then you take food away. And when they lose their beauty and health and so on, they are *not* human anymore. When he's reduced to a skin-colored skeleton, you have taken away his humanity. It is much easier to kill nonhumans than humans.

Springer aptly captures what I believe is the critical psychological component of genocide. It is how we see ourselves in relation to others that is key. These perceptions then set and delineate the options we find available, empirically and morally. People who shift their perceptions of neighbors enough to make fellow country-men less human will be able to justify acts that seemed unthinkable during the long years in which the two groups lived together in peace. It is this shift in perception that transforms long-standing ethnic cleavages within a society into the horror of genocide.

NOTES

1. Funding was provided by the Research Group on Identity, sponsored by the University of California Center for German and European Studies. The author would like to thank Nancy Bermeo, Terry Nardin, Etel Solingen, and Michael Urben for their comments and encouragement.

2. Canada provides an excellent example of a society with such cleavages but low levels of violence.

3. Although the practice of genocide has existed for centuries, the term itself was coined around 1933 by Raphael Lemkin as part of his campaign to obtain an international convention outlawing genocide. For further discussion of this, see Lemkin's 1944 study, *Axis Rule In Occupied Europe* (1944; New York: Howard Fertig, 1973), or Leo Kuper's excellent book *Genocide: Its Political Uses in the Twentieth Century* (New Haven: Yale University Press, 1981). Kuper also discusses the extent to which persecution of political groups constitutes genocide in his book *The Prevention of Genocide* (New Haven: Yale University Press, 1985).

4. Different definitions of genocide are used in the literature. Fein pays particular attention to these definitional differences. Ethnocide is not considered as serious as genocide under existing international conventions.

5. Although some analysts (such as Fein) find this definition lacking, it remains the preeminent definition codified in international law.

6. Miller and Miller, *Survivors,* 45; Kuper, *Genocide,* 19.

7. See Kuper, *Genocide* and *The Prevention of Genocide,* or Lawrence J. LeBlanc, *The United States and the Genocide Convention* (Durham: Duke University Press, 1991), 2–3. Also quoted in Miller and Miller, *Survivors,* 209, n.4.

8. Some analysts (for example, Kuper) believe a plural society is a prerequisite of genocide. I remain unconvinced since this would eliminate genocides between two countries or between societies, such as the genocides that occurred in colonial situations where it could be argued that two societies meet. Regardless of how one defines society, all analysts agree that the persistent nature of the cleavages between social groups is significant. Genocide has a long memory. The current fighting in Bosnia, for example, can be viewed as a continuation of the genocide *against* Serbs in the Second World War, which arose out of a long history of religious conflict between Orthodox Serbs and Roman Catholic Croats, assisted by the Muslims.

9. Such formal institutionalization of political inequalities would guarantee that no more than 40 percent (for example) of the legislative seats would go to a particular religious, linguistic, or ethnic group.

10. Sartre, for example, claimed that colonization was a major creator of plural societies that lead to genocide.

11. Indeed, the present situation for Armenians is complicated by their existence in more than one nation.

12. The Armenian survivors, who believe the first step in forgiveness is the acknowledgment that a crime was committed, complained bitterly about this to the Millers.

13. See also Burleigh and Wippermann (1991) for an excellent analysis of the racial foundations of the Nazi state.

14. It is important that shared goals are not assumed to be volitional but are instead related to characteristics endowed by birth. For example, a Christian living in a predominantly Islamic region is presumed by virtue of being born a Christian to be opposed to the goal of creating an Islamic state. While the Christian could convert to Islam and then share this goal, it is considered most unlikely that one would do so while remaining Christian.

15. The Northern Ireland situation may differ from this scenario in this regard; that is, Protestants may share Unionist goals and vice versa. Whether this is related to the containment of ethnic violence in Northern Ireland provides intriguing speculation.

16. For the Native Americans in North and South America the white man's burden of bringing civilization and Christianity served this function.

17. Lerner's book makes a powerful and disturbing argument that the biological justification preceded Hitler. In particular, Lerner points to the importance of biological determinism, Social Darwinism, and eugenics as contributors to this justification for such inhumane treatment of human beings. He also makes the important point that this movement extended into "negative eugenics" such as infanticide, not just of Jewish children but of any children who were "diseased." These included bedwetters, those with malformed ears, or merely those children marked by someone as "difficult to educate." (p. 33.)

Browning also touches on the connection between biology and anti-Semitic policy in *Path to Genocide,* where the discussion focuses more on the role of medical authorities in closing the Polish ghettos and acquiescing in the eventual murder of the Jews as a way to restrict diseases the Jews supposedly carried. While Jews were singled out as the "eternal bloodsuckers, vampires, germ carriers, people's parasites, and maggots in the rotting corpse," the "genetic determinist thinking in Germany prior to the advent of the Nazi era—involving the Social Darwinist Monist League, the eugenics movement, and the "new science" of racial hygiene—indicate that neither racist doctrines of National Socialism nor the ideas for their application to the social world either began with Hitler and his cohorts or were concentrated in a small group of socially marginal fanatics" (Lerner, p. 31). Lerner's chapter 2 is particularly informative on the historical precedents for Nazi genocide, although chilling in its suggestion that Hitler was only one of many such advocates of biological determinism.

18. "[F]or at least two thousand years . . . social actions have been implemented based on the belief that certain people had something inherent in them, something in their blood, that made them less than human and consequently deserving of persecution or even death. It was not until the mid-nineteenth century, however, that this doctrine became broadly legitimated in society and science." (Lerner, p. 11) Lerner spells out the relationship between Darwin's view of evolution, Spencer's social evolution, eugenics, and genocide, while making clear that the "connection between the doctrine of biological determinism (or, more specifically, of genetic determinism) . . . and racism and political movements . . . is neither a necessary nor an isomorphic one." (Lerner, p. 17)

The British delegation to the first international eugenics conference, called to improve the race through the science of eugenics, was led by Winston Churchill.

19. Although much of the anti-Jewish legislation was in place by the end of 1933, Browning's volume pays special attention to the series of decisions (made between 1939 and 1941) which set up the Final Solution.

20. The intentionalists focus on Hitler and his ideology. They explain the Jewish policies as "primarily determined by the decisions of Adolf Hitler, which in turn were calculated or 'intended' to realize the goals of an ideologically derived 'program' to which he had clung with fanatical consistency since the 1920s." In contrast, the functionalists emphasize the structure and institutions of the Third Reich, arguing that what occurred was an "unplanned 'cumulative radicalization' produced by the chaotic decision-making process of a polycratic regime and the 'negative selection' of destructive elements from the Nazis' ideological arsenal. . . . " (p. 86)

21. *Millet* is a religious sect in the Arabic language. The Turks borrowed this term to refer to the national corporations set up by Sultan Mohammed II in his attempt to reorganize the Ottoman state as the heir to the Eastern Roman empire in 1453. As originally established, each *millet* had a written charter and was presided over by a patriarch who was elected by his community and who served as liaison between this community and the government, at whose pleasure he held office. The *millets* had effective authority over religion, culture, education, and social life, but their political power was limited.

22. Many of the writers on genocide are driven by their own family experiences. Lerner opens his book with a touching story from his Jewish grandmother. Lorna Miller's parents were survivors of the deportations and the Millers are quite open about the extent to which their book constitutes an act of love on their part for her parents, the Armenian community, and the other children who endured these deportations. Given this emotional involvement, it is worth remarking on the extent to which all the books reviewed here reflect both the scholars' sense of fairness and respect for the truth and the passion of the partisan.

23. In fact, the Armenians were given quotas, and if they did not have enough guns they had to buy them from their Turkish neighbors before they could hand them in to authorities.

24. The similarity of this to the Nazi pattern is striking; the use of the murder of a minor German official (not even a Nazi Party member) in Paris by a Jewish refugee as the excuse for Kristallnacht is but one example.

25. The fact that Armenians were given the option of converting also differs from the situation for the Jews under the Nazis. Such conversions are referred to as white genocide, for although the individual member of a group is not killed the culture itself is effectively destroyed when its members are assimilated into the dominant culture through conversion or dispersion into the diaspora.

26. Two nationalistic physicians were heavily involved in organizing the killer units. Other physicians were also involved in the Armenian genocide. One was accused in postwar trials of having gassed and poisoned infants and children, others of poisoning or of disposing of bodies.

27. Since bullets are an expensive way to kill people, state-induced famine has been an effective tool of genocide in places like Stalin's Ukraine (James E. Mace, in Fein, 113).

28. The mass starvations that occurred under Stalin are frequently described as deliberate genocide. Starvation of the Jews in the ghettos was a conscious part of the Nazi genocide, as Browning makes clear in *The Path to Genocide.*

29. Some scholars argue that the number was as low as 800,000. Much of the controversy centers on the size of the Armenian population in Turkey at this time and whether or not to calculate statistics from the period 1894 to 1923 or to use the narrower time frame of 1915 to 1916.

30. Michael Urben has suggested in private conversation that genocidal psychology oscillates between two stages. In the first phase, the genocidalist constructs an enemy who is prepared to victimize him and his people. This sets up the genocidalist as pure victim. The emotions are focused on the need to protect oneself and family. This is what Urben calls the energy-building moment, the moment at which moral culpability enters. (My killing others is justified as a preemptive attack on those who threaten me.) Urben notes that this passive moment actually contains the hot emotions. The second moment is the dehumanizing moment. Here, the emotions are no longer hot but cold as the genocidalist engages in the physical act of murder, as we would coldly and ruthlessly exterminate insects. Ironically, then, genocide seems the opposite of the frenzied killing during battle in which one goes beserk.

31. Talaat, quoted in Miller and Miller, *Survivors,* 90.

32. In mid-March of 1942, some 75 to 80 percent of all victims of the Holocaust were still alive, while some 20 to 25 percent had already perished. A mere eleven months later, in mid-February 1943, the situation was exactly the reverse. Some 75 to 80 percent of all Holocaust victims were already dead, and a mere 20 to 25 percent still clung to a precarious existence. . . . The center of gravity of this mass murder was Poland" (Browning, *Path to Genocide,* 168).

33. Although Buchmann received another assignment, a cruel fate meant that after the war he was one of the few men in Battalion 101 to receive punishment for his actions.

34. Bittner, one of the few men to openly oppose the battalion's actions toward the Jews, tells that he was assigned Sunday duties and special watches because of this opposition:

> [F]rom the first days I left no doubt among my comrades that I disapproved of these measures and never volunteered for them. Thus, on one of the first searches for Jews, one of my comrades clubbed a Jewish woman in my presence, and I hit him in the face. A report was made, and in that way my attitude became known to my superiors. I was never officially punished . . . but anyone who knows how the system works knows that outside official punishment there is the possibility for chicanery that more than makes up for punishment. (p. 129)

35. Babi Yar was a ravine near Kiev and the site of one of the largest massacres in history, in which 100,000 bodies were found, 35,000 of whom were Jews believed massacred on September 29–30, 1941.

36. Lerner offers further disturbing evidence of the limited extent to which the Nazi perpetrators of genocide were ever prosecuted.

37. This special identity did not exempt these Jews from being killed but it did often forestall death or, ironically, mean that the death would be sudden and unexpected, something that in the bizarre world of the Nazis was meant as a special kindness. "By 1942 standards of German-Jewish relations, a quick death without the agony of anticipation was considered an example of human compassion!" (p. 154–55)

38. The cynic might draw the following general moral principle from this: Better to slaughter innocent women and children than lose face in front of one's comrades.

39. Frenzy has been used to explain the kind of brutality that occurs in war (as at My Lai) and in domestic situations where there appears to be the overuse of power by authorities, as in the 1992 Rodney King beating in Los Angeles.

40. "Many scholars of the Holocaust . . . have emphasized the bureaucratic and administrative aspects of the destruction process. This approach emphasizes the degree to which modern bureaucratic life fosters a functional and physical distancing in the same way that war and negative racial stereotyping promote a psychological distancing between perpetrator and victim. . . . Such a luxury, of course, was not enjoyed by the men of Reserve Police Battalion 101, who were quite literally saturated in the blood of victims shot at point-blank range. No one confronted the reality of mass murder more directly than the men in the woods at Jozefow. Segmentation and routinization, the depersonalizing aspects of bureaucratized killing, cannot explain the battalion's initial behavior there." (Browning, *Path to Genocide,* 162)

41. Steiner, "The SS Yesterday and Today: A Sociopsychological View," in Joel E. Dimsdale, ed., *Survivors, Victims, and Perpetrators: Essays on the Nazi Holocaust* (Washington: Hemisphere Publishing, 1980), 431–43.

ROBERT E. GOODIN

International Ethics and the Environmental Crisis

The problems of the environment have long been seen as global in scope.[1] "Only One Earth" was, after all, the motto of the 1972 Stockholm conference founding the United Nations Environmental Program and the title of the book that served as its semiofficial "manifesto."[2] Even before that, attention had been firmly fixed on considerations such as the carrying capacity of the planet and the exhaustion of the earth's stocks of mineral and other resources.

Still, there is something new and distinctively global about the current concern with the environment. The "first environmental crisis" was essentially a concern with problems that, though recurring the world over, could in principle be resolved perfectly well on a country-by-country basis.[3] When environmental problems were essentially matters of dirty air or water, they were very largely matters of domestic political concern. Ill winds and shared waterways apart, pollution generally stayed in the same political jurisdiction as that in which it was generated. Of course, since all industrial nations used broadly the same dirty technologies, they all experienced similar problems of pollution. But problems that were in that sense common among a number of nations were not "shared problems" in a stronger sense, requiring concerted action among all countries for their resolution.

That is not to minimize the seriousness of the problems forming the focus of earlier environmental crusades. London's "killer fogs" were no less lethal for being purely domestic products. Neither, politically, are these traditional environmental problems necessarily all that tractable just because they are purely domestic in nature. Even in purely domestic terms, producers with a vested interest in not cleaning up after themselves will always be a political force to be reckoned with. Still, whatever obstacles politicians face in mounting effective action against domestic polluters, those obstacles will be multiplied many times over with the addition of a genuinely international dimension to the problem.

What is striking about the environmental crisis as it is currently understood is how genuinely global it is, in contrast to traditional environmental problems. The problems at the forefront of present environmentalist discussions are problems like the degradation of the ozone layer and the "greenhouse effect." These problems are shared internationally, in the stronger sense. They are not just problems for each nation, taken one by one. They simply cannot be resolved by isolated actions of individual nations.

London's dirty air could effectively be cleaned simply through local regulations requiring domestic users to burn smokeless coal in their fireplaces and industrial users to install scrubbers in their smokestacks. No such purely local remedies will patch the hole in the ozone layer. The voluntary decision of the United States—or indeed the whole Organization for Economic Cooperation and Development (OECD)—to ban the use of aerosols may serve as a useful start and an important precedent; the United States produces something like 28 percent of global CFC-11 and CFC-12, and Western Europe another 30 percent, all told.[4] However, if our goal is genuine stabilization of the ozone layer, and if we want to be reasonably certain of accomplishing it, then we cannot (working with present knowledge, anyway) be sufficiently sure of achieving it, even through dramatic reductions in emissions by such major producers.

In and of themselves, initiatives by single countries or even small groups of countries cannot really solve such problems. These new environmental concerns, unlike the core concerns of the "first environmental crusade," are truly global. The whole world, or some very large proportion of it, must be involved in the solution.

My argument here will build on that observation. I shall have little to say about particular environmental issues or political maneuvers surrounding them. My concern will instead be with the deeper structure of these problems, concentrating first on philosophical aspects: what alternative normative structures are logically available to us for handling such situations? Ultimately, however, this recourse to moral philosophy will be only incidental and instrumental. The fundamental point will be essentially political. The aim is to use philosophical insights to assist us in deciding the appropriate structure of an international regime for resolving the full range of environmental problems that we now know we face.

To foreshadow, my conclusion will be that the traditional structure of international law—guided as it is by notions of autonomous national actors with strong rights that all other national actors similarly share—is wildly inappropriate to many of these new environmental challenges. A system of shared duties or, better yet, shared responsibilities is a more fitting model, given the nature of the tasks at hand.

Normative Structures

The first task, then, is to explore alternative normative structures for coping with issues of the international environment. Here I shall identify three. One is a system of shared rights, giving each nation absolute and total control over what happens within its own boundaries. Another is a system of internationally shared duties, specifying particular performances for each nation that are the duty of that nation alone; the effect is to exempt others from any obligation to pick up the slack left, should any one nation fail to do its duty. A third is a system of shared responsibilities, stipulating outcomes that all nations are responsible for helping to produce; the effect there is to enjoin all nations, individually and collectively, to help take up the slack, should any among them default, in whole or in part.

Shared Rights

The fundamental principles of international law, from Grotius and Vattel forward, are all based on premises of national autonomy and noninterference with the domestic affairs of other nations. These, in turn, seem to follow from a normative structure in which each nation is thought to have a strong right to do whatever it likes to people, property, and natural resources within its own jurisdiction.

Just as a system of personal rights gives individuals a "protected sphere" within which they can act without interference from others, so too does a system of international law that accords analogous rights to political entities protect the autonomy of nation-states. And just as modern liberal political theory accords to each individual maximal rights to liberty consistent with like liberty for all, so too does liberal international law accord only such fundamental rights to any one nation as are consistent with like rights being accorded to all other nations as well.[5] The rights in question are, thus, shared rights—"shared" in the sense that all other agents possess rights strictly similar to one's own.

Of course, there are limits to what liberal political theory will let agents do to themselves—as individuals or as nations. At the personal level, we standardly refuse to respect people's decisions to sell themselves into slavery on the grounds that respecting autonomy cannot commit us to respecting decisions (even autonomously reached ones) to renounce autonomy. At the international level, we might sometimes want to impose standards of decent conduct—respecting basic human rights, for example—even upon regimes that might want to renounce them autonomously.

But those practices constitute the exceptions rather than the rule, both in liberal political theory and in the regime of international law that flows from it. By and large, if we are to interfere in the affairs of some other person or nation, we must find justification for it. That, in turn, usually amounts to showing that some of our own rights would somehow be infringed upon by the conduct in question.

If we can succeed in showing that the actions of others actually violate some of our own rights, then we can justifiably intervene in those actions, however sovereign or autonomous they may be. In the case of genuine spillovers, where others' activities impose external costs upon us—and, crucially in this rights-based context, we actually have a right that they not impose such costs upon us—it is relatively easy to invoke notions of rights to justify our interfering with their activities. Transboundary spillovers are, within a regime of shared rights, akin to aggression, an infringement of the prerogatives of another autonomous actor with rights identical to one's own. Thus, it is far from surprising that the case for international environmental protection long has been—and still largely continues to be—couched in terms of damage done beyond one's own borders.[6]

Absent a demonstration of transboundary spillovers, however, we must, within a regime of shared rights, simply concede that environmental policy is entirely within a nation's sovereign sphere. What is then left for us to do is to try to persuade all nations that—either because it is in their interests or for some other, less self-serving reason—they should exercise their sovereign rights so as to produce the outcomes we want.

It is far from absurd to believe that we might be able to do so. Ward, Dubois, and participants at the 1972 Stockholm Conference on the Human Environment more generally saw no real need to "reconsider national sovereignty" to solve the problems they were considering: simply sharing information worldwide would, they supposed, be more than enough; once nations realize what environmental threats they actually face, they will have no hesitation in agreeing to concerted international action to counter them.[7] In a similar vein, Jessica Tuchman Matthews's recent *Foreign Affairs* article attempts to cast the environmentalist case explicitly in terms of national interest, inviting nations to "redefine" conceptions of their "national security" so as to include environmental interests preeminently alongside their other "vital interests."[8]

The whole aim of rights, though, is to carve out a "protected sphere" within which agents can act with complete autonomy. What they do within that sphere—a sphere that in international law tends to be defined in basically territorial terms—is, under a regime of shared rights, purely their own business. As the much-vaunted Principle 21 of the 1972 Stockholm Declaration on the Human Environment declares, "States have, in accordance with the Charter of the United Nations and the principles of international law, the sovereign right to exploit their own resources pursuant to their own environmental policies," constrained only by the correlative "responsibility to ensure that activities within their jurisdiction . . . not cause damage to the environment of other States or . . . beyond the limits of national jurisdiction."[9] Unless we can either show that our rights have somehow been transgressed or else persuade others to exercise their rights in line with our preferences, a regime of shared rights effectively blocks us from interfering in the actions of others—however environmentally destructive or shortsighted they may be.

Shared Duties

Whereas classical international law revolves around notions of shared rights and sovereign prerogatives, we have recently added an overlay of shared duties. We now tend to assume, for example, that each nation must respect the fundamental human rights of its subjects, whether or not it wants to do so.[10] Among these, it is sometimes said, is a "fundamental right to an environment adequate for their health and well-being."[11]

Shared duties may correlate with—and indeed derive from—the rights of others. In the particular example listed above, they actually do so. But even where they do, they are rights of the nation's own subjects rather than of any other national actor. No other nation necessarily has any rights in the matter to press against the offending nation. That is what is crucial in differentiating this model from the last.

Under an international regime organized around notions of shared rights, the only circumstance in which there exists anything that could, strictly speaking, be called a "duty" to restrain any one nation's autonomous action would be if the proposed action violated the rights of some other nation. Under a regime of shared duties, by contrast, one nation may well be bound by genuine duties, even where no other nation has any strict rights.[12]

Notice, however, that only truly fundamental duties can justifiably be imposed in this way upon nations, regardless of their particular preferences or circumstances. What follows from that fact is a rule of universality. Truly fundamental duties are equally fundamental for all agents alike. The duties thus imposed can therefore be said to be shared duties—"shared" in the sense that each nation is under the very same duties for the very same reasons as is every other nation.

For an example of this sort of normative structure drawn from the more familiar terrain of personal morality, consider the duty that each of us has to tell the truth. This is not, first and foremost, a duty that derives from any right owed to others: it rings untrue to say that the only reason we should tell the truth is simply that others have a right to be told the truth.[13] The duty is freestanding, in that sense. Furthermore, it is a duty that is imposed upon all agents alike. Whatever reasons we have for thinking that moral agents should be bound by a duty to tell the truth, those reasons are the same for all agents. The duty in question is, therefore, a shared duty.

The striking thing about duties that are shared in this way, however, is that they are also very much "personalized" (or, in the current jargon, "agent-relative"). If I fail in my duty to tell you the truth, no one else is under any duty to right the wrong by disabusing you of the falsehood that I have planted in your head. The lie would be my lie; it would be charged to my moral account. Others cannot clear my account—they cannot make me any less of a liar—simply by telling the truth on my behalf. Nor can they somehow restore the moral balance of the universe by being doubly honest themselves to make up for my dishonesty.

It is indisputably true that duties such as those of truth telling are shared duties, in the sense that everyone is under one and the same duty. The nonetheless peculiar thing about shared duties, thus construed, is that they are so weakly shared. They bind each of us individually but none of us collectively. If one agent defaults on his duty, there is nothing any other agent should do—indeed, within this moral structure, there is nothing that any other agent even can do—to remedy the situation.

International duties are sometimes said to be like that. Consider the classic case of human rights once again. Many of those who are most anxious that their own nation respect the rights of its subjects will also insist that it would be wrong for other nations to interfere if it did not. Sometimes that position reflects simple hypocrisy, revealing that the person only halfheartedly agreed to the principle of human rights in the first place. But sometimes, at least, people urge that view because of a particular view they take about why human rights are morally important. They might think, for example, that the reason for insisting upon respect for human rights has to do with a duty that nations have to display a certain attitude—an attitude of equal consideration and respect—toward their subjects. While external pressure might force a nation to perform the right actions, these would be no more than morally empty gestures if performed for the wrong reasons.[14] What would follow from this way of thinking about human rights is that every nation should respect the human rights of its own subjects but no nation should (because none usefully could) intervene if other nations fail to respect the rights of their own subjects.

That model of "tending our own garden" has been applied fairly widely by those commentators on international relations inclined to move somewhat beyond—but not too far beyond—a minimalist regime of shared rights. "Pursuing the Good" in this way, one step at a time and one country at a time, has obvious attractions. It is laudably realistic, appreciating that we cannot reasonably expect to persuade everyone in the world to do exactly the right thing at the very same instant. And if the problems in view are genuinely decomposable in that way—if they genuinely can be resolved through country-by-country action—that may well be the most effective way to pursue "The Good" in an inevitably imperfect world.

There are, however, genuine problems with that model. The first and most obvious is, of course, the simple fact that not all internationally significant problems are necessarily decomposable in that way. But that is merely an objection to the impracticality of that way of proceeding. In a more principled vein, what is perhaps morally most unattractive about this model is that it makes altogether too many concessions to realism. It lets off the hook altogether too easily those who actually do take their moral duties seriously. Under this model, they are morally in the clear just so long as they do not themselves do anything wrong. If others around them are doing wrong, even wrong of a sort that they could take action easily and without cost to correct, they are on this account under no duty to do so. Of course, it would be good if they did. But morally, such a performance would count as supererogatory—above and beyond the call of duty. Critics of this model might reasonably remark that if this is so, then duty seems not to be calling loudly enough.

Shared Responsibilities

Whereas a regime of shared duties is act-oriented, a regime of shared responsibilities is outcome-oriented.[15] What duties demand of agents are specific performances. What responsibilities demand of agents are specific results, leaving the agents themselves to choose which among various possible, morally permissible actions might best achieve the mandated results. Under a system of duties, an agent is morally off the hook once he has performed precisely those actions demanded of him, even if the overall results are utterly catastrophic. A system of responsibilities does not let an agent off the hook until he has actually accomplished the prescribed ends through some judicious choice among permissible means.

Some responsibilities—such as the responsibility of a bodyguard to protect the dignitary he or she is assigned to watch over—are peculiar to one particular agent. But many responsibilities are shared among several agents. Consider, as an example, the responsibility that is shared by both parents to care for their offspring: there is a single outcome in view (healthy and happy children), which the two partners, jointly and separately, are responsible for producing.[16]

Notice, however, that the implications of sharing a responsibility are markedly different from those of sharing a duty. The principal difference derives, in turn, from the difference between act-oriented and result-oriented moral systems. To share a duty is to have a duty just like another's; but it is still very much your own duty, and if you fail to do it, no one else can do it for you. To share a responsibility, by contrast, is to be responsible together with various others for producing certain outcomes. And since it is the outcome that each is responsible for producing, there is usually something each can (and should, if possible) do to pick up the slack, if any of the others default in their responsibility. Thus, for example, parents are, insofar as they are able, jointly and separately responsible for ensuring that their children's basic needs are met. What that means, in turn, is that each parent is responsible for assuming complete responsibility for catering to the basic needs of the couple's children, should the other partner prove unable or unwilling to shoulder his or her share of the burden.[17]

That leads to the second important point of difference in a regime of shared responsibilities. Under the other sorts of regimes, it is inappropriate (wrong, under a regime of shared rights; pointless, under a regime of shared duties) to force people to do what, in some larger sense, they should. Under a regime of shared responsibilities, by contrast, it is perfectly proper to do what one can—within limits—to force others to shoulder their share of a responsibility that is jointly shared. It is your business to do so, precisely because their default would increase the share of the burden that would morally fall to you to bear. Thus, in the example of family relations, it is thought to be perfectly proper to use the force of the law to extract child support payments from financially solvent parents who have chosen to leave their families.

Transpose this family model, now, from hearthside settings to the international arena. What would it mean to say, then, that what nations shared were genuine responsibilities rather than mere duties? First of all, it would fix the moral focus upon the outcomes that they were collectively supposed to produce, rather than upon specific acts of specific agents. Second, it would mean that each nation would be responsible for making good any shortcomings, should other nations fail to do their full part toward producing those ends. And third, it would mean that each could properly press others to do their part toward producing those shared ends.

In the context of international human-rights policy, for example, a regime of shared responsibilities would have quite clear and distinctive implications. Under such a regime, it most definitely is the business of the international community as a whole to ensure that states respect human rights, even if they are not so inclined. It would be legitimate for other nations to do whatever they can, within limits, to force delinquent nations to respect human rights. And it would be not only morally permissible but morally mandatory for nations, insofar as possible, to respect human rights on behalf of any delinquent nation—by offering political asylum to that nation's persecuted subjects, for example.

In the context of international environmental policy, a regime of shared responsibilities would imply, first of all, that it is morally permissible for environmentally conscientious nations to bring pressure, at least in certain ways, upon nations that fail to discharge their environmental responsibilities. It would be perfectly permissible, rather than a gross infringement of another nation's sovereign prerogatives, for one nation to grant licenses to fish in its territorial waters only to the ships of nations that comply with international standards to protect fish stocks within their own territorial waters. It would also be perfectly permissible for bilateral- or multilateral-aid donors to attach strings to loans, making receipt conditional upon effective policies to protect the environment within the recipient nations.

Such a model would imply, second, that it would be both fitting and proper for environmentally conscientious nations to do double duty, should others refuse to do their duty at all. If some nations are not going to do their part, then the others must do more than their share if the task is going to get done at all. On this analysis, therefore, there should be no moral qualms about paying Brazil to stop destroying the Amazon rain forests, even though this would amount to paying Brazilians to do no more than what morally they should be doing anyway. And on this analysis, it is perfectly proper for environmentally conscientious nations to overcomply with international agreements protecting the environment—reducing their whale catch or their production of chlorofluorocarbons (CFCs) or "greenhouse gases" by more than the treaty requires—once it becomes clear that some other nations are going to undercomply.

Mixed Models

Naturally, these are all highly stylized models, and the distinctions between them tend to blur in practice. It is, nevertheless, worth setting out distinctions as clearly as possible, even at the risk of some artificiality, so that the advantages and disadvantages of any particular component in the larger mixture can be clearly assessed.

While conceding that actual cases may always be mixed, it would be a mistake to jump to the conclusion that actual cases will inevitably be mixed. It is commonly said, for example, that rights entail responsibilities; and that might lead us to suppose that those two models of international ethics are necessarily complementary, rather than competing. Whether or not that is true, however, depends upon what account is given of the entailment relationship. According to one very standard interpretation, rights entail only a responsibility to respect the analogous rights of others. If that is all there is to the relationship, then the rights and corollary responsibilities both work strictly within one and the same model of shared rights, as described above. There are, of course, other ways of interpreting the rights-responsibilities entailment relationship. One, for example, deals in terms of the duties that the powerful have to protect the less powerful.[18] But genuinely distinctive responsibilities, akin to those to be imposed under the model of shared responsibilities described above, will arise only within stronger and more contentious accounts of the entailment relationship.

Applying the Structures

With all this philosophical apparatus in place, let us return to the actual policy problems—problems of the environment—that motivated this inquiry in the first place. Of course, there are many problems with the environment, each subtly different from the other. Different sorts of policy responses, and different structures of international regime, are therefore going to be best suited to solving all the various problems of the global environment.

Let us, however, try to cut through all those subtleties and focus instead on fundamentals. Different as they may be in other respects, notions of shared rights and notions of shared duties both deal in terms of the actions of individual nations. Some, perhaps many, environmental problems are indeed decomposable in that way: the more nations there are implementing a policy, the more likely it is that the desired outcome will be achieved, and the relationship is thus a smoothly increasing function of how many, and to what extent, actors are working toward that end. In such a case, isolated actions of individual nations are, in principle, perfectly capable of producing—or at least of contributing usefully to the production of—the desired outcome. And it is therefore perfectly defensible for us to pursue those goals through normative structures focusing upon the actions of individual nations.

Some of the most worrisome environmental problems are not like that at all, however. Instead, they are more akin to "lumpy public goods": instead of policy inputs translating smoothly into environmental outputs, the response curve is more of a "step function," and inputs must pass a certain threshold before they make any difference whatsoever to the outcome.[19] As alluded to earlier, ozone depletion and resulting climate change might be like that.

In such cases, concerted action among a large group of countries will be required to make any difference at all to the outcome, and normative structures focusing upon the isolated acts of single states are wildly inappropriate to the situation. For these second-wave problems that characterize the "new environmental crisis," therefore, a regime of shared responsibilities is the normative structure that is prudentially required.

To say that a regime of shared responsibilities is the normative structure that the situation requires, however, is not to say that it will be set in place automatically. Politically, we must start from where we find ourselves, and that is in a world of sovereign states. Even the most committed environmentalist must take due account of that fact.[20] In such a setting, shared responsibilities can acquire practical political force only if (and only to the extent that) they are recognized by nations themselves, through treaties and other similar international instruments.

There are good grounds for suspecting that this strategy is morally suboptimal, second-best, or worse. Of course it is perfectly possible, in a regime of shared rights, for states, through the exercise of their sovereign prerogatives, to sign treaties assuming various responsibilities to be shared with other cosignatories. But the shared responsibilities that emerge in that way are very different from those in models built around these notions directly. Whereas the shared responsibilities under the latter models would be foundational, treaty-based responsibilities would be merely derivative—derivative from the rights that sovereign states have to sign such agreements with other sovereign states.

The disadvantage of their being derivative, in turn, is that they are virtually always revocable, at least in principle. What sovereign states do through the exercise of their sovereign prerogatives they can typically undo in the same manner. As the old saying in constitutional law has it, sovereigns cannot bind their future selves—or at least they cannot do so without undermining the sovereignty of those future sovereigns.[21]

Under regimes based directly upon notions of shared responsibilities, by contrast, the responsibilities are regarded as foundational. Having in that way an existence independent of the actions of sovereign states, they cannot simply be revoked at the pleasure of the states concerned in quite the same way that responsibilities deriving merely from treaties typically can. Such is the great disadvantage of deriving shared responsibilities from treaty commitments alone.

Even if the treaty-based strategy is morally suboptimal, though, at least it has realism to recommend it. Given where we are starting—in a world of sovereign states—perhaps the treaty-based strategy is the only way to move toward a regime of shared responsibilities.

Still, if a regime of shared responsibilities can only emerge in present circumstances from treaties, not all sorts of treaties are equally good for the purpose. Some treaties institute a regime of shared responsibilities, whereas others just serve to reinforce regimes of shared rights.

Compare, for example, the 1985 Vienna Convention for the Protection of the Ozone Layer with the 1987 Montreal Protocol on Substances That Deplete the Ozone Layer.[22] Notice how the Montreal protocol was set to go into force not (as with the Vienna convention) when a fixed number of signatories ratified it but, rather, when it was ratified by countries accounting for two-thirds of the estimated 1986 consumption of ozone-depleting substances. The idea—which, in terms of a model of shared responsibilities, is obviously the right idea—is that what matters is not how many members there are in the club but whether the members that are in it have the capacity to make the relevant difference to the outcomes.[23] Or again, notice how, rather than just encouraging systematic observation, research, and information exchange, as under the Vienna convention, the Montreal protocol actually imposes some rather onerous burdens upon signatory states, committing them first to freezing and then to sharply reducing their emissions of ozone-depleting substances. Or notice, yet again, how the Montreal protocol commits signatories, in a way the Vienna convention patently does not, to the attempt to influence the ozone-depleting actions of other, nonsignatory states. That might be regarded by advocates of a shared-rights model of international relations as an unwarranted interference with the domestic affairs of another nation, but it would be perfectly permissible in pursuit of genuinely shared moral responsibilities. In all these respects, the Montreal protocol is a model of how to—and the Vienna convention a model of how not to—draft treaties institutionalizing a regime of shared responsibilities.[24]

The primary recommendation of this article—which for reasons given at the outset of this section is still very much a second-best solution, morally—is for the recognition of such responsibilities through many more treaties along the lines of an extended version of the Montreal protocol. Pending such international developments, however, there are still useful steps that individual nations can take. A model of shared moral responsibilities for environmental protection would, for example, legitimize a nation refusing to allow the manufacture or export of CFCs or the technology to produce them. Or, for another example, it would legitimize a nation unilaterally refusing to provide aid or loans to countries that manufacture CFCs.

Other nations may protest that this constitutes interference in their own domestic affairs. And, of course, in a way it does. But that objection bites only if we are thinking in terms of rights of sovereign states. The point of this paper is that this is the wrong way to be thinking about the new wave of environmental concerns.

NOTES

1. I am grateful to James Crawford and Joel Rosenthal for comments on an earlier draft of this article.

2. Barbara Ward and René Dubois, *Only One Earth* (Harmondsworth, England: Penguin, 1972). See also Peter B. Stone, *Did We Save the Earth at Stockholm?* (London: Earth Island, 1973).

3. That certainly is what is suggested by the policy-specific portions (e.g., parts 3 and 4) of Ward and Dubois's *Only One Earth.* Only in part 5 do they turn—briefly, and almost as an afterthought—to consider the larger questions of the "planetary order," among them questions of climate modification that I here present as paradigmatic of the "new environmental crisis." Similarly, the 1972 Stockholm Declaration on the Human Environment, article I, section 7, concedes that, inevitably, "local and national government will bear the greatest burden for large-scale environmental policy and action within their jurisdiction," even while acknowledging a "growing class of environmental problems . . . [that] are regional or global in extent or . . . affect the common international realm" and will therefore "require extensive cooperation among nations and action by international organizations in the common interest"; see *International Legal Materials* 11 (1972), 1416–21.

4. David A. Wirth, "Climate Chaos," *Foreign Policy* 74 (1989), 3–22 at 7.

5. H. L. A. Hart, "Are There Any Natural Rights?" *Philosophical Review* 64 (1955), 175–91.

6. Note, for example, the extent to which the "Proposed Legal Principles for Environmental Protection and Sustainable Development," adopted by the World Commission on Environment and Development (WCED) chaired by Gro Harlem Brundtland, all still largely pertain to problems of "transboundary environmental interferences"; WCED, *Our Common Future* (Oxford: Oxford University Press, 1987), annex 1, 348–51.

7. Ward and Dubois, *Only One Earth,* 292–95. The detailed recommendations in the "Action Plan for Human Environment," adopted at the Stockholm conference, all tend toward this same implication; the text is reprinted in *International Legal Materials* 11 (1972), 1421–69.

8. Jessica Tuchman Matthews, "Redefining Security," *Foreign Affairs* 68 (Spring 1989), 162–77.

9. United Nations Conference on the Human Environment, "Declaration on the Human Environment," adopted in Stockholm on June 16, 1972; reprinted in *International Legal Materials* 11 (1972), 1416–21.

10. These duties may sometimes correlate with, or indeed derive from, the rights of others. In this particular example, they actually do so. But even where they do, they are rights of the nation's own subjects, rather than of any national actor. What is crucial in differentiating this model from the last is precisely that fact: no other nation (necessarily) has any rights in the matter. (Of course, they may, as cosignatories of international agreements; but morally, nations arguably lie under such a duty even if they have not signed any relevant international instruments.)

11. "Proposed Legal Principles for Environmental Protection and Sustainable Development," WCED, *Our Common Future* (Oxford: Oxford University Press, 1987), 348–51. Principle 1 of the 1972 Stockholm Declaration on the Human Environment—reprinted in *International Legal Materials* 11 (1972), 1416–21 at 1417–18—puts an identical point in rather more florid language.

12. To sample this way of thinking, see the *Philosophy and Public Affairs* debate between Michael Walzer and his critics; it is reprinted in Charles Beitz et al., eds., *International Ethics* (Princeton: Princeton University Press, 1985), 165–246.

13. They may or may not, in any particular case. But even where we think they do, it seems somehow wrong to say that the duty derives from the right. Surely the duty would exist, even in the absence of any particular right (or right holder) in the matter.

14. John Locke argues similarly in his *Letter Concerning Toleration* that there is no point in compelling outwardly pious religious performances from people whose hearts are not in it, since pious acts performed for fear of external sanction and not motivated by genuine belief will not procure a person's salvation.

15. In terms of contemporary moral philosophy, the former is deontological whereas the latter is consequentialist. For further elaboration of the distinction between duties and responsibilities at work here, see Robert E. Goodin, "Responsibilities," *Philosophical Quarterly* 36 (1986), 50–56.

16. See further, Philip Pettit and Robert E. Goodin, "The Possibility of Special Duties," *Canadian Journal of Philosophy* 16 (1986), 651–76.

17. See further, Robert E. Goodin, "Apportioning Responsibilities," *Law and Philosophy* 6 (1987), 167–85.

18. Robert E. Goodin, *Protecting the Vulnerable* (Chicago: University of Chicago Press, 1985).

19. For an application of such a model to environmental problems, see Michael Taylor and Hugh Ward, "Chickens, Whales, and Lumpy Public Goods: Alternative Models of Public Goods Provision," *Political Studies* 30 (1982), 350–70.

20. As, indeed, the 1972 Stockholm Declaration does in Principle 24: "International matters concerning the protection and improvement of the environment should be handled in a cooperative spirit by all countries, big or small, on an equal footing. Cooperation through bilateral or multilateral arrangements or other appropriate means is essential, [but it must work] in such a way that due account is taken of the sovereignty and interests of all states."

21. Sometimes, of course, treaties do explicitly renounce sovereignty in certain respects, in which case the obligations arising under them may well be irrevocable.

22. These are reprinted in *International Legal Materials* 26 (1987), 1529–40 and 1550–61, respectively. For the purely illustrative purposes here, I shall simply gloss over the fact that the latter is a protocol concluded under the former convention; the differences here described may reflect no more than the inevitably different levels of generality in such different documents.

23. A similar idea informs the classic paper by George F. Kennan, "To Prevent a World Waste Land: A Proposal," *Foreign Affairs* 48 (1970), 401–13.

24. In other respects, however, the Montreal protocol is less than a perfect paradigm. Instead of requiring fixed performances from each nation, regardless of how many other nations have signed and how much of the world emissions they account for, a regime of shared responsibilities would imply that the required performance should vary with those factors. The more signatories there are and the more emissions they account for, the less each should have to do, and vice versa. (Treaty obligations under this model would be more like the obligations falling to "names" in Lloyds insurance syndicates: how much each owes depends upon how many others there are in the syndicate and upon the size of the claims against the syndicate as a whole.) In fairness, it should be said that the Montreal protocol does also provide for regular meetings of signatories to update the list of ozone-depleting substances and requirements for their control, in light of subsequent research. Perhaps that, in practice, is the mechanism by which such adjustments would be made.

Thomas Donaldson

Moral Minimums for Multinationals[1]

When exploring issues of international ethics, researchers frequently neglect multinational corporations. They are prone to forget that these commercial leviathans often rival nation-states in power and organizational skill, and that their remarkable powers imply nonlegal responsibilities. Critics and defenders agree on the enormity of corporate multinational power. Richard Barnet and Ronald Muller, well-known critics of multinationals, remark that the global corporation is the "most powerful human organization yet devised for colonizing the future."[2] The business analyst, P. P. Gabriel, writing in the *Harvard Business Review,* characterizes the multinational as the "dominant institution" in a new era of world trade.[3] Indeed, with the exception of a handful of nation-states, multinationals are alone in possessing the size, technology, and economic reach necessary to influence human affairs on a global basis.

Ethical issues stemming from multinational corporate activities often derive from a clash between the cultural attitudes in home and host countries. When standards for pollution, discrimination, and salary schedules appear lower in a multinational's host country than in the home country, should multinational managers always insist on home-country standards? Or does using home standards imply a failure to respect cultural diversity and national integrity? Is a factory worker in Mexico justified in complaining about being paid three dollars an hour for the same work a U.S. factory worker, employed by the same company, is paid ten dollars?[4] Is an asbestos worker in India justified in criticizing the lower standards for regulating in-plant asbestos pollution maintained by a British multinational relative to standards in Britain, when the standards in question fall within Indian government guidelines and, indeed, are stricter than the standards maintained by other Indian asbestos manufacturers? Furthermore, what obligations, if any, do multinationals have to the people they affect indirectly? If a company buys land from wealthy landowners and turns it to the production of a cash crop, should it ensure that displaced farmers will avoid malnutrition?

I

It is well to remember that multinational power is not a wholly new phenomenon. Hundreds of years ago, the East India Company deployed over 40 warships, possessed the largest standing army in the world, was lord and master of an entire subcontinent, had dominion over 250 million people, and even hired its own church bishops.[5] The modern multinational is a product of the post–World War II era, and its dramatic success has stemmed from, among other factors, spiraling labor costs in developed countries, increasing importance of economies of scale in manufacturing, better communication systems, improved transportation, and increasing worldwide consumer demand for new products.[6] Never far from the evolution of the multinational has been a host of ethical issues, including bribery and corrupt payments, employment and personnel issues, marketing practices, impact on the economy and development of host countries, effects on the natural environment, cultural impacts of multinational operations, relations with host governments, and relations with the home countries.[7]

The formal responsibilities of multinationals as defined in domestic and international law, as well as in codes of conduct, are expanding dramatically. While many codes are nonbinding in the sense that noncompliance will fail to trigger sanctions, these principles, taken as a group, are coming to exert significant influence on multinational conduct. A number of specific reasons lie behind the present surge in international codes and regulations. To begin with, some of the same forces propelling domestic attempts to bring difficult-to-control activities under stricter supervision are influencing multinationals.[8] Consider, for example, hazardous technology, a threat which by its nature recognizes no national boundaries yet must be regulated in both domestic and foreign contexts. The pesticide industry, which relies on such hazardous technology (of which Union Carbide's Bhopal plant is one instance), in 1987 grossed over $13 billion a year and has been experiencing mushrooming growth, especially in the developing countries.[9] It is little surprise that the rapid spread of hazardous technology has prompted the emergence of international codes on hazardous technology, such as the various UN resolutions on the transfer of technology and the use of pesticides.

Furthermore, just as a multiplicity of state regulations and laws generates confusion and inefficiency, and stimulates federal attempts to manage conduct, a multiplicity of national regulations stimulates international attempts at control. Precisely this push for uniformity lies behind, for example, many of the international codes of ethics, such as the WHO Code of Marketing Breast Milk Substitutes. Another well-known instance illustrating the need for uniformity involved the collision of French and U.S. law in the sale of equipment by Dresser Industries to the Soviets for the planned European pipeline. U.S. law forbade the sale of such technology to the Soviets for reasons of national security while French law (which affected a Dresser subsidiary) encouraged it in order to stimulate commercial growth. It was neither to the advantage of Dresser Industries nor to the advantage of the French and U.S. governments to be forced to operate in an arena of conflict and inconsistency. For months the two governments engaged in a public standoff while Dresser, and Dresser's public image, were caught in the middle.

National laws, heretofore unchallenged in authority, are now being eclipsed by regulatory efforts falling into four categories: namely, inter-firm, inter-government, cooperative, and world-organizational efforts.[10] The first category of "inter-firm" standards is one which reflects initiatives from industries, firms, and consumer groups, and it includes the numerous inter-industry codes of conduct that are operative for international business, such as the World Health Organization's Code on Pharmaceuticals and Tobacco, and the World Intellectual Property Organization's Revision of the Paris Convention for the Protection of Industrial Patents and Trademarks. The second category of "inter-government" efforts includes specific-purpose arrangements between and among nation-states, such as the General Agreement on Tariffs and Trade (GATT), the International Monetary Fund (IMF), and the World Bank.[11] "Cooperative" efforts, which comprise the third category, involve governments and industries coordinating skills in mutual arrangements that regulate international commerce. The European Community (EC) and the Andean Common Market (ANCOM) are two notable examples of such cooperative efforts.[12]

Finally, the fourth or "world-organizational" category includes efforts from broad-based global institutions such as the World Court, the International Labor Organization (ILO), the Organization for Economic Cooperation and Development (OECD), and the various sub-entities of the United Nations.

II

The growing tradition of international business codes and policies suggests that the investigation of ethical issues in international business is pressing and proper. But what issues deserve attention?

One key set of issues relates to business practices that clearly conflict with the moral attitudes of most multinational's home countries. Consider, for example, the practice of child labor, which continues to plague developing countries. While not the worst example, Central America offers a sobering lesson. In dozens of interviews with workers throughout Central America conducted in the fall of 1987, most respondents said they started working between the ages of 12 and 14.[13] The work week lasts six days, and the median salary (for all workers including adults) is scarcely over a dollar a day. The area is largely non-unionized, and strikes are almost always declared illegal. There is strong similarity between the pressures compelling child labor in Central America and those in early nineteenth-century England during the Industrial Revolution. With unemployment ranging from a low of 24 percent in Costa Rica to a high of 50 percent in Guatemala, and with families malnourished and older breadwinners unable to work, children are often forced to make growth-stunting sacrifices.[14]

Then, too, there are issues about which our moral intuitions seem confused, issues which pose difficult questions for researchers. Consider an unusual case involving the sale of banned goods abroad—one in which a developing country argued that being able to buy a banned product was important to meeting its needs. Banned pharmaceuticals, in contrast to other banned goods, have been subject to export restrictions for over 40 years. Yet, in defense of a recent Reagan initiative, drug manufacturers in the United States argued by appealing to differing cultural variables. For example, a spokesman for the American division of Ciba-Geigy Pharmaceuticals justified relaxing restrictions on the sale of its Entero-Vioform, a drug he agrees has been associated with blindness and paralysis, on the basis of culture-specific, cost-benefit analysis. "The government of India," he pointed out, "has requested Ciba-Geigy to continue producing the drug because it treats a dysentery problem that can be life threatening."[15]

III

The task for the international ethicist is to develop or discover concepts capable of specifying the obligations of multinational corporations in cases such as these. One such important concept is that of a human right.

Rights establish minimum levels of morally acceptable behavior. One well-known definition of a right construes it as a "trump" over a collective good, which is to say that the assertion of one's right to something, such as free speech, takes precedence over all but the most compelling collective goals, and overrides, for example, the state's interest in civil harmony or moral consensus.[16] Rights are at the rock bottom of modern moral deliberation. Maurice Cranston writes that the litmus test for whether something is a right or not is whether it protects something of "paramount importance."[17] Hence, it may help to define what minimal responsibilities should be assigned to multinational corporations by asking, "What specific rights ought multinationals to respect?"

The flip side of a right typically is a duty.[18] This, in part, is what gives aptness to Joel Feinberg's well-known definition of a right as a "justified entitlement *to* something *from* someone."[19] It is the "from someone" part of the definition which reflects the assumption of a duty, for without a correlative obligation that attaches to some moral agent or group of agents, a right is weakened—if not beyond the status of a right entirely, then significantly. If we cannot say that a multinational corporation has a duty to keep the levels of arsenic low in the work place, then the worker's right not to be poisoned means little.

Often, duties associated with rights fall upon more than one class of moral agent. Consider, for example, the furor over the dumping of toxic waste in West Africa by multinational corporations. During 1988, virtually every country from Morocco to the Congo on Africa's west coast received offers from companies seeking cheap sites for dumping waste.[20] In the years prior, dumping in the U.S. and Europe had become enormously expensive, in large part because of the costly safety measures mandated by U.S. and European governments. In February of 1988, officials in Guinea-Bissau, one of the world's poorest nations, agreed to bury 15 million tons of toxic wastes from European tanneries and pharmaceutical companies. The companies agreed to pay about $120 million, which is only slightly less than the country's entire gross national product. In Nigeria in 1987, five European ships unloaded toxic waste containing dangerous poisons such as polychlorinated biphenyls, or PCBs. Workers wearing thongs and shorts unloaded the barrels for $2.50 a day, and placed them in a dirt lot in a residential area in the town of Kilo.[21] They were not told about the contents of the barrels.[22]

Who bears responsibility for protecting the workers' and inhabitants' rights to safety in such instances? It would be wrong to place it entirely upon a single agent such as the government of a West African nation. As it happens, the toxic waste dumped in Nigeria entered under an import permit for "non-explosive, nonradioactive and non-self-combusting chemicals." But the permit turned out to be a loophole; Nigeria had not meant to accept the waste and demanded its removal once word about its presence filtered into official channels. The example reveals the difficulty many developing countries have in creating the sophisticated language and the regulatory procedures necessary to control high-technology hazards. It seems reasonable in such instances, then, to place the responsibility not upon a single class of agents, but upon a broad collection of them, including governments, corporate executives, host-country companies and officials, and international organizations.

One list receiving significant international attention is the Universal Declaration of Human Rights.[23] However, it and the subsequent International Covenant on Social, Economic and Cultural Rights have spawned controversy, despite the fact that the Declaration was endorsed by virtually all of the important post–World War II nations in 1948 as part of the affirmation of the UN Charter. What distinguishes these lists from their predecessors, and what serves also as the focus of controversy, is their inclusion of rights that have come to be called, alternatively, "social," "economic," "positive," or "welfare" rights.

Many have balked at such rights, arguing that no one can have a right to a specific supply of an economic good. Can anyone be said to have a "right," for example, to 128 hours of sleep and leisure each week? And, in the same spirit, some international documents have simply refused to adopt the welfare-affirming blueprint established in the Universal Declaration. For example, the European Convention of Human Rights omits mention of welfare rights, preferring instead to create an auxiliary document (The European Social Charter of 1961) which references many of what earlier had been treated as "rights," as "goals." Similar objections underlie the bifurcated covenants drawn up in an attempt to implement the Universal Declaration: one such covenant, entitled the Covenant on Civil and Political Rights, was drawn up for all signers, including those who objected to welfare rights, while a companion covenant, entitled the Covenant on Social, Economic, and Cultural Rights, was drawn up for welfare rights defenders. Of course, many countries signed both; but some signed only the former.[24]

Many who criticize welfare rights utilize a traditional philosophical distinction between the so-called negative and positive rights. A positive right is said to be one that requires persons to act positively to *do* something, while a negative one requires only that people not directly deprive others. Hence, the right to liberty is said to be a negative right, whereas the right to enough food is said to be a positive one. With this distinction in hand, the point is commonly made that no one can be bound to improve the welfare of another (unless, say, that person has entered into an agreement to do so); rather, they can be bound at most to *refrain* from damaging the welfare of another.

Nonetheless, Henry Shue has argued persuasively against the very distinction between negative and positive rights. Consider the most celebrated and best accepted example of a negative right: namely, the right to freedom. The meaningful preservation of the right to freedom requires a variety of positive actions: for example, on the part of the government it requires the establishment and maintenance of a police force, courts, and the military, and on the part of the citizenry it requires ongoing cooperation and diligent (not merely passive) forbearance. The protection of another so-called negative right, the right to physical security, necessitates "police forces; criminal rights; penitentiaries; schools for training police, lawyers, and guards; and taxes to support an enormous system for the prevention, detention, and punishment of violations of personal security."[25]

This is compelling. The maintenance and preservation of many non-welfare rights (where, again, such maintenance and preservation is the key to a right's status as basic) require the support of certain basic welfare rights. Certain liberties depend upon the enjoyment of subsistence, just as subsistence sometimes depends upon the enjoyment of some liberties. One's freedom to speak freely is meaningless if one is weakened by hunger to the point of silence.

What list of rights, then, ought to be endorsed on the international level? Elsewhere I have argued that the rights appearing on such a list should pass the following conditions:[26] (1) the right must protect something of very great importance; (2) the right must be subject to substantial and recurrent threats; and (3) the obligations or burdens imposed by the right must satisfy a fairness-affordability test.[27]

In turn, I have argued that the list of fundamental international rights generated from these conditions include: (1) the right to freedom of physical movement; (2) the right to ownership of property; (3) the right to freedom from torture; (4) the right to a fair trial; (5) the right to nondiscriminatory treatment (e.g., freedom from discrimination on the basis of such characteristics as race or sex); (6) the right to physical security; (7) the right to freedom of speech and association; (8) the right to minimal education; (9) the right to political participation; and (10) the right to subsistence.

This seems a minimal list. Some will wish to add entries such as the right to employment, to social security, or to a certain standard of living (say, as might be prescribed by Rawls's well-known "difference" principle). The list as presented aims to suggest, albeit incompletely, a description of a *minimal* set of rights and to serve as a point of beginning and consensus for evaluating international conduct. If I am correct, many would wish to add entries, but few would wish to subtract them.

As we look over the list, it is noteworthy that, except for a few isolated instances, multinational corporations have probably succeeded in fulfilling their duty not to actively deprive persons of their enjoyment of the rights at issue. But correlative duties involve more than failing to actively deprive people of the enjoyment of their rights. Shue, for example, notes that three types of correlative duties (i.e., duties corresponding to a particular right) are possible: (1) to avoid depriving; (2) to help protect from deprivation; and (3) to aid the deprived.[28]

While it is obvious that the honoring of rights clearly imposes duties of the first kind, i.e., to avoid depriving directly, it is less obvious, but frequently true, that honoring them involves acts or omissions that help prevent the deprivation of rights. If I receive a note from Murder, Incorporated, and it looks like business, my right to security is clearly threatened. Let's say that a third party (X) has relevant information which, if revealed to the police, would help protect my right to security. In this case, there is no excuse for X to remain silent, claiming that it is Murder, Incorporated, and not X, who wishes to murder me.

Similarly, the duties associated with rights often include ones from the third category, i.e., that of aiding the deprived, as when a government is bound to honor the right of its citizens to adequate nutrition by distributing food in the wake of famine or natural disaster, or when the same government, in the defense of political liberty, is required to demand that an employer reinstate or compensate an employee fired for voting for a particular candidate in a government election.

Which of these duties apply to corporations, and which apply only to governments? It would be unfair, not to mention unreasonable, to hold corporations to the same standards for enhancing and protecting social welfare to which we hold civil governments—since frequently governments are formally dedicated to enhancing the welfare of, and actively preserving the liberties of, their citizens. The profit-making corporation, in contrast, is designed to achieve an economic mission and as a moral actor possesses an exceedingly narrow personality. It is an undemocratic institution, furthermore, which is ill-suited to the broader task of distributing society's goods in accordance with a conception of general welfare. The corporation is an economic animal; although its responsibilities extend beyond maximizing return on investment for shareholders, they are informed directly by its economic mission. Hence, while it would be strikingly generous for multinationals to sacrifice some of their profits to buy milk, grain, and shelter for persons in poor countries, it seems difficult to consider this one of their minimal moral requirements. If anyone has such minimal obligations, it is the peoples' respective governments or, perhaps, better-off individuals.

The same, however, is not true of the second class of duties, i.e., to protect from deprivation. While these duties, like those in the third class, are also usually the province of government, it sometimes happens that the rights to which they correlate are ones whose protection is a direct outcome of ordinary corporate activities. For example, the duties associated with protecting a worker from the physical threats of other workers may fall not only upon the local police but also upon the employer. These duties, in turn, are properly viewed as correlative duties of the right—in this instance, the worker's right—to personal security.

This will become clearer in a moment when we discuss the correlative duties of specific rights.

The following list of correlative duties reflects a second-stage application of the fairness-affordability condition to the earlier list of fundamental international rights, and indicates which rights do, and which do not, impose correlative duties upon multinational corporations of the three various kinds.[29]

Minimal Correlative Duties of Multinational Corporations

	To Avoid Depriving	**To Help Protect From Deprivation**	**To Aid the Deprived**
FUNDAMENTAL RIGHTS			
Freedom of physical movement	X		
Ownership of property	X		
Freedom from torture	X		
Fair trial	X		
Nondiscriminatory treatment	X	X	
Physical security	X	X	
Freedom of speech and association	X	X	
Minimal education	X	X	
Political participation	X	X	
Subsistence	X	X	

Let us illustrate the duty to protect from deprivation with specific examples. The right to physical security entails duties of protection. If a Japanese multinational corporation operating in Nigeria hires shop workers to run metal lathes in an assembly factory, but fails to provide them with protective goggles, then the corporation has failed to honor the workers' moral right to physical security (no matter what the local law might decree). Injuries from such a failure would be the moral responsibility of the Japanese multinational despite the fact that the company could not be said to have inflicted the injuries directly.

Another correlative duty, to protect the right of education, may be illustrated through the example mentioned earlier: namely, the prevalence of child labor in developing countries. A multinational in Central America is not entitled to hire an eight-year-old for full-time, ongoing work because, among other reasons, doing so blocks the child's ability to receive a minimally sufficient education. While what counts as a "minimally sufficient" education may be debated, and while it seems likely, moreover, that the specification of the right to a certain level of education will depend at least in part upon the level of economic resources available in a given country, it is reasonable to assume that any action by a corporation which has the effect of blocking the development of a child's ability to read or write will be proscribed on the basis of rights.

In some instances, corporations have failed to honor the correlative duty of protecting the right to political participation from deprivation. The most blatant examples of direct deprivation are fortunately becoming so rare as to be nonexistent, namely, cases in which companies directly aid in overthrowing democratic regimes, as when United Fruit, Inc., allegedly contributed to overthrowing a democratically elected regime in Guatemala during the 1950s. But a few corporations have continued indirectly to threaten this right by failing to protect it from deprivation. A few have persisted, for example, in supporting military dictatorships in countries with growing democratic sentiment, and others have blatantly bribed publicly elected officials with large sums of money. Perhaps the most celebrated example of the latter occurred when the prime minister of Japan was bribed with $7 million by the Lockheed Corporation to secure a lucrative Tri-Star Jet contract. The complaint from the perspective of this right is not against bribes or "sensitive payments" in general, but against bribes in contexts where they serve to undermine a democratic system in which publicly elected officials are in a position of public trust.

Even the buying and owning of major segments of a foreign country's land and industry have been criticized in this regard. As Brian Barry has remarked, "The paranoia created in Britain and the United States by land purchases by foreigners (especially the Arabs and the Japanese, it seems) should serve to make it understandable that the citizenry of a country might be unhappy with a state of affairs in which the most important natural resources are in foreign ownership."[30] At what point would Americans regard their democratic control threatened by foreign ownership of U.S. industry and resources? At 20 percent ownership? At 40 percent? At 60 percent? At 80 percent? The answer is debatable, yet there seems to be some point beyond which the right to national self-determination, and in turn national democratic control, is violated by foreign ownership of property.[31]

Corporations also have duties to protect the right to subsistence from deprivation. Consider the following scenario. A number of square miles of land in an underdeveloped country has been used for years to grow black beans. The bulk of the land is owned, as it has been for centuries, by two wealthy landowners. Poorer members of the community work the land and receive a portion of the crop, a portion barely sufficient to satisfy nutritional needs. Next, imagine that a multinational corporation offers the two wealthy owners a handsome sum for the land, and does so because it plans to grow coffee for export. Now if—and this, admittedly, is a crucial "if"—the corporation has reason to *know* that a significant number of people in the community will suffer malnutrition as a result—that is, if it has convincing reasons to believe either those persons will fail to be hired by the company and paid sufficiently or, if forced to migrate to the city, will receive wages insufficient to provide adequate food and shelter—then the multinational may be said to have failed in its correlative duty to protect persons from the deprivation of the right to subsistence. This despite the fact that the corporation would never have stooped to take food from workers' mouths, and despite the fact that the malnourished will, in Coleridge's words, "die so slowly that none call it murder."

In addition to articulating a list of rights and the correlative duties imposed upon multinational corporations, there is also a need to articulate a practical stratagem for use in applying the home-country norms of the multinational manager to the vexing problems arising in developing countries. In particular, how should highly-placed multinational managers, typically schooled in home-country moral traditions, reconcile conflicts between those traditions and ones of the host country? When host-country standards for pollution, discrimination, and salary schedules appear substandard from the perspective of the home country, should the manager take the high road and implement home-country standards? Or does the high road imply a failure to respect cultural diversity and national integrity?

What distinguishes these issues from standard ones about corporate practices is that they involve reference to a conflict of norms, either moral or legal, between home and host country. Consider two actual instances of the problem at issue.

Case #1: A new American bank in Italy was advised by its Italian attorneys to file a tax return that misstated income and expenses and consequently grossly underestimated actual taxes due. The bank learned, however, that most other Italian companies regarded the practice as standard operating procedure and merely the first move in a complex negotiating process with the Italian internal revenue service. The bank initially refused to file a fallacious return on moral grounds and submitted an "American-style" return instead. But because the resulting tax bill was many times higher than what comparable Italian companies were asked to pay, the bank changed policy in later years to agree with the "Italian style."[32]

Case #2: In 1966 Charles Pettis, employee of an American multinational, became resident engineer for one of the company's projects in Peru: a 146-mile, $46 million project to build a highway across the Andes. Pettis soon discovered that Peruvian safety standards were far below those in the United States. The highway design called for cutting through mountains in areas where rock formations were unstable. Unless special precautions were taken, slides could occur. Pettis blew the whistle, complaining first to Peruvian government officials and later to U.S. officials. No special precautions were taken, with the result that 31 men were killed by landslides during the construction of the road. Pettis was fired and had difficulty finding a job with another company.[33]

One may well decide that enforcing home-country standards was necessary in one of the above cases, but not in the other. One may decide that host-country precautions in Peru were unacceptable, while at the same time acknowledging that, however inequitable and inefficient Italian tax mores may be, a decision to file "Italian style" is permissible.

Thus, despite claims to the contrary, one must reject the simple dictum that whenever the practice violates a moral standard of the home country, it is impermissible for the multinational company. Arnold Berleant has argued that the principle of equal treatment endorsed by most U.S. citizens requires that U.S. corporations pay workers in less developed countries exactly the same wages paid to U.S. workers in comparable jobs (after appropriate adjustments are made for cost of living levels in the relevant areas).[34] But most observers, including those from the less developed countries, believe this stretches the doctrine of equality too far in a way that is detrimental to host countries. By arbitrarily establishing U.S. wage levels as the benchmark for fairness, one eliminates the role of the international market in establishing salary levels, and this in turn eliminates the incentive U.S. corporations have to hire foreign workers. Perhaps U.S. firms should exceed market rate for foreign labor as a matter of moral principle, but to pay strictly equal rates would freeze less developed countries out of the international labor market.[35] Lacking a simple formula such as "the practice is wrong when it violates the home-country's norms," one seems driven to undertake a more complex analysis of the types and degrees of responsibilities multinationals possess.

What is needed is a more comprehensive test than a simple

appeal to rights. Of course the earlier rights-based approach clarifies a moral bottom line regarding, say, extreme threats to workers' safety. But it leaves obscure not only the issue of less extreme threats, but of harms other than physical injury. Granted, the celebrated dangers of asbestos call for recognizing the right to workers' safety no matter how broadly the language of rights is framed. But what are we to say of a less toxic pollutant? Is the level of sulphur-dioxide air pollution we should tolerate in a struggling nation, one with only a few fertilizer plants working overtime to help feed its malnourished population, the same we should demand in Portland, Oregon?

In the end, nothing less than a general moral theory working in tandem with an analysis of the foundations of corporate existence is needed. But at the practical level a need exists for an interpretive mechanism or algorithm that multinational managers could use in determining the implications of their own moral views.

The first step in generating such an ethical algorithm is to isolate the distinct sense in which the norms of the home and host country conflict. If the practice is morally and/or legally permitted in the host country, but not in the home country, then either: (1) the moral reasons underlying the host-country's view that the practice is permissible refer to the host-country's relative level of economic development; or (2) the moral reasons underlying the host-country's view that the practice is permissible are independent of the host-country's relative level of economic development.

Let us call the conflict of norms described in (1) a type 1 conflict. In such a conflict, an African country that permits slightly higher levels of thermal pollution from electric power generating plants, or a lower minimum wage than that prescribed in European countries, would do so not because higher standards would be undesirable per se, but because its level of economic development requires an ordering of priorities. In the future, when it succeeds in matching European economic achievements, it may well implement the higher standards.

Let us call the conflict of norms described in (2) a type 2 conflict. In such cases, levels of economic development play no role. For example, low-level institutional nepotism, common in many developing countries, is justified not on economic grounds, but on the basis of clan and family loyalty. Presumably the same loyalties will be operative even after the country has risen to economic success—as the nepotism prevalent in Saudi Arabia would indicate. The Italian tax case also reflects an Italian cultural style with a penchant for personal negotiation and an unwillingness to formalize transactions, more than a strategy based on level of economical development.

The difference in norms between the home and host country, i.e., whether the conflict is of type 1 or 2, does not determine the correctness, or truth value, of the host country's claim that the practice is permissible. The practice may or may not be permissible, whether the conflict is of type 1 or 2. This is not to say that the truth value of the host country's claim is independent of the nature of the conflict. A different test will be required to determine whether the practice is permissible when the conflict is of type 1 as opposed to type 2. In a type 1 dispute, the following formula is appropriate:

> The practice is permissible if and only if the members of the home country would, under conditions of economic development similar to those of the host country, regard the practice as permissible.

Under this test, excessive levels of asbestos pollution would almost certainly not be tolerated by the members of the home country under similar economic conditions, whereas higher levels of thermal pollution would be tolerated. The test, happily, explains and confirms our initial moral intuitions.

Since in type 2 conflicts the dispute between the home and host country depends upon a fundamental difference of perspective, a different test is needed. In type 2 conflicts, the opposing evils of ethnocentrism and ethical relativism must be avoided. A multinational must forego the temptation to remake all societies in the image of its home society, while at the same time rejecting a relativism that conveniently forgets ethics when the payoff is sufficient. Thus, the ethical task is to tolerate cultural diversity while drawing the line at moral recklessness.

Since in type 2 cases the practice is in conflict with an embedded norm of the home country, one should first ask whether the practice is necessary to do business in the host country, for if it is not, the solution clearly is to adopt some other practice that is permissible from the standpoint of the home country. If petty bribery of public officials is unnecessary for the business of the Cummins Engine Company in India, then the company is obliged to abandon such bribery. If, on the other hand, the practice proves necessary for business, one must next ask whether the practice constitutes a direct violation of a basic human right. Here the notion of a fundamental international right outlined earlier, specifying a minimum below which corporate conduct should not fall, has special application. If Toyota, a Japanese company, confronts South African laws that mandate systematic discrimination against nonwhites, then Toyota must refuse to comply with the laws. In type 2 cases, the evaluator must ask the following questions: (1) Is it possible to conduct business successfully in the host country without undertaking the practice? and (2) Is the practice a clear violation of a fundamental international right? The practice would be permissible if and only if the answer to both questions is "No."

What sorts of practice might satisfy both criteria? Consider the practice of low-level bribery of public officials in some developing nations. In some South American countries, for example, it is impossible for any company, foreign or national, to move goods through customs without paying low-level officials a few dollars. Indeed, the salaries of such officials are sufficiently low that one suspects they are set with the prevalence of the practice in mind. The payments are relatively small, uniformly assessed, and accepted as standard practice by the surrounding culture. Here, the practice of petty bribery would pass the type 2 test and, barring other moral factors, would be permissible.

The algorithm does not obviate the need for multinational managers to appeal to moral concepts both more general and specific than the algorithm itself. It is not intended as a substitute for a general theory of morality or even an interpretation of the basic responsibilities of multinationals. Its power lies in its ability to tease out implications of the moral presuppositions of a manager's acceptance of "home" morality, and in this sense to serve as a clarifying device for multinational decision-making. The algorithm makes no appeal to a universal concept of morality (as the appeal to fundamental rights does in type 2 cases), save for the purported universality of the ethics endorsed by the home-country culture. When the home country's morality is wrong or confused, the algorithm can reflect this ethnocentricity, leading either to a mild paternalism or to the imposition of parochial standards. For example, the home country's oversensitivity to aesthetic features of the environment may lead it to reject a certain level of thermal pollution, even under strained economic circumstances. This results in a paternalistic refusal to allow such levels in the host country, despite the host country's acceptance of the higher levels and its belief that tolerating such levels is necessary for stimulating economic development. It would be a mistake, however, to exaggerate this weakness of the algorithm; coming up with actual cases in which the force of the algorithm would be relativized is extremely difficult. Indeed, I have been unable to discover a single, non-hypothetical set of facts fitting this description.

IV

How might multinational corporations improve their moral performance and come to embody the normative concepts advanced in this article? Two classes of remedies suggest themselves:

external remedies, that is, those that rely on international associations or agreements on the one hand; and internal remedies, i.e., those that rely on internal, corporate initiatives on the other.

Earlier we discussed the dramatic expansion of external remedies in the form of international laws, agreements, and codes of conduct. Again, while many of these are nonbinding in the sense that noncompliance will fail to trigger sanctions, they are as a group coming to exert significant influence on multinational conduct. One of the principal advantages of such global and industry-wide initiatives is that they distribute costs more fairly than initiatives undertaken by individual corporations. When, in line with the WHO Code of Marketing Breast Milk Substitutes, Nestle curtails questionable marketing practices for the sale of infant formula, it does so with the confidence that the other signers of the WHO Code will not be taking unfair advantage by undertaking the same questionable practices, for they must adhere to its provisions. Still another advantage of external remedies stems from the fact that many nation-states, especially developing ones, are unable to gather sufficient information about, much less control, the multinational corporations that operate within their borders. Thus, the use of supranational entities, whether of an international or interindustry form, will sometimes augment, or supplement, the power and information-gathering abilities of developing nations. It seems difficult to deny that the growth and maturation of such entities can enhance the ethical conduct of multinational corporations.

The most important change of an internal nature likely to enhance the ethical behavior of multinationals is for multinationals themselves to introduce ethical deliberation, i.e., to introduce factors of ethics into their decision-making mechanisms. That they should do so is a clear implication of the preceding discussion, yet it is a conclusion some will resist. Those who place great confidence in the efficacy of the market may, for example, believe that a corporate policy of moral disinterest and profit maximization will—*pace* Adam Smith's invisible hand—maximize overall global welfare.

This kind of ideological confidence in the international market may have been understandable decades ago. But persisting in the belief that market mechanisms will automatically ensure adequate moral conduct today seems recklessly idealistic. Forces such as Islamic fundamentalism, the global debt bomb, and massive unemployment in developing countries have drastically distorted the operation of the free market in international commerce, and even though a further selective freeing of market forces may enhance global productivity, it cannot solve automatically questions of fair treatment, hazardous technology, or discrimination.

Even adopting the minimal guidelines for corporate conduct advanced here would involve dramatic changes in the decision-making mechanisms of multinational corporations. Such firms would need to alter established patterns of information flow and collection in order to accommodate new forms of morally relevant information. The already complex parameters of corporate decision-making would become more so. Even scholarly research about international business would need to change. At present, research choices tend to be dictated by the goals of increased profits, long-term access to basic commodities needed for manufactured items, and increased global market share; but clearly these goals sometimes conflict with broader moral ends, such as refraining from violating human rights. Revised goals call for a revised program of research. And although we have rejected the view that multinational corporations must shoulder the world's problems of poverty, discrimination, and political injustice because, as economic entities, they have limited social missions, their goals nonetheless must include the aim of not impeding solutions to such problems.

Are such changes in the decision making of multinational corporations likely or even possible? Resistance will be intense; clearly, there should be no delusions on this score. Yet, without minimizing the difficulties, I do not think the task impossible. At a minimum, corporations are capable of choosing the more ethical alternative in instances where alternative courses of action yield equal profits—and I believe they are capable of even more. Corporations are run by human beings, not beasts. As multinationals continue to mature in the context of an ever-expanding, more sophisticated global economy, we have reason to hope that they are capable of looking beyond their national borders and recognizing the same minimal claims, made in the name of our shared humanity, that they accept at home.

NOTES

1. Much of this article is extracted from Thomas Donaldson's book *The Ethics of International Business* (Oxford: Oxford University Press, 1989). The book provides a framework for interpreting the ethics of global business. Excerpts reprinted by permission of Oxford University Press.

2. Richard Barnet and Ronald Muller, *Global Reach: the Power of Multinational Corporations* (New York: Simon and Schuster, 1974), 363.

3. P. P. Gabriel, "MNCs in the Third World: Is Conflict Unavoidable?" *Harvard Business Review* 56 (March–April 1978), 83–93.

4. An example of disparity in wages between Mexican and U.S. workers is documented in the case study by John H. Haddox, "Twin-Plants and Corporate Responsibilities," in Patricia Werhane and Kendall D'Andrade, eds., *Profits and Responsibility* (New York: Random House, 1985).

5. Barnet and Muller, *Global Reach,* 72.

6. J. R. Simpson, "Ethics and Multinational Corporations vis-à-vis Developing Nations," *Journal of Business Ethics* 1 (1982), 227–37.

7. I have borrowed this eight-fold scheme of categories from researchers Farr and Stening in Lisa Farr and Bruce W. Stening, "Ethics and the Multinational Corporation" (an unpublished paper) p. 4.

8. An analysis of such reasons, one which also contains many observations on the evolution of international public policy, is Lee E. Preston's "The Evolution of Multinational Public Policy Toward Business: Codes of Conduct," a paper read at the annual meeting of the American Academy of Management, New Orleans, August 1987.

9. Jon R. Luoma, "A Disaster That Didn't Wait," *The New York Times Book Review,* November 29, 1987, 16.

10. While I personally have coined the terms, "inter-industry," "inter-government," etc., the basic four-fold division of international initiatives is drawn from Preston, *op. cit.*

11. See, for example, Raymond J. Waldman, *Regulating International Business through Codes of Conduct* (Washington, D.C.: American Enterprise Institute, 1980).

12. See, for example, P. S. Tharp, Jr., "Transnational Enterprises and International Regulation: A Survey of Various Approaches to International Organizations," *International Organization* 30 (Winter 1976), 47–73.

13. James LeMoyne, "In Central America, the Workers Suffer Most," *The New York Times,* October 26, 1987, 1 and 4.

14. Ibid.

15. Quoted in "Products Unsafe at Home are Still Unloaded Abroad," *The New York Times,* August 22, 1982, 22.

16. Ronald Dworkin, *Taking Rights Seriously* (Cambridge: Harvard University Press, 1977). For other standard definitions of rights, see: James W. Nickel, *Making Sense of Human Rights: Philosophical Reflections on the Universal Declaration of Human Rights* (Berkeley: University of California Press, 1987) especially chapter 2; Joel Feinberg, "Duties, Rights and Claims," *American Philosophical Quarterly* 3 (1966), 133–44. See also Feinberg, "The Nature and Value of Rights," *Journal of Value Inquiry* 4 (1970), 243–57; Wesley N. Hohfeld, *Fundamental Legal Conceptions* (New Haven: Yale University Press, 1964); and H. J. McCloskey, "Rights—Some Conceptual Issues," *Australasian Journal of Philosophy* 54 (1976), 99–115.

17. Maurice Cranston, *What Are Human Rights?* (New York: Taplinger, 1973), 67.

18. H. J. McCloskey, for example, understands a right as a positive entitlement that need not specify who bears the responsibility for satisfying that entitlement. H. J. McCloskey, "Rights—Some Conceptual Issues," 99.

19. Joel Feinberg, "Duties, Rights and Claims," *American Philosophical Quarterly* 3 (1966), 137–44. See also Feinberg, "The Nature and Value of Rights," 243–57.

20. James Brooke, "Waste Dumpers Turning to West Africa," *The New York Times,* July 17, 1988, 1 and 7.

21. Ibid.

22. Ibid., p. 7. Nigeria and other countries have struck back, often by imposing strict rules against the acceptance of toxic waste. For example, in Nigeria officials now warn that anyone caught importing toxic waste will face the firing squad.

23. See Ian Brownlie, *Basic Documents on Human Rights* (Oxford: Oxford University Press, 1975).

24. James W. Nickel, "The Feasibility of Welfare Rights in Less Developed Countries," in Kenneth Kipnis and Diana T. Meyers, eds., *Economic Justice: Private Rights and Public Responsibilities* (Totowa, N.J.: Rowman and Allenheld, 1985), 217–26.

25. Henry Shue, *Basic Rights: Subsistence, Affluence, and U.S. Foreign Policy* (Princeton: Princeton University Press, 1980), 37–38.

26. Donaldson, *The Ethics of International Business,* see especially chapter 5. My formulation of these three conditions is an adaptation from four conditions presented and defended by James Nickel in James W. Nickel, *Making Sense of Human Rights: Philosophical Reflections on the Universal Declaration of Human Rights* (Berkeley: University of California Press, 1987).

27. The fairness-affordability test implies that in order for a proposed right to qualify as a genuine right, all moral agents (including nation-states, individuals, and corporations) must be able under ordinary circumstances, both economically and otherwise, to assume the various burdens and duties that fall fairly upon them in honoring the right. "Affordable" here means literally capable of paying for; it does not mean "affordable" in the vernacular sense that something is not affordable because it would constitute an inefficient luxury, or would necessitate trading off other more valuable economic goods. This definition implies that—at least under unusual circumstances—honoring a right may be mandatory for a given multinational corporation, even when the result is bankrupting the firm. For example, it would be "affordable" under ordinary circumstances for multinational corporations to employ older workers and refuse to hire eight-year-old children for full-time, ongoing labor, and hence doing so would be mandatory even in the unusual situation where a particular firm's paying the higher salaries necessary to hire older laborers would probably bankrupt the firm. By the same logic, it would probably not be "affordable" for either multinational corporations or nation-states around the world to guarantee kidney dialysis for all citizens who need it. The definition also implies that any act of forbearance (of a kind involved in not violating a right directly) is "affordable" for all moral agents.

28. Shue, *Basic Rights,* 57.

29. It is possible to understand even the first four rights as imposing correlative duties to protect from deprivation under highly unusual or hypothetical circumstances.

30. Brian Barry, "The Case for a New International Economic Order," in J. Roland Pennock and John W. Chapman, eds., *Ethics, Economics, and the Law, Nomos XXIV* (New York: New York University Press, 1982).

31. Companies are also charged with undermining local governments, and hence infringing on basic rights, by sophisticated tax evasion schemes. Especially when companies buy from their own subsidiaries, they can establish prices that have little connection to existing market values. This, in turn, means that profits can be shifted from high-tax to low-tax countries, with the result that poor nations can be deprived of their rightful share.

32. Arthur Kelly, "Italian Bank Mores," in T. Donaldson, ed., *Case Studies in Business Ethics* (Englewood Cliffs, N.J.: Prentice-Hall, 1984), 37–39.

33. Charles Peters and Taylor Branch, *Blowing the Whistle: Dissent in the Public Interest* (New York: Praeger, 1974), 182–85.

34. Arnold Berleant, "Multinationals and the Problem of Ethical Consistency," *Journal of Business Ethics* 3 (August 1982), 182–95.

35. Some have argued that insulating the economies of the less developed countries would be advantageous to the less developed countries in the long run. But whether correct or not, such an argument is independent of the present issue, for it is independent of the claim that if a practice violates the norms of the home country, then it is impermissible.

Contributors

Jacques Barzun is University Professor Emeritus, Columbia University, where he also held various administrative posts, including serving as the first Dean of Faculties and Provost of the University and as Special Adviser on the Arts to the president. A collection of his essays from 1940 to 1980 was published in 1982 as *Critical Questions*. He is the author of *A Stroll with William James* (1983).

Sissela Bok is Professor of Philosophy at Brandeis University. She is the author of *Lying: Moral Choice in Public and Private Life* (1978), *Secrets: On the Ethics of Concealment and Revelation* (1982), and *A Strategy for Peace: Human Values and the Threat of War* (1989).

Alberto R. Coll is the Charles H. Stockton Professor of International Law at the United States Naval War College. He has also taught at Georgetown University. In addition to numerous articles on ethics, grand strategy, and the use of force, Dr. Coll is the author of *The Wisdom of Statecraft* and *The Western Heritage and American Values: Law, Theology and History*. He was also a former Deputy Assistant Secretary of Defense for Special Operations and Low Intensity Conflict in the Bush administration.

Cho-yun Hsu is University Professor of History and Sociology at the University of Pittsburgh. He is the author of *Western Chou Civilization* (1988) in addition to numerous other books and articles on Chinese history.

Thomas Donaldson is the Mark O. Winkelman Professor at the Wharton School of the University of Pennsylvania, where he teaches in the area of business ethics. He has written broadly in the area of business values and professional ethics. Books that he has authored or edited include: *Ethics in International Business; Ethical Issues in Business*, 5th edition, co-edited with Patricia Werhane; *Issues in Moral Philosophy;*

and *Corporations and Morality*. He is a founding member and past president of the Society for Business Ethics, and a member of the editorial boards of *Business Ethics Quarterly* and the *Academy of Management Review*.

Jack Donnelly is Associate Professor of Political Science at the University of Denver. He is the author of *International Human Rights* (1998), *The Concept of Human Rights* (1985), *Universal Human Rights in Theory and Practice* (1989), and numerous articles on the theory and practice of human rights.

John Lewis Gaddis teaches history at Yale University. He is the author, most recently, of *We Now Know: Rethinking Cold War History* (1997), a reassessment of the Cold War in the light of newly opened Soviet, East European, and Chinese archival sources.

Lyn S. Graybill teaches African politics at the University of Virginia. She is the author of *Religion and Resistance Politics in South Africa* (1995).

Frances V. Harbour is Assistant Professor of Government at George Mason University's Department of Public and International Affairs. She has written about ethics and war, arms control, chemical weapons, and international law. She is the author of the forthcoming *Thinking About International Ethics: Applying Moral Theory to Cases in American Foreign Policy*.

David C. Hendrickson is Associate Professor of Political Science at Colorado College. He is the author of *The Future of American Strategy* and *Reforming Defense: The State of American Civil-Military Relations*. He has also written three books with Robert W. Tucker, including *The Imperial Temptation: The New World Order and America's Purpose*.

Stanley Hoffmann is Professor of Government at Harvard University and Chairman of Harvard's Center for European Studies. He is the author of numerous works relating to ethics and international affairs, most notably his book *Duties Beyond Borders* and his published lecture *The Political Ethics of International Relations*.

Kristen Renwick Monroe is Professor of Politics and Society at the University of California at Irvine. She is the editor of *Contemporary*

Empirical Political Theory (1997) and *The Economic Approach to Politics* (1991), and author of *The Heart of Altruism* (1996).

Robert J. Myers is president emeritus of the Carnegie Council on Ethics and International Affairs. He is the author and editor of several books on ethics and international affairs, including *International Ethics in the Nuclear Age* and *The Political Morality of the IMF.* His recent articles include pieces on democracy and foreign policy, the development of democracy in the Far East, and human rights. Prior to joining the Carnegie Council in 1981, he served as publisher of *The New Republic.*

Amir Pasic is Deputy Director of the Project on World Security at the Rockefeller Brothers Fund. He is also a Visiting Scholar at Brown University's Thomas J. Watson Jr. Institute for International Studies.

Augustus Richard Norton is Professor of International Relations at Boston University. During the closing years of the Cold War he was a consultant to the Vice President's Task Force on Terrorism, and from 1989 to 1991 he participated in a series of unofficial U.S.-Soviet meetings on cooperation to combat terrorism. He is the author of numerous books and articles, including *Amal and the Shi'a: Struggle for the Soul of Lebanon* (1987), and Senior Editor of *The International Relations of the Palestine Liberation Organization* (1989).

Joel H. Rosenthal is President of the Carnegie Council on Ethics and International Affairs. In addition to several articles on ethics and U.S. foreign policy, he is the author of the book *Righteous Realists: Political Realism, Responsible Power, and American Culture in the Nuclear Age* (1991) and editor of the Carnegie Council's journal, *Ethics & International Affairs.*

Amartya Sen is Master of Trinity College, Cambridge. Winner of the 1998 Nobel Prize in Economics, he is the author of numerous books and articles, including *On Ethics and Economics* (1987), *Collective Choice and Social Welfare* (1970), *Inequality Reexamined* (1992), *Poverty and Famines* (1981), and *Hunger and Public Action* (1989, with Jean Drèze). He has served as President of the International Economic Association, the American Economic Association, the Indian Economic Association, and the Econometric Society.

Michael J. Smith is Associate Professor of Government and Foreign Affairs at the University of Virginia, where he also codirects the Program in Political and Social Thought. He is the author of *Realist Thought from Weber to Kissinger* (1989). He is also co-author and editor of *Ideas and Ideals: Essays on Politics in Honor of Stanley Hoffmann.* Professor Smith regularly teaches courses on ethics and international affairs, and for several years has served as the Project Coordinator of the Carnegie Council's faculty development seminars on teaching ethics and international relations. He contributes frequently to *Ethics & International Affairs* and is currently working on a book-length manuscript with Stanley Hoffmann on ethics and international relations.

Thomas G. Weiss is Distinguished Professor of Political Science at the Graduate School and University Center, City University of New York. He also serves as Executive Director of the Academic Council on the United Nations System. He has authored or edited numerous books on various aspects of international organization, conflict management, North-South relations, and humanitarian action. His books include *Humanitarian Challenges and Intervention: World Politics and the Dilemmas of Help,* with Cindy Collins (1996), and *The News Media, Civil War, and Humanitarian Action,* with Larry Minear and Colin Scott (1996).